Cinema and the Swastika

Also by David Welch

NAZI PROPAGANDA: The Powers and the Limitations

PROPAGANDA AND THE GERMAN CINEMA 1933–45

THE THIRD REICH: Politics and Propaganda

HITLER: Profile of a Dictator

Cinema and the Swastika

The International Expansion of Third Reich Cinema

Edited by

Roel Vande Winkel

and

David Welch

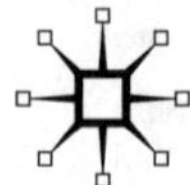

First published 2007 by
PALGRAVE MACMILLAN
Houndmills, Basingstoke, Hampshire RG21 6XS and
175 Fifth Avenue, New York, N.Y. 10010
Companies and representatives throughout the world

PALGRAVE MACMILLAN is the global academic imprint of the Palgrave Macmillan division of St. Martin's Press, LLC and of Palgrave Macmillan Ltd. Macmillan® is a registered trademark in the United States, United Kingdom and other countries. Palgrave is a registered trademark in the European Union and other countries.

ISBN-13: 978–1–4039–9491–2 hardback
ISBN-10: 1–4039–9491–9 hardback

This book is printed on paper suitable for recycling and made from fully managed and sustained forest sources.

A catalogue record for this book is available from the British Library.

Library of Congress Cataloging-in-Publication Data
Cinema and the swastika: the international expansion of Third Reich cinema/edited by Roel Vande Winkel and David Welch.
p. cm.
Includes bibliographical references and index.
ISBN-13: 978–1–4039–9491–2 (cloth)
ISBN-10: 1–4039–9491–9 (cloth)
1. Motion pictures, German—Foreign countries. 2. Motion pictures, German—Foreign countries—Influence. I. Vande Winkel, Roel. II. Welch, David, 1950–
PN1993.5.G3C555 2007
791.430943—dc22 2006048784

10 9 8 7 6 5 4 3 2 1
16 15 14 13 12 11 10 09 08 07

Printed and bound in Great Britain by
Antony Rowe Ltd, Chippenham and Eastbourne

Contents

List of Illustrations

Notes on the Contributors

Brett Bowles is Assistant Professor of French Studies at the State University of New York, Albany, and book review editor for the *Historical Journal of Film, Radio and Television*. He has published widely on French cinema of the 1930s and 1940s, particularly the fiction films of Marcel Pagnol and French-language newsreels made during the Second World War. His book on Pagnol is forthcoming in 2007 from Manchester University Press.

David Culbert is John L. Loos Professor of History at Louisiana State University, Baton Rouge, and Editor of the *Historical Journal of Film, Radio and Television*. He is co-author of *Propaganda and Mass Persuasion: A Historical Encyclopedia, 1500 to Present* (2003), and Editor-in-Chief of *Film and Propaganda in America: A Documentary History* (5 volumes, 1990–93).

Michael Eckardt, PhD-candidate, is visiting scholar at Stellenbosch University (Journalism) and the author of *Film Criticism in Cape Town, 1928–1930* (2005).

Jo Fox is Senior Lecturer of European History at the University of Durham. She is the author of *Filming Women in the Third Reich* (Berg, Oxford, 2000) and *Film Propaganda in Britain and Nazi Germany: World War II Cinema* (Berg, Oxford, 2006).

David S. Frey is Assistant Professor of History at the United States Military Academy at West Point. He received his PhD from Columbia University in 2003 and his research interests involve interwar Central Europe. He is, at the time of writing, working on a manuscript titled *The National Spirit Doesn't Stick to Celluloid. The Transnational Development of the Hungarian National Sound Film Industry, 1929–44.*

Janine Hansen received her master's degree in Japanese studies from the Ostasiatisches Seminar at Freie Universität Berlin. She has written on film in Japan and German–Japanese film policy with a focus on the 1930s.

Gianni Haver is Professor at the Institut de sociologie des communications de masse (ISCM) at the Université de Lausanne. His books include *Les lueurs de la guerre: écrans vaudois 1939–1945* (2003) and many edited volumes, including *La Suisse les Alliés et le cinéma. Propagande et représentation, 1939–1945* (2001).

Lisa Jarvinen is Visiting Assistant Professor of History at Colgate University. She has finished her doctoral dissertation entitled *Hollywood's Shadow: the American Film Industry and Spanish-Speaking Markets During the Transition to*

Sound, 1929–1936 at Syracuse University (New York). She also holds an MA in Cinema Studies from New York University.

Aristotle A. Kallis is Senior Lecturer in European Studies at the University of Lancaster, Department of European Languages and Cultures. He had previous appointments at the University of Bristol and the University of Edinburgh. His publications include *Fascism: A Reader – Historians and Interpretations of Fascism* (2003), *Nazi-propaganda and the Second World War* (2006) and *Fascism and Genocide* (2007).

Tim Kirk teaches European history at the University of Newcastle upon Tyne. He is author of *Nazism and the Working Class in Austria* (1996 and 2002), and co-editor (with Anthony McElligott) of *Working Towards the Führer* (2003). He is, at the time of writing, working on a book on the Nazi new order in Europe.

Ivan Klimeš has worked since 1981 in the National Film Archive in Prague, where, since 1990, he has headed the department of film theory and history. Since 1996, he has also lectured at the Department of Film Studies at the Faculty of Philosophy of Arts, Charles University. The focal points of his research over recent years include the relationship between cinematography and the state, the development of the Czech film industry and the genesis of centralised film dramaturgy Czechoslovakian film.

Paul Lesch (PhD Ghent University, 2006) teaches film and history at the Miami University John E. Dolibois European Center in Luxembourg. He directed the documentary film *Call Her Madam* (1997) and is the author of *René Leclère. Pionnier du cinéma luxembourgeois* (1999), *Heim ins Ufa-Reich? NS-Filmpolitik und die Rezeption deutscher Filme in Luxemburg 1933–1944* (2002) and *In the Name of Public Order and Morality. Cinema Control and Film Censorship in Luxembourg 1895–2005* (2005). Paul Lesch has published articles in journals such as the *Historical Journal of Film, Radio and Television*, *Film History* and *Cinema & Cie.*

Benjamin George Martin (PhD Columbia University, 2006) is a postdoctoral fellow at the Berlin Program for Advanced German and European Studies at the Freie Universität Berlin, where he is preparing a book manuscript on Nazi Germany and Fascist Italy's effort to create a 'New Order' in European cultural life between 1936 and 1945.

Julio Montero is Senior Lecturer at the Universidad Complutense de Madrid, where he delivers lectures on History and Cinema, Social History of the Cinema and History of Informative Cinema. He has written, in collaboration with his colleague María A. Paz, several books about these subjects: *Historia y Cine. Realidad, ficción y propaganda* (1995), *La Historia que el cine nos cuenta* (1997), *Creando la realidad. Cine informativo 1895–1945* (1999) and

La imagen pública de la monarquía. Alfonso XIII en la prensa y los noticiarios cinematográficos de su época (2001).

Luiz Nazario is Professor of Film History at the Fine Arts School of the Federal University of Minas Gerais. Author of a PhD thesis on the role movies played in the preparation of the Holocaust: *Imaginários da destruição* (*Imaginaries of Destruction*, 1994) and of several books, including *Da natureza dos monstros* (1998), *As sombras móveis* (1999), *Segredos* (2001), *A cidade imaginária* (2005) and *Autos-de-fé como espetáculos de massa* (2005).

María A. Paz is Professor at the Faculty of Information Science at the Complutense University of Madrid. She works in the Department of the History of Social Communication. Her research and teaching interests focus on informative cinema-newsreels and documentaries, the cinema as a historical source and the social history of the cinema. In recent years she has, apart from articles journals such as the *Historical Journal of Film, Radio and Television*, published several books, mostly in collaboration with her colleague Julio Montero (see pg. xii).

Francisco Peredo-Castro is Professor/Researcher in the Faculty of Political and Social Science of the National Autonomous University of Mexico (UNAM). He worked for 2 years at the General Direction of Cinematography Activities of UNAM. He is member of the National Researchers System (*Sistema Nacional de Investigadores*) in Mexico and Director of the MA Programme on Teaching for High School Education at the National Autonomous University of México. He is the author of *Cine y propaganda para Latinoamérica. México y Estados Unidos en la encrucijada de los años cuarenta* (2002).

Daniel Rafaelić was born in Bitola, Macedonia. After his degree in history, at Philosophic Faculty in Zagreb, Croatia, he became film historian and, at the time of writing, is working in Croatian cinematheque. Aside from editing several books on history of Croatian cinema, he is also an assistant at the Academy of Dramatic Arts in Zagreb where he is teaching history of Croatian Cinema. In 2005, he wrote screenplay, and together with Leon Rizmaul he directed documentary called *The Other Side of Welles*, about life and work of Orson Welles in Croatia.

Ingo Schiweck (PhD) studied History and Political Science in Germany and the Netherlands. He has published books on the German feature film in the occupied Netherlands (*'[...] Weil wir lieber im Kino sitzen als in Sack und Asche...'*, 2002) and on Dutchmen in German show business (*Laß dich überraschen...*, 2005). He held a guest lectureship in Media History at Heinrich-Heine-Universität Düsseldorf in 2005. In 2006, he founded his own publishing company, MaveriX Verlag, specialising in books on cultural subjects like music, film and sports.

Eirini Sifaki teaches film history at the School of Film Studies at the Aristotle University of Thessaloniki in Greece (Faculty of Fine Arts). Her PhD thesis focused on Greek film history during the 1940–1960s emphasising the economic and political factors as well as trans-national player's strategies that influenced Greek cinema-going practices. She has participated in many international conferences on international communication, cultural studies and film history. Her recent publications focus on film production and consumption in Greece and migrant and diasporic cinema in contemporary Greek cinema.

Bjørn Sørenssen is Professor at the Department of Art and Media Studies (Norwegian University of Technology and Science – NTNU) in Trondheim. His books include *Å fange virkeligheten. Dokumentarfilmens århundre* (2001) and *Kinoens mørke – fjernsynets lys* (1996, with co-authors Hans Fredrik Dahl, Jostein Gripsrud, Gunnar Iversen and Kathrine Skretting).

Keyan Tomaselli is Professor of Culture, Communication and Media Studies, University of KwaZulu-Natal, Durban, and author of the *Cinema of Apartheid* (1988) and *Encountering Modernity: 20th Century South African Cinemas* (2006). He is also editor in chief of *Critical Arts: A Journal of South–North Cultural and Media Studies*.

Roel Vande Winkel is Postdoctoral Fellow at the Belgian *Research Foundation – Flanders*, member of the *Working Group Film & TV Studies* (Ghent University) and Visiting Professor at the *Sint Lukas Hogeschool Brussel*. He has published on various topics relating to Belgian and German film and media history. He is the European book review editor for the *Historical Journal of Film, Radio and Television* and preparing the book publication of his PhD thesis on Nazi newsreels in occupied Europe, 1939–45.

Robert von Dassanowsky is Professor of Languages and Cultures and Director of Film Studies at the University of Colorado, Colorado Springs. A specialist in Austrian studies, he is also known for his work as a film and cultural historian. Dassanowsky is a founding Vice President of the Austrian American Film Association, Editor of the *Gale Encyclopedia of Multicultural America*, Editorial Advisor to the *International Dictionary of Films and Filmmakers*, and is active as an independent film producer. His latest book is the first English-language survey of the Austrian film industry, *Austrian Cinema: A History* (2005).

David Welch is Professor of Modern History and Director of the Centre for the Study of Propaganda and War at the University of Kent. His books include *Modern European History, 1871–2000* (1999), *Germany, Propaganda and Total War 1914–18* (2000), *Hitler: Profile of a Dictator* (2001), *The Third Reich: Politics and Propaganda* (2002) and *Propaganda and the German Cinema, 1933–45* (2001, 2006). He is co-author of *Propaganda and Mass Persuasion: A Historical*

Encyclopedia, 1500 to Present (2003) and is the General Editor of Routledge's Sources in History series.

Rochelle Wright, Professor of Scandinavian and Comparative Literature, Cinema Studies, and Gender and Women's Studies at the University of Illinois, specialises in Swedish film and modern Swedish prose. In addition to *The Visible Wall: Jews and Other Outsiders in Swedish Film*, she has published essays on the films of Alf Sjöberg; iconographic representations of 'Swedishness'; recent trends in 'immigrant film'; and Ingmar Bergman's *The Best Intentions*. Publications on literary topics include the chapter 'Literature after 1950' in *A History of Swedish Literature* and a dozen articles on the prose fiction of Kerstin Ekman. She has also translated three Swedish novels.

Disclaimer

Jacket picture designed by Stephan Demeulenaere, based on this Belgian poster from the Ufa film *Münchhausen* (1943). *Source*: Warie Collection.

Introduction

Roel Vande Winkel and David Welch

Most film scholars and enthusiasts will agree that, from an aesthetic viewpoint, German films produced between 1933–45 are rather uninteresting. In contrast, a number of films produced during the Weimar Republic (1919–33) are considered milestones in the history of film art: silent films such as *The Cabinet of Dr. Caligari* (*Das Cabinet des Dr. Caligari*, 1920), *Nosferatu* (1922), *The Last Laugh* (*Der letzte Mann*, 1924), *The Joyless Street* (*Die freudlose Gasse*, 1925) and *Metropolis* (1927); and also early sound films such as *The Blue Angel* (*Der Blaue Engel*, 1930) and *M – The Murderers are Among Us* (*M. Eine Stadt sucht einen Mörder*, 1931). Under Nazi rule, the German film industry failed to produce a single film that is considered a major contribution to the development of the seventh art. The only possible exceptions to this may be found in Leni Riefenstahl's *Triumph of the Will* (*Triumph des Willens*, 1935) and *Olympia* (1938), propagandistic documentaries that, from a technical viewpoint, were revolutionary. It is, in retrospect, ironic that these films were commissioned by the Nazi Party and patronised by Adolf Hitler but produced outside the constraints imposed by Joseph Goebbels' Ministry of Popular Enlightenment and Propaganda (RMVP).[1] What is unquestionable is that none of the films Goebbels and his collaborators monitored from the first drafts of the screenplay to the censorship of the final cut will be remembered for outstanding artistic qualities. Remarkably, this does not stop such films, or at least a significant sample of them, from being studied in detail by many film researchers and students.

In spite of their rather limited aesthetic quality, films produced in the Third Reich and German films produced during the Second World War, in particular, have received massive attention from film scholars and continue to do so. Early studies such as Erwin Leiser's *Deutschland Erwache!* (1968),[2] Gerd Albrecht's *Nationalsozialistische Filmpolitik* (1969)[3] and David Stewart Hull's *Film in the Third Reich* (1969, the very first English-language book on the subject)[4] are now criticised for their flaws – which they certainly had[5] – but were important steps in the coming of age of an area of research that is now often referred to as the 'traditional' school of Nazi film historiography. This school, the best known works of which are by Richard

Taylor and David Welch,[6] investigate the Nazi use of film for propaganda purposes – or more specifically, examine Nazi film propaganda as a reflection of National-Socialist ideology. They therefore tend to focus on a rather limited corpus of films. It is no coincidence that these largely are the same films that the Nazi regime considered 'politically especially valuable' (*staatspolitisch besonders wertvoll*)[7] and labelled as such – which for cinema owners made the films more financially attractive to screen. It is precisely the propagandistic potential the Nazi regime attached to such films that makes them such an interesting artefact. The consequence of this scholarly focus on a selected film corpus, a practice based on a rather strict dichotomy between films that are either 'propagandistic' or 'non-political', is that a large majority of films produced in the Third Reich received little to no attention. Films starring popular actors and actresses like Heinz Rühmann and Marika Rökk, who mainly played in 'non-political' entertainment features, are barely mentioned in many 'traditional' studies of Third Reich cinema.[8] The same went for the films of the leading actress Zarah Leander. While the propagandistic intentions of a film such as *The Great Love* (*Die grosse Liebe*, 1942) have been recognised, her films are not as immediately associated with overt political 'propaganda' as those of Veit Harlan and his wife, the actress Kristina Söderbaum.

In the 1990s, what is now commonly accepted as a new school of Nazi film studies emerged. The ideas elaborated by scholars such as Stephen Lowry[9] and Karsten Witte[10] were important steps in the development of revisionist theories, the academic breakthrough of which is marked by the 1996 publications of literary scholars Eric Rentschler[11] and Linda Schulte-Sasse.[12] What these authors and their followers have in common – in spite of the sometimes very different theoretical frameworks they use – is a determination to look beyond the 'traditional' canon[13] and to approach these films as complex cultural texts that, apart from their 'preferred reading' (intended messages and dominant themes, as reflected in screenplays and archival sources), contain unintended discursive elements that can be read in a variety of non-simultaneous or contradictory ways, which are also relevant to our understanding of the culture and society that produced and received them. The work of this new school has advanced the scholarly tools of (Nazi) cinema studies, and their readings of formerly neglected entertainment films have simultaneously improved and differentiated our understandings of film production and consumerism in the Third Reich. There are, however, two sides to every question and it must be clear that, while it has become fashionable for some exponents of the new generation to dispense with more traditional, historical examinations of Nazi cinema, several followers of the new school could benefit from some historical awareness before making their assertions. In the future, researchers will hopefully cross the history/cultural divide that hitherto separates both schools:[14] both the 'traditional' and 'new' studies of Nazi cinema can benefit from incorporating the insights of the other.

Whether they are part of the 'traditional' or the 'new' school, most of the internationally established scholarly works on the cinema of the Third Reich have one thing in common. It is their strict focus on the production, distribution, screening or reception of films in the so-called 'Old Empire' (*Altreich*): the territories that were already part of the Third Reich in 1933–37. Some studies also pay attention to regions that were annexed afterwards but often focus only on territories that became important production centres like Austria. With the exception of Boguslaw Drewniak[15] and Jürgen Spiker,[16] virtually no author pays sufficient attention to the expansionist policy the German film industry pursued before and during the Second World War, attempting to turn Berlin into Europe's very own Hollywood. Students of this era are of course aware that, apart from 'reorganising' the cinema of Nazi-occupied countries, the German film industry also tried to increase its influence over friendly or neutral states, like Italy, Spain or Sweden. It is also understood that this process, stimulated by Propaganda Minister Joseph Goebbels, not only represented an economic takeover, but also had important cultural and political implications. What has been lacking, however, is concrete information on the success or failure of the Third Reich film industry to influence, infiltrate or take over the film sector of such countries.

The main reason for this blind spot in Third Reich film studies is a linguistic one. In many countries, scholars have already conducted ground-breaking research on the German influence over their national film industries (1933–45). Unfortunately, access to most of these publications is restricted to scholars who read the local language. *Cinema and the Swastika* aims to bring together comparative research in this field. This book investigates various attempts to infiltrate – economically, politically and culturally – the film industries of 20 countries or regions Nazi Germany occupied, befriended or entertained 'neutral' relationships with. Countries and regions covered include Western and Central Europe, Italy, Japan, Scandinavia, Spain, South American countries and the United States. Many of the specialists who contributed chapters to this book have already published extensively on the topic in their mother tongue, but now do so for the first time in English. To place the 'local' studies in a broader framework, the book opens with an assessment of the German film industry (1933–45), of the International Film Chamber through which Germany tried to take the lead of the 'Film Europe' movement, and of Hispano Film, through which German cinema tried to conquer Spanish markets.

Obviously, this book has blind spots too. The current state of affairs of research in or about most countries that after 1945 became part of the Soviet sphere of influence does not yet allow for analyses of German film activities in those regions. We have, for instance, tried, to no avail, to locate research on film distribution and exhibition in the Baltic republics and the occupied zones of the Soviet Union. Hopefully this book will stimulate the undertaking of such research in the near future. Also, most chapters have a political–economical approach and pay more attention to the superstructures (the activities of big companies such as Ufa, the diplomatic and economic manoeuvres made by German officials and businessmen, the larger historical and political context against which such processes are to be understood) than to the experiences of local film-goers. On the other hand, this does not mean that the tastes and preferences of local audiences have been ignored. One of the recurring themes of this book is the international popularity of films and actors/actresses that were so often neglected in early studies of Third Reich cinema.

Editing this book has been a slow but rewarding process. We are indebted to our contributors and hope that their and our efforts will encourage further comparative research on the influence Nazi Germany had on the international film industry.

Notes

1. Riefenstahl's relationship with Goebbels was nevertheless much better than she preferred to remember after 1945. J. Trimborn, *Riefenstahl – Eine deutsche Karriere* (Berlin: Aufbau-Verlag, 2002), pp. 156-A171; D. Culbert, 'Leni Riefenstahl and the Diaries of Joseph Goebbels', *Historical Journal of Film, Radio and Television,* 13:1 (1993), pp. 85–93.
2. E. Leiser, *'Deutschland, erwache!' Propapaganda im Film des Dritten Reiches* (Reinbek bei Hamburg: Rowohlt Taschenbuch Verlag, 1968).
3. G. Albrecht, *Nationalsozialistische Filmpolitik. Eine soziologische Untersuchung über die Spielfilme des Dritten Reiches* (Stuttgart: Ferdinand Enke Verlag, 1969).
4. D. S. Hull, *Film in the Third Reich. A Study of the German Cinema 1933–1945* (Berkeley–Los Angeles: University of California Press, 1969).
5. This is above all true for Hull. See, for instance, J. Petley, *Capital and Culture. German Cinema 1933–1945* (London: British Film Institute, 1979), pp. 1–8.
6. R. Taylor, *Film Propaganda. Soviet Russia and Nazi Germany* (London–New York: I.B. Tauris, 1998 rev.); D. Welch, *Propaganda and the German Cinema 1933–45* (London–New York: I.B. Tauris, rev. 2001 20061 rev.).
7. K. Kanzog, *Staatspolitisch besonders wertvoll: ein Handbuch zu 30 deutschen Spielfilmen der Jahre 1934 bis 1945* (München: Diskurs-Film-Verlag, 1994).
8. Of course, in a highly politicised society such as the Third Reich, even the apolitical becomes significant in that so-called 'entertainment films' tend to promote the official 'world view' of things and reinforce the existing political, social and economic order. See, Welch (rev. 2001), pp. 35–8.
9. S. Lowry, *Pathos und Politik. Ideologie im Spielfilm des Nationalsozialismus* (Tübingen: Max Niemeyer Verlag, 1991).
10. K. Witte, *Lachende Erben, toller Tag. Filmkomödie im Dritten Reich* (Berlin: Vorwerk 8, 1995).
11. E. Rentschler, *The Ministry of Illusion. Nazi Cinema and its Afterlife* (Cambridge, London: Harvard University Press, 1996).
12. L. Schulte-Sasse, *Entertaining the Third Reich: Illusions of Wholeness in Nazi Cinema* (Durham NC: Duke University Press, 1996).
13. Nevertheless, films such as *Jew Süss* and *Hitler Youth Quex* (*Hitlerjunge Quex*, 1933) remain a very popular object of research even among this 'new' school.

14. S. Spector, 'Was the Third Reich Movie-Made? Interdisciplinarity and the Reframing of "Ideology"', *American Historical Review* 106:2 (2001), pp. 460–84; R. Vande Winkel, 'Nazi Actresses as Trojan Horses? "New" and "Traditional" Interpretations of Third Reich Film Representations of Women', *Historical Journal of Film, Radio and Television,* 25:4 (2005), pp. 647–54. For a discussion of this historiographical debate see, D. Weinberg, 'Approaches to the Study of Film in the Third Reich: A Critical Appraisal', *Journal of Contemporary History* 19:1 (1984), pp. 105–26.
15. B. Drewniak, 'Die Expansion der Kinematographie des Dritten Reiches in den Jahren des Zweiten Weltkrieges', in C. Madayczyk (ed.), *Inter armae non silentae Musae. The war and the culture 1939–1945* (Warszawa: Panstowowy Instytut Wydawniczy, 1977), pp. 89–116; B. Drewniak, *Der deutsche Film 1938–1945* (Düsseldorf: Droste Verlag, 1987).
16. J. Spiker, *Film und Kapital* (Berlin: Verlag Volker Spiess, 1975).

1

Europe's New Hollywood? The German Film Industry Under Nazi Rule, 1933–45

David Welch and Roel Vande Winkel

This chapter, together with the following chapters on the International Film Chamber and the Hispano-Film-Produktion Company, serves as an introduction to the many case studies of German activities on the international film market, and offers a brief introduction to the National-Socialist 'reorganisation' of the domestic film market. For the purpose of this book, it provides an overview of how the German government, and most notably its propaganda ministry, streamlined German film production and regulated film distribution and exhibition.

The Nazi party and film before the takeover of power[1]

The film activities of the Nazi Party before 1933 were of little relevance to the film industry of the time, but they illustrate the Nazi party's growing awareness of the importance of a well-coordinated organisation and opportunism for learning and adapting new propaganda techniques. The knowledge that film was an important propaganda medium was present from the early beginnings of the Party. But at this stage they had little finance and even less experience in their propaganda department of the complexities of film. Films produced by the party were amateurish and mainly shown to closed party gatherings.

Towards the end of 1930, Joseph Goebbels, who had been steadily building up the Party following in Berlin since 1926, decided to establish the Reich Film Cells (*NSDAP-Reichsfilmstelle*, RFS) in the capital for the purpose of distributing films throughout Germany. However, the project proved to be optimistically premature as the Nazi leadership was not convinced of its necessity and refused to supply the necessary capital. It was only by October 1932 that all *Nationalsozialische Deutsche Arbeiterpartei* (NSDAP) film activities were finally transferred to Berlin under Goebbels' control. During this period the film industry in general was still recoiling from the continuing effects of the recession in world trade and the advent of sound films, which involved considerable expenditure at a time when total receipts were falling, companies were going bankrupt, and cinemas were changing hands at an alarming rate. The German film industry responded with the so-called *SPIO Plan* of 1932. The *Spitzenorganisation der Deutschen Filmindustrie* (SPIO) was the industry's main professional representative body and its principle concern was to strike a satisfactory relationship between the production, distribution, and exhibition sectors while at the same time retaining the traditional structure of the industry. Significantly SPIO was dominated by the large combines and it was no surprise that they should produce a plan that discriminated so blatantly against the German Cinema Owners' Association (*Reichsverband Deutscher Lichtspieltheater*) whom they accused of flooding the market with too many cinemas, price cutting, and retaining a disproportionate share of total receipts.

This conflict within the film industry placed the NSDAP in a rather delicate position. On the one hand, the Nazis did not have to worry about making their own propaganda films at this stage. Alfred Hugenberg, press baron, leader of the German National People's Party (*Deutschnationale Volkspartei*) and sympathiser of the Nazis, had bought the largest and most prestigious German film company, Ufa (*Universum-Film-Aktiengesellschaft*).[2] Hugenberg had acquired Ufa to 'preserve it for the national outlook', which in practice meant producing overt nationalist films; but on the other hand, they had believed for some time that the cinema owners were an important element in their future operations. There were also at this stage divisions within the NSDAP itself over the nature of the German film industry. The struggle between these elements both within the industry and the NSDAP and the questions they posed for the future of the German film industry would be answered by the new Nazi government in less than a year after assuming power.

The Gleichschaltung (coordination) of the German film industry[3]

As early as the 1920s the National Socialists had infiltrated their members into many spheres of public life. The entire organisation of the Party, the division into administrative sectors, and the structure of leadership were built up as a state within a state. The Nazis were therefore well placed to take control of a film industry which had to a large extent prepared itself to be controlled. The *Gleichschaltung* (coordination)[4] of the German cinema was affected behind the scenes by a process of which the ordinary citizen was largely unaware. To achieve this end, a plethora of complex laws, decrees, and intricate state machinery was instigated to prevent any form of nonconformity. Pursuing a policy that was to become traditional in the Third

Reich, the Party organisation was kept separate from state administration at both national and regional levels, while at the same time remaining closely linked.

In the months following Hitler's appointment to Chancellor in January 1933, the divisions within the Party which had flared up in 1932 became an issue again. Certain organisations such as the Nazi Trade Union (*Nationalsozialistische Betriebszellen Organisation*, NSBO) and the Fighting League for German Culture (*Kampfbund für deutsche Kultur*, KfdK – led by Alfred Rosenberg) put forward radical solutions to the film industry's problems, demanding centralisation and the banning of all films which offended the National-Socialist world-view (*Vőlkische Weltanschauung*). Goebbels, on the other hand, was more realistic, and appreciated that the German film community did not welcome these forces of Nazi extremism. He was unwilling to undertake an immediate nationalisation of the industry not only on ideological grounds but for the pragmatic reasons that Hugenberg, who owned Ufa, was in the new cabinet as Minister of Economics and that the Party in general depended on big business for its finances.

Cinema owners were not the only sector of the industry to be effectively 'coordinated' in this manner. Throughout March and April the NSBO had been active in all spheres of film production – from cameramen to film actors and composers. When the Nazis banned all trade unions in early May, the industry's 'official' trade union DACHO was dissolved and absorbed initially into the NSBO[5] which was itself transferred automatically to the German Labour Front (*Deutsche Arbeitsfront*, DAF), the only permissible trade union. It was during these months that Goebbels was making final plans for a Propaganda Ministry that would assume control over all aspects of mass communication. Eventually Goebbels was appointed head of the Reich Ministry for Popular Enlightenment and Propaganda (*Reichsministerium für Volksaufklärung und Propaganda*, RMVP) on 13 March 1933. In June Hitler was to define the scope of the RMVP according to which the new Minister would be responsible for 'all tasks of spiritual direction of the nation'.[6] Not only did this vague directive give Goebbels room to manoeuvre against the more radical elements within the Party (like Party ideologue Alfred Rosenberg, who also tried to exercise influence over the German film industry[7]), it also gave the mark of legality to what was soon to be the Ministry's complete control of all that mattered most in the functioning of the mass media in the Third Reich.

The film industry presented a number of structural, economic, and artistic problems for the builders of the new German society. Corresponding to its importance as a medium of propaganda, film was immediately reorganised after the takeover of power. The RMVP was already established when a provisional Reich Film Chamber (*Reichsfilmkammer*) was set up in July 1933. Shortly afterwards, in September 1933, Goebbels decided to extend the idea to the whole of German life and form the Reich Culture Chamber (*Reichskulturkammer*). The Reich Film Chamber became one of the seven Chambers which made up the Reich Culture Chamber, the others being literature, theatre, music, fine arts, press, and radio.

The creation of the Reich Film Chamber is an excellent example of the process of coordination in that it allowed the RMVP to exert *its* control over both film-makers and the film industry as a whole. As Propaganda Minister, Goebbels acted as President of the seven Chambers, and through him their jurisdiction spread down to both the nation's regional administrations (*Länder*) and the Party's own specifically political areas (*Gaue*). This not only facilitated the RMVP's control over individual Chambers but, equally importantly, it allowed the Ministry to coordinate its propaganda campaigns. The structure of the Reich Film Chamber was scarcely changed after it had been incorporated into the Reich Culture Chamber. Its head and all-responsible President was subordinate only to the President of the Reich Culture Chamber, that is the Propaganda Minister. The various sections of the German film industry were grouped together into 10 departments. These 10 departments controlled all film activities in Germany. The centralisation, however, did not lead to what the Propaganda Minister claimed – the harmonisation of all branches of the industry – but it did harm the substance of the German film by limiting personal and economic initiative and artistic freedom.

To gain control over film finance, a Film Credit Bank (*Filmkreditbank*) was established. It was announced on 1 June 1933 as a provider of credit and help for a crisis-ridden film economy. The Film Credit Bank was to create the beginnings of the National Socialists' disastrous film policy and to result in the dependence of the private film producers on the Nazi state. However, at the time, the Film Credit Bank was greeted with great enthusiasm from all sides of the film industry. The Film Credit Bank took the form of a private, limited liability company and functioned to all intents and purposes as a normal commercial undertaking except that it was not expected to make large profits. The procedure for securing finance from the Bank was that a producer had to show that he could raise 30 per cent of the production costs as well as convincing the Film Credit Bank that the film stood a good chance of making a profit. The film then became the property of the Bank until the loan was repaid. Thus, private finance was excluded from all freedom of credit and opportunities for profit. Within a short time this financial body would also become an important means of securing both economic and political conformity. The Bank, acting on behalf of the government, could refuse all credit at the pre-production stage until a film reflected the wishes of the new regime. Significantly, there is no evidence to suggest that the film industry was unwilling to accept this form of self-censorship.

Originally the Film Credit Bank was inaugurated to assist the small independent producer; however, by 1936 it was financing over 73 per cent of all

German feature films dealing almost exclusively with distributors who could guarantee that a film would be shown nationwide.[8] The result was that the smaller companies' share of the market continued to decline as the process of concentration was relentlessly increased. This was a further step towards creating dependence and establishing a state monopoly in order to destroy any form of independent initiative.

Apart from regulating the financing of films, one of the main purposes of establishing the Reich Film Chamber was the removal of Jews and other 'degenerate artists' from German cultural life, since only racially 'pure' Germans could become members. Whoever wished to participate in any aspect of film production was forced to become a member of the Reich Film Chamber. Goebbels was, however, given the power to issue exemptions to these conditions should he require to do so.[9] The man entrusted by Goebbels for the *Entjudung* (removal of Jews) was Hans Hinkel, who in May 1935 was given overall responsibility for all matters relating to Reich Culture Chamber personnel policy. Hinkel brought about a radicalisation of the Reich Culture Chamber policy. Eventually, by arranging for the Jews to have their own separate cultural organisation, Hinkel justified the total elimination of Jews from German cultural life. Not surprisingly the result of such policies was the emigration of all those who either could not or would not submit to these conditions. The loss of talent was naturally severe but the Nazis were able to retain the services of many highly qualified technical and artistic staff, and a veritable reservoir of talented actors.

Tightening the straitjacket: The new Reich Cinema Law[10]

To consolidate his position Goebbels still desired more power than he had hitherto secured through the Reich Culture Chamber legislation. He also needed some form of legal confirmation to be able to supervise films in the early stages of production. Goebbels settled both these issues by creating a revised version of the Reich Cinema Law (*Reichslichtspielgesetz*), which became law on 16 February 1934 after long and careful preparation. This decree attempted to create a new 'positive' censorship by which the State undertook to encourage 'good' films instead of merely discouraging 'bad' ones. The new Cinema Law anticipated three ways of achieving this positive censorship: a compulsory script censorship, an increase in the number of provisions under which the Censorship Office (*Filmprüfstelle*) might ban a film, and a greatly enlarged system of distinction marks. The most significant innovation of the new Cinema Law was the institution of a pre-censor (*Vorzensor*) undertaken by an RMVP official called the Reich Film Director (*Reichsfilmdramaturg*). The Reich Film Director could supervise every stage of production. The orders issued and the changes suggested by him were binding. As the representative of the RMVP, he could even interfere with the censorship exercised by the Censorship Office (*Prüfstelle*) in Berlin. After the 1934 Cinema Law had been in operation for just 10 months, the law was changed (13 December 1934) to make the submission of scripts optional instead of compulsory.

According to the new Cinema Law, all kinds of films were to be submitted to the censor. Public and private screenings were made equal in law. Even film advertising in the cinemas was censored. In all matters concerning censorship, the Propaganda Minister had the right of intervention. In the second amendment to the Cinema Law (28 June 1935) Goebbels was given extra powers to ban, without reference to Censorship Office, any film if he felt it was in the public's interest. Not only was the entire censorship apparatus centralised in Berlin but the previous rights of local governments to request a re-examination of films was now the exclusive prerogative of the RMVP.

In addition to direct censorship the film industry depended on a system of distinction marks (*Prädikate*), which was really a form of negative taxation. As film allegedly improved, the range of the *Prädikat* system was extended. Before 1933 the distribution of *Prädikate* was an honour and an opportunity to gain, according to the degree of the distinction mark, tax reductions, but now every film had to obtain a *Prädikat* not only to benefit from tax reductions but to be allowed to be exhibited at all. Films without these distinction marks needed special permission to be shown. A further incentive was that producers with a *Prädikat* now received an extra share of the film's profits. By 1939 the law provided for the following distinction marks:[11] Instructional (1920); National education (1924); Politically and artistically especially valuable (awarded from 1933); Politically especially valuable (1933); Artistically especially valuable (1933); Politically valuable (1933); Artistically valuable (1933); Culturally valuable (1933); Valuable for youth (1938); Nationally valuable (1939); and Film of the Nation (1939).

The highest distinction marks meant that the entire programme would be exempt from entertainment tax while the lower *Prädikate* reduced the tax proportionate to their value. The system not only produced certain financial advantages but also helped to establish the appropriate expectations and responses on the part of cinema audiences. 'Politically valuable' was clearly a film which completely reflected the aims of the NSDAP. This title was given not only to documentaries like *Triumph of the Will* (*Triumph des Willens,* 1935) but also to feature films with a political message such as the pro-euthanasia production *I Accuse* (*Ich klage an,* 1941). The combination of 'politically and artistically especially valuable' signified a special quality and credibility. The distinction marks 'artistically valuable' were understood in the sense of cultural propaganda and were given only to prestige films and those reserved for export.

Under the pretence of discarding all the old hypocrisies surrounding the film industry, the Cinema Law assumed powers which in fact only served

O. K. Farb-Film-Foto

Reich Propaganda Minister Joseph Goebbels and some of his closest collaborators in the field of cinema. From left to right: Leopold Gutterer, State Secretary in the RMVP (1941–44) and chair of the Ufa and Ufi board; Max Winkler, Goebbels's financial genius and Reich Appointee (*Reichsbeauftragter*) for the German film industry; Fritz Hippler, Head of the RMVP's film department since 1939 and *Reichsfilmintendant* from 1939 to 1943; Ludwig Klitzsch, Chairman of Ufa. *Source*: Unnumbered pages of O. Kriegk, *Der Deutsche Film Im Spiegel Der UFA – 25 Jahre Kampf Und Vollendung* (Berlin: Ufa-Buchverlag, 1943).

to create the formation of a film monopoly controlled by the Party and the State. The result was the adjusting of cinema terminology to fit the ideas of National Socialism, in terms of both the language used in Nazi films and the phrasing of the film law which was kept as ambiguous as possible so that it could be applied according to the wishes of the moment and the official viewpoint. The producer was informed of the current aims of the government by having his particular film project checked by both the Film Credit Bank and the *Reichsfilmdramaturg.* A film was often passed by the Censorship Office only one or two days before its première.[12] This suggests that within a short period of time legal censorship became a mere formality, the real censorship being done elsewhere at an earlier stage in the process of the film's production.

When discussing the implementation of the Nazi Cinema Law it is important to consider the attempts to control film criticism at this time. On 13 May 1936, Goebbels issued a proclamation that banned the writing of critical reviews on the same evening as the performance (*Nachtkritik*). In November of the same year, the RMVP banned all art criticism by confining critics to writing merely 'descriptive' reviews.[13] In practice film criticism came more and more to resemble publicity material associated with any film company attempting to promote a new product. A film deemed important by the RMVP would be introduced to the film public before its première by progress reports on its production. The first performance would be accompanied by an extravagant illustrated report and then, perhaps one or two days later, by a favourable analysis which would place the film within its political context. Thus with slogans following the propaganda principle of repetition, the press introduced the public to the films, explained them, and fitted the events of the film into the topical context. Even for a patently bad film a positive review had to be found and 'politically valuable' films were praised on principle. The press were guided in the formation of definitions and the use of language by directives from the RMVP, enabling it to present a common approach in its film reviews.

It should not, however, be assumed that all films produced under the aegis of the RMVP were *overtly* propagandistic. An analysis of the different types of film made during the Third Reich reveals a good deal about Goebbels' *Filmpolitik*. Of the 1097 feature films produced between 1933 and 1945 only about one-fifth were, according to assessments of the regime,[14] overtly propagandistic with a direct political content. Less than half of these films (96 out of 229) were 'state-commissioned films' (*Staatsauftragsfilme*), which included the most important films from a political standpoint and were given disproportionate funding and publicity. Of the entire production of feature films, virtually 50 per cent were either love stories or comedies, and 25 per cent dramatic films, such as crime thrillers or musicals.[15] Regardless of the genre, all of these films went through the pre-censorship process and all were associated with the National-Socialist ideology in that they were produced and performed in accordance with the propagandistic aims of the period. From the breakdown of films made, it can be seen that there was no clearly formulated policy regarding the percentage of films that were to be allocated to each particular genre. However, it is discernible that as the war dragged on – particularly after Stalingrad, when disillusionment set in – the number of political films declined, and the Nazi cinema served increasingly to facilitate escapism (*Wirklichkeitsflucht*) that would divert people's attention from the war. These figures both reflect the diversification of the film programme and illustrate Goebbels' intentions of mixing entertainment with propaganda.

It should also be mentioned that, in spite of all the efforts to streamline film production, the RMVP failed to condition the actual content of the films, let alone the ways in which audiences interpreted them – if only because the meaning of a film can be interpreted in so many ways.[16] Also, it has been demonstrated that even well-produced propaganda films failed to exercise long time influence over its audiences.[17]

Conditioning film exhibition: Newsreel, *Kulturfilm*, and feature film[18]

Cinema owners were tied by the regulations mentioned above and had, which was especially true for the larger cinemas in cities, virtually no say in the composure of 'their' film programme. The state-controlled companies decided which film went to what cinema and which productions were to be shown before or after the feature. But that was not the end of it. The RMVP wished not only to control national cinematographic production/distribution, but also to condition circumstances under which audiences (Aryan audiences, as Jews were not allowed) viewed films. In 1934, the RMVP obliged all cinemas to include a non-fiction short, known as the *Kulturfilm*, in the supporting programme of each feature film. In November 1938, the screening of a newsreel was also made obligatory. This way the ministry established a compulsory 'cinematic trinity' of newsreel, *Kulturfilm* and feature film that was often – but not always and everywhere – shown in that order. When, in subsequent years, Nazi Germany conquered many European countries, allowing the Propaganda Ministry to 'reorganise' local film industries and orientate them towards Berlin, most occupied territories were forced to adopt this three-pronged cinema programme. While German cinemas already often showed such programmes before it became obligatory, the system was new to many foreign cinemas that used to have a 'double bill' of two feature films, sometimes headed by a newsreel. The advantage of this film programme was twofold: it diminished the need for feature films (a need the German industry could not fulfil without imports) and it increased the propagandistic potential of film screenings. Indeed, 'propaganda and enlightenment' were often a stronger presence in the *Kulturfilm* and (particularly) in the newsreel than in the feature.

The notion of *Kulturfilm* is specifically German and to be preferred over the English translation ('cultural short') for *Kulturfilme* did not only treat cultural subjects. Hilmar Hoffmann described their thematic variety as follows:

> From the cellular division of an amoeba to an artistic giant such as Michelangelo, the *Kulturfilm* deals with everything that is being investigated by biology and medicine, by research and technology, art and literature, ethnology and geography and incorporates it all into a more elevated way of looking at the world that is peculiar to this genre.[19]

Although the educational component was crucial, it was not unique to the genre. In other words: every *Kulturfilm* was at some level educational, but not every educational short was a *Kulturfilm*. Long before the Nazi takeover, Ufa and many other enterprises produced *Kulturfilme*. Since their educational component was widely known and accepted, it was manifestly logical that Nazi propagandists show an interest in the *Kulturfilm*. Nevertheless, Nazi's ascension to power did not result in a real break in *Kulturfilm* production. It is true that everyone involved in the *Kulturfilm* sector was subject to the Reich Film Chamber and was therefore controlled by the Propaganda Ministry. It is also true that some professionals produced propagandist *Kulturfilme*, which had been specifically commissioned by the party or the state. The fact that a number of *Kulturfilme* were deployed for propaganda purposes should, nevertheless, not be interpreted as a goal-oriented direction of the entire *Kulturfilm* production. A first attempt to centralise the sector was only made around March 1939, when preparation for war required a halt to an uncoordinated accumulation of similar *Kulturfilm* projects. This led to the creation of the German *Kulturfilm* Centre that was officially established in August 1940. The setting up of the German *Kulturfilm* Centre (*Deutsche Kulturfilmzentrale*) served a political as well as an economic purpose because it facilitated the production of propagandist *Kulturfilme* while assuring the production of a sufficient number of *Kulturfilme* during the war years. In February 1942, the duties of the German *Kulturfilm* Centre were transferred to another service but remained controlled by the Propaganda Ministry.

Although their efficacy in terms of real influence on public opinion has often been exaggerated, newsreels were undoubtedly an important Third Reich propaganda medium, especially during the war years. Soon after its foundation, the Propaganda Ministry created a department that facilitated the work of newsreel cameramen and suggested topics that could/should be covered. In 1935, the RMVP increased its influence on German newsreel production by establishing a German Film News Office (*Deutsches Film-Nachrichtenbüro*, 1935). By that time, the number of different newsreels distributed in German cinemas was, taking into account the size of Germany, surprisingly low. This can mainly be attributed to the expansionist politics of Ufa owner Alfred Hugenberg, under whose guidance several smaller newsreels had been taken over and absorbed by Ufa. There were only four different newsreels, two of which were produced and distributed by Ufa: the *Ufa-Tonwoche* and *Deulig-Tonwoche*. The other two newsreels were the *Tobis-Woche* and the *Fox-Tönende-Wochenschau*, respectively produced/distributed by Tobis firm and by the German branch of the American Fox company. In 1938, the German Film News Office transferred its tasks of controlling newsreel editorial offices and censoring the final results to another service within the ministry, the so-called German Newsreel Bureau (*Deutsche Wochenschauzentrale*). As responsibilities for newsreels were transferred from one ministerial department to another, they increased slightly. Until the war broke out, the above-mentioned ministerial services successively controlled the four existing newsreels to an increasing extent but nevertheless allowed their separate editorial offices to co-exist. Replacing all of them with a single department would certainly have facilitated the Propaganda Ministry's tasks but it would also have highlighted the ministry's role. The full reason for Goebbels' reluctance to nationalise and monopolise the German newsreels is to be found here, in his clear preference to conceal propaganda mechanisms. As the Wehrmacht made its final preparations to invade Poland, the Propaganda Ministry nevertheless realised that to control newsreel coverage of the campaign it would have to combine the different editorial offices. From September 1939 onwards, coinciding exactly with the German invasion, the *Ufa-Tonwoche, Deulig-Tonwoche, Tobis-Woche,* and *Fox-Tönende-Wochenschau* were merged into a single war newsreel. They kept their respective opening titles until June 1940. After that the merger was made public by the use of a single new opening title: *Die Deutsche Wochenschau* (DW) or the German Weekly Newsreel. As the Propaganda Ministry's newsreel centre transformed from a powerful watchdog into a proper newsreel editorial office, Goebbels considered subcontracting it to a separate organisation. These plans were finalised with the foundation of the German Newsreel Company (*Deutsche Wochenschau GmbH*), officially set up on 21 November 1940. Although legally speaking, a subsidiary of the (in the meantime state-owned) Ufa film company, all of its employees were directly subordinate to the Propaganda Ministry. The German Newsreel Company also produced a foreign weekly newsreel, or *Auslandstonwoche* (ATW). The ATW was not just a foreign version of the DW, but a fully fledged newsreel in its own right, a continuation of the newsreels Ufa had exported since 1927. From late 1940 onwards, foreign editorial boards making local versions of the ATW were established all over Europe, in occupied as well as in neutral territories. In Germany as in many occupied regions these Nazi newsreels were compulsory before each film screening, which made them accessible to a wide audience.[20]

Enlarging the German film market and nationalising the German film industry[21]

In 1934, an NSDAP handbook claimed that German films should continue to sell extremely well in international markets. It calculated that foreign sales would take an upward turn and that the industry should be striving to achieve 40 per cent of its total income from the sale of German films abroad.[22] But in 1934–35, instead of rising, German film exports went into an alarming decline, accounting for only 8 per cent of the industries' income and in 1938–39 this figure dropped to 7 per cent.[23] A number of reasons accounted for this catastrophic state, the most important being the growing political hostility towards Germany. The film industry found itself in a difficult position; on the one hand the government wanted to reduce film imports, but because of foreign countries' quota systems, this made exporting difficult. Moreover, many foreign Jewish distributors simply refused to accept German films. The situation was further complicated by the Censorship Office, which tended to object to foreign films on ideological and racial grounds. The result was that within a short time, foreign distributors gave up trying to exhibit their films in Germany. This led German artists with an international reputation to leave the country and German films became even more parochial and nationalistic.

The decline in exports would not have been so alarming had it not been accompanied by a sharp increase in production costs in 1935–36. In the same year the President of the Reich Film Chamber (Dr Fritz Scheuermann) warned Goebbels that production expenditure had increased by 50 per cent since 1933. Two years later, the Film Chamber Yearbook (*Jahrbuch der Reichsfilmkammer*) was gloomily reporting that costs had risen by 35 per cent since the previous year. As far as the RMVP was concerned, this situation called for state intervention. There were a number of options open to Goebbels, he could either support the independent film-makers or he could increase the government's hold over the large production companies. In choosing the latter, the gradual nationalisation of the film industry, the concentration of film as a propaganda medium was carried out with great care. The task of clearing up the economic problems of the nationalisation and disguising them was given to a private company.

Goebbels' agent in these transactions and later Reich Delegate to the German film industry was Max Winkler, who had been active as a trustee on behalf of successive German governments since 1919.[24] By disguising the real nature of the transactions, Goebbels was able to claim that the government takeover had been motivated by purely artistic and not commercial reasons. Winkler, in fact, had convinced Goebbels that the best way of achieving the ideologically committed films that he had been demanding was not to force the film industry to become National-Socialists but instead to guarantee them financial stability. In this way, both production and distribution sectors would be drawn into the Nazi *Weltanschauung* without realising that they were becoming increasingly the political instruments of the Propaganda Ministry.

In 1936, the shaky financial position of the two major film companies, Ufa and Tobis (*Tonbild-Syndikat AG*, a German company owed by international investors and dominated by Dutch shareholders[25]), gave the RMVP the opportunity they had been seeking. Winkler's method of control was to establish a trust company, *Cautio Treuhand GmbH,* which was to act as a majority shareholder and would administer the assets of the various companies. The preparations for the state monopoly took place in almost complete secrecy. The takeover of these firms was achieved by the purchase of the majority of the shares and the transactions were always carried out as separate dealings. The film press scarcely commented on them, or, if so, only briefly. Thus the process of nationalisation went completely unnoticed. Cautio simply bought out ailing companies and administered them for the State as trustee. Interestingly enough, they were referred to as *staatsmittelbar* (indirectly state-controlled), rather than state owned.

Ufa, which itself had swallowed many smaller companies in the 1930s, was the first company to be acquired in March 1937. Two months later, Winkler decided that Tobis should be broken up. In August of that year, Terra Film AG (an Ufa subsidiary of Swiss origin[26]) was amalgamated with one of Tobis' distribution companies (Tobis Rota) to form a new production company, *Terrakunst GmbH*. Four months later, in December, the original Tobis was transformed and given the new title, *Tobis Filmkunst GmbH.*[27] The most pressing problem at this stage, however, was how to finance these *staatsmittelbar* companies. If nationalisation was to be effective, Winkler appreciated that a radical reorganisation of film finance was needed. This came in the form of a new company called Film Finanz GmBH. Film credit was determined by a supervisory board consisting of representatives of the RMVP, the Reich Finance Ministry, the Reich Credit Company, Cautio, and the *staatsmittelbar* companies. The first meeting was held in November 1937 and RM 22 million was allocated (RM 10 million to Tobis and RM 6 million each to Ufa and Terra).[28]

Shortly afterwards, Cautio purchased the holding of Bavaria Film AG and on 11 February 1938 it became known as *Bavaria Filmkunst GmbH*. It was during this time that Goebbels announced that a National Film School, the *Deutsche Filmakademie,* would be entrusted with the task of training new technicians and artists in the service of the National Socialist State.[29] There were 23 different courses, including scenario writing, direction, set and costume design, photography, sound recording, acting, even distribution, house management, and laboratory work. The new German cinema, it was claimed, now rivalled Hollywood in terms both of scope and resources. While this was an exaggeration, it is true that when war came in 1939, the German cinema had attained an expertise and technical mastery that was unequalled in Europe.

Some of the greatest stars of Third Reich cinema. From left to right: Zarah Leander; Marika Rökk; Kristina Söderbaum; Heinz Rühmann. *Source*: Vande Winkel/De Paepe Collection.

Winkler, meanwhile, had not finished the process of state intervention. In 1938 the *Anschluss* (annexation) of Austria provided further opportunities. Because of a common language and culture the Austrian film industry had always had close ties with Germany. On 16 December 1938, the whole industry amalgamated to form a new *staatsmittelbar* company, *Wien Film GmbH*, which immediately came under the jurisdiction of Winkler's Cautio.[30] Later a similar reorganisation was carried out in Czechoslovakia with the formation of the *Prag-Film AG*.[31]

By 1939, all the major film companies were *staatsmittelbar*. Not surprisingly they quickly dominated film output. In 1939, they accounted for 60 per cent of all feature film production; in 1941, this figure had risen to 70 per cent. The aim behind this reorganisation was to rationalise film-making so that it could respond quickly and efficiently to the demands of the RMVP; in practice this meant simplifying the financing of films and maintaining a strict control over the content of feature films. *Staatsmittelbar* film companies were not intended to compete with each other but to cooperate in producing quality films that would represent the intrinsic values of National Socialism both at home and abroad.

The outbreak of war in September 1939 created initial problems for the film industry in that shortages of labour and raw materials tended to increase production costs. Another factor which increased costs still further was the disruptive effect of tighter censorship during the making of films. However, there emerged as a result of the war important developments that offset these difficulties. First, the military conquests of 1939–40 had created a German-dominated film monopoly in Europe. At the end of 1939 German distributors were in the fortunate position of having 8300 cinemas at their disposal.[32] This number increased in 1940–41, as the Wehrmacht conquered territory in Western and Eastern Europe. Several measures, notably the enforced closure of American film distributors inside and outside the Reich, further expanded the market for German films. This also allowed for the exploitation of films that had not been authorised for screenings in Germany. All over Europe, Ufa and Tobis either established new distribution branches or were able to strengthen the market position of already existing subsidiaries.

Sometimes new production centres (which often incorporated existing local companies) were established as well: *Wien-Film* in Austria,[33] *Prag-Film* (above) in Czechoslovakia,[34] and *Continental Films* in France,[35] and the *Zentrallfilmgesellschaft Ost* and its subsidiaries (*Ostland Filmgesellschaft* and *Ukraine-Filmgesellschaft*) in Poland and the occupied zones of the Soviet-Union.[36] In other countries too, the Netherlands[37] for instance, local studio facilities were primarily used to produce German (instead of local) films. Meantime, Max Winkler's Cautio openly or secretly acquired foreign theatres (preferably prestigious film palaces that attracted large audiences) in order to recuperate more ticket office revenues. Such tasks were usually carried out by plenipotentiaries such as Alfred Greven.

This unprecedented growth also created problems for the German film industry. The major problem at this stage, in spite of the establishment of new production centres, was the supply of films. Winkler was particularly concerned that if Germany was to exploit her position in Europe the industry should be producing at least 100 feature films per year. However, during 1941 it became increasingly clear that the target of 100 films was not going to be reached. The only solution seemed to lay in a complete take-over by the state. On 10 January 1942, a giant holding company, *Ufa-Film GmbH* (called Ufi to distinguish it from its predecessors), assumed control of the entire German film industry and its foreign subsidiaries. This resulted, for instance, in Ufa subsidiaries all over Europe incorporating local branches of Tobis. The Ufi umbrella organisation would not only facilitate a much closer supervision of the industry's economic and political development but from Goebbels' point of view it would also protect the film industry from the financial demands of the Finance Ministry who were causing him considerable anxiety.

Ufi had a capital of RM 65 million, which was initially held by Cautio and represented the entire assets of the *staatsmittelbar* firms. Although they remained largely unchanged, they were now referred to as 'state-owned' (*staatseigen*). To facilitate the purchasing of film theatres throughout Greater Germany a single company, the *Deutsche Filmtheater GmbH*, was set up with the intention of regulating the profits from exhibition. Similarly, in order to keep distribution costs to a minimum, the *Deutsche Filmvertriebs-GmbH* was formed; although a centralised, non-profit-making distribution organisation, it is significant that all films were still distributed under their old production companies' names. This served to retain a link with the past and also to disguise the State's monopoly.

Finally on 29 February 1942, Goebbels announced to an audience of film-makers a new body within the Ufi called the *Reichsfilmintendanz*. It would be headed by Dr Fritz Hippler who was already in charge of the Film Section of the RMVP and was the director of the virulent anti-Semitic film *The Wandering/Eternal Jew* (*Der ewige Jude*, 1940).[38] The *Reichsfilmintendanz* was to concentrate on matters of film 'art' allowing the RMVP to dictate the political affairs of the industry. In practice there was no duplication of labour in that Goebbels was overlord of both bodies and therefore the *Reichsfilmintendant* (Head of the Reichsfilmintendanz) was directly subordinate to him.

The Propaganda Minister's weaponry was now complete. Ufi had taken over the responsibilities of the Cautio with Winkler once again in charge. The Nazi film industry would remain virtually unchanged for the rest of its existence. Every aspect of film-making, from the selection of subject-matter to production distribution and eventually exhibition, was now the immediate responsibility of Ufa-Film GmbH. The Reich Film Chamber had become merely a bureaucratic administrative machine and Ufi, thanks to its vertical organisation, was a mere receiver of orders from the RMVP. This represented an enormous concentration of a mass medium in the hands of the National-Socialist State and more specifically, the Minister for Popular Enlightenment and Propaganda.

Notes

1. D. Welch, *Propaganda and the German Cinema, 1933–45* (London: IB Tauris, 2001 rev.), pp. 5–8; T. Hanna-Daoud, *Die NSDAP und der Film bis zur Machtergreifung* (Köln–Weimar–Wien: Böhlau, 1996).
2. K. Kreimeier, *Die Ufa story. Geschichte eines Filmkonzerns* (München: Wilhelm Heyne Verlag, 1992).
3. D. Welch (2001 rev.), pp. 10–18; W. Becker, *Film und Herrschaft. Organisationsprinzipien und Organisationsstrukturen der nationalsozialistischen Filmpropaganda* (Berlin: Verlag Volker Spiess, 1973); J. Spiker, *Film und Kapital* (Berlin: Verlag Volker Spiess, 1975).
4. *Gleichschaltung* was the term employed by the Nazis which loosely referred to the obligatory assimilation within the state of all political, economic, and cultural activities.
5. NSBO had to share DACHO with Alfred Rosenberg's KfdK.
6. The decree is reproduced J. Wulf, *Theater und Film im Dritten Reich* (Gütersloh: Sigbert Mohn Verlag, 1964), p. 94.
7. See, for instance, Chapter 23.
8. Bundesarchiv (Barch), R55/484, *Akten des Reichsministeriums für Volksäfklarung und Propaganda, Filmkreditbankbilanz,* 1943.
9. G. Albrecht, *Nationalsozialistische Filmpolitik. Eine soziologische Untersuchung über die Spielfilme des Dritten Reiches* (Stuttgart: Ferdinand Enke Verlag, 1969), pp. 208–9. In fact a number of 'half Jews' and 'quarter Jews' did remain in the Reich Film Chamber.
10. D. Welch (2001 rev.), pp. 10–18; Becker (1973); Spiker (1975).
11. The dates refer to the year when the *Prädikate* were first awarded.
12. K.-J. Maiwald, *Filmzensur im NS-Staat* (Dortmund: Nowotny, 1983); W. Moritz, 'Filmzensur während der Nazi-Zeit', in S. Barron (eds), *Entartete Kunst: das Schicksal der Avantgarde im Nazi-Deutschland* (München: Hirmer Verlag, 1992), pp. 185–91.
13. The decree was issued on 27 November and is reproduced in Wulf (1964), pp. 119–20.
14. G. Albrecht (1969); Welch (2001 rev.).
15. A full breakdown of the different genres can be found in Welch (2001 rev.), p. 36.
16. This goes for other cultural products too. 'In contrast to what the Nazis envisioned, it was impossible to streamline popular culture; instead a strange parallelism permeated the popular, allowing a number of non-simultaneous discourses to exist.' A. Ascheid, *Hitler's Heroines: Stardom and Womanhood in Nazi Cinema* (Philadelphia: Temple University Press, 2003), p. 7.
17. D. Welch (2001 rev.).
18. D. Welch, 'Nazi Wartime Newsreel Propaganda', in K. R. M. Short (ed.), *Film & Radio Propaganda in World War II* (Knoxville: The University of Tennessee Press, 1983), pp. 202–19; R. Vande Winkel, 'Nazi Newsreels in Europe, 1939–1945: The Many Faces of Ufa's Foreign Weekly Newsreel (Auslandstonwoche) versus the German Weekly Newsreel (Deutsche Wochenschau)', *Historical Journal of Film, Radio and Television*, 24:1 (2004), pp. 5–34; P. Zimmermann and K. Hoffmann

(eds), *Geschichte des dokumentarischen Films in Deutschland. Band 3: 'Drittes Reich' (1933–1945)* (Stuttgart: Philipp Reclam, 2005).

19. H. Hoffmann, *'Und die Fahne führt uns in die Ewigkeit.' Propaganda im NS-Film* (Frankfurt: Fischer Verlag, 1991).
20. For an analysis of some of these newsreels see, D. Welch, 'Goebbels, Götterdämmerung and the Deutsche Wochenschauen', in K. R. M. Short and S. Dolezel (eds), *Hitler's Fall. The Newsreel Witness* (London, New York, Sydney: Croom Helm, 1988), pp. 88–99.
21. D. Welch (2001 rev.), pp. 23–9; M. S. Phillips, 'The Nazi Control of the German Film Industry', *Journal of European Studies*, 1(1) (1971), pp. 37–68; Spiker (1975), pp. 182–239.
22. W. Plugge, 'Wesen und Aufgaben des Films und der Reichsfilmkammer', in E. A. Dreyer (ed.), *Deutsche Kultur im neuen Reich. Wesen, Aufgabe und Ziel der Reichsfilmkammer* (Berlin: Schlieffen-Verlag, 1934), p. 123.
23. Barch, R2/4799, *Akten des Reichsfinanzministeriums.*
24. M. Behn and M. Töteberg, 'Diskrete Transaktionen: Bürgemeister Winkler und die Cautio; Die graue Eminenz: Bürgemeister Max Winkler', in H.-M. Bock and M. Töteberg (eds), *Das Ufa-Buch* (Frankfurt am Main: Zweitausendeins, 1992), pp. 389–91.
25. K. Dibbets, 'Tobis, Made in Holland', in J. Distelmeyer (ed.), *Tonfilmfrieden/Tonfilmkrieg: Die Geschichte der Tobis vom Technik-Syndikat zum Staatskonzern* (München: Edition text + kritik, 2003), pp. 25–33.
26. T. Kramer and D. Siegrist, *Terra. Ein Schweizer Filmkonzern im Dritten Reich* (Zürich: Chronos Verlag, 1991).
27. Details taken from Barch, R109 1/431, *Akten derUfa-Film GmbH.*
28. Barch, R2/4807.
29. The decree is dated 18 March 1938. It is reproduced in Wulf (1964), p. 302. See also H. Traub, *Die Ufa-Lehrschau: Der Weg des Films von der Planung bis zum Vorführung* (Berlin: Ufa-Buchverlag, 1941).
30. See Chapter 4.
31. See Chapter 8.
32. Barch, R2/4799.
33. See Chapter 4; Spiker (1975), pp. 183–6.
34. See Chapter 8; Spiker (1975), pp. 187–9.
35. See Chapter 9.
36. Spiker (1975), pp. 190–2; Becker (1973), pp. 216–17.
37. See Chapter 15.
38. R. Vande Winkel, 'Nazi Germany's Fritz Hippler (1909–2002)', *Historical Journal of Film, Radio and Television*, 23:2 (2003), pp. 91–9.

2
'European Cinema for Europe!' The International Film Chamber, 1935–42

Benjamin George Martin

Beginning in the mid-1930s and accelerating during the Second World War, Nazi Germany sought to create a German-dominated European film-bloc oriented in opposition to the United States. In pursuit of this goal, German political and economic leaders pursued both a project of political–economic organisation, designed to enshrine German dominance in new international networks and institutions, and a large-scale cultural campaign, celebrating the idea of a distinctly 'European' cinema defined by its cultural depth and national rootedness, in contrast to what critics saw as the vapid cosmopolitanism and empty materialism of American film. At the heart of both efforts was the International Film Chamber (*Internationale Filmkammer*, IFK). Founded in 1935 to support a German-led drive to create a trans-European economic bloc that could rival the United States, under the tense but still peaceful circumstances of the mid-1930s, this was an international organisation of national film industry representatives from 22 nations. The IFK held several meetings before mounting political tensions condemned the body to irrelevance on the eve of the outbreak of war in September 1939. In 1941, after Hitler's military victories had placed Nazi Germany and its allies in control of the continent, the organisation was revived on a European basis as part of a new effort to consolidate German control over a coordinated European film economy, now under the sign of Hitler's 'New Order' in Europe.

In its first phase, the IFK was an interesting but weak structure of international cultural cooperation designed to promote German influence; under the new conditions of the Second World War, the Nazis were able to make a reconfigured IFK into a central organisational and coercive tool of the expansion of German cinema in wartime Europe. This expansionist, hegemonic project was supported by the IFK's European rhetoric. In both of its incarnations, the IFK mobilised well-established economic arguments as well as an idealistic appeal to the idea of Europe's distinctive cultural identity. Based on the power and centrality of Germany's film industry, the prestige of Germany's cinematic and cultural traditions, and the apparently unstoppable German military machine, the Nazis could make a credible claim to be able finally to lead the sort of unified 'Film-Europe', with the economic power and cultural self-confidence to meet the challenge of American film, which had been widely discussed since the 1920s.

The poor state of the archival record on the IFK has meant that it has occupied a minor position in scholarly literature on Nazism and cinema.[1] In this chapter, I use the IFK's publications and its coverage in the press to reconstruct the important role this institution's activities and rhetoric played in the Nazi's bid to establish hegemonic control over an integrated European economic and cultural space.

The First International Film Chamber, 1935–39

German film industry leaders first proposed the idea of a new international cinema organisation at the lavish International Film Congress in Berlin (26 April–1 May 1935), to which Joseph Goebbels' Reich Ministry for Popular Enlightenment and Propaganda (*Reichsministerium für Volksaufklärung und Propaganda*, RMVP) had invited over 2000 representatives of the world's film industries.[2] Carefully guided by the staff of Goebbels' Reich Film Chamber (*Reichsfilmkammer*, RFK), this conference presented Berlin as the centre of a cosmopolitan vision of international cooperation, while giving imposing support for Germany's claim to be its new leader, through events designed to highlight the wealth, technological power, cultural sophistication, and glamour of the German film industry. Between the conference's sessions in the Reichstag and Kroll Opera House, delegates could wander through an exhibition of German cameras, projectors, and sound equipment from firms including AEG, Siemens, and Zeiss.[3] Later, nearly 60 buses were commissioned to take some 1800 delegates on a tour of the Ufa studios at Babelsberg, led by studio General Director Ludwig Klitsch.[4] Germany also showed off its commitment to the preservation of film history as over 300 foreign delegates were taken on a tour of the newly founded Reich Film Archive (*Reichsfilmarchiv*), one of the first state-sponsored film archives in the world. Housed with scholarly dignity in the offices of Germany's prestigious Kaiser-Wilhelm-Gesellschaft in the Berlin suburb Dahlem, this institution had already collected some 1500 films since opening in February 1935 under RFK official Frank Hensel.[5] Finally, the glamour associated with Germany's 'Ufa-style' was mobilised at a formal ball in the Marble Hall of the Berlin Zoo on Saturday night, 27 April, at which Goebbels showed off a glittering array of German stars, directors, and celebrities, including Carola Höhn, Willy Fritsch, Gerhard Menzel, Carl Froelich, and boxer Max Schmeling, while playing host to glamorous foreign stars including Czech beauty Lida Baarová and Shanghai actress Butterfly Wu. On Thursday 2 May, international delegation leaders were even taken to a private audience with Hitler.[6]

The conference's most lasting contribution took place when its General Commission, made up only of representatives of European film industries, approved a German-led resolution calling for a new permanent institution.[7] After a preparatory meeting only of representatives of Europe's 11 largest film industries in Munich in July, the IFK's statute was presented at the Venice International Film Festival in September 1935, and was signed in Paris on 7 November 1935. The IFK's meetings were attended by delegations from China, Japan, and India, but the institution's leadership was entirely European: its first president was the head of the Nazi Reich Film Chamber Fritz Scheuermann; vice-presidents were representatives of major European studios, like Svensk Filmindustri's Olof Andersson, French director Felix Gandera, and Carlo Roncoroni, head of Italy's Cines.[8] This continental European leadership reflected the organisation's central goal: facilitating exchange among Europe's film industries in order to create an organised European market. To this end, IFK meetings planned the creation of an international commission to standardise international copyright practices, an office to coordinate international film distribution, a bank for coordinating currency exchanges, and an international court of arbitration to settle disputes.[9] These measures sought to respond to what was universally recognised as the central structural crisis of European cinema: while the Hollywood 'majors', having covered the production costs of their films on America's vast home market, could export their films for low rental rates and turn large profits, none of Europe's national cinemas had a home market big enough to keep up with the steady rise in production costs.[10]

The introduction of sound films in 1929 had exacerbated the situation by dividing and restricting the potential export market for European films; fatefully, this coincided with the onset of the global economic crisis. If the situation was bad in 1935, it was not new. The IFK's proposals reflected the same concerns that had motivated the calls for a unified 'Film-Europe' that had been much discussed from the mid-1920s.[11] In 1924, for example, Erich Pommer, the renowned producer of Germany's powerful Ufa film conglomerate, had called for the 'production of European films, of films [that are] no longer French, English, Italian or German but continental; works of a rapid and broad European diffusion which will thus allow for the easy amortisation of the costs of production, which have become enormous everywhere'.[12] This vision of a 'European film' which would itself have the power to transcend national boundaries and resolve financial difficulties retained its attractive force long after Pommer left Berlin for Hollywood. But by 1935 the IFK's vision reflected the belief that creating the ideal 'European' film would not be enough. Rather, in keeping with the economic protectionism and cultural nationalism of the 1930s, IFK leaders proposed that the way to respond to the crisis was to use political and legal means to create a more coherent and defensible European market.

The IFK found much of Europe ready to look to Germany's powerful film industry for leadership, just as they had since the mid-1920s.[13] Leading figures in Italy's film industry, for example, had no illusions about the German goals that stood behind the new 'international' body.[14] But seeing cooperation with Germany as a means to revive Italy's struggling industry, in 1935 Mussolini's Italy placed the prestigious Venice International Film Festival at the disposal of the IFK, whose members were accorded places on the festival's jury. The IFK also succeeded in drawing France into a closer relationship with Germany by offering the institution's second presidency to French producer Georges Lourau, and allowing the organisation's seat to move with him to Paris in 1937.[15] Moreover, the International Federation of Cinema Journalism (*Fédération Internationale de la Presse Cinématographique*, Fipresci), founded in Brussels in 1930, began to coordinate its meetings with those of the IFK in 1937. But the Americans – who had been conspicuously absent from the 1935 conference – declined to participate, seeing the IFK not incorrectly as a German ploy for dominance that would attempt to block the free circulation of American films in Europe. Even after the IFK's presidency had moved to Paris, the Motion Picture Producers and Distributors of America defined it in 1937 as 'a European block that has Germany at its head – officially or not – and is directed against American films'. They were joined in their refusal by the Dutch and the British, whose participation in the 1935 Berlin conference was not repeated in 1937.[16]

With the world's most powerful film industry hostile to it, and with intra-European political relations under mounting pressure, the IFK was not able to achieve much. The institution's 5–10 July 1937 meeting in Paris – the sole accomplishment of which was to pass a German-led resolution against so-called 'incitement films' (*Hetzfilme*) – was to be the IFK's last, in this form. The IFK was already effectively defunct when president Lourau resigned and dissolved the Paris office on 3 May 1939. By that point, Nazi Germany had instead begun to consolidate German cinema's position in Europe through imperialist military expansion.

'European' Film in Hitler's New Order, 1941–45

On 16 July 1941, delegates from 17 European nations gathered in Berlin for a 6-day meeting and solemn ceremony that officially refounded the International Film Chamber. Meeting in the offices of Joseph Goebbels' RMVP, representatives of the governments and film industries of Belgium, Bulgaria, Denmark, Germany, Bohemia and Moravia, Finland, Holland, Italy, Croatia, Norway, Romania, Slovakia, Spain, Sweden, Switzerland, Turkey, and Hungary signed on to a German-led programme to create a new arrangement of intra-European cooperation in film in the spirit of the 'New European Order' being created by Hitler's conquest of the continent.[17] The IFK was among the first of a wave of new international and 'European' cultural institutions founded under German leadership, including an International Chamber of Law, a European Writers' Union, a Union of National

Journalists' Associations, and a European Youth Federation, through which Nazi Germany, with close cooperation from Fascist Italy and other allies, created institutional structures designed to ensure German cultural hegemony in support of the new Nazi European empire.[18]

The IFK's changed membership reflected wartime Europe's imperial realities. Austria and Luxembourg had been absorbed into the Reich; dismembered Czechoslovakia and Yugoslavia were now represented by the German-dominated Protectorate of Bohemia and Moravia and the German satellites Slovakia and Croatia; recently occupied Greece was excluded, Poland obliterated, and France, although the focus of much attention from Nazi film organisers, was barred from its previously central position in the IFK. The Germans' expansionist interest in south-eastern Europe was reflected by the new presence as full members of Romania, Bulgaria, and Turkey. The Netherlands, which had refused to join the IFK of its own accord, was now a member, too.[19] Moreover, as the war kept British India from participating, the already predominantly European institution now became exclusively so.

Speaking 'not as a German, but as a European!,' Goebbels declared, 'I can assure you that in the cooperation of European peoples in the area of film, Germany . . . pursues no selfish goals. We have here entirely altruistic motives.'[20] The IFK's new statute, however, signed at the end of the refoundation ceremony in Berlin on 18 July 1941, sharply established the Germans' dominance, locating the body's permanent seat in Berlin and creating a proportional voting system in which votes were distributed 'in proportion to the significance of the film-economy of each country'.[21] This statute also divided the IFK into several 'sections', the most important of which, like the powerful Section for Distribution, Import and Export, and the Section for Film Law, were led by long-time staff of the RFK, Günther Schwarz and Georg Roeber.[22] Germany highlighted its 'Axis' partnership with Fascist Italy by appointing Venetian industrialist Count Volpi di Misurata, founder and President of the Venice International Film Festival, as the IFK's new president, and surrounded him with a gaggle of vice-presidents, carefully selected to reflect the cultural and political hierarchies of the 'New Europe', including Hungarian Culture and Education Ministry representative László Balogh, Sweden's Olof Andersson, Director of the Film Division of the Romanian Propaganda Ministry Mihai V. Puscariu, Spanish representative Antonio Pacheco Picazo, and RFK president and prominent director and producer Carl Froelich.[23] The institution's most powerful figure was, however, its general secretary Karl Melzer, a 44-year-old SS officer who had worked in the film division of Goebbels' RMVP since 1933 and had led the organisation of the 1935 International Film Congress in Berlin.[24] Vice-president of the Reich Film Chamber since 1939, Melzer enjoyed a 6-year term as IFK General Secretary (compared to the president's 3 years), sat on the IFK's Board, and attended virtually all of its frequent meetings.[25]

If the Germans' claim to leadership was blunt, it also appeared justified. Backed up by Germany's crushing military dominance, the IFK's old core idea – using political means to create a trans-European film economy under German leadership – seemed more plausible than ever. The German film industry was by far Europe's strongest, having been centralised, streamlined, and enriched by the process of state consolidation and expansion that had begun in 1936 and would reach its pinnacle in the creation of the giant Ufi concern (Ufa-Film-Gesellschaft) in 1942. Expanded and enriched through the seizures of cinemas, studios, and other assets in Austria and the former Czechoslovakia, and from dispossessed Jews all over Europe, Germany now also had a huge home market of its own.[26] Although much talent had been driven from the German film industry since 1933, Berlin was the capital of a growing multi-national central European film culture.[27] This role was supported by innovative institutions designed to train a new generation of film specialists, including the *Ufa-Lehrschau*, an ambitious permanent exhibition that opened on the grounds of Ufa's legendary Babelsberg studios on 31 January 1936, illustrating all aspects of modern film production.[28] This exhibition, a prototype of which had been shown to guests at the 1935 conference in Berlin, was to serve along with an archive and library as the core of a new German Institute for Film Studies. A rival model of film education was instead inaugurated in March 1938 with Goebbels' support as the *Deutsche Filmakademie Babelsberg*.[29] Since 1936, Germany had also made itself the centre of a new web of international cultural relations, including close bilateral cultural accords with Italy and Hungary, which had come to be Europe's second and third largest producers of films.[30] Above all, Germany's claim to lead a unified European film market made sense in the light of the intensely debated idea of the 'New Order', the phrase with which Nazis, Fascists, and their allies referred to the continental reordering of European politics, economics, and cultural life that was supposed to follow the Axis' apparently imminent victory.[31]

The prospects for German leadership of a unified Film-Europe had been improved not simply by Nazi military dominance, but by the prospect this created of at last closing Europe off to American films. Beginning in August 1940 – over a year before the US entered the war – the Nazis banned American movies in countries under German occupation. This was seen as the first step towards the development of what IFK President Volpi called 'the autarkic European cinematographic complex of today and tomorrow' – a closed, internally integrated European film economy.[32] At the Ninth Venice Film Festival in September 1941, which Volpi helped make into the showcase of the revived IFK, the exclusion of Hollywood movies was presented as a celebration of what one German newspaper called 'Film-Europe without Hollywood', inaugurating a new era of 'the independence of European film'.[33] This was a necessary condition for the development of a European film that, while culturally superior to its crass American competition, was delicate and in need of protection from American 'stimulants', 'effects', and 'sensations'. 'Next to such strong American tobacco', one German journalist remarked, 'the Europeans' much gentler, more sensitive films seemed weak... It is indeed quite clear: a *double-entendre* joke elicits louder applause from the crowd than a poem by Rilke.' Thus it was 'excellent for the production of individual countries that they no longer see Hollywood films – these countries are beginning to develop their own film style'.[34] For the Germans, moreover, this American-free zone was one that Germany would be ideally placed to dominate. As Goebbels declared privately to the staff of the RFK on 15 February 1941, 'We can view Europe today as our export zone. The Americans have disappeared as competition.'[35]

As Goebbels knew, however, American films had not yet fully disappeared from European screens. (As a matter of fact, even Italy never entirely banished American films.[36]) Accordingly, when the IFK held its first real working session in Berlin in March 1942, its leaders' primary concern was to induce – and coerce – its members into definitively banning American movies from their national markets. At the meeting of the Distribution Section in Berlin's Hotel Bristol on 2–3 March 1942, section head Günther Schwarz, himself an employee of the Germans' powerful Deutsche Filmexport Company and the export officer of the Reich Film Chamber, threatened IFK members who did not comply with the IFK's resolution, passed in Munich in December 1941, to ban all films of 'anti-European tendency', with a list of harsh penalties. These included barring the export of the offending country's films, cutting off that country's supply of film stock (a valuable commodity that only Germany and Italy could produce economically), and blocking its provision with films from the rest of IFK's members.[37] This threat was amplified at the IFK's general meeting in Rome in April 1942 with a resolution calling for economic sanctions against member nations that failed to show serious efforts to purge their countries of American films by the end of the year.[38]

The IFK's reliance on coercive measures reflected the fact that even as the IFK officially celebrated the possibilities offered by 'Film-Europe without Hollywood', the sudden withdrawal of American films represented a crisis for many of Europe's film industries. Distributors were left with too little product to satisfy theatre owners' demands for new films, profits were lost, and audiences were restless. Thus when the Hungarian delegation opposed the American ban order at the IFK's April 1942 meeting in Rome, they earned 'roars of joy' from other IFK delegates; they also incurred the wrath of the IFK's German masters, who quickly mobilised the coercive powers of Germany's powerful network of cultural institutions. Germany's delegates to the German–Hungarian Committee for Cultural Exchanges, a legacy of the two nations' 1936 cultural accord, enforced the IFK's order by cutting off Hungary's supply of film stock. This tactic succeeded in pressuring the Hungarians into announcing a total ban on American film in December 1942.[39]

If these coercive measures were the IFK's stick, its carrot was the promise of greater intra-European trade in films within a protected, autarkic European block. In this new system, Europe's film demand would be met entirely by a new European film production, which the IFK would help to expand and improve under the guiding slogan, 'European cinema for Europe!'[40] This slogan was backed up by a series of concrete economic and legal measures which sought to extend the model of the German film industry – vertically integrated, centralised, state controlled, and operating profitably according to sound capitalist principles – to each European country, and thence to Europe as a whole.

Already at the IFK's July 1941 refoundation, the newly reconfigured presidency called on each member nation that had not already done so to develop a single 'central leading organisation' on the German or Italian model, empowered to represent its national film industry at the international level, and to apply IFK decisions at the local level.[41] These powerful national bodies, subordinated to the German-dominated IFK, would allow Nazi Germany to penetrate and standardise the local workings of Europe's heterogeneous film industries, making possible the centralised, Europe-wide coordination of film distribution, exhibition, and production with a minimum of direct German intervention. In turn, the Germans could present these measures as steps towards the creation of a streamlined, integrated European market, which would provide them with more than enough films to replace the American movies on which cinemas had depended, and to which Europe's film industries, protected from American competition, would have privileged access.

The distribution of Europe's films to Europe's cinemas – a problem given the lack of existing networks and the generally protectionist nature of wartime Europe's national economies – would be facilitated, for example, by a 'clearing' in Berlin, to manage the balance of payments among European national economies, avoiding the complexities of many transfers among Europe's protected, non-convertible currencies. The Film Law section prepared standardised model contracts to facilitate cross-national relations among producers, distributors, and theatre owners,[42] while the IFK's new statute founded a Court of Arbitration, also in Berlin, the binding decisions of which would 'overcome' the differences among European nations 'in the higher interest of a European film-economy'.[43] At Rome in April 1942, IFK delegates agreed not to apply protectionist 'luxury taxes' on film; in July, Finland received a stern warning for having violated this resolution.[44]

Regarding film exhibition, the IFK sought to regulate competition among cinema owners in order to create a rationalised European film market with a more predictable annual demand that could be met by fewer films. At Munich in November 1941, IFK delegates resolved, for example, to create a European standard film programme – one newsreel, one feature, and one documentary (or *Kulturfilm*) – that would not exceed 2 hours and would strictly ban double-features.[45] Subsequent meetings discussed regulating the opening of new cinemas, standardising the length of time new films would be shown, and establishing minimum admission prices through a standardised European 'ticketing system'.[46] The continental application of these centralising, rationalising 'measures of National Socialist *Filmpolitik*' – measures that had been compulsory in Germany since 1938, and throughout occupied Europe since 1940 – would reduce the number of films Europe's cinemas needed annually to about 400. And, as IFK leaders enthusiastically claimed throughout 1942, member nations were slated to produce at least 427 films.[47] The IFK had thus brought Europe within reach of autarky, finally meeting European demand with European supply.

But while the number of films produced in Europe was more than enough to meet European demand in theory, very few of the films made in Europe in 1942 could in practice replicate the strengths of American feature films, in terms of their production quality, star value, or ability to appeal to audiences in multiple national markets. As Günther Schwarz declared to an audience of 20 representatives from 8 countries at the July 1942 meeting of the Amortisation Commission and Cinema Management Section at Brussels' Hotel Metropole, Europe's apparent excess of supply consisted of 'too many little, not exportable films'. Europe's national cinemas were not producing 'a sufficient member of big, exportable films that in the long view – that is, even after the war – can guarantee a high level of European film'.[48] There was therefore an intimate relationship between the twin tasks that General Secretary Melzer outlined at the IFK's general meeting in Rome's Cinecittà studios on 8 April 1942: the *economic* project of creating 'an autarkic Film-Europe', capable of meeting Europe's film demand exclusively with European films, depended upon Europe's success in the *cultural* project of developing 'a European film . . . which one day will bear the same world-significance that until now the American film has had in Europe'.[49]

This call for the production of a more 'European' film was to be the main demand the IFK made of its members for the remainder of its existence. But what did 'European' mean? Vittorio Mussolini, the son of the Italian dictator and prominent film personality, spoke for many when he declared in December 1941 that the new 'European' cinema would be defined by 'the imprimatur of European civility, disinfected from Jewish poison'.[50] Count Volpi reflected the IFK's rather softer official position in Rome in 1942, explaining that the IFK's main goal was 'to establish common guidelines for the art, technique, and economy of film so that the European film-world can create . . . a production that will distinguish itself from that of all other countries of the world, a production that is worthy of Europe's high cultural traditions'.[51] 'European' cinema should be a film-art, with a commitment to cultural rather than economic values. The 1941 Venice Film Festival was thus celebrated as marking a shift from an American to a European way of valuing cinema, a historic transition 'From Commodity to Artwork'.[52]

In the IFK's most detailed programmatic statement on this issue, General Secretary Melzer pronounced 'quality' – understood in a transcendent sense, unconnected to whims of the market, and rooted in tradition – to be the distinguishing feature of the new European cinema. Writing in *Interfilm*, the monthly journal of the IFK, Melzer argued that 'a European film of high artistic value' would 'contribute to the European audience freeing itself from the imaginings of the American civilisation that seeks to make the world happy, and finding its way back to a European bearing that rests on a centuries-old *Kultur*'.[53] Here Melzer deployed concepts made famous during the cultural struggle of the First World War, in which German intellectuals defended the profound, transcendent, and yet nationally rooted values of *Kultur* against the universalising pretensions of Western Europe's materialist and superficial *Zivilisation*. Now, however, in a rhetorical move common to much wartime Nazi cultural politics, Melzer insisted that this anti-materialist concept of culture was in fact characteristic of Europe as a whole, and should be reflected in the new 'European' film.

At the same time, IFK rhetoric and policy insisted that the new 'European' film should retain a strong national character, reflecting the distinctive identity of its country of origin. 'Even when a European format is demanded of it,' Melzer declared, 'film is and remains a national matter.'[54] Carl Froelich had stressed this same idea at the refoundation of the IFK in July 1941, telling the assembled delegates that 'the good film' was generally 'a national film': 'It is incidentally my experience,' he suggested, 'that it leads nowhere to tune a film to the key of so-called international taste.'[55] According to Italian Minister of Popular Culture, Alessandro Pavolini, a more national film was in fact better suited to the new European market: 'absolutely national films, with authors and artists and subjects that are a typical expression of the race . . . beyond fulfilling an irreplaceable function in the Fatherland, often also constitute, for foreign countries, the genuine revelation of a determined atmosphere, of a given mentality. Often a film is international on the strength of being national.'[56] Germany's delegation to the March 1942 IFK meeting in Berlin made a similar point, declaring that German audiences preferred films that were 'typical' of their country of origin: 'so if, for example, a Finnish film is surprisingly, originally Finnish, such as [Germans] have never seen before, it will certainly find greater success than a half-baked and poorly executed comedy'.[57] The IFK promised moreover to support and defend Europe's smaller film industries in their effort to produce a characteristically national style. 'Alongside the demand for films of European format', Schwarz said at the Brussels meeting, the IFK recognised 'the smaller countries' justified aspiration to maintain and expand their national productions. This production will, for cultural reasons, also be maintained after the war, even if this produces . . . economic losses.'[58]

This emphasis on the values of cultural nationalism, although apparently in conflict with the IFK's 'European' message, was a crucial element of the IFK's European vision. The model of a European market composed of exchange among cinemas with stable and distinct national identities effectively responded to real crises: it offered Europe's national film industries the prospect of access to an expanded and protected market, while relieving worried cultural elites' concerns about the cultural degeneration and social upheaval associated with uncontrolled trans-national cultural and economic transfers, which they perceived as threatening national cultural sovereignty. More broadly, the IFK's 'European' model eased concerns about the significance of film overall: the IFK promised to place film in the hands of nationalist regimes and their intellectual, economic, and cultural elites, where it could serve as a tool of state and elite influence over the masses. By fostering a cinema rooted in national traditions, and removed from the hands of American studios and Jewish financiers, the IFK would help neutralise the socially destabilising effect of cinema, which had encouraged the masses, especially the youth and women, to imitate foreign styles of dress and manner, and to question local values and hierarchies.

This model was consistent with Nazi ideology's commitment to the idea of a *völkisch* culture, rooted in values and traditions that were particular to a specific race, and purified of the cosmopolitanism associated above all with the Jews. It also reflected a specifically Nazi ideology of international cultural relations, which called for a form of 'cultural contact' among pure nations, which could enrich both without leading to cultural 'contamination' or 'degeneration.'[59] Significantly, it also allowed the IFK's German leaders to present themselves as the defenders of Europe's national traditions; many of the continent's smaller national cinemas did in fact enjoy significant development under German hegemony.[60] Finally, the suggestion that Europe's nations would be allowed to maintain their cultural sovereignty in the Nazi New Order was particularly significant for those countries whose political sovereignty, or existence, was very much in doubt in 1942.

Even as the IFK offered an attractive vision to Europe's cinema leaders, its actions and ideology served nothing so much as the establishment of absolute German hegemony. The goal of the IFK's measures streamlining intra-European exchange was not, for example, the creation of a European free trade zone, but rather the establishment of a planned European film economy under centralised German control. As several European industries soon discovered, the IFK's smooth exchange mechanisms did not in fact offer the improved access to the lucrative German market that its leaders promised. The IFK's export quotas were enforced by Transit Film GmbH, the monolithic distribution company that Goebbels had founded in May 1942 to consolidate all German-dominated regional distributors. With total control over the German market and occupied Europe, Transit Film vigorously exported German films while restricting the import of foreign films, even from erstwhile allies like Italy and Hungary.[61] Moreover, the IFK's insistence that member nations produce typically national films, while apparently supportive of threatened cultural traditions, in fact served Goebbels' desire, as recorded in his diary in May 1942, to make Germany 'the dominating power on the European continent. In so far as pictures are produced in other countries they must be only of a local or limited character.'[62] Only Germany would be able to develop the spectacular, internationally successful blockbusters that would affirm its position as Europe's unquestioned cultural leader.

The IFK, then, was meant to create a supple tool for the support of lasting German empire in Europe. But the Nazis' effort to create a German-dominated new order of European film, rendered possible only by the forcible closure of the European market to American cinema, was soon rendered impossible by the collapse of the Axis military dominance on which, in the end, the project depended. By the time the IFK gathered for its last major meeting in Budapest from 28 November to 4 December 1942, the German Sixth Army had been surrounded by Russian forces outside Stalingrad, losing the battle that marked the turning point of the war. The German effort to forge a trans-European counter-weight to Hollywood had been greeted with serious interest and widespread collaboration. But based on the brutal pursuit of absolute German dominance, in the service of a New Order of exploitation, racism, and genocide, the IFK turned out to be an episode of European cultural cooperation that most of its participants were happy to forget.

Propaganda Minister Joseph Goebbels welcomes members of the International Film Chamber in his ministry in July 1941. *Source*: Ullstein-Bild.

Reception for delegates to the 1935 International Film Congress, in Berlin's Rheingold Restaurant. *Source*: *Der Internationale Filmkongress Berlin 1935. Seine Organisation und seine Ergebnisse/Le Congrès International du Film. Organisation et résultats* (Berlin: Reichsfilmkammer, 1935).

Notes

1. The IFK is discussed in most detail in M. Argentieri, *L'asse cinematografico Roma-Berlino* (Naples: Libreria Sapere, 1986); E. Offermanns, *Internationalität und europäischer Hegemonialanspruch des Spielfilms der NS-Zeit* (Hamburg: Kovacs, 2001); V. de Grazia, 'Mass Culture and Sovereignty: The American Challenge to

European Cinemas, 1920–1960', *Journal of Modern History*, 61 (1989), pp. 53–87; V. de Grazia, 'European cinema and the idea of Europe, 1925–95,' in Geoffrey Nowell-Smith and Steven Ricci (eds), *Hollywood and Europe: Economics, Culture, National Identity: 1945–95* (London: British Film Institute, 1998), pp. 9–33; and V. de Grazia, *Irresistible Empire: America's Advance through Twentieth-Century Europe* (Cambridge, MA: Belknap Press of Harvard University Press, 2005), pp. 324–5.

2. See *Der Internationale Filmkongress Berlin 1935. Seine Organisation und seine Ergebnisse/Le Congrès International du Film. Organisation et résultats* (Berlin: RFK, 1935); and Y. C. Choy, 'Inszenierungen der völkischen Filmkultur im Nationalsozialismus. Der Internationale Filmkongress Berlin 1935' (PhD Dissertation, Technische Universität Berlin, 2006).
3. 'Rundgang durch die technische Kongreß-Ausstellung', *Licht-Bild-Bühne* (27 April 1935).
4. '1800 in Neubabelsberg', *Film-Kurier* (27 April 1935); 'Wochenschau des Kongresses', *Film-Kurier* (4 May 1935).
5. 'Es wurde gute Arbeit geleistet', *Der Film* (4 May 1935). See also 'Reichsfilmarchiv: Akademie der deutschen Filmkunst', *Film-Kurier* (25 April 1935) and 'Ehrung der Pioniere. Film-Archiv als Kulturwert', *Film-Kurier* (30 April 1935).
6. Photographs from the ball and visit with Hitler are reproduced in *Internationale Filmkongress* (1935).
7. See *Internationale Filmkongress* (1935), p. 21.
8. Countries that participated officially in the IFK in 1935–1937 were: Austria, Belgium, Czechoslovakia, Denmark, Finland, France, Germany, Greece, Hungary, Italy, Luxemburg, Norway, Poland, Portugal, Spain, Sweden, Switzerland, and Yugoslavia. India joined during the 1937 meeting in Paris, at which point the IFK claimed 21 members, according to 'Die Ergebnisse der Pariser Filmkongresse', *Licht-Bild-Bühne* (12 July 1937), which does not list these member nations. This count probably included Bulgaria, Romania, and Turkey, whose IFK membership in 1935–1939 has been otherwise impossible to confirm. Several other countries were represented unofficially at the 1935 International Film Conference by small delegations, including China, Japan, Britain, and the Netherlands.
9. 'Die Internationale Filmkammer zusammengetreten', *Völkischer Beobachter*, n. 314, 10 November 1935.
10. On the crisis of interwar European cinema, see de Grazia (1989), passim; J. Petley, *Capital and Culture. German Cinema 1933–45* (London: British Film Institute, 1979); and A. Higson and R. Maltby (eds), *'Film Europe' and 'Film America.' Cinema, Commerce and Cultural Exchange 1920–1939* (Exeter: Exeter University Press, 1999).
11. See Higson and Maltby (1999), passim.
12. Quoted in Argentieri (1986), p. 31.
13. de Grazia (1989), p. 79.
14. Argentieri (1986), p. 33.
15. The IFK's new vice-presidents under Lourau in 1937 were Roncoroni, Reval (Czechoslovakia), Ryzsard Ordynski (Poland), and RFK president and outgoing IFK president Oswald Lehnich, who had succeeded Scheuermann in 1936. See Choy (2006), 253, and *Licht-Bild-Bühne* (9 July 1937).
16. Argentieri (1986), p. 41; and M. S. Phillips, 'The German Film Industry and the New Order', in P. D. Stachura (ed.), *The Shaping of the Nazi State* (London: Croom Helm, 1978), p. 266, n. 32.

17. See IFK, *Tagung der Internationalen Filmkammer. Berlin 16–21. Juli 1941* (Berlin, n.d. [1941]), p. 5. Portugal joined in 1942. Switzerland maintained observer status before withdrawing late in 1942, followed by Sweden in 1943.
18. See F.-R. Hausmann, *Dichte, Dichter, tage nicht! Die Europäische Schriftsteller-Vereinigung in Weimar 1941–1948* (Frankfurt am Main: Vittorio Klostermann, 2004); R. E. Herzstein, *When Nazi dreams come true: the Third Reich's internal struggle over the future of Europe after a German victory: a look at the Nazi mentality, 1939–45* (London: Abacus, 1982); and B. G. Martin, 'A New Order for European Culture: the German-Italian Axis and the Reordering of International Cultural Relations, 1936–1943' (PhD Dissertation, Columbia University, 2006).
19. 'Tagung der Internationalen Filmkammer in Berlin', *Der Deutsche Film*, 6 (2/3), (August/September 1941), 56–8.
20. IFK (1941), pp. 10–11.
21. See text of the 'Satzung' in Ibid., pp. 58–67.
22. The IFK's other *Sektionen* included Production, Film Theatre Management, Film Technology, and one for Educational, Cultural, and Documentary Films. The Distribution section also included an Amortisation Commission. A complete list of the sections' members was published in *Interfilm*, 3 (November 1942), 22–3.
23. IFK (1941), pp. 39, 45; Argentieri (1986), p. 51.
24. Bundesarchiv, Berlin-Lichterfelde (henceforth: BA), SSO (former Berlin Document Center), Melzer, Karl. See also *Internationale Filmkongress* (1935), p. 3.
25. The meetings of all or part of the IFK included the following: Berlin, 16–21 July 1941; Venice, 6–9 September 1941; Munich, 24–27 November 1941; Berlin, 2–3 March 1942; Rome, 8–10 April 1942; Florence, 10–11 May 1942; Brussels, 28–30 July 1942; Strbské Pleso, Slovakia, 3–6 August 1942; Venice, 2–4 September 1942; Dresden, 1–4 October 1942; Budapest, 29 November–4 December 1942. This final meeting was also attended by representatives of France, Greece, and Japan. See IFK (1941); IFK, *Tagungen der Internationalen Filmkammer* (Berlin, n.d. [1942]); and IFK, *Tagungen der Internationalen Filmkammer* (Berlin, n.d. [1943]). A meeting was planned for Baden-Baden, 18–21 June 1944, but does not appear to have taken place (Argentieri (1986), p. 62). In addition, the IFK sponsored a European narrow film conference (Erster europäischer Schmalfilm-Kongreß) in Agram, Croatia, on 18 May 1943 with representatives from Germany, Italy, Hungary, Croatia, Slovakia, Bulgaria, Romania, Sweden, Denmark, Norway, France, Spain, Portugal, and Switzerland: see 'Erster europäischer Schmalfilm-Kongreß mit Vertretern aus 14 Ländern in Agram eröffnet', *Deutsche Allgemeine Zeitung* (18 May 1943).
26. See Petley (1979) and Phillips (1978).
27. de Grazia (2005), p. 330.
28. M. Lichtenstein, 'Der Lebenslauf des Films. Die Ufa-Lehrschau', in H.-M. Bock and M. Töteberg (eds), *Das Ufa-Buch. Kunst und Krisen, Stars und Regisseure, Wirtschaft und Politik; die internationale Geschichte von Deutschlands größtem Film-Konzern* (Frankfurt: Zweitausendeins, 1992), pp. 396–8; UFA, *Führer durch die Lehrschau der Universum-Film Aktiengesellschaft* (Berlin: Universum-Film Aktiengesellschaft, 1936).
29. *Deutsche Filmakademie mit dem Arbeitsinstitut für Kulturfilmschaffen* (Babelsberg Ufastadt, 1938).
30. See Argentieri (1986); D. S. Frey, 'National Cinema, World Stage: A History of Hungary's Second Film Industry, 1929–44', PhD dissertation, Columbia University, 2003; and J.-P. Barbian, ' "Kulturwerte im Zeitkampf". Die Kulturabkommen des

"Dritten Reiches" als Instrumente nationalsozialistischer Außenpolitik', *Archiv für Kulturgeschichte*, 74 (1992), 415–59.

31. See B. Kletzin, *Europa aus Rasse und Raum: die nationalsozialistische Idee der Neuen Ordnung* (Münster: Lit, 2000); M. Mazower, *Dark Continent: Europe's Twentieth Century* (New York: Vintage, 1998), 138–81; Alan S. Milward, *War, Economy and Society, 1939–1945* (London: Allen Lane, 1977).
32. Argentieri (1986), p. 58.
33. 'Film-Europa ohne Hollywood', *Dresdner Neueste Nachrichten* (17 September 1941).
34. H. Karbe, 'Die Entstehung der neuen Filmstile Europas. Aufzeichungen während der Biennale', *Nationalzeitung* (Essen) (18 September 1941).
35. Quoted in Offermanns (2001), p. 73.
36. See Chapter 12.
37. IFK (1942), p. 13.
38. Ibid., pp. 74–5.
39. Frey (2003), pp. 409–15. In fact, as Frey notes, some American films played in Hungary until the 1944 German invasion.
40. From Italian Minister of Popular Culture Alessandro Pavolini's speech at the closing session of the IFK's general meeting in Rome, 10 April 1942. Published in the Italian weekly *Film*, 16 (18 April 1942) and in IFK (1942), p. 37.
41. IFK (1941), p. 47. This repeated the essence of a resolution passed by Commission III of the 1935 International Film Congress in Berlin, urging all nations to create a unified Film Chamber 'which makes possible the balance of interests among cinema owners, distributors, and producers.' See *Internationale Filmkongress* (1935), p. 21.
42. This was the topic of the August 1942 meeting of the IFK's Film Law section with the *Internationale Rechtskammer* (International Chamber of Law) in the Slovakian mountain resort town of Strbské Pleso. IFK (1943), p. 38ff.
43. Melzer, speaking in Rome, 8 April 1942. IFK (1942), p. 45.
44. IFK (1942), p. 25.
45. Argentieri (1986), p. 55.
46. See, for example, IFK (1942), pp. 7–17.
47. These statistics, presented by Günther Schwarz at the July 1942 meeting in Brussels (see IFK (1942), p. 10), were repeated in *Interfilm*, 3 (1942), p. 20. Reichsfilmintendant Fritz Hippler claimed there would be 475 films, in the Italian magazine *Cinema* (25 September 1942) (see Argentieri (1986), p. 23) and in 'Probleme des europäischen Films', *Film-Kurier* (16 October 1942).
48. IFK (1942), pp. 9–10.
49. Melzer, at Rome, 8 April 1942, in IFK (1942), p. 43.
50. Quoted in Argentieri (1986), p. 16; and de Grazia (2005), p. 328.
51. IFK (1942), p. 42.
52. D. Schmidt, 'Von der Handelsware zum Kunstwerk. Zur 9. Internationale Filmkunstschau in Venedig', *Hamburger Tageblatt* (24 August 1941).
53. Melzer, 'Europäische Filmversorgung im Zeichen der Qualität', *Interfilm*, 3 (November 1942), 20–9, here p. 25.
54. IFK (1941), pp. 23–8.
55. Ibid., p. 21.
56. Pavolini, speech at IFK meeting, Rome, April 10, 1942.
57. IFK (1942), pp. 22–3.
58. IFK (1943), p. 10.

59. V. Laitenberger, 'Theorie und Praxis der "Kulturellen Begegnung zwischen den Nationen" in der deutschen auswärtigen Kulturpolitik der 30er Jahre', *Zeitschrift für Kulturaustausch*, 31:2 (1981), pp. 196–206.
60. de Grazia (2005), p. 327.
61. On Transit Film, see Frey (2003), pp. 418–20. Relevant documents are in BA R 56 VI/31.
62. L. P. Lochner (ed.), *The Goebbels Diaries 1942–1943* (Garden City: Doubleday, 1948), p. 221. Quoted in B. Drewniak, 'Die Expansion der Kinematographie des Dritten Reiches in den Jahren des Zweiten Weltkrieges', in C. Madajczyk (ed.), *Inter arma non silent Musae. The War and the Culture 1939–1945* (Warsaw: Panstwowy Instytut Wydawniczy, 1977), p. 98.

3
German Attempts to Penetrate the Spanish-speaking Film Markets, 1936–42

Lisa Jarvinen and Francisco Peredo-Castro

When the Second World War began, the belligerent countries were already conscious that the battles would also be fought on the cinema screens, as had happened during the First World War. However, even prior to the outbreak of the Second World War, the fascists in both Germany and Spain were particularly concerned with gaining political, economic and ideological influence over the strategically important countries and vast movie markets of Latin America. Although Germany and Spain were sometimes at cross-purposes, they had, by the late 1930s, a decided headstart over Great Britain and the United States.[1]

This chapter traces the history of the *Hispano-Film-Produktion Company* (HFP), a joint German–Spanish endeavour that dates from the start of the Spanish Civil War, which was created to produce and distribute fascist films addressed to audiences in Spain and Latin America. The history of this company illuminates some of the tensions in the alliance between the German Nazis and the Spanish Nationalists. This chapter also shows how the disparate interests of these allies and competition between film businesses associated with them led to conflicting attempts by both the Germans and the Spanish to conquer the most important Latin American film industries. By the early 1940s, the Allies began to contest all of the fascist efforts to influence Latin America.

Nazi Germany and the Spanish-speaking film markets

Nazi Minister of Propaganda Joseph Goebbels devoted much of his time and attention not just to the uses of film as propaganda, but also to the growth of the film industry which came under increasing Nazi control over the course of the 1930s. This industry, which Goebbels envisioned replacing Hollywood as the dominant global power, would similarly have to rely on foreign exports – and on a star system with international appeal.[2] Thus, as with fascist Italy and Japan, once the Spanish fascists had entered into alliances with Nazi Germany, Goebbels sought ways to gain some control over Spanish film-making through co-productions. The joint endeavour held particular attractions given the vast Spanish-speaking film markets and the strategic importance of Spain and Latin America.

The introduction of sound into the cinema had revitalised film production in Spain, Mexico and Argentina all of which had capitalised on audience interest in films made in Spanish. After English, Spanish speakers constituted the largest language market for films in terms of number of speakers and access to cinemas wired for sound.[3] Hollywood studios had tried the direct production of films in Spanish in the early 1930s, but later in the decade had moved in the direction of co-production and distribution deals with Mexico, Spain and Argentina. With the revolt of fascist elements within the Spanish military against the country's Republican government on 18 July 1936, Spain became engulfed in Civil War. The major centres of Spanish film production (Madrid and Barcelona) would remain under Republican control for most of the war (1936–39).[4] This lack of production facilities was one factor which motivated some to take advantage of the diplomatic and commercial relationships established between Nazi Germany and Nationalist Spain to renew film production using German film studios. For the Nazis, who envisaged a unified fascist Europe, offering support to the Spanish Nationalists gave them the chance to influence the ideological content of propaganda films about the Spanish Civil War. Furthermore, the Spanish film industry had close ties with Spanish-speaking Latin America and could offer Nazi Germany a new outlet for its film exports, which had been in decline since 1933.[5]

A series of agreements between the two countries made Spain dependent on German film supplies, although the Spanish Nationalists also relied on Italy, Portugal and some French fascist sympathisers for help in producing films during the Civil War. The formation of the most significant German–Spanish venture, the HFP, is described in the next section. However, there were other strong links between German and Spanish film companies. Tobis established relations with the *Departamento Nacional de Cinematografía de España* (*Spanish National Department of Cinematography*) and with the CEA studios, through Tobis' subsidiary in Madrid, *Hispania-Tobis, S. A* (created in 1935). The *Compañía Industrial Film Española* (Cifesa), a key distributor for HFP, also made propaganda films with *Lisboa Filme de Portugal Studios*, which in turn was related to the German Tobis. Another company, *Hispano–Italo–Alemana Films*, which was linked to the German Bavaria and Terra, was created later to exploit the strong commercial and ideological relations between Nazism and fascism in Europe, and to advance their common propaganda crusade against communism and the Allies, and to gain Latin America for the Axis side of the war.[6]

The formation of the Hispano-Film-Produktion Company

In Spain one integrated production and distribution company had developed which was organised along the lines of a Hollywood studio. Founded in 1932 in Valencia by Manuel Casanova, Cifesa became the leading producer and exporter of Spanish-language films in the 1930s. Spain's top directors, Florián Rey and Benito Perojo, made films with Cifesa. Both men had started in the silent era and had significant international experience. Rey had worked with his future wife Imperio Argentina when he was a production supervisor on Spanish-language features for Paramount at its Joinville studios in France. Perojo had made a series of films in the French industry, and had worked briefly in Germany's Ufa studios in 1930 and on Spanish-language features for Paramount and Fox. By 1936, the box office successes of Cifesa films in Spain and throughout Latin America had provided the company with sufficient capital to open distribution branches first in Buenos Aires and later in the Netherlands, France, French Morocco and Germany.[7]

The HFP was created in late 1936 in Berlin as a joint Spanish–German venture. Evidence suggests that Goebbels played a role in founding the company, although his direct intervention has yet to be established.[8] The company's founder and public face on the German side was Johann Wilhelm Ther. He had worked as Cifesa's representative in its German branch and was an early Nazi party member. During the Second World War, Ther not only went to Spain ostensibly to continue his work with the HFP, but he also served as a spy for the German Security Service (*Sicherheitsdienst*, SD).[9] The key individuals on the Spanish side include Joaquín Reig Gonzalbes and Norberto Soliño. Early in the Spanish Civil War, Reig was sent to Berlin to represent the propaganda arm of the *Falange Española y de las Juntas de Ofensiva Nacionalsindicalista* (Spanish Phalanx of the Assemblies of National-Syndicalist Offensive, FE JONS). Soliño, born in Spain but raised in Cuba, was working as Cifesa's Cuban representative in 1936.[10]

Despite the close connections between Cifesa and HFP, the companies were distinct from each other. Originally, the HFP produced propaganda films and it was most likely funded by the Nazi Ministry of Propaganda and with the possible participation of FE JONS.[11] Nevertheless, soon after its founding, HFP moved into commercial fiction film-making. The company's principle star, the Spanish–Argentine actress and singer Imperio Argentina, has always insisted that she and her husband, Florián Rey, were invited to work in Germany by Goebbels. This suggests that Goebbels had a hand in moving the company in this direction. Furthermore, when the HFP could not come up with the capital it had promised the German Ufa studios for production costs on one of its films, Goebbels personally intervened to force Ufa to cooperate.[12]

The diva and the propaganda masters

The tensions between Nazi Germany and Nationalist Spain over the ideological direction and ultimate commercial control of their respective film industries can be seen clearly in the experiences of Imperio Argentina, the premier Spanish-speaking artist who worked in the Nazi cinema. The actress, according to her own account, first came to the attention of Hitler after he saw her in the German dubbed version of Rey's *Aragonese Virtue* (*Nobleza baturra*, 1935), a film she has claimed the Führer watched repeatedly.[13] Having arrived in Berlin in 1937 to begin work for the HFP, Goebbels believed she would be a key weapon in the German film industry's drive towards domination of the world's movie screens. However, he quickly became exasperated with her. He praised her in his diaries for her talent and personality, but then declared her 'a typical Spanish woman', who 'must also learn and work'.

Prior to captivating Goebbels and Hitler (who was, according to Goebbels, 'totally charmed' by her in their famous private meeting), Imperio Argentina had captivated the entire Spanish-speaking world through her films and records.[14] One of the most popular performers of the 1930s, the acquisition of Argentina for the German film industry represented a real coup. In early 1937, Norberto Soliño began offering contracts to many Spanish stars who had formerly worked for Cifesa. While the Spanish Civil War raged, Soliño arranged for Argentina (accompanied by her husband, Rey), the singing star Estrellita Castro and actor Miguel Ligero to get to Havana, Cuba, by offering them theatre work. Argentina notes that the contract for Ligero was 'faked' as a way of getting him out of Republican-held Madrid.[15] Once there, Argentina reports receiving the actual offer to work in Berlin via a telegram from Ther.[16] Perojo was offered a contract while in Paris. Although quite a few of the best known Spanish actors and actresses of the day accepted, at least one, Rosita Díaz Gimeno, declined. This star who had made her name in American-made Spanish-language films had nearly been executed by Nationalists just after the war's start before escaping to France.[17] Although not all of those who went to work for the HFP in Berlin necessarily sympathised with Nationalists in Spain, many did.

Rey and Argentina were both members of FE JONS and went to work in Berlin as part of their service to the party. Evidence indicates that Rey may have collaborated on one of the propaganda films.[18] Argentina has insisted that she and her husband did not support the Nazis, refused to make a film version of the life of Lola Montez (the nineteenth-century dancer and lover of Ludwig I of Bavaria) because Goebbels wanted to turn it into a pro-Nazi fable, and left Berlin in part because of their horror at witnessing the devastation of the Jewish neighbourhoods following *Kristallnacht* (the *Night of Broken Glass*, 9 November 1938). Argentina claims that Rey proposed to film an emphatically Spanish project, a version of Prosper Merimée's *Carmen*, which they titled *Carmen, la de Triana* (1938) in reference to a famed neighbourhood of Seville.[19] Given that fascist Spain and Nazi Germany had frequent conflicts over their diplomatic, cultural and commercial relationships, as well as over ideological goals, their work in Berlin need not be construed as directly supportive of the Nazi political project. In a private letter from Rey and Argentina to Luis Casaus, the head of FE JONS in Spain, they enthusiastically describe Hitler's offer to support *Spanish* film-making.[20]

Nevertheless, both Argentina's account and Goebbels' diaries make clear that Argentina had special significance for her German hosts. She remarked upon it herself, writing later that '[we] were not the only Spanish film-makers present in Berlin, but not everyone received the same official consideration'. Even the well-known director Perojo stayed at a hotel while Argentina and Rey were given the former home of the British ambassador – and had the Goebbels as neighbours. Argentina attributed this to the fact that they, unlike the others, were 'official guests of the German government'.[21] Furthermore, Argentina seems to have been the only star who was being prepared to act in German-language films. She studied German intensively with Lucy Höfling, Emil Jannings' first wife. In her various memoirs, Argentina tends to suggest that her German training was for the purpose of making a German-language version of *Carmen*.[22] In *Andalusian Nights* (*Andalusische Nächte*, 1938) directed by Herbert Maisch and completed shortly after the Spanish version, Argentina played the lead but spoke and even sang entirely in German and was supported by a German-speaking cast. The HFP made no other dual-version films.

Goebbels' diary suggests that he may have envisaged Argentina as a key player in a Nazi German film industry with global aspirations. Immediately after her arrival and initial meeting with Goebbels and Hitler in 1937, Goebbels wrote that she was a valuable addition to 'our band of artists' and that he would pay attention to her development. He continued:

> And first and foremost this question of the great later developments [must be] very carefully handled. It must in the end also be successful. The Führer supports me fully in this.[23]

Goebbels wrote later that year that they would turn Argentina into a 'great advertisement' and that she was 'a great victory for us'.[24] Goebbels' plans for her ultimately did not come to fruition. He writes that she did not want to learn German, but that he was pressuring her to do so.[25] He mentions on several occasions that Argentina was causing problems and that those at Ufa did not wish to work with her. In one entry, he writes in connection with these problems that '[Zarah] Leander has deliberately insulted [Imperio Argentina]'.[26] Leander, a Swedish actress brought in to work in the German industry in 1936, did become a major star who appeared in several of the most successful entertainment films made during the Nazi years. Leander may have seen Argentina as a competitor given that both played similar kinds of roles. Goebbels, however, notes on two occasions that he would force Ufa to work with Argentina.[27]

Argentina, who never fully did master German, may not have fully perceived Goebbels' plans for her. In her memoirs, she only identifies the Lola Montez project as a source of conflict. Although she suggests that they rejected it almost immediately, a private account indicates that they had initially agreed to do it after completing *Carmen*.[28] Goebbels placed great importance on the Montez script and personally supervised its creation and revision throughout 1937. His diaries give the best indication of what eventually must have caused Rey and Argentina to reject it: Goebbels insisted that his writers make the film 'sharply anticlerical'.[29] Later he wrote that a revised version was a 'sharp attack on priest and Jesuit ridden Bayer. So it is meant to be.'[30] Anti-Catholicism would of course have been anathema to Rey and Argentina. They had gone to work in Berlin partly to support the cause of the Spanish Nationalists who believed that Roman Catholicism constituted the core of Spanish national identity.[31] The difficulties caused by Argentina combined with her and Rey's refusal to make the Lola Montez story must have put an end to Goebbels' hopes for promoting her as a major star in the German industry. Although he comments favourably on her performance in *Andalusian Nights* in 1938, this is the last entry he writes about the actress.[32] The anti-religious and racial politics of German fascism complicated the assimilation of the militant Catholicism of Spanish fascism.

The Films of the HFP

Despite Goebbels' ultimate frustration, HFP's five Spanish-language features were mostly successful films which helped cement the stardom of their actors and directors. Rey directed Argentina in *Carmen* and subsequently in *Africa* (*La canción de Aixa*, 1939). Benito Perojo made three films, all starring Estrellita Castro: *The Barber of Seville* (*El barbero de Sevilla*, 1938), *Sighs of Spain* (*Suspiros de España*, 1938) and *Mariquilla Terremoto* (1939). With the exception of *Africa* which is set in the Spanish protectorate of Morocco and features an all-Spanish cast playing Moroccans, the rest of the films are all *españoladas*, or a highly romanticised and simplistic vision of Spain. These films tend to be set in Andalusia, feature musical numbers and emphasise the Spain of gypsies, bullfights and flamenco. Indeed, Rey's *Carmen* is a masterpiece of the genre. An ultimately tragic melodrama, the film concerns the seduction of a brigadier in the Spanish army by a captivating gypsy. Perojo's lightly ironic films emphasised instead the humorous side of typically Spanish characters. Such films took advantage of one area of cultural politics on which the Nazis and Spanish Nationalists agreed: the anti-modern values of traditional Spanish folkloric culture.

All of these films were dubbed into German and released with either German or Spanish soundtracks and subtitles in appropriate local languages. All were widely exported and, as most appeared before or in the early stages of the Second World War, were not rejected because of their provenance. Of the fiction films made by the HFP, *Carmen* has the most clearly fascistic message in its exaltation of the military and of traditional values. Perojo's two films set in contemporary Spain, *Mariquilla Terremoto* and *Sighs of Spain*, are most notable for the striking absence of any reference to the ongoing Spanish Civil War. The commercial successes of these films undoubtedly owe much more to the compelling performances by their leads and the skill of their directors.

All of the HFP films played widely in Europe and Latin America, and some even showed in Spanish-language theatres in the United States prior to the outbreak of the Second World War. *Sighs of Spain* and *Carmen* were the most successful.[33] Much like Argentina's earlier films, *Carmen* had extraordinarily long runs at some movie theatres in Paris, Lisbon and throughout Latin America. In Mexico City, it played for more weeks at a first-run theatre than any other film of the 1930s.[34] Despite successes, the end of the Spanish Civil War in 1939 and the outbreak of war in Germany ended the conditions which had favoured the production of Spanish-language films in German studios. Furthermore, rather than collaborate, the German and Spanish distributors of films made by the HFP competed with each other for rights to different territories.[35] The HFP officially moved its offices to Madrid in 1940, but produced only one further feature film, as both Germany and Spain turned their attention to other ways to influence Spanish-language cinemas.

Competing Fascist Interests in Latin America

The Nazis had hoped to take advantage of their diplomatic and commercial relationships with the Spanish Nationalists and use the HFP as a springboard to wrest primary control of the Spanish-speaking film markets away from any competitors and ultimately to dominate the global film industry. However, Germany had difficulty competing with other traditionally influential powers in Latin America. In the two largest and most significant film-producing countries, Argentina and Mexico, the Nazis had some initial successes but eventually ran into opposition from the governments of Britain, the United States, Mexico and even its sometimes ally Spain, once the Civil War had ended and Francisco Franco began to consolidate his control over the country.

Diplomatic records of the Allies indicate that Germany took advantage of the traditional Argentine antipathy to American leadership in the continent, and established the headquarters of its propaganda machine in Buenos Aires, although Germany also considered Mexico to be a main target. At the start, Germany outstripped both Britain and America in the number of staff and 'diplomatic' resources dedicated to propaganda.[36] The Allied files suggest their concern about the distribution of German shorts and feature films through the German embassies and legations in Latin America.[37] The disadvantage suffered by the British cinema led the British Embassy in Argentina (BEA) to inform the British Ministry of Information (MoI)[38] in London on 11 April 1941 that 'Argentina itself is the worst territory in Latin America so far as the distribution of our films is concerned', and added that in Brazil 'the distribution situation is almost as bad as in Argentina'.[39]

These documents reveal Britain's perception of the importance of some of the Latin American republics in terms of Allied efforts to stop the influence of Nazi cinema in Latin America: '*We regard Mexico, Buenos Aires and Rio de Janeiro as our principal centres* for supervising the Caribbean area, Spanish speaking South America and Brazil, *and the officers in Mexico and Buenos Aires have a certain advisory functions* [. . .].'[40] As we have noted, the Nazis concurred with this diagnosis of the Latin American film market and its main countries and cities not only for business from the very beginning of sound cinema, but also for propaganda activities from 1933 onwards.

Spanish Attempts to Infiltrate the Mexican Cinema

The Nazis were not, however, the only fascist power the Allies had to worry about. Although the German–Spanish agreements had helped open the door for Nazi and fascist penetration of Latin America in a joint effort, Cifesa also independently tried to penetrate the Mexican film industry. On 17 February 1940, Quirico Michelena Llaguno, acting as Cifesa's agent in Mexico and Latin America, was denounced to the Mexican embassy in Colombia, and later to the Mexican Foreign Affairs Ministry. Michelena, on behalf of Cifesa, had sought to start a new company which would serve as a front for an ideological offensive. It would build on the highly successful Mexican infrastructure for distribution and exhibition of its films in the Spanish-speaking world.

What shocked Mexican officials and diplomats was that Cifesa–Michelena's new company, *Dulcinea Productions* (*Producciones Dulcinea*, DP), grew out of the Franco government's creation in 1940 of the *Consejo de la Hispanidad* (*Council of the Hispanic Culture*), which was intended to influence Latin America towards Spanish fascism. One of Michelena's documents, aimed to convince South American distributors of Mexican cinema to participate in the venture: 'Dulcinea Productions will be a regular collective society managed by men willing to sacrifice everything to introduce Spanish speaking films at least in all the Spanish speaking markets. *These men should not only pursue profit. They shall base their actions on ideological motives, according to the spiritual orientations of the New Spanish State.*'[41] Michelena affirmed that he was in contact with other distributors and exhibitors of Mexican films all over Latin America, and he also assured that there were already signed contracts with them to produce the first great project of the new company, which should be *Marianela* (based on Benito Pérez Galdós' novel).

Taking into account Cifesa, along with CEA and Ufilms, the three Spanish film companies most committed with the Franco regime and with the Nazi and fascist interests in Europe (through their agreements with German, Italian and Portuguese film companies) and with their aims to infiltrate Latin America with Nazi–fascist propaganda films, it was evident that by 1940 Spain and Argentina were the countries that, although not occupied by the Third Reich, were however at the peak of their symbiosis with the Nazi film industry.[42]

The German Project in Argentina

A series of communications between the BEA and the Films Division of the MoI during 1941–42 demonstrate the depth of German implication in the Argentine film industry. Several reports prepared by the heads of the main American film distributors in Buenos Aires explained that German entertainment films were very popular in Argentina up to 1933. The later relative decline of Nazi films in that country seems to have given rise to Nazi strategies to penetrate the Argentinean film industry. The reports contain illuminating descriptions of German steps to achieve this goal. *Agfa de la Argentina* (a German supplier of film stock) began giving credits to Argentine film companies from the early 1930s onwards. Later, between 1938 and 1940, after certain Argentine companies, such as *PAF, SIDE, Tecnograf, Laboratorios Mendez Delfino and Laboratorios Cristiani* filed for bankruptcy, Agfa and Mr Von Simpson, its German managing director in Buenos Aires, appeared as the principal creditors. As Agfa had precedence over the rest of the creditors, it became 'liquidator [sic] of two companies and member of the administrative board of another two, his vote being the deciding one in the future production of these companies'.[43] The same report highlighted the power of Agfa in Argentina:

> The reason why Agfa has been able to gain such a firm foot-hold in the virgin film market, to the point of being almost the only means of supply to the Argentine producers is due (1) to the liberal way in which they grant credit, (2) to the introduction of the 'Suprema' supersensitive film, (3) to the difficulties Kodak had in obtaining exchange and (4) because of the total elimination of competition which 'Gevaert' signified, although really this was never of major importance.[44]

Poster for the Spanish-language version of Florián Rey's *Carmen la de Triana* (1938). *Source*: Filmoteca Española.

Also according to these reports, when the Argentine SIDE Company appeared in bankruptcy court in 1939, Mr Von Simpson, apparently acting upon instructions received from Berlin, suggested that, as Agfa was also SIDE's principal creditor, there was an opportunity to consolidate the German task. Such a project would have implied bringing in (to Argentina) German directors, technical advisors and artists (art directors, designers and so on) to produce German films, but spoken in Spanish. Although the events in Europe brought a momentary end to Simpson's plans (the report added), German interests in the Argentine industry continued to expand.

Agfa, together with Siemens Schuckert, was also the main creditor of *Argentina Sono Film*, the most important Argentine film company, among others. Furthermore, the *Banco Germánico* (*Deutsche Bank* or *German Bank* in Argentina) granted liberal credits to almost all the Argentine cinema companies that were experiencing financial difficulties, and later became also creditor of some of them. We have to take into account that these German corporations (particularly Agfa and the Deutsche Bank) had strong and lengthy past relationships, as they also had with Ufa since its inception in 1917.[45] Therefore, the Allies could observe that Agfa and the Deutsche Bank were apparently acting almost as Ufa's subsidiaries in Argentina, and if we also consider the strong relationship between Agfa and Siemens Schuckert, we can see that the Argentine film companies seemed to be trapped in a complex and strong liaison of political, economical and propagandistic interests acting from Germany. This explains that a report dated on 10 February 1941 concluded that:

> Summarising, we can deduct that a *Nazi infiltration in the distribution* of material received from the totalitarian countries *has commenced*. That *they have almost entirely dominated the sale of virgin film* and as regards production, although nothing concrete exists, it is evident that by means of liberal credit *they are trying to take a hand in the Argentine production*, waiting the opportune moment to obtain a greater gravitation over this phase of the business.[46]

Another long communication issued on 26 February 1941, given to the BEA by the representative of Columbia Pictures at Buenos Aires, showed the attention that the British and the Americans devoted to this question, as well as the fruitfulness of their intelligence activities.

According to information supplied to Herdman by the local publicity agent for Columbia Pictures, an official German envoy, named Hans Heinrich Biester, arrived at Buenos Aires by Condor Plane at the end of the last month, for the purpose of

> supervising the distribution of German propaganda films throughout Latin America [. . .] Biester was formerly an attaché at the German embassy in Madrid and organised the distribution of German films throughout Spain [. . .] In Latin America he is apparently authorised to build cinemas, should he be unable to make satisfactory arrangements with existing ones. He is also prepared to finance Argentine film companies, with a view to arranging for German propaganda to be introduced into local films and newsreels [. . .] Biester's preliminary negotiations with certain exhibitors have not been very encouraging since they are afraid of American reprisals.[47]

In the field of distribution, Nazi and anti-British films, as well as German propaganda in general, were being distributed and screened by Mr Nicolás Di Fiori.[48] Born Italian and naturalised Argentine, and the proprietor of a large number of theatres, Di Fiori had been denounced for receiving subsidies from the German Embassy, in return for agreeing to screen Nazi propaganda through his distribution company, *Organización Cinematográfica Argentina* (Argentine Film Organisation).[49]

This situation in Argentina, in addition to evidence that German film interests were also active in Chile and elsewhere, motivated British and American initiatives to block German infiltration. Both Britain and America lagged far behind the Germans. They, like the Germans, had to confront the problem of Latin America's large illiterate population who could not read sub-titled propaganda films. They aimed to intervene in Spanish-language film production to counterattack the Axis' film propaganda in Spanish already being produced in Germany, Italy, Portugal and Spain, and to prevent such propaganda also being produced in Latin America.[50]

The British and United States' Counter Offensive

Britain's proposal was to 'take over, organise and expand wherever possible, the distribution in Latin America' of British newsreels, propaganda shorts and feature films. The MoI planned to create an Argentine film company, supported by British local interests in Buenos Aires, whose aim would be 'to encourage production by local units of films *in the vernacular* which would have *a suitable propaganda angle*'.[51] There was a short period of intense negotiations between the Latin American sections at the MoI and the British Foreign Office (BFO) in London, the BEA and the British Information Services Office in New York. The British staff in Buenos Aires was encouraged to 'inspire' local companies to produce propaganda films with a sympathetic view of the Allies.[52] American producers, however, objected to British competition and pressured the British to cancel their project in Argentina.[53]

The United States planned instead to disseminate propaganda through Mexico to the Spanish-speaking world through coordinated action by the White House, the State Department and the Office of the Coordinator of Inter American Affairs (OCIAA) and the Mexican Government. As soon as the OCIAA emerged, John Hay Whitney, head of the most influential of the OCIAA's divisions, the Motion Picture Division, toured Latin America in 1941, to explore Spanish-speaking film industries and to find a suitable candidate for fostering 'democratic' ideals through movies in Latin American audiences.[54] At the beginning of 1942 the OCIAA's project was well advanced. By then, Whitney had written the first draft of a *Plan to Stimulate Production of Motion Pictures by Mexican Industry in Support of War Effort*.[55] The project was part of a wider plan to develop the film industries of several

Imperio Argentina, the wife and favourite lead actress of Florián Rey. *Source*: Vande Winkel/De Paepe Collection.

of the Latin American republics. However, Mexico was selected because of its proximity to the United States and because Mexican cinema was one of the best established in the region. The two governments also had good diplomatic relationships.[56] Thus, the final plan was drawn up and signed on 15 June 1942 on the following grounds: the main objective was to aid the Mexican film industry in the production of films with a 'desirable effect of propaganda on the Latin American Audiences', which gave support to the war effort and the hemisphere solidarity as a means of combating Spanish-language films from the Axis – 'wherever they were produced' – and as a means 'to forestalling the development of such industries in other republics contrary to the interests of the United States'.[57]

The success of the Mexican–American agreement was perhaps one of the main reasons for the failure of the Nazi film industry's effort to penetrate Spanish-speaking film industries. Additionally, most Latin American countries either broke off diplomatic relations with Germany or declared war on the Axis after the Japanese attack on Pearl Harbor. Mexico stopped Cifesa's project for Spanish entry into the Mexican film industry, and took measures that made German financial intervention in the Mexican cinema impossible. Once the United States imposed a film stock quota and the war made film supplies from Europe unavailable, Argentine film production decreased significantly. Hollywood, too, blacklisted any Latin American company which collaborated with Axis countries during the war. By 1943 Mexico and the United States reached the peak of their collaboration, whereas the beginning of the end had already started for the Nazis and fascists, in the war as in the film propaganda race all over the world.

Notes

1. J. Chapman, *The British at War. Cinema, State and Propaganda, 1939–1945* (London: I.B. Tauris Publishers, 1998), p. 41; G. D. Black and C. R. Koppes, *Hollywood Goes to War* (New York: The Free Press, 1987), pp. 48–64.
2. Michael H. Kater, 'Film as an Object of Reflection in the Goebbels Diaries: Series II (1941–45)', *Central European History*, 33:3 (2000), pp. 394–404.
3. Estimates typically suggested that there were 100–120-million Spanish speakers. See Román Gubern, *El cine sonoro en la II República, 1929–1936* (Barcelona: Editorial Lumen, 1977), p. 71.
4. See also Chapter 19.
5. Manuel Nicolás Meseguer, *La intervención velada: el apopyo cinematográfico alemán al bando franquista (1936–1939)* (Murcia: Universidad de Murcia; Lorca: Primavera Cinematográfica de Lorca, 2004), pp. 79–100.
6. E. Diez Puertas, 'Los acuerdos cinematográficos entre el franquismo y el tercer Reich (1936–1945) [The Film Agreements Between the Franquism and the Third Reich (1936–1945)]', *Archivos de la Filmoteca*, 33 (1999), pp. 35–59.
7. Gubern (1977), pp. 78–9.
8. Meseguer (2004), p. 104.
9. Ibid., pp. 101, 108, 117.
10. Ibid., pp. 110–11.
11. Ibid., p. 105.
12. Ibid., p. 116.
13. Agustín Sánchez Vidal, *El cine de Florián Rey* (Zaragoza: Caja de Ahorros de la Inmaculada de Aragón, 1991), p. 228; Román Gubern, *Benito Perojo: Pionerismo y supervivencia* (Madrid: Filmoteca Española, 1994), p. 292; Imperio Argentina with Pedro M. Víllora, *Imperio Argentina: Malena Clara* (Madrid: Ediciones Temas de Hoy, 2001), p. 109.
14. 29 October 1937, in Elke Fröhlich (ed.), *Die Tagebücher von Joseph Goebbels*, part 1/volume 4 March–November 1937 (München: K.G. Saur, 2000a), p. 381. My thanks to Thomas Bach for the translations from the original German.
15. Argentina (2001), p. 102; Gubern (1994), p. 294.
16. Martín de la Plaza, *Imperio Argentina: una vida de artista* (Alianza: Madrid, 2003), p. 106.
17. Gubern (1994), p. 294.
18. Meseguer (2004), p. 114.
19. Argentina (2001), pp. 105–12, 125–7; Carlos Manso, *Imperio Argentina (mito y realidad)* (Buenos Aires: El Francotirador Ediciones, 1999), pp. 70–3, 80–4.

20. Aytor Iarola, 'Mision españolista: los camaradas Florián Rey y Argentina con Hitler y el Dr. Goebbels', *Filmhistoria*, 9:3 (1999), p. 289.
21. Argentina (2001), p. 111; Manso (1999), p. 73.
22. Manso (1999), p. 79; Argentina (2001), pp. 115, 119.
23. Goebbels, 13 May 1937 in Fröhlich (2000a), p. 136.
24. Goebbels, 14 May and 23 November 1937 in Fröhlich (2000a), pp. 138, 418.
25. Goebbles, 18 August 1937 in Fröhlich (2000a), p. 270.
26. Goebbels, 17 July 1937 in Fröhlich (2000a), p. 241.
27. Goebbels, 31 July and 20 August 1937 in Fröhlich (2000a), pp. 241, 273.
28. Meseguer (2004), pp. 113–14.
29. Goebbels, 20 June 1937 in Fröhlich (2000a), p. 189.
30. Goebbels, 18 November 1937 in Fröhlich (2000a), p. 410.
31. Meseguer (2004), p. 121.
32. Goebbels, 24 June 1938 in Elke Fröhlich (ed.), *Die Tagebücher von Joseph Goebbles*, 1:5 December 1937–July 1938 (München: K.G. Saur, 2000b), p. 359.
33. Gubern (1994), p. 306.
34. Sánchez Vidal, p. 209; María Luisa Amador and Jorge Ayala Blanco, 'Películas taquilleras de los treinta', *Revista Filmoteca*, 1:1 (November 1978), pp. 26–69.
35. Meseguer (2004), pp. 116–17.
36. Public Record Office (hereafter PRO), Kew, London. Archives of the British Ministry of Information (hereafter MoI). Archival documents on British efforts through the MoI, to diminish 'the very active German propaganda being carried out' in both countries between 1939 and 1943. Hereafter this archive will be referred as PRO/INF1, followed by the names of those involved in the issue, the file's title, number and date, when all this information was clearly stated. In this case the file codes are PRO/INF1/375, British Official Wireless Services to Argentina, and PRO/INF1/376, on the same issue for Mexico.
37. PRO/INF I/607/F109/31 MoI's Memoranda, 9 December 1940.
38. See also Chapter 22.
39. PRO/INF1/537. Report from Vizcount Lord Davidson to K. G. Grubb, both of them at the MoI, 28 January 1941, pp. 2–3; PRO/INF1/607/F109/31/BEA to MoI, 11 April 1941.
40. Ibid., p. 3. Emphasis added.
41. Genaro Estrada Archive of the Mexican Foreign Affairs Ministry. Letter from Quirico Michelena to Jorge Jaramillo Villa, distributor and exhibitor of Mexican films in Colombia, 26 December 1939. File code AGE/SRE/III-419-4. Emphasis added.
42. Diez Puertas (1999), p. 36.
43. PRO/INF1/607. Report sent by the BEA to the MoI's Films Division, 10 February 1941, p. 1.
44. Ibid., p. 2.
45. K. Kreimeier, *The Ufa Story. A History of Germany's Greatest Film Company 1918–1945* (Berkeley: University of California Press, 1999).
46. PRO/INF1/607. BEA to MoI's Films Division. 10 February 1941, p. 4. Emphasis added.
47. PRO/INF1/607/F109/31. BEA to Latin American Section of MoI's American Division, 26 February 1941. Emphasis added.
48. Ibid., p. 3.
49. Ibid., p. 2 on the list of cinema theatres owned by Nicolás de Fiori.
50. T. Barnard (ed.), *Argentine Cinema* (Toronto: Nightwood, 1986), p. 35.

51. PRO/INF1/607/F/109/31/1/ MoI to BEA, 30 April 1941. Emphasis added.
52. Ibid., EUP Fitzgerald from MoI's Latin American Section to T. W. Pears at the Information Department in the BEA, 17 May 1941.
53. PRO/INF1 632/ BEA to MoI. 7, 9, 13, 14, and 17 June 1941.
54. National Archives of Washington (hereafter NAW). Communication of Sub-secretary of State to George S. Messersmith, American Ambassador at Mexico City. File code: NAW812.4061MP/273 27 May 42. See also for more reference G. S. de Usabel, *The High Noon of American Films in Latin America* (Ann Arbor, Michigan: The University of Michigan Research Press, 1982), p. 156.
55. NAW812.4061MP/269.
56. Ibid.
57. Ibid. Emphasis added.

4

Between Resistance and Collaboration: Austrian Cinema and Nazism Before and During the Annexation, 1933–45

Robert von Dassanowsky

The future of the film industry in a country that was to become a province of the German Reich was conceived throughout most of the 1930s, long before the Austrian Chancellor's radio broadcast to the nation surrendering to the Nazi invasion on 12 March 1938. Hitler's arrival speech, given from the balcony of the imperial Hofburg palace in Vienna, announced the 'return' of his homeland into the Reich and thus marked Austria as the first national victim of Nazi aggression, but given the significant numbers of Austrian National Socialists, also as a collaborator.[1] Five years of Nazi Germany's systematic infiltration of Austrian film production through investment, racial dictates, and blatant corporate absorption had so prepared the industry for its new form and role that Berlin was in complete control in a matter of days following annexation.[2]

Upon Hitler's assumption of power in Germany in January 1933, the *Nationalsozialische Deutsche Arbeiterpartei* (NSDAP) began the *Gleichschaltung* (coordination)[3] of society and culture to its ideology. The first indication of the nationalisation and 'Aryanisation' of the German film industry was given in Propaganda Minister Joseph Goebbels' speech to representatives of the German film industry on 28 March 1933. From that point on, the German film industry would be subordinate to Goebbels' ministry (*Reichsministerium für Volksaufklärung und Propaganda*, RMVP) and the goals of National Socialism. Germany's most dominant and now nationalised central film studio, Ufa, immediately severed contracts with all Jewish artists and organisational staff. Subsequently, the Austrian film industry became the haven for talent fleeing Germany. Vienna might have benefited from such an influx if it were not for the plans Hitler had set in motion from his first days in office – to isolate, impoverish and bring Austria to its knees in order to foster a Nazi coup and accomplish annexation. Even tourism, Austria's most important industry, was to be hampered: Nazi Germany instituted the *1000 Mark Sperre*, which required a deposit of 1000 Reich marks for Germans who desired to travel to Austria for either business or pleasure.

Austria's film market was highly dependent upon Germany for production and distribution. Many German companies had bought into Austrian firms during the early years of sound, and Austrian film's largest export audience was Germany. The showing of Austrian films that were made with Jewish or with known or perceived anti-German/anti-National-Socialist talent was officially refused German release beginning in March 1933. Of the 14 Austrian films in distribution at the time of the first National-Socialist industry guidelines (March 1933–February 1934), 5 were blocked from release, 1 was pulled from distribution, and 3 sold to Germany were rejected for their 'poor quality' by the new arm of the RMVP, the Reich Film Chamber. The actual reason was that Jewish artists had been involved in their creation.

The Film Agreement of 1934 placed the Austrian film industry under strangulating external pressure by Nazi Germany, which forbade the importing and showing of any Austrian film that included among cast or crew 'non-Germans' (émigrés from Nazi Germany) or 'non-Aryan' Austrians. That this was specifically aimed at destabilising the Austrian economy and 'Aryanising' Austrian cinema from outside, in preparation of annexation, was clear to Oskar Pilzer, the director of the largest studio in Austria, Tobis-Sascha, and president of the Association of Producers (*Gesamtverband der Produzenten*), a branch of the authoritarian state's official film culture establishment. Additionally, his Pilzer Group (with brothers Kurt, Severin and Viktor) had part or direct ownership of other Austrian film companies as well. Pilzer maintained that the Third Reich was not as insistent on 'Aryan' talent in other foreign films as it was in Austrian product.[4] Others in the Austrian film industry believed that the Germans were not targeting Austrian citizens, only ex-German nationals in Austrian film, and that the racial laws of Germany did not apply to Austria, nor would Austria institute an *Arierparagraph* (Aryan Law) of its own to suit Germany. Unfortunately, Austrian film did exactly that with its concessions to Germany for the sake of film distribution. Film credits were edited to remove the 'undesirable' names and by 1935, the previous agreement was replaced with a new one that put the now seriously disadvantaged and dependent Austrian film industry one step closer towards mandatory 'Aryanisation'. Austria was limited to the distribution of 12 films annually in Germany through German companies, whereas Germany could export an unlimited amount to Austria. Cases involving permission to work now no longer needed German citizenship, Austrian citizenship would be acceptable, but this was a worthless concession since the German proof of Aryan status, the *Ariernachweis*, was still demanded. This gave Germany substantial control in the creation and casting of Austrian film. Exceptions would be approached on an individual basis, but only in the same manner Berlin dealt with its own film talent, meaning that this was nearly impossible.

The discord that Germany caused the Austrian film industry and practically every other aspect of its economy and culture was no doubt intended to be a brief and fruitful policy by the National Socialists. On 25 July 1934, Austrian Nazis assassinated Chancellor Dollfuss in an attempted coup that was to enable the annexation (*Anschluss*). But no internal collapse occurred and Kurt von Schuschnigg, the Minister of Education in Dollfuss' government, was named Chancellor. Although von Schuschnigg continued the authoritarian-corporate state (often called 'Austrofascism') instituted by Dollfuss in 1934, he was quite different in many ways from his predecessor. His regime, which lasted until the German Anschluss in 1938, intended to reduce the government's authoritarian aspects. Austrians who were illegal members of the Austrian National Socialist Party (all traditional parties were forbidden) openly aided Germany's involvement in the Austrian film industry. German producer Serge Otzoup and Austrian banker Wilhelm Gaik founded a company, known as the Kombination Otzoup, that would help Austrian productions locate 'Aryan' cast and crew in order to allow for easy German approval and distribution. Austrian producers were encouraged to make bilateral agreements with the firm and the leader of the outlawed Austrian National Socialist Party, Josef Leopold. The former president of the Austrian film industry's umbrella organisation, the *Filmbund*, silent film pioneer Heinz Hanus, also assisted in providing racial information about the talent being employed.

The Nazi racial laws made about 900 members of the German film industry unemployable in Germany and ultimately stateless.[5] Many of these headed towards Hollywood but a substantial portion sought out Vienna and Budapest, to be able to work in the German language and often because Austria or Hungary had been their origin. Since they were now not able to work with most of the major Austrian film companies, a secondary or independent film industry developed around this talent. These new companies were non-dependent on Germany for investment or distribution and therefore rejected Germany's racial guidelines. Their *Emigrantenfilm* (emigrant film) would utilise émigré and Austrian 'non-Aryan' talent, often co-produce their films with foreign studios and in multi-language versions, and market them across Europe. Austrian co-production with Hungary, Czechoslovakia, the Netherlands and Sweden dominated this second film industry between 1934 and 1938.

By 1936, there were strong contradictions regarding the condition of the Austrian film industry. The state-led Austrian Film Conference was held that year, and suggesting that film had certainly come into its own as a major national art form, made impressive plans for a film academy as well as for an archive and a museum. But the possibilities of independent Austrian film-making had begun to fade. The new film agreement between Germany and Austria in March of that year stipulated that the agreement would have to be renewed annually and the Germans now demanded that all German performers and crew (except the extras or atmosphere players) in Austrian film bound for German release would have to present their *Ariernachweis*, or documentation of 'Aryan' status. Only 14 Austrian films would be allowed into Germany per year. The Berlin–Rome Axis lost Austria its erstwhile protector, Mussolini, who aligned with Hitler and abandoned Austria to Hitler's goals of Nazi infiltration and the eventual annexation of his former homeland to the German Reich. Moreover, the removal of the Pilzer Group from the board of Tobis-Sascha indicated the extent of German influence within the Austrian film industry. The studio was subsequently transformed into a German 'scout' which swallowed up many smaller Austrian production companies by purchase rather than merger in an attempt to control the industry landscape and prepare it for the Nazi *Gleichschaltung*. The summit meeting between Hitler and Chancellor von Schuschnigg at Berchtesgaden in February 1937 was to have normalised the German–Austrian political situation, but it was in fact a major step for the Nazification of Austria. Although the Austrian corporate state was a non-party or national front system, Hitler demanded and received concessions to allow Austrian National-Socialist representation in the government. The mainstream film industry seemed to ignore the ominous possibilities, perhaps because they had already been 'Aryanised' and their productions found distribution in Germany with little problem. A roster of fascinating projects were announced for 1938, all of course unrealised due to the Anschluss and re-organisation of the former Austrian film industry according to Goebbels' dictates.

The first transportation of Austrians bound for Dachau concentration camp began on 1 April 1938. Nine days later, Schuschnigg's intended referendum regarding the rejection of German annexation, which was to have alerted the world to Austria's plight, was supervised by Hitler's new interim 'Chancellor' of Austria, Arthur Seyss-Inquart. In best ballot-fixing tradition, the results gave a 99 per cent vote in favour of Anschluss. Austria disappeared from the map and was integrated into the Third Reich as the *Ostmark* or Eastern March. Dissatisfied with this new name, which still recalled 'Austria' in German (*Österreich*), Hitler later degraded the annexed country into the even more fragmented and vague *Alpen- und Donaugau* (Alpine and Danube District). In response to the New Order, the Austrian film publication, *Mein Film* (*My Film*), insisted that 'true' Viennese films had always been examples of good 'German' cinema, both in theme and execution. That they were Viennese because of 'a certain something that one could not place into words',[6] no longer made them Austrian. At first, this statement seems to attempt an absurd sense of continuity for Austrian film coupled with acceptance of German leadership, but one can read between the lines. The idea that despite all external appearances of Nazi pan-Germanisation, the spirit of what was Viennese film, indeed what was Austria, would live on in memory and in subtle, even subversive cultural elements, was the hope and intention of many in this Berlin-controlled film world. With the dissolution of all film organisations and the transfer of their activities to the Reich Film Chamber, *Mein Film* was soon obliged to call for loyalty to and confidence in the man who would now be in charge of the film talents of the *Ostmark*, Joseph Goebbels. Several film personalities were quoted in print as encouraging the vote for 'yes' in April's sham referendum.

All aspects of film-making and presentation would now be controlled by the Reich Film Chamber, and membership was required for a 'former Austrian' to work in the unified all-German industry. This was, of course, only possible with documentation of 'Aryan' status.

The Tobis-Sascha group was transformed into the new Wien-Film firm on 16 December 1938. As the Reich's centralised production unit in the *Ostmark*, it would control the great Tobis-Sascha complex also known as the Rosenhügel studio, the secondary facilities as well as all film transfer plants and post-production sites. Centralisation and expansion of film theatres was also instituted. As early as July 1938, all Austrian film theatres, including those owned by Ufa prior to the Anschluss, were absorbed into RMVP control. Given its specific cultural mission, the new Vienna mega-studio Wien-Film echoed the concept of the Hollywood studio system more closely than had been normal in previous Austrian cinema development. Many Austrian talents working at Ufa in Berlin returned home to participate in this new phase of Vienna's industry. Fritz Hirt was named managing director of the new studio and Austrian director Karl Hartl became production head. Hartl utilised his power to keep Vienna's film industry as autonomous as possible from the dictates of Berlin and the influence of its big-sister studio Ufa, which would release all Wien-Film productions. Goebbels foresaw a specific mission for Vienna as one of the three production centres (along with Berlin and eventually Prague) of the Reich. Wien-Film was to produce romantic fare, operetta films and musicals as the more entertainment-oriented and more exportable aspect of the Reich's film-making, while Ufa would focus on the dramas, historical spectacles, and on propaganda 'documentaries'. Even the logo of the new company, a treble clef, blatantly associated Wien-Film with Vienna as the 'German' city of music. Viennese-associated traditions and images, even the dialect, was to be utilised as an indication of the Reich's multivalent Germanic culture, to appeal to the audiences of allied and occupied lands, and most importantly, to cinematically annex the historical/cultural Vienna (and by extension, Austria). This coopting of a mythic Vienna intended to contain and exploit actually allowed Wien-Film to distance itself from, and to some extent subvert, the dictates of the pan-German ideology. One of the primary missions of the Reich's film industry was the production of biographical features (known as the 'genius' genre), which would suggest the importance of Germans in world history and elevate the public's sense of national superiority. Wien-Film would also have to produce its share of films about Austrian musicians, composers and writers who had now become historical figures of the Greater Germany.

Wien-Film's musical-romance escapism: Maria Holst and Willi Forst in Forst's *Operette* (1940). *Source*: Deutsches Filminstitut Frankfurt.

With four exceptions, the 50-plus features produced or distributed by Wien-Film between 1939 and 1945 were not overtly political; indeed this entertainment angle completely suited the designs of the RMVP, especially as it later provided a diversion from the war. Most Wien-Film product found box-office success and remain classics today primarily because of their avoidance of National-Socialist ideology, and due to their significant artistic and technological aspects. The studio launched its programme for escapism through regression into a romanticised Viennese past almost immediately: the first production was E. W. Emo's Johann Strauss family saga, *Immortal Waltz* (*Unsterblicher Walzer*, 1939). The lavish imperial setting and the memorable waltzes might have been claimed by the regime as a part of the Reich's history and as a work displaying a family of '*German* geniuses', but the film generates nothing if not sentimentality for a lost *Austrian* world.

There was a strict hierarchy among the actors and the directors regarding assignments and studio promotion at Wien-Film and its few semi-autonomous satellites. Willi Forst and Geza von Bolvary dominated the musical and the Viennese Film genre;[7] another actor-turned-director Hans Thimig created theatre and literary-based features, and E. W. Emo made comedies and two of Wien-Film's four political-propaganda features. Gustav Ucicky and his usual collaborator, screenwriter Gerhard Menzel, tended to specialise in a contrived form of social drama, which offered allegories on the general values of the Reich and managed to achieve high government ratings.[8] *A Mother's Love* (*Mutterliebe*, 1939) was the first in several Ucicky Wien-Film productions that, although not blatantly political, expounded on the themes of self-denial, self-sacrifice and the concept of a greater destiny.

It was Willi Forst, however, that dominated Wien-Film's reputation and style. He had secured his reputation as a major star, director, screenwriter and producer with his 1939 production of *Bel Ami*, based on the novel of

Paula Wessely as a victimised ethnic German (*Volksdeutsche*) in Poland. Gustav Ucicky's *Heimkehr*, a Wien-Film production (*Homecoming*, 1941), justified the 1939 invasion of Poland. *Source*: Deutsches Filminstitut Frankfurt.

the soon to be banned Guy de Maupassant, and followed it with the test of any great film actor – the double role – in *I Am Sebastian Ott* (*Ich bin Sebastian Ott*, 1939). His most important work of the period is the lavish set of period musical dramas (Viennese Film) known today as his Wien-Film trilogy: *Operetta* (*Operette*, 1940), *Viennese Blood* (*Wiener Blut*, 1942), and *Viennese Girls* (*Wiener Mädeln*, begun 1944; completed 1949). While he certainly used the Reich to further his career, Forst was nonetheless aware of the distinct opportunity that he had to continue Austrian content and style in these entertainment films while appearing to satisfy the official mission of Wien-Film. He would later reflect on his involvement with the Nazi propaganda machine and the effort to create both personal and specifically 'Austrian' cinema in the German totalitarian state: 'My native country was occupied by the National Socialists, and my work became a silent protest. Grotesque though it may sound, it is true that I made my most Austrian films at a time when Austria had ceased to exist.'[9] Gertraud Steiner suggests that this was no simple hind-sighted self-justification. Forst's Wien-Film projects managed to provide a subtle resistance to the dictates of Nazi socio-culture. His popular success in presenting what seemed to be harmless excursions into a romanticised Viennese culture of the past provided him an escape from having to create an overt propaganda film, but his allusions and references often contradicted National-Socialist dictates and became a point of friction with the censors: 'One step further and he would have been barred from making films.'[10] Sabine Hake, however, finds such a subversive aesthetic strategy little more than 'fantasy resistance', since the unreal and the masquerade, which now might represent difference, had always been part of the Viennese operetta construct. Nevertheless, she concedes that transformed through Forst's 'deceptive lightness and ironic self-awareness, the Vienna myth became a game between the film-maker and his audience'.[11]

The Vienna-based cinema of the Third Reich provided a cultural-theoretical counterpoint to the Berlin style that ultimately divided rather than united. Film scholar Linda Schulte-Sasse finds either direct use of or influence from the literature, history and philosophy of the eighteenth-century Enlightenment as a strong basis for the German narrative films of the Reich, ranging from the ionisation of Prussia and blatant anti-Semitism to the genius genre of Ufa's *Friedrich Schiller, Triumph of a Genius* (*Friedrich Schiller – Triumph eines Genies*, 1940).[12] These distorted versions of Enlightenment paradigms offer security to the viewer through familiar material, valorisation of bourgeois culture, and illusion of classical harmony and wholeness. In a similar fashion, Wien-Film productions can be read to find a comforting underlying cultural–historical paradigm in the nineteenth-century Biedermeier period, and its message of humble values and victories: love, family, modest creativity – all in the service of social harmony. Regardless of how one interprets the concept of a Greater German Reich and negates Austria with the idea of a provincial *Ostmark* and the even more culturally diluted notion of the *Alpen- und Donaugau*, the very success of Wien-Film's mission rested on the conjuring of 'an *Austrian* past, not a greater German one'.[13] Despite the 'Aryanisation' of history, Vienna's Belle Époque could not offer the same pro-German messages as Prussian historical or German literary models might. Lingering imperial era class-consciousness and strong multiculturalism, as well as Catholicism, had made the creation of a socially levelled and more German interwar Austria an impossible challenge to pan-German movements, and this 'problem' was not resolved by the race-based illusions of Nazism.

The most interesting intentional failure of Nazi ideological *Gleichschaltung* in Wien-Film product occurs in Karl Hartl's 1942 Mozart biography *Whom the Gods Love* (*Wen die Götter lieben*), written by Eduard von Borsody. To read Hartl's biopic as a genius genre film is to realise the difficulty of an Austrian cultural *Gleichschaltung* with Nazi German norms. Like Schiller, Mozart represents the genius that can be reflected on both high and popular cultural planes. For Nazi purposes, it becomes a 'narcissistic mirror'[14] for the masses in their identification with the German genius. Also like Schiller, Mozart is known for his commonness and his role as a rebel hero against forces that do not comprehend his art. But this is where the similarity ends. Unlike Schiller or the other German genius figures in Nazi cinema, Mozart had no true adversary against which he needed to realise himself. He composed for, against, and regardless of the authority figures that he attempted to manipulate and which could not deal with him. Mozart may be interpreted as a genius that rises from the people and falls to them again, but his transcendence is in his art rather than in a perceived 'heroic' life, and Hartl's film emphasised this. Despite the posturing of the title, Hartl's Mozart appears to be the unruly target of a regimented world that would have him appropriately submissive or disappear – much like Austrian cultural identity in the Nazi Reich.

Geza von Cziffra created one of the most famous of the entertainment films from Wien-Film in 1943. *The White Dream* (*Der weisse Traum*) was intended to be Wien-Film's answer to the novelty musicals of Hollywood's Sonja Henie. This was Austria's first ice revue film and the only one during the Wien-Film era, although the concept would be revisited again after 1945 and became a popular postwar genre. At a cost of more than 2 million Reich marks, the film was among the most expensive of the era, but also one of the most successful throughout the Reich and occupied Europe, eventually earning back 35 million Reich marks. As the war progressed, however, official criticism of the non-conformist aspects of the Wien-Film product increased. Although Goebbels appreciated Forst's work as a director, he found his presence as a leading man too soft for the times, and believed that there was perhaps even something 'Jewish' about his on-screen persona.[15] Forst's elegant cinematic gentlemen did not present the ideal of a National-Socialist hero and Goebbels lamented that the hit film *Operetta* was actually hindered by Forst's performance. He had probably no knowledge of Forst's bisexuality, which was a secret widely known within the industry, but if exposed would have immediately ended Forst's career and imperilled his life.

In 1942, all film production in the Reich, including the nominally autonomous Wien-Film studio was consolidated as part of the larger Ufa concern, the Ufi Trust. The few director-led subsidiaries such as Forst-Film or Emo-Film, regional satellites such as Styria-Film, and all semi-independent post-production facilities were now completely absorbed by a totally centralised industry that was ideologically and financially controlled by the state as an actual branch of the government. Goebbels explained this reorganisation as increased recognition of the great achievement of cinema in the Reich, but he now also asked that the industry become more budget-minded. Unless previously approved, no film could be longer than 2500 m and cost more than 1 million Reich marks. The Wien-Film costume epics and musicals seemed to have standing permission to overspend, but by 1943, only minimum pay would be forthcoming to the talent of the Reich's film industry.

Although it was never truly understood for the subversive power it possessed, the heavy Viennese or Austrian dialects of Wien-Film productions finally did become too much for Berlin to take. In 1944, Wien-Film head Karl Hartl informed directors Forst, Ucicky, Thimig and von Cziffra that the authorities expected them to be 'particularly careful . . . that our films will be understood by a German public of all regional origins'.[16] Accents or regional flavourings would still be acceptable, but the full-blown dialects that had been so flagrantly used in Wien-Film productions were now forbidden. The studio had retained its semi-autonomy not only because it was so adept at creating highly entertaining and escapist box-office successes, but because it also made good on fulfilling the order for an occasional *Tendenzfilm* or ideological propaganda film to show that it was not totally lost in Viennese nostalgia and soft on the ideas of the Reich. Ufa and its stars were mostly responsible for this type of film, but there were also Wien-Film talents that found these projects to be worthy cinematic art. Most, however, did not. Heinz Helbig directed the first of the four Wien-Film propaganda features. His anti-Semitic period film, *Linen from Ireland* (*Leinen aus Irland*, 1939), tells the story of Dr Kuhn (Siegfried Breuer), a Jewish secretary at the Prague (then in Austria–Hungary) Libussa textile firm, who attempts to sabotage the Bohemian industry by importing Irish linen. His plot also involves the seduction of Lilly (Irene von Meyendorff), the daughter of the firm's president. A heroic weaver ultimately exposes Kuhn's intrigue and the corruption of the Trade Ministry. The industry is saved and Lilly finds love with the only honest civil servant in the Ministry (Rolf Wanka).

The 1941 E. W. Emo comedy, *Love is Tax-Free* (*Liebe ist Zollfrei*), is also considered a *Tendenzfilm*. Written by Fritz Koselka from a play by Fritz Gottwald, it was designed as a vehicle for comic star Hans Moser, who portrays a customs officer in a fictionalised First Republic Austria led by an incompetent chancellor (Oskar Sima). In his famous curmudgeon manner, Moser's insignificant but honest civil servant exposes a corrupt regime while attacking democracy, capitalist bureaucrats, and practically every aspect of the former Austria. The survival of Moser's Jewish wife was at the mercy of the regime, so he never protested the Reich's film politics or official plans for his career. In addition to this brazen satire, Moser also made several films with German producers and directors between 1939 and 1945. E. W. Emo returned to the propaganda feature in 1943, with the biographical drama, *Wien 1910* (*Vienna 1910*). These two political concessions to Berlin at Wien-Film earned him the gratitude of the regime and the short-lived position as production head of the Reich's film industry in Prague. Like *Love is Tax-Free* and *Linen from Ireland,Vienna 1910* returns to the particular focal point of the *Tendenzfilme* at Wien-Film – the defamation of the culture, society and/or politics of imperial or republican Austria. Unlike E. W. Emo's other *Tendenzfilm*, however, the targets here are actual historical figures. The film is set during the final days of Vienna's controversial but popular mayor Karl Lueger (Rudolf Forster), and attempts to display the roots of German nationalism (read Nazism) in imperial Vienna vis-à-vis the 'corrupt' Christian Social and 'Jewish' Socialist political movements prior to the First World War. Historically, Georg von Schönerer (portrayed in the film by Heinrich George), who founded the Pan-German Party in 1885, led a violent anti-Semitic assault in 1888, which resulted in his loss of noble title, deprivation of his parliamentary seat and imprisonment. Menzel's script portrays him as a hero who sacrifices his social standing and nearly himself for the cause against a 'Slavic-Jewish' Austrian Empire. The Habsburg-loyal Lueger, however, appears to be the more sympathetic and interesting character. Was this an intentional sabotage of a propaganda film? The director never commented on the matter, but the expensive (approximately 2.5 million Reichs marks) historical drama was ultimately deemed unacceptable for showings to former Austrians in the *Ostmark*, and after re-editing, it was only screened in distant Reich territories and in Axis states.

Ucicky took the ultimate step into overtly propagandistic film-making with his *Homecoming* (*Heimkehr*, 1941), the most notorious of the four political features from Wien-Film. Curiously, the film has nothing to do with Vienna or even former imperial or republican Austrian history, although it does borrow style from Austrian social dramas of the 1920s and 1930s. It was honoured as few films of the Reich had been, achieving official recognition from the Italian Ministry of Culture and receiving the highest German rating directly from Goebbels as *Film der Nation* (*Film of the Nation*) as well as the additional kudos, 'of particular political and artistic value' and 'valuable for youth'. *Homecoming* contrives the plight of a German minority in Polish territory prior to the 1939 'liberation' to justify the attack and destruction of Poland. Austria's great dramatic stars, Paula Wessely and Attila Hörbiger (also husband and wife), would later never escape criticism for having portrayed the lead characters in the film, which included a mostly German-supporting cast, the Vienna Boys Choir, and for the sake of 'authenticity', several Polish performers and Jewish actor Eugen Preiss, who was forced to do an anti-Semitic characterisation. It was one of the most expensive projects undertaken by Wien-Film at 3.7 million Reich marks, but it earned far less (4.9 million) than the more popular and less costly entertainment films.

Willi Forst's unfinished *Viennese Girls* may have been the only colour feature to eventually come out of Wien-Film, but the studio had used colour since 1943 in its programme of culture and nature films (*Kulturfilme*) produced by Otto Trippel. Unlike the disappointing box office of the propaganda films, the *Kulturfilm* enjoyed great popularity. Not only did they highlight the cultural and nature subjects of the *Ostmark*, they also did their south-eastern European duty in co-productions with Romanian (and in planned films with Bulgarian and Greek) studios. Wien-Film produced nearly 60 of these documentaries for the Reich between 1939 and 1944. During the Second World War, as elsewhere in the Reich, only the German Weekly Newsreel (*Deutsche Wochenschau*) was shown in Austrian cinemas.

The film that has come to represent the ultimate work of the studio, and which was in fact the last one to be completed, was Geza von Bolvary's Viennese Film, *Schrammeln* (1945), based on the life and times of the famed Schrammel Quartet, which helped bring Vienna's folk and waltz music to international fame in the nineteenth century. The film focuses on the creation of the Quartet by the violin-playing brothers Johann and Josef Schrammel. The music style of this historic group is still known today as *Schrammelmusik* (Schrammel music) and is considered one of Vienna's important contributions to Austrian folk culture. The choice to make such a film as the war front and Nazism collapsed is perhaps a final demonstration of the dissident quality of Wien-Film productions. By the time *Schrammeln* was shown in theatres in the 'Austrian province' in 1944, the messages Wien-Film had slipped in between the lines, or the waltzes were no longer just quietly appreciated. The word *Österreich* (Austria) had been forbidden in film even as historical reference. This required a rewriting of one of the Schrammel Brother's songs, *Was Öst'reich ist* (*What Austria is*) as *Wie schön das ist* (*How beautiful that is*). During the screenings in Austrian cities, audiences would break into wild applause each time the masked line was sung. The ideological Anschluss, at least, had ended with spontaneous reaction in the cinemas.

By 1944, the war had altered the Reich's film industry significantly. Bombings had destroyed studio facilities and cinema theatres. Hans Hinkel replaced Fritz Hippler as the *Reichsfilmintendant*. This new head of film culture in the Reich, a staunch National Socialist and a self-proclaimed expert in the 'Aryanisation' of the German film industry since 1933, believed that film should be a war industry and that the various production chiefs of the

Reich would now be totally under his military-style command. Although a 1-year labour service had been mandatory in the Reich for youth, members of the artistic sector were often excused, given their contribution to the culture of the Reich. Hinkel saw to it that beginning in 1944, even members of the film industry should perform such service. All age groups were expected to participate, and only major stars like Paula Wessely or the very elderly were excused.[17] Additionally, he decided that the work force of the industry might better serve the war effort and conscripted a majority of its male personnel into the army, and later as the Reich's territory decreased, into the home defence. Even the regime's trustworthy liaison at Wien-Film, Fritz Hirt, protested against this total drain of the industry, but to no avail. Resistance to the final self-annihilation of the Reich in the cause of a hopeless war was particularly strong in Austria, and found resonance among the film-makers. In February 1945, the Gestapo arrested popular actor Paul Hörbiger (brother of Attila) for alleged involvement with an Austrian resistance group. According to actress Marte Harell, wife of studio head Karl Hartl, plans were made by Hinkel's office to detonate the Wien-Film studio complex prior to the Soviet arrival as part of the general 'scorched earth' policy Hitler ordered as the Reich disappeared, but her husband and his staff managed to derail this plan.[18] The liberation of Vienna by Soviet troops scattered members of the industry into the western region of Austria in hopes of escaping the brutality of the Red Army and surviving the final days of the war. Karl Hartl remained with the remnants of Wien-Film in Vienna and was arrested by Allied occupation officials in August 1945.

Notes

1. T. Weyr offers an excellent introduction to the Anschluss in *The Setting of The Pearl: Vienna Under Hitler* (London: Oxford UP, 2005). Analysis of Austria's film industry in the 1930s can be found in A. Loacker, *Anschluss im 3/4-Takt: Filmproduktion und Filmpolitik in Österreich 1930–1938* (Trier: WVT Wissenschaftlicher Verlag, 1992) and in A. Loacker and M. Prucha (eds), *Unerwünschtes Kino: Der deutschsprachige Emigrantenfilm 1934–1937* (Wien: Filmarchiv Austria, 2000). For an English language survey of Austria's film history, see R. von Dassanowsky, *Austrian Cinema: A History* (Jefferson and London: McFarland, 2005).
2. G. Steiner, *Traumfabrik Rosenhügel* (Wien: Compress, 1997), p. 37.
3. See the introductory chapter by Welch and Vande Winkel.
4. Loacker (1992), pp. 150–1. Translation by R. von Dassanowsky.
5. *Filmemigration aus Nazideutschland*, dir. Günter Peter Straschek, WDR, W. Germany, 1975.
6. W. Fritz, *Im Kino erlebe ich die Welt. 100 Jahre Kino und Film in Österreich* (Wien: Brandstätter, 1997), p. 179. Translation by von Dassanowsky.
7. Screenwriter/director Walter Reisch and Willi Forst created what became known as the 'Viennese Film' in the early 1930s. The genre consisted of opulently stylised musical melodrama often dealing with the romanticised lives of historical or fictional artists who must chose between personal happiness or self-sacrifice for their art.

8. Fritz (1997), p. 185.
9. G. Steiner, *Film Book Austria* (Wien: Bundespressedienst, 1995), p. 35.
10. Steiner (1997), p. 45.
11. S. Hake, *Popular Cinema of the Third Reich* (Austin: UP Texas, 2001), p. 159.
12. L. Schulte-Sasse, *Entertaining the Third Reich: Illusions of Wholeness in Nazi Cinema* (Durham: Duke UP, 1996).
13. T. Kramer and M. Prucha, *Film im Lauf der Zeit: 100 Jahre Kino in Deutschland, Österreich und der Schweiz* (Wien: Überreuter, 1994), p. 168.
14. Schulte-Sasse (1996), p. 150.
15. Steiner (1997), p. 41.
16. Fritz (1997), p. 188. Translation by von Dassanowsky.
17. Ibid., p. 208.
18. *Das Kleine Volksblatt*, 18 August 1945.

5

German Influence on Belgian Cinema, 1933–45: From Low-profile Presence to Downright Colonisation

Roel Vande Winkel

The parliamentary monarchy of Belgium is divided by a 'language frontier', separating the Dutch-speaking Flanders (north) from the French-speaking Wallonia (south); a frontier with historic cultural and social differences. In the first half of the 20th century, the Belgian elite, including the bourgeoisie of the Flemish-speaking cities, was mainly francophone. This francophone ascendancy also influenced cultural life and film preferences. In many respects, international film companies considered Belgium as an extension of the French film market. In the Second World War, Nazi Germany grabbed the opportunity to temporarily change that situation.

German films on the Belgian market, 1933–40

In between both world wars, Belgium had neither a film industry worthy of mention nor a legislation protecting or stimulating national film production or exploitation. Belgian theatres (between 1100 and 800, with a seating capacity of at least 500 000)[1] therefore formed an attractive outlet for foreign production companies. Belgium was a particularly inviting market as, though this was partially compensated by a very active catholic film movement,[2] state censorship was quite open-minded. Only films to be played for minors (children under 16 years old) were to be submitted to a censorship board.[3]

Though many small distribution companies were active – often as subsidiary activity of cinema owners – the Belgian film market was in large measure dominated by American and French companies. Fox, Gaumont, Paramount, Pathé, RKO, United Artists, Universal and Warner Brothers each had their own branch in Brussels while Columbia and MGM shared one joint representative. However, no important German film company seems to have had its own branch in Belgium. Tobis was represented by the Belgian firm of Mercure/Mercator Film.[4] It also had ties with Films Sonores

Tobis, which had been founded in 1932 as a branch of the likewise named Paris-based Tobis company.[5] (In 1938, Films Sonores Tobis changed its name to 'Filmsonor'.)[6] Ufa was represented in Belgium by the Alliance Cinématographique Européenne (ACE Brussels). The latter was at its turn a Paris-based subsidiary of Ufa.[7]

The ACE Brussels distributed, apart from Ufa productions such as *La Habanera* (Detlef Sierck, 1937), also French-language films that Ufa produced between 1933 and 1938[8] and films it bought from other production companies. Other companies distributed German films too. For instance, Atlas Films, one of the many small players on the Belgian market, released Paul Verhoeven's *The Bat* (*Die Fledermaus*, 1937), an operetta (starring Lida Baarová), which in Germany was distributed by Tobis.[9] Nevertheless, the overall presence of German films in Belgian cinemas remained rather weak. In 1929–39, only 11 per cent of all films submitted to Belgian censors were entirely or partially produced by German companies. From 1938 onwards, this number even sank below 5 per cent.[10] It is not unlikely that the latter was influenced by anti-German sentiments among the Belgian population, the majority of which – only 20 years had passed since the German invasion and occupation of 1914–18 – was alarmed by Nazi Germany's aggressive foreign policy.

Although Nazi Germany made great efforts to charm the 'Germanic' Flanders throughout the 1930s by stimulating all kinds of cultural exchange, it had no intention to offend the Belgian government. This probably explains why Germany – similar to the policy it pursued vis-à-vis France but unlike its activities in the 'Germanic' Netherlands and the Grand Duchy of Luxembourg[11] – did not aggressively export transparently propagandistic productions to Belgium. Productions such as *Triumph of the Will* (*Triumph des Willens*, 1935) were either not released at all or only shown to limited audiences, for instance during private screenings.[12] An exception to this rule was made for Riefenstahl's *Olympia* (1938) that was distributed by Filmsonor, probably in the special edit (minus two scenes featuring Hitler and many swastika banners) that had also been shown in Paris.[13] The Brussels premiere of the first part of the film was patronised by *Le Front Sportive Belge*, an organisation created by former minister Maurice Lippens to promote Belgian participation for the 1936 Olympics. The film screening at the Palace of Fine Arts on 23 June 1938 was organised by Lippens and therefore attended by King Leopold III. The king had learned only after his acceptance that, on invitation of the German embassy, the director herself would also attend the screening. Though Riefenstahl remembers sitting in the royal box at the king's left hand during the projection,[14] archival evidence suggests that she remained in her own box and did not meet with the king.[15]

The German invasion of Poland and the outbreak of the so-called Phoney War between Germany, France and Great Britain (September 1939)

Belgian poster for Veit Harlan's anti-Semitic feature *Jew Süss* (*Jud Süss*, 1940), a gala premiere of which was organised at the Palace of Fine Arts (Palais-des-Beaux-Arts) in Brussels, to give the film more prestige. *Source*: Gillespie Collection.

Veit Harlan's *The golden City* (*Die goldene Stadt*, 1942) was, as in most other European countries, one of the most popular films shown during the Nazi occupation of Belgium. Lead actress Kristina Söderbaum was extremely popular. *Source*: Vande Winkel/Warie Collection.

heightened the distress of the Belgian population. Gaston Schoukens' *They who watch over us* (*Ceux qui veillent*, 1939), a documentary sponsored by the Ministry of Defence to 'demonstrate' that the Belgian army could ward off any invasion, became a hit at the box-office. While the Belgian government desperately stuck to its strict neutrality, most Belgians were far more sympathetic towards France and Great Britain. Again this was also visible in the field of cinema. The announcement that Ufa personnel would travel to Belgium in the spring of 1940, to produce a documentary about Peter-Paul Rubens (in collaboration with the city of Antwerp, who was to celebrate the painter's 500th anniversary in May 1940), lead to such press controversy that the whole project was cancelled.[16] Meantime, ACE Brussels quit promoting German films and focused on French-language productions such as the Fernandel vehicle *The Mondesir Heir* (*L'Héritier des Mondésir*, 1940).[17] However, the company had been pressurised by the German Ufa board into distributing its Foreign Weekly Newsreel (*Auslandstonwoche*, ATW).[18] These newsreels inspired protest actions before and in cinemas, protests that were not aimed against newsreels of French origin. Incidents like these encouraged cinema owners to censor the newsreels themselves and even urged local authorities (mayors and city councils) to forbid the screening of newsreels altogether. The public screening of propagandistic features was sometimes forbidden by such authorities on the same ground. However, this did not stop thousands of people attending 'private' screenings of British propaganda films such as *The Lion Has Wings* (1940).[19] Also during the Phoney War, Lilian Harvey, who had migrated from Germany to France, was heartily welcomed when she came over to promote her new French film, Jean Boyer's *Sérénade* (1940).[20]

First activities of the Propaganda Division Belgium (PAB) in Nazi-occupied Belgium (June–August 1940)[21]

Nazi Germany invaded Belgium on 10 May 1940. Acting against the explicit will of his government, Leopold III had the capitulation signed on 28 May. The king hoped to convince Hitler into restoring Belgian independence, preferably under an autocratic government that he (Leopold) would lead. Hitler, who never revealed the political future he envisaged for Belgium, did not even consider granting the king any powers. Although he briefly toyed with the idea of installing a civil administration (like he had done in the Netherlands), Hitler eventually imposed a military administration on Belgium. Since Belgium fell under military rule, all propaganda issues in these regions came under the sole responsibility of the Wehrmacht, more specifically of its *Propaganda-Abteilung Belgien* (Propaganda Division Belgium, PAB). By supplying information, qualified staff and considerable financial support, Goebbels' Ministry of Propaganda (RMVP) nevertheless managed to exercise tight control over the PAB.[21]

Through the PAB Film Group, the RMVP started reorganising Belgian cinema and assisting the German industry in colonising this commercially important outlet. (The same went for cinemas in the northern French departments of Lille and Pas-de-Calais, regions that for economic reasons were also ruled by the military administration of Brussels instead of its counterpart in Paris.) Little is known about the concrete collaboration between the PAB and Alfred Greven, officially Goebbels' *Reich* appointee for Belgium, France and the Netherlands. Whether or not Greven's involvement was substantial, it is clear that the reorganisation of Belgian cinema (1940–44) lived up to German expectations. Where Greven played a crucial role was the acquisition of big cinemas in Belgium's largest cities through Bruciné, a company with a Belgian history that Greven (on behalf of the Cautio-Treuhandgesellschaft) acquired by Belgian figureheads. According to a post-war assessment, Bruciné represented 25 per cent of all revenues created by film screenings in Belgium.[22]

The PAB Film Group announced almost immediately after the capitulation that all distribution companies and cinema owners were allowed to resume their activities as soon as 'certain formalities' had been fulfilled:

1. All film screenings were to include the screening of a newsreel, to be projected without cuts or modifications. This newsreel was to be rented from Ufa Brussels, the newly founded Ufa branch that continued and expanded the activities of ACE Brussels. In other words, Ufa's ATW was granted an absolute newsreel monopoly. (The ATW was originally imported from Berlin, but later on modified by a local editorial board, headed by a German chief-editor.)[23]
2. Apart from the newsreel and a complementary short, the programme could include one feature film only. In other words, the pre-war standardised 'double programme' (two features in one programme) was forcibly replaced by the model German cinemas had already adopted in 1938: newsreel–*Kulturfilm*–feature. This measure assured the need for (German) *Kulturfilme* while reducing the need for feature films.[24]
3. Only features accompanied by a German censor's card were allowed. These cards, revocable at any time, were presented upon payment of a special tax. Since German officers could not possibly view every film for which an authorisation was requested by its distributor, the censorship was to be carried out with Belgian help, based on the reading of a summarised scenario. Before supplying the censors with a summary, the distributor had first to place the production in one of three categories: (a) films that were neither connected with war nor with Germany; (b) films that were related to war or to the Russian revolution; and (c) films acting against German interests, in which 'German interests' had to be interpreted 'in their broadest sense'.[25] Most films falling in the latter two categories were prohibited and the available prints confiscated. Distributors also needed to indicate whether the director, screenwriter or actors

were Jewish or anti-German. In these cases also, the film was most likely to be banned and confiscated.
4. No other shows, meetings and so on were allowed to take place inside cinemas.
5. A fifth rule that was not even mentioned specifically as it had already been proclaimed on 31 May 1940 regarding all Belgian economic sectors: Jewish people were not allowed to continue their activities at all. (In October 1940, another regulation would seize all theatres and film companies that belonged, to the tune of 25 per cent or more, to Jews.)

Not all distribution companies were given the possibility to work under these new rules. Jewish film distributors were, as mentioned above, not authorised to stay in business at all. British films were also immediately banned. The Brussels outlets of United Artists, Universal and Warner Bros were closed down immediately 'for having distributed anti-German films' (before the German invasion) such as Charlie Chaplin's *The Great Dictator* (1940). Branches of other Hollywood firms were initially allowed to open their doors again. In July, some cinemas were showing Laurel and Hardy's *A Chump at Oxford* (MGM, 1940) as well as other 'innocent' American films.

The rules listed above, which the PAB Film Group issued in early June, prepared for a 'reorganisation' of Belgian cinema. This reorganisation, which took several years to complete, was officially heralded on 6 August 1940, when the Military Administration announced its 'First Order concerning the New Regulation for Cinema in Belgium'. The order laid down several rules that can be summarised as follows:[26]

1. All film distributors and cinema owners were to be members respectively of the Chamber of Film Distributors or the Union of Cinema Directors.[27]
2. Membership of these organisations was granted exclusively by the Military Administration (PAB Film Group) and was, as the order explicitly specified, not a right that could be extorted. The PAB Film Group would, for instance, refuse membership to anyone unable to prove that he/she was Aryan. Membership could also be revoked at any time.
3. Companies were strictly forbidden to change owner or director without permission. (This measure was directly aimed at non-Aryan Belgians, who had to be prevented from selling their businesses rapidly.)
4. Further, the order confirmed several rules which had already been laid down. The screening of a newsreel and a *Kulturfilm* were compulsory components of each cinema programme. Every film was to be accompanied by a censor card.
5. Contravention of any of these rules would be punished with imprisonment and/or a financial penalty, possibly including the confiscation of all properties belonging to the violating company.

Three days later, on 9 August 1940, the Military Administration decided because of the 'anti-German tendencies in American film productions' to ban the distribution and screening of all American films. The direct expulsion of all remaining American companies – an operation that was carried in out in several other German-occupied territories too – was, together with the order of 6 August 1940, one of the only direct interventions ever made regarding the cinema by the Military Administration.

Further reorganising Belgian cinema: The corporate straitjacket (1940–44)

As in many other economic fields, the occupying forces chose to procure their plans for the reorganisation of Belgian cinema from within existing Belgian structures and organisations rather than overtly carrying them out themselves. All interference, either direct or indirect, worked towards the same goal: the formation of a Belgian cinema corporation. The term 'corporation' should thereby be interpreted in a historic, fascist manner. In that context, corporations, which were subordinate to the state, united all employers and employees of a particular (branch of) industry. Replacing all labour unions and pressure groups, corporations were, in theory, to defend the interests of the entire economic group they represented. In reality, largely controlling all people and activities within their jurisdiction, corporations were deployed to impose the will of the state, in this case of the PAB Film Group. Steering an industry through a corporate system requires that everyone within the industry branches be tied to the corporation in question. The obligation for all film distributors and cinema directors to become member of their respective associations, imposed by the above-mentioned 'First Order concerning the New Regulation of Cinema in Belgium', must be understood in that sense.

The PAB Film Group would use the Belgian Chamber of Film Distributors and the Union of Cinema Directors, which from 6 August 1940 included all Belgian film professionals, to force the Belgian film world into the straitjacket of corporatism. When the Union of Cinema Directors refused to collaborate, it was simply disbanded and replaced by a new, similar organisation that listened better to its master's voice. An important corporate step was taken when both organisations approved in May 1941 a long text specifying the general conditions of film rental. The agreement mainly codified the rules and arrangements that had already been brought into force previously but bringing them together into one agreement facilitated control over their application and penalising infringements. There is no doubt that the PAB Film Group played an important role in producing this treaty, which probably explains why its rules became valid (30 May 1941) before the representatives of the corporate organisations had even signed it (9 June 1941).[28] However, officially all leading positions in the corporate organisations were occupied by Belgian film personalities. After the war some of them, including the 'Leader' of the corporation (Jan Vanderheyden), were tried for collaboration.

The corporate process was finalised in June–July 1943, when both organisations effectively amalgamated into one big organisation. Oddly, this corporation, a newly created administrative body, was not called the 'Belgian Cinema Corporation' but the 'Belgian Film Guild'.[29]

The corporation/guild joined the International Film Chamber (IFK)[30] in July 1941. One of the newly founded IFK departments (Film Exploitation) was headed by a 'leading' member of the Belgian corporation (Camille Damman) and therefore located in Brussels. In July 1942, Belgium even hosted an international meeting of the IFK.[31]

Film production, distribution and screening

Initially, several Belgian film people hoped that the disappearance of popular Anglo-American film productions would allow them to build up a film industry of their own. This was particularly true for Flemish film professionals like Jan Vanderheyden, who hoped to benefit from the pro-Flemish policy (*Flamenpolitik*) Hitler had personally ordered. German film companies, however, as the Belgians soon found out, intended to bridge the film gap themselves. Stimulating local film production – the pre-war quality of which had been low already – was not an option. This became clearer than ever in 1942, when director Boleslaw Barlog and his German crew travelled to Belgium and filmed exteriors for *When the sun shines again* (*Wenn die Sonne wieder scheint*, 1943), a Terra produced adaptation of the famous Flemish novel *De Vlaschaard* (*The Flax Field*) by Stijn Streuvels.[32]

During the four years of German occupation, only six Belgian feature films went into premiere: four by Jan Vanderheyden, one by his German companion Edith Kiel (who worked for his company and actually managed it) and one by Gaston Schoukens. It is probably no coincidence that each of these three people had connections with the PAB Film Group.[33] Each of these titles was released before 1 January 1943. After that date, when raw film stock became increasingly scarce, Belgian feature film production was entirely brought to a standstill, which the authorities tried to compensate for from late 1943 onwards by having some local short documentaries (Belgian *Kulturfilme*) produced.[34] It was within this framework that Henri Storck, who also played a role in the Belgian film corporation, completed the production of several documentary shorts that after the war were edited together into *Peasant Symphony* (*Symphonie paysanne*, 1942–44).

As mentioned earlier, Belgium counted many small film enterprises, companies that combined the distribution of some films with the exploitation of one or more cinemas. It were such companies whose distribution activities next fell victim to the corporate politics of the PAB Film Group. Of the 114 distribution companies that were active on the Belgian market before the German invasion, only 75 were still operating by the end of

December 1940: over one-third had been eliminated by anti-Jewish measures, the closing down of Anglo-American companies and the 'First Order concerning the New Regulation for Cinema in Belgium'. The activities of the remaining distributors were further clipped through several injunctions and regulations by their corporatist association. The obligatory withdrawal of all films released before 1 June 1937 and the subsequently enforced closure of all companies whose catalogue contained less than 10 films further downsized the distribution market. In March 1941, a mere 10 months after Belgian capitulation, only 19 companies remained. By 1944 there were only 15.[35] These decisive actions, purging the Belgian market of innumerable films that had initially survived the obligatory censorship, further paved the way for a German takeover of the Belgian film market. This takeover was carried out through the German Ufa branch, with assistance from Tobis.

Ufa Brussels (officially Ufa-Films SPRL Brüssel) was officially founded on 22 August 1940, but already active more than 2 months before. In June 1940 it had occupied the buildings of ACE Brussels and officially taken over all its assets. The former Belgian owners, who reportedly owed money to the German Ufa headquarters, were not compensated. Ufa Brussels, fully owned by the German parent company, was just like its predecessor first and foremost a distribution company, in other words an instrument to disseminate German productions (including the ATW) on the Belgian market. It basically represented all major German film companies except for Tobis, which initially kept its own branch.

Tobis Brussels (officially Tobis Films SPRL Brüssel, later on Tobis-Films S.A. Brüssel) was founded on 25 September 1940. It incorporated the former representative of Tobis Berlin (Mercure/Mercator Film, the Belgian owner of which was compensated with shares) but, oddly, not Filmsonor, the representative of the Parisian Tobis branch. Filmsonor continued to exist separately. Though apparently distributing only films it had already exploited before the occupation, Filmsonor was allowed to continue its activities, even after the severe restructuring of the entire Belgian sector.

Tobis Brussels was officially independent from Ufa Brussels, but actually had a complementary function. In a report to the Propaganda Ministry, Berlin's Ufa headquarters stipulated: 'In Belgium too, rental interests are concentrated within Ufa AG. The renting of German films is carried out through Ufa Brussels [...] If the concentration of trade through one firm proves unsuitable, a cover in the guise of Tobis Brussels is available.'[36] Tobis Brussels had its own offices and administration until August 1942, when all its services were merged with those of Ufa Brussels. Although the name Tobis remained in use, the company was practically swallowed up by Ufa. This operation was carried out simultaneously throughout Europe as Ufa (the Ufi Concern) was given widespread control over the foreign distribution of all German films.

A smaller role was played by Orbis Film SPRL Brüssel, a Belgian branch of the German Descheg (*Deutscher Schmallfilm-Vertrieb*) Company, which rented out small film projectors and distributed 16 mm prints of German films.[37] Orbis Film SPRL Brüssel was a subsidiary of Tobis Berlin. Originally called Tobis-Degeto Films SPRL Brüssel, Orbis Film SPRL Brüssel had formed part of the German Degeto Company (*Deutsche Gesellschaft für Ton und Film*) that also was part of Tobis.

Belgian film exhibitors were handcuffed by the rules of the corporation. Numerous rules meticulously prescribed how films were to be shown, advertised and so on. The only positive element was that the corporation made the long-needed training of film projectionists, which among others was to reduce the fires (caused by the inflammable nitrate film stock) that occasionally destroyed cinemas, obligatory.

Conclusion

The PAB Film Group, operating under the Wehrmacht-Propaganda but equally acting on behalf of the RMVP, made no attempt to promote the development of the Belgian film industry. Instead it paved the way, with the assistance of Belgian collaborationists, for the German film industry. Spearheaded by Ufa Brussels and Tobis Brussels, German films flooded the market with a huge quantity of German films. The disappearance of Anglo-American productions as well as of the back catalogue that many small film distributors used to provide left Belgian cinemas little choice but start screening German films. Within that context it should be pointed out that, although German films formed the majority of the new film supply, there was a relatively large number of French films. Many of these films were produced by Greven's Continental. Hispano Film productions[38] and a handful of films produced by IFK members such as Hungary, Italy and Spain were also imported.

Although the propagandistic newsreels occasionally inspired hostile reactions (which were forbidden), Belgian audiences quickly reconciled themselves to the new situation. German film stars such as Marika Rökk, Kristina Söderbaum, Heinz Rühmann and Zarah Leander – whose films had been distributed before the war – developed a large fan base in Belgium.[39] It may seem bizarre that German film-stars became very popular with a population that by and large opposed the German occupation of its fatherland. On the other hand this was, as other contributions to this book demonstrate, absolutely not unique to Belgium. In 1954, 10 years after the liberation, Zarah Leander toured Belgium. Sold-out concert halls listened rapturously to her performing songs from *The Great Love* (*Die grosse Liebe*, 1942) and other audience favourites.

Notes

1. The number of 1100 (with a seating capacity of 650 000) is mentioned in J. Alicoate (ed.), *The 1939 Film Daily Year Book of Motion Pictures* (New York: The

Film Daily, 1939), pp. 1168–9. This probably also included occasional venues like pubs and community houses. In 1944, German officials counted 788 regularly active cinemas: 783 public cinemas and five theatres that had been turned into military cinemas (*Soldatenkinos*). Bundesarchiv (hereafter Barch), *R 109 II/48*.

2. D. Biltereyst, '"Healthy films from America". The Emergence of a Catholic Film Mass Movement in Belgium and the Realm of Hollywood, 1928–1939', in R. C. Allen, R. Maltby and M. Stokes (eds), *Hollywood's Audiences: The Social Experience of Movie-Going* (Exeter University Press – California University Press, in press).
3. L. Depauw and D. Biltereyst, 'De kruistocht tegen de slechte cinema. Over de aanloop en de start van de Belgische filmkeuring (1911–1929)', *Tijdschrift voor Mediageschiedenis*, 8:1 (2005), 4–26.
4. Bundesarchiv (here after Barch), R 109 I/512, Berichte der Revisionsabteilung der Universum Film AG.
5. Ibid., Films Sonores Tobis S.A. in Brüssel: Gründungsanzeige.
6. Announcement in *Revue Belge du cinéma*, 28:24 (1938).
7. ACE Brussels, Paris, was founded in 1926, ACE Brussels in 1928. The latter was, though this was not publicised, clearly a subsidiary of the French parent company. Barch, R 109 I/515, *Alliance Cinématographique Européenne SA Paris*.
8. See Chapter 9.
9. Advertisement in *Revue Belge du cinéma*, 28:11 (1938). A. Bauer, *Deutscher Spielfilm Almanach 1929–1950* (Berlin: Filmblätter Verlag, 1950), p. 364.
10. These data were supplied by the ongoing research project *Forbidden images* (funded by the Belgian *Research Foundation – Flanders*). I am most indebted to its promoter (Prof. Dr D. Biltereyst) and collaborators (L. Depauw and Dr L. Desmet) for their assistance.
11. See Chapters 9, 14 and 15.
12. More research into this subject is needed.
13. L. Kinkel, *Die Scheinwerferin: Leni Riefenstahl und das 'Dritte Reich'* (Hamburg – Wien: Europa, 2002) pp. 86–7.
14. L. Riefenstahl, *Memoiren* (München – Hamburg: Albrecht Knaus Verlag, 1987), pp. 314–15. Riefenstahl's memoirs are notoriously unreliable.
15. Archives of the Royal Palace, *GM-LIII 83*. It is of course possibly that a private, informal meeting was arranged nevertheless.
16. Barch, R 109 I/5265 and 5465.
17. Advertisement in *Revue Belge du cinéma*, 30:11 (1940).
18. R. Vande Winkel, 'Nazi Newsreels in Europe, 1939–1945: The Many Faces of Ufa's Foreign Weekly Newsreel (Auslandstonwoche) Versus the German Weekly Newsreel (Deutsche Wochenschau)', *Historical Journal of Film, Radio and Television*, 24:1 (2004a), pp. 14–34; J. Flament, 'Les deux neutralités', *Revue belge du cinéma*, 29:41 (1939), pp. 2–4.
19. These incidents were reviewed (rather favourably) before the war in trade journals such as the *Revue Belge du cinéma*. During the occupation they were repeatedly referred to (unfavourably) by collaborationist newspapers such as *Volk en Staat*.
20. *Revue Belge du cinéma*, 30:5 (1940).
21. The rest of this chapter offers a preview on the ongoing research project *Visual media, propaganda and politics: research into Nazi film politics in Belgium and Europe* (funded by the Belgian *Research Foundation – Flanders*). This (hi)story was reconstructed with the use of many archival sources, only the most important of which can be mentioned here.

22. Barch, R 109 I/1663, Gesellschaftlisrechtliche Bindungen: Aufstellug und Erläuterung des in Belgien belegenen Ufa-vermögens.
23. Vande Winkel (2004a), pp. 16–17. See also R. Vande Winkel, *Nazi newsreel propaganda in the Second World War* (Ghent: Academia Press, 2007).
24. The International Film Chamber would try to have this 'European standard film programme' taken over by all of its members. See Chapter 2.
25. A.-M. Poels, 'De organisatie van het filmbedrijf tijdens de bezetting van '40-'44: de censuur', *Belgisch tijdschrift voor nieuwste geschiedenis – Revue belge d'histoire contemporaine*, 27:3–4 (1997), pp. 419–30.
26. 'De nieuwe organisatie van het Belgisch cinemabedrijf – L'organisation nouvelle du cinéma en Belgique', *CINEMA*, 1:1 (1940), p. 1.
27. Both organisations repeatedly changed their names during the occupation.
28. The agreement is printed and commented upon in several articles in the 1 July 1941 issue of *CINEMA*.
29. The founding charter of the Film Guild was published in the Belgian law gazette of 18 July 1943.
30. See Chapter 2.
31. See Chapter 2.
32. R. Vande Winkel and I. Van linthout *De Vlaschaard 1943* (Kortrijk: Groeninghe, 2007).
33. Schoukens held office on a committee of the Belgian Chamber of Film Distributors.
34. R. Vande Winkel, 'De cameraman, de dichter en de kapelaan. Alfred Ehrhardt draait cultuurfilms met de hulp van Wies Moens en Cyriel Verschaeve', *Wetenschappelijke tijdingen op het gebied van de geschiedenis van de Vlaamse beweging*, 62:1 (2003), pp. 32–47.
35. These calculations are based on data printed in *CINEMA*, collected and processed by the author.
36. Barch, R 55/1319, Produktionsgesellschaften, Universum Film GmbH (Ufi), p. 199.
37. Barch, R 109 I/1663, Gesellschaftlisrechtliche Bindungen: Aufstellug und Erläuterung des in Belgien belegenen Ufa-vermögens.
38. See Chapter 3.
39. R. Vande Winkel, 'Die Grosse Liebe – De Groote Liefde: Getuigenissen over de populariteit van Duitse film(sterren) in bezet België (1940–1944)', *Mores: Tijdschrift voor Volkscultuur in Vlaanderen*, 5:4 (2004), pp. 15–20.

6

Nazi Film Politics in Brazil, 1933–42

Luiz Nazario

In the 1930s, Brazil became one of the main targets for Nazi propaganda strategies in South America – due to its continental dimensions (a vast 'vital space'); its numerous German immigrants established in colonies in the Southern States (800 000 to a million, to which should be added 80 000 to 100 000 resident Reich citizens[1]); its large reserve of mineral resources, a desired source of raw material for the Reich economy. One of the most insidious means of ideological dissemination used by the Nazis in Latin America was the cinema.

German colonies, German films

Although no specific research has been published on the subject, it is possible to verify that during the two consecutive mandates of President Getúlio Vargas many Nazi films were being shown in movie houses throughout the country (1933–42). Brazil was also used for the diffusion of ideology from Fascist Italy.[2] The Italian Embassy promoted lectures, provided local newspapers with abundant proselytisation material and sponsored the exhibition of films such as *Black Shirt* (*Camicia Nera,* 1933) by Giovacchino Forzano and *Scipio the African* (*Scipione L'Africano,* 1937) by Carmine Gallone. As pointed out by the historian João Fábio Bertonha, due to the difficulties in attracting the Brazilian public, whose cinematographic taste had been deeply influenced by the American movies, the Italian government held long negotiations between 1936 and 1939 with the local film distributors trying to introduce Italian films in Brazilian movie houses. As a result, Italian news items were included in the frequently exhibited Ufa newsreels (Ufa's Foreign Weekly Newsreel or *Auslandstonwoche,* ATW). Documentaries on ancient Greek and Roman ruins in Paestum and Pompeii, films on the Spanish Civil War and Italian Luce newsreels were also exhibited. But Italian infiltration was hindered by a language barrier (French was the only foreign tongue taught

The Ufa Film Palace (*Cine UFA-Palácio*) in São Paulo. *Source*: R. Anelli, A. Guerra, and N. Kon, *Rino Levi – arquitetura e cidade* (São Paulo: Romano Guerra Editora, 2001), p. 103.

in traditional elite schools) as well as by the need of the Italian Embassy to concentrate their scarce funds on propaganda directed to the local Italian immigrant community.[3]

Nazi infiltration, on the other hand, was facilitated by the large German colonies, which preserved their native tongue and Prussian values. Pan-Germanist ideologists considered these German colonies as ideal subjects for the development of a 'leading race'.[4] There were three different groups within these colonies. A majority of traditionalists maintained their native language, art and traditions, but showed no interest in Nazi ideas. A smaller group wanted to assimilate local culture while a minority with close links to the German diplomats in Brazil supported Hitler and considered it their right to retaliate against 'Teutonic' Brazilians that did not share their ideas.

Even before Hitler came to power, the *Nationalsozialische Deutsche Arbeiterpartei* (NSDAP), the Brazilian branch of which had been founded in Rio de Janeiro in 1931 with 40 000 members, had been acting in these local German communities. Another facilitating fact was that during the 1930s, Germany had been Brazil's most important economic partner by exporting arms and machinery while importing rubber, coffee and cotton. The German Embassy, with an annual propaganda fund of 10 000 Reichmarks, tried to influence the Brazilian press. It also published the Nazi weekly *Deutscher Morgen* in Rio de Janeiro and the *Urwaldsbote* in Blumenau. Through these publications, German meetings in clubs and in halls were organised and promoted. National-Socialism was exalted in German schools and flags with the swastika were hoisted on 1 May.[5]

By the end of 1934, Hans Hening Von Cossel, whose headquarters were in São Paulo, was in charge of all the National-Socialist organisations in Brazil. Copying the party structure of the Reich, the Brazilian NSDAP divided the country into polling districts (*Gauen*), and each state had its own district leaders and deputy-leaders, judges, secretaries, treasurers and agents with the responsibility of disseminating Nazi propaganda via the radio, press and cinema; infiltrating schools, clubs and factories; editing and distributing newspapers and pamphlets; organising meetings, parades and marches which emulated those held in Germany. The swastika decorated their meeting places, where they toasted Hitler's health and criticised Brazil's politics – a 'land of monkeys' that did not appreciate German orderliness. On the occasion of his visits to the German Choir (*Deutscher Männer Gesangverein*) of São Paulo, after being received with the Nazi salute, the German consul pleaded for the union of all Teutons in accordance with the Führer's wishes. Members of the Teuton-Brazilian Working Circle, founded in 1935, travelled frequently to Germany. One of its directors, Karl-Henrich Hunsche, published *Der brasilianische Integralimus*, a book on the Brazilian Integralist Action (AIB) movement,[6] in which he preached in favour of an independent 'Southern Brazil', separated from the 'inferior population' of the rest of the country. The German Embassy in Rio de Janeiro financed not only such organisations as *Pró-Arte*, which represented the *Deutsche Akademie* and *Cultura Artística*, a branch of the AIB, but also Integralist associations and German firms. It bought the Guanabara Radio Station and placed Integralist Alberto Mane as its director to ensure favourable attitudes towards the Third Reich. Nazis and Integralists fraternised at the *Ira Gesangverein Club* exchanging *Anauês* and 'Heil-Hitlers' and those who participated in the *Deutsche Vereinigung* were offered jobs in German firms – such as the Transatlantic and the South American German Banks – which distributed swastika badges to their staff.[7]

American cinema, which had been the model for Brazilian film makers, critics and the general movie-going public, became the target of Integralist attacks. In 1935, Oswaldo Gouvêa released a pamphlet called 'The Jews of the Cinema' in which he blamed Hollywood for promoting decadence in moral values and for sabotaging the production of 'national movies'.[8] In another pamphlet, 'The Mysteries of the National Cinema', he claimed 'National cinematography is being discredited by a campaign of the North American Jewish companies which completely dominate the market due to their huge economical power [. . .] Brazilian movie house owners are tied down to the hands of the Jews from Metro, Fox, Universal, United Artists, and Warner Bros. As soon as the release of a new film is announced, Jewish persecution goes into action.'[9] Anti-Semitism was also disseminated to the general public trough caricatures of Jews – replicas of those used in Nazi propaganda – published in illustrated magazines and newspapers, such as *Careta* and *Acção*.[10]

At the same time, imported German newsreels, Ufa *Kulturfilme* and feature films, began to be distributed in Brazil, in order to captivate not only the German community but also all spectators. The newsreels (ATW), dubbed into or subtitled in Portuguese, included advertisements of products from German companies established in Brazil, such as the medicine 'Instantina', manufactured by Bayer.[11] Two important movie houses in Fortaleza (Ceará State capital), 'Cine Moderno' and 'Cine Majestic', exhibited, between 1935 and 1938, *Farewell Waltz* (*Abschiedswalzer*, 1934) by Geza von Bolvary; *The Csardas Princess* (*Die Czardas Fürstin*, 1934) by George Jacoby; and *Varieté* (1935) by Nicolaus Farkas.[12] A crucial role in the attempts to embed Germ film culture was undertaken/played by the 'Cine Ufa-Palácio', in São Paulo. The building, designed in 1936, by Modernist architect Rino Levi[13] – and provided with sophisticated acoustic devices appropriate to the performance of Martha Eggert's and Jan Kippura's operettas – was the principal Ufa movie theatre in Brazil. It was dedicated exclusively to the exhibition of German productions and it housed the prestigious premiere of *Olympia* (1938) by Leni Riefenstahl.[14]

Plinio Moraes and the German Cinema

From Porto Alegre (Rio Grande do Sul State capital), one of the pioneer professional film critics was Plinio Moraes, alias Jacob Koutzii (1908–75), a Russian Jew who had emigrated to Brazil as a child.[15] He reviewed several German films and pointed out that 'Aliança has distributed excellent films, especially musicals'[16] and mentioning three he thought 'had all the qualities of a magnificent spectacle':[17] *Lover Divine* (*Leise Flehen Meine Lieder*, 1933) by Willi Forst; *Farewell Waltz* (*Abschiedswalzer*, 1934); and *Dreaming of Love* (*Liebesträume*, 1935) by Heinz Hille. In another review, he analysed *Mazurka* (1935), by Willi Forst, praising the camera work: 'the film exhibits [. . .] unprecedented takes in terms of photographic expression'.[18] Carried away by the artistic quality of the films, Moraes was unable to detect the propaganda imbedded in 'entertainment films' such as *Black Roses* (*Schwarze Rosen*, 1935) by Paul Martin:

> It is a magnificent show of intense dramatic colouring in which the director, evincing special knowledge, puts in movement great human masses gathered in patriotic action: Finland's fight for independence from the Czar, in 1890, assumes gripping proportions. Saint John's festivity, involving thousands of participants, is transformed from an innocent traditional celebration into a mass political meeting followed by the charge of the Cossack Cavalry. Then, there is the scene in the theatre, when Collin addresses his enthused fellow citizens with the proclamation of independence and, the moment they believe the Governor has been arrested, a company of soldiers in shoulder-to-shoulder formation emerges on stage, pointing their rifles to the audience. They are both scenes of admirable emotion.[19]

It is evident that Moraes was not aware of the metaphors that, through spectacular staging, by associating national liberation crusades to the Nazi movement and by identifying Czarism to Communism and Hitler to the independence heroes of other countries stimulated local National-Socialist movements. When reviewing *The Czar's Courier (Der Kurier des Zaren*, 1935), by Richard Eichberg, he stated,

> All the filmic resources have been completely exploited by the talent and intelligence of a great director [. . .] each scene vibrates with intense realism and vivid humanness. The collective scenes, including a great number of extras, which require discipline and coordination, are presented with extreme precision. The collisions, the sudden onsets, the battles, the displacement of military troops, the charges of the Tartar cavalry, all cause vivid emotions. The attacks on the cities with terrorist action, murderous ravaging and robbery are also worthy of mention [. . .] it is a film that honours German cinematography.[20]

Dazzled by the spectacular techniques used in these films, the Brazilian critic failed to notice the contemporary political associations established by German historical films to exalt militarism and the *Führerprinzip* (leadership principle). Reviewing *Forget me not* (*Vergiss mein Nicht*, 1935), by Augusto Genina, Moraes exalted, 'It is a film that exhibits, with all the wonderful cinematographic possibilities, the extraordinary voice of Beniamino Gigli [. . .] surprising us with the perfect adaptation of the lyrical theatre atmosphere to the movie scene.'[21] And he also commended what he considered the best lyrical film, *Martha* (1936), by Karl Anton, produced by Tobis. Once again without taking into account the Nazi aesthetic references in peasant festivities and chores he wrote,

> A real masterpiece of modern cinematography [. . .] almost perfect, a model for the lyrical gender [. . .] the pastoral scenes [. . .] possess a wonderful suggestive beauty. The march of the workers down the road, the path to the traditional festivity, the chorus followed by the take on the peasants on their chores, surprise us by the poetic world they reveal.[22]

Not long afterwards, Moraes would loose his enthusiasm for German films. By 1936, with the German and Italian involvement in the Spanish Civil War, he came to realise that: 'Frightening gloomy days [. . .] are approaching. The Spanish people have been used as an experience field for the exhibition of the destructive potential of a group of powerful nations that live in a constant state of war.'[23] In 1937, he wrote critical comments on *One Hundred Days* (*Hundert Tage*, 1935), by Franz Wenzler, based on the play written by Benito Mussolini and Giovacchino Forzano:

> With Werner Krauss, the German cinema presented Napoleon as if conceived by Mussolini's totalitarian spirit with only the figure and gestures of a human being. Although it was the best cinematographic type created by the notable German actor, there was hardly any revelation of the character and intimate feelings of the great Corso. It has been said that from all the existing interpretations of Napoleon this is the most faithful. I doubt it. In concentrating only in the belligerent and dictatorial aspects of the Emperor's personality, Mussolini did not capture the intimate drama of a man capable of modifying his political conduct moved by the intensity and diversity of his emotional experiences.[24]

It is worth noting that Mussolini had been present during the shooting of the film and gave Krauss personal directions on the interpretation of the character.[25] The general applause with which the film was received proved that moviegoers were not yet aware of what Moraes had began to detect: that the *Unterhaltungfilm* (entertainment film), even with high quality aesthetics and advanced technology, was a vehicle to the totalitarian policies of the Third Reich.

Influences of Nazi Film Structures on the 'reorganisation' of Brazilian Cinema

During the 1930s, President Getúlio Vargas had considered Hitler's regime a 'model of progress' and adopted some of its 'prophylactic' and 'educational' measures. His government also became aware of the far-reaching possibilities of cinematographic propaganda. The official of the cabinet of the Secretary of the Presidency, Luis Simões Lopes, was so impressed by the despotism of the Nazi regime that suggested to Vargas the creation of a 'miniature' of the Goebbels' Reich Culture Chamber in Brazil.[26] In 1935, the magazine *Cinearte* in a sequence of six articles praising the policies adopted by the Third Reich for the German cinema recommended the application of the same methods in Brazil.[27] In June 1936, the Minister of Education, Gustavo Capanema, invited Roberto Assumpção – a young professional swimmer and a cinema enthusiast – to work at the recently created National Institute of Educational Cinema (*Instituto Nacional de Cinema Educativo*, INCE). Since Assumpção was going to participate in the Berlin Olympic Games, he was asked to gather information on the Reich's educational cinema. In December of the same year, the Minister also asked the director of INCE, anthropologist Edgard Roquette-Pinto – who was going to Europe to participate in a Congress – to collect information on the educational programmes of the countries he would visit. He brought back the news that both Italy and Germany were favourable to an exchange programme with Brazil. The country was invited to integrate the *Luce* Institute, directed by Vittorio Mussolini. In Germany, Assumpção visited the German Reich Office for the Educational Film (*Reichsstelle für den Unterrichtsfilm*), which formed part of Bernard Rust's Ministry of Education and in 1940 would change its name to Reich Institution for Film and Photography in Science and Education (*Reichsanstalt für Film und Bild in Wissenschaft und Unterricht*). The Reich Office for the Educational Film had already produced 322 educational films in cooperation with German universities, technical schools and scientific institutions; INCE decided to adopt the same practices and produced its first sound movie destined to Brazilian schools: *Dia da Pátria* (1936).[28] During the same year, the chief of the Specialised Departement for Political and Social Order (*Departamento de Ordem Política e Social*, DEOPS), Filinto Müller, a man of German descent and a Nazi enthusiast, signed a cooperation agreement between the Brazilian Police Force and the Gestapo to combat communism.[29] A Committee for the Repression of Communism promoted popular proselytising campaigns,[30] while some Jews of both sexes were cruelly tortured and deported to Germany. Soon afterwards President Vargas asked the Integralists to forge a plan with a Jewish name that would justify a coup d'état (the 'Plano Cohen'). Vargas also dissolved the government, postponed elections, exiled the opposition candidate to the presidency (Armando Sales de Oliveira) and extended his mandate. Thus, without finding any resistance, he established the 'Estado Novo' (the New State).

In March 1937, Captain Affonso Henrique de Miranda Correia, chief of the DEOPS in Rio de Janeiro, travelled to Berlin in order to help Germany to control Jewish immigration. He was warmly welcomed by the Gestapo, visited secret facilities, police schools, counter-espionage files and labs in which forged documents were produced. As a result of his collaboration, more imprisonments, tortures and extraditions occurred in Brazil. At the same time, commercial exchange between the two countries increased. In 1937, President Vargas referred to Hitler as 'a great friend' and wished to 'tighten even further their good friendly relationship'. The

NSDAP also grew in Brazil. By 1937, the Party had 87 sections linked to the *Auslandsorganisation* and counted with 3000 members.[31] Detlef Sierck's *La Habanera* (1937) was a good example of this cooperation. In this movie, a Swedish doctor goes to Puerto Rico, in Central America, to study a mysterious virus contaminating the local population. He is accompanied by a 'non-Aryan' colleague, a Brazilian doctor, who acts as a co-adjutant hero helping to identify the spreading plague. The virus can be interpreted as a metaphor for the Jews.[32]

It is no coincidence that, around this time, German film imports reached a peak. Although it remained small in comparison to American film imports, German film imports were much higher than its European competitors. In 1937,[33] Brazil imported 1324 films from the United States, 138 from Germany, 51 from France, 35 from Italy, 23 from the United Kingdom, 11 from Portugal.

Deteriorating German–Brazilian relations and their impact on the import of German films

The Brazilian Ambassador to the United States, Oswaldo Aranha, was a fierce opponent of his country's cooperation with Italy and Germany. He contested from the very beginning the Fascist-oriented new Constitution stating it seemed to be 'conceived by an abnormal person'.[34] Aranha resigned from his position but, since President Vargas insisted that he should remain in the government (Aranha was immensely popular), he became the Minister of Foreign Affairs, which would allow him to tighten relationships with the United States and to act against the totalitarian members of Vargas' administration. Although Getúlio Vargas had resorted to the Integralists for the creation of the New State, he limited the participation of the AIB in the government. Plinio Salgado resented this, he did not accept the post of Minister of Education offered to him and organised demonstrations to remind Vargas of the force of his movement. As a result, the President forbid all political party activities in the country as well as the use of flags, uniforms, badges and other party symbols, establishing a regime of 'social peace' and 'constructive political action'.[35]

In retaliation, the Integralists, supported by the German and Italian Embassies, planned a coup lead by Plínio Salgado, Miguel Reale and Gustavo Barroso, under the military command of Severo Fournier. Their plan failed, the NSDAP leaders were imprisoned and the German–Brazilian Youth Circle was banished. The German Embassy, disreputed for its participation in the unsuccessful coup, suppressed all its visible activities in the country.[36] Oswaldo Aranha requested the German Ambassador, Karl Ritter (not to be confused with the German director), to leave the country. The Italian Ambassador organised a massive escape of Integralist leaders to Italy and Aranha had to force him to leave his post.[37] The victorious fascist campaign in Brazil could have shaken the whole South American democratic system but, through Aranha's interventions, the Brazilian administration changed positions and approached the Allied Forces: by 1938, the German language was prohibited in the country and schools, clubs and associations that had been under the control of the NSDAP were closed.

But supporters of totalitarianism continued to act both within and outside the government. The INCE sent Brazilian film maker Humberto Mauro to participate in the 1938's Venice Film Festival, where he did not win any prizes but appreciated *Mannesmann* (1937), by Walter Ruttmann, as a model of educational film to be followed,[38] noticed that Germany had heavily invested in propaganda for Leni Riefenstahl's *Olympia* (1938), and met both Riefenstahl and Veit Harlan.[39]

On 2 January 1939, Von Levetzow, Councillor to the German Embassy, stated that 'American filmed propaganda against Germany had been banned in Brazil as a result of the success of my activities.'[40] The films in question were American newsreels on German espionage. Later Chaplin's *The Great Dictator* (1940) was 'liberated' – with cuts on the subtitles of Chaplin's speech that were considered inappropriate by the government[41] – only after the intervention of the US State Department.

When the Second World War was declared, Friedrich Karl Gustav Schulze hid the registers of the Nazi party members in the cellar of the German Consulate in São Paulo and the NSDAP adopted underground activities. Although many members of the Brazilian government still supported the German–Italian Axis – among them Lourival Fontes, chief of the Departement of Press and Propaganda (DIP)[42] – commercial relations with the Axis diminished significantly in favour of new trading with the United States, which doubled the rate of exportation to Brazil. Even so, the supply of Italian documentaries duplicated between 1939 and 1940, and Nazi propaganda continued to be released in this country.[43]

The fall of France reinforced the Axis appeal over their Brazilian government supporters, and President Vargas was reminded by Karl Ritter that Germany, which had increased its numbers of consumers and producers to 90 million, continued interested in collaborating with the development of Brazil's natural resources. Although Vargas was interested in this proposal, the importation of war equipment from Germany was impossible due to the watchful presence of the British Navy on the Atlantic Ocean. In his efforts to sabotage German plans, Oswaldo Aranha managed to sign an agreement with the United States for the construction of an iron and steel industry in the city of Volta Redonda and for the exportation of coffee, rubber and cotton.[44]

Investigations of the Office of Coordinator Inter-American Affairs (OCIAA), created by the National Security Council of the United States, coordinated by Nelson Rockefeller, revealed that fifth column propaganda was subsidised by Axis agencies which also controlled radio stations and produced films destined to schools, cultural centres, sport clubs and other associations. The OCIAA had 1100 people in the United States and 300 in Latin America working in combined actions of the National Security Council and cultural private enterprises to develop programmes related to the arts, science, education, travelling, the radio, the press and the cinema. American actors and film makers, such as Orson Welles, John Ford, Walt Disney, Gregg Toland, Henry Fonda, Errol Flynn and Douglas Fairbanks Jr, came to visit Brazil, or to shoot films here, and many Brazilian actors, technicians and musicians were signed up to work in Hollywood.

Although the operation of new air routes opened in Brazil were thus granted to American companies, Pan Am and Pan Air, the Transcontinental Italian Airlines (LATI) provided the location of allied merchant ships to German and Italian submarines. So as to counteract American influence in the region, German Embassies bought, rented or subsidised radio stations, newspapers and cinemas throughout Latin America.[45] Nazi agents from the South American Political Department of Broadcasting visited 19 cities, 4 in Brazil (Rio de Janeiro, São Paulo, Recife, Porto Alegre), and guaranteed access to 35 radio stations, 14 in Brazil. In 1941, in the cinema quarter of Rio de Janeiro (Cinelandia) they rented the 'Cine-teatro Broadway' to show exclusively German movies.

After the 'Brazilian Pearl Harbor'

When the Japanese attacked Pearl Harbor, on 7 December 1941, the United States entered the war and Brazil had to break diplomatic and economic relations with Japan, Germany and Italy. On 23 December, the first American soldiers arrived in Recife.[46] Having lost all hope of influencing the Brazilian government, the Axis attacked the merchant ships travelling to and from the United States, destroying 13 of them and killing hundreds of people. And in August, 1942, when three more ships were sunk and more than 780 persons disappeared (the 'Brazilian Pearl Harbor'), for the first time in the history of the country, the Brazilian people reacted in huge street demonstrations, led by the National Students Union, in support of the Allies. President Vargas was forced to dismiss Filinto Müller, Lourival Fontes, and only then was DIP able to effectively prohibit the exhibition of Nazi propaganda films in the country. A 'state of war' was declared against Berlin and Rome (but not against Tokyo) on 31 August. Roosevelt promised moral and material support to Brazil;[47] millions of dollars were invested on national industries and military agreements were signed for the protection of the Brazilian territory and the repression of German espionage.

This situation also affected the cinema. In 1943, no longer dazzled by the technical qualities of the German cinema, Plínio Moraes wrote a letter, published in the *Jornal da Tarde* newspaper, rebuking the statements of the film critic Adil, who had commented on the lack of interest on anti-Nazi films in Porto Alegre. In it he said,

Sensationsprozess Casilla (1939), an Ufa film by Eduard von Borsody starring Heinrich George, premiered in the Ufa theatre at Rio de Janeiro in July 1941. *Source*: H. Traub, *Die Ufa. Ein Beitrag zur Entwicklungsgeschichte des deutschen Filmschaffens* (Berlin: Ufa-Buchverlag, 1943), p. 258.

> The fifth column is still very strong in this country. Not all the Nazis have been imprisoned yet, and the Integralists are wandering around coffee houses and newspapers spreading a demoralising defeating campaign [...] What in good faith you judged as the cause of public disinterest, is no other than the well organised work of the fifth column. [...] What we need to do now is to transform anti-Nazi shows into democratic demonstrations. Let us fight against the fifth column in our movie theatres. Let us organise the applause against the silence of Nazi saboteurs.[48]

Brazil participated in the allied war efforts with the supply of raw materials and strategic products; the defence of the Atlantic Ocean; the protection of the route Natal/Dakar; the creation of the Brazilian Expeditionary Forces (FEB) and of the squadron 'Senta a Pua!', of the Brazilian Air Force (FAB), to fight against Nazi forces in Europe. With a contingent of 49 pilots and 417 service men, this group of Brazilian fighter planes participated in 5 per cent of the total manoeuvres and destroyed or badly damaged 15 per cent of the vehicles, 28 per cent of the bridges, 36 per cent of the fuel deposits and 85 per cent of the ammunition deposits. The FEB participated in the Italian Campaign, especially in Monte Cassino, in the Apennines, from July 1944 to May 1945, with an effective of 25 334 men.[49] Brazil was the only

Latin-American country to fight and win over the German forces in Europe. In a series of paradoxes, the country was being governed by a dictator, Vargas, who was deposed by the Army, which called for a general election won by General Gaspar Dutra, who had lead the pro-Axis wing of the government, and later became the Commander of the Brazilian Expeditionary Forces in the liberation of Italy and, as the new president, started the democratisation of his country.

Notes

1. In 1938, German Ambassador in Brazil Karl Ritter declared himself responsible for the protection of 100 000 *Reich* citizens, according to a report by Von Cossel, the NSDAP director in Brazil, who also stated there were 1 million Teuton-Brazilians and 2000 German schools in this country. Herbert Guss, ex-NSDAP director, who had been dismissed from the post and excluded from the Party for political dissidence, questioned this information: 'There are around: 800 000 elements of German race in Brazil. At most, 30 000 of them were born in Germany and from these, not even 2000 belong to the Party. There are here some 1120 German schools, with which the National-Socialist Party has nothing to do.' [GUSS, Herbert. *Letter to Dr M-r.*, August 9, 1936. Apud: DA SILVA PY, Aurélio. *A 5ª coluna no Brasil*, p. 36]. According to journalist and writer Maria Kahle, who knew well the German colonies in Brazil, there would be, in 1934: 500 000 a 600 000 Germans in the State of Rio Grande do Sul; 220 000 in the State of Santa Catarina; 80 000 a 90 000 in the State of São Paulo; 60 000 a 70 000 in the State of Paraná; 15 000 in the State of Espírito Santo; 25 000 in the State of Rio de Janeiro, in an approximate total of 900 000 to 1 020 000. M. Kahle, *Deutsche Heimat in Brasilien* (Berlin: Verlag Grenze und Ausland, 1937), p. 29; R. Gertz, *O fascismo no sul do Brasil* (Porto Alegre: Mercado Aberto, 1987), p. 20. In 1940, 89 038 *Reich* citizens were registered. These numbers and Maria Kahle's are closer to the count claimed by Von Cossel.
2. See Chapter 12.
3. J. F. Bertonha, 'Divulgando o Duce e o fascismo em terra brasileira: a propaganda italiana no Brasil, 1922–1943', *Revista de História Regional*, 5:2 (2000), pp. 83–110.
4. A. Da Silvy Py, *A 5ª coluna no Brasil* (Porto Alegre: Edição da Livraria Globo, 1942), pp. 11–31.
5. M. L. Tucci Carneiro and B. Kossoy, *A imprensa confiscada pelo Deops 1924–1954* (São Paulo: Ateliê Editorial/Imprensa Oficial do Estado, 2004).
6. *Der brasilianische Integralimus* (Stuttgart, 1938). The AIB was founded in 1932 by the writer Plínio Salgado. Two years before he had met Mussolini, and had admired 'his capacity of totalising individual and social elements with an integral view of the world, in which there would be no clashes nor dissociating tendencies'. The AIB attracted numerous followers (up to a million, by 1938), with the support of the Church, the Armed Forces, the economic elite and the intellectuals. Preaching a dictatorial ultra-nationalist government, its followers wore uniforms with green shirts, such as the black shirts of Italian Fascists and the brown shirts of the *Stürmabteilungen*. The 'green-shirts' adapted the Fascist motto *Believe! Obey! Fight!* to *God!, Fatherland!, Family!*. The *Sieg Heil!* was transformed into *Anauê!*, an Indian expression, that was shouted with the right arm extended in front of the chest. As the Nazis adopted the swastika, the Integralists adopted Greek

sigma: Σ. In allusion to the Italian *Duce* and the German *Führer*, Plínio Salgado was called *Our Leader* or *Great Constable*. Integralist demonstrations emulated those of the Fascists and the Nazis, exhibiting a profusion of flags, uniforms, badges and medals. They created a magazine, *Hierarchia* – a title inspired in the name of the official newspaper of Italian Fascism – to which contributed Plínio Salgado, San Tiago Dantas, Hélio Viana, Obiano Mello, Madeira de Freitas, Antonio Galotti. The movement admitted as members coloured people and Jews. But anti-Semitic discourse appeared in the works of Oswaldo Gouvêa and of Gustavo Barroso, who lived in Berlin during 1940 and was president of the Historical Museum of Rio de Janeiro.

7. N. Cruz, *O integralismo e a questão racial* (unpublished thesis UERJ: Niterói, 2004), pp. 62–5.
8. O. Gouvêa, *Os judeus do cinema* (Rio de Janeiro: Graphica São Jorge, 1935). The author justified the recent measures adopted by Hitler in Germany: preventing Jewish participation in cultural and productive activities throughout the country.
9. Cruz (2004), p. 62.
10. M. Tucci Carneiro, *O anti-semitismo na Era Vargas* (São Paulo: Brasiliense, 1988), pp. 432–58.
11. Director Chico Faganello salvaged copies of these Nazi newsreels from archives in Germany and included segments from them in his film *Outra memória* (2005), a mixture of fiction and documentary.
12. A. Leite, *O Mundo da 7ª Arte* (http://paginas.terra.com.br/arte/memoriadocinema/1930a1939.html.)
13. R. Anelli, *Rino Levi: Arquitetura e cidade* (http://www.vitruvius.com.br/romanoguerra/rino/rino.asp.); M. L. Tucci Carneiro (1988), pp. 432–58.
14. Personal communication from Jacó Guinsburg to Luiz Nazario, 15 June 2005.
15. His film reviews were published in the newspapers *Diário de Notícias* and *Folha da Tarde*. They were transcribed, identified and dated by Marcus Mello.
16. J. Koutzil, *A tela branca* (Porto Alegre: Unidade Editorial, 1997), p. 33.
17. Ibid., p. 31.
18. Ibid., p. 46.
19. Ibid., pp. 58–9.
20. Ibid., pp. 59–60.
21. Ibid., pp. 62–3.
22. Ibid., pp. 63–4.
23. Ibid., pp. 9–11.
24. Ibid., pp. 94–5.
25. B. Drewniak, *Der deutsche Film 1938–1945* (Düsseldorf: Droste Verlag, 1987), p. 567.
26. A. Simis, *Estado e cinema no Brasil* (São Paulo: Annablume, 1996), p. 60.
27. C. Almeida, *O cinema como 'agitador de almas* (Annablume: São Paulo, 1999), pp. 87–90.
28. S. Schwarzman, *Humberto Mauro e as imagens do Brasil* (São Paulo: UNESP, 2004), pp. 200–3.
29. R. Seitenfus, *O Brasil de Getúlio Vargas e a formação dos blocos: 1930–1942* (São Paulo: CEN/INL/Fundação Pró-Memória, 1985), pp. 434–5.
30. E. Dutra, *O ardil totalitário: imaginário político no Brasil dos anos 30* (Rio de Janeiro: UFRJ; Belo Horizonte: UFMG, 1997), pp. 260–1.
31. According to studies by historian Ana Maria Dietrich.

32. L. Nazario, 'Diversão e terror: dos autos-de-fé ao cinema nazista', in M. L. Tucci Carneiro and L. Gorenstein (eds), *Ensaios sobre a intolerância* (FAPESP: São Paulo), pp. 375–417; L. Nazario, 'O "judeu" no cinema nazista', in H. Lewin (ed.), *Judaísmo, Memória e Identidade* (Rio de Janeiro: Universidade Federal do Rio de Janeiro, 1997), pp. 257–76; L. Nazario, 'O cinema na herança de Goebbels', *Revista de Estudos Judaicos*, 2 (1995), pp. 79–82.
33. Bertonha (2000).
34. Seitenfus (1985), p. 158.
35. Ibid., pp. 160–1.
36. Ibid., p. 205.
37. Ibid., p. 221.
38. Almeida (1999), pp. 167–72.
39. Schwarzman (2004), p. 216.
40. Seitenfus (1985), p. 454.
41. Memorandum from Murray to Alstock, 21/08/42, NA RG 229/99. S. Mesquita, *A política cultural norte-americana no Brasil* (UERJ: Rio de Janeiro, 2002), pp. 81–3.
42. The Press and Propaganda Department (DIP) was created through decree no. 1.915 of 27 December 1939. It functioned as a propaganda and censorship agency, of Nazi–Fascist inspiration, in charge of controlling the whole cultural production in the country (literature, the press, the radio, the theatre and the cinema). By 1941, stimulated by German newsreels, the DIP had produced, 250 propaganda films. S. Souza Ferreira, *Cinema carioca nos anos 30 e 40* (Belo Horizonte: Annablume/PPGH-UFMG, 2003), pp. 89–98.
43. Seitenfus (1985), pp. 271–6.
44. Ibid., p. 343.
45. F. Texeira *et al.*, *Nas ondas do Reich.* (http://www.habonimdror.com.br/sifria/reich.html.)
46. Seitenfus (1985), p. 368.
47. Ibid., pp. 410–19.
48. Koutzil (1997), pp. 82–3.
49. Seitenfus (1985), p. 421.

7

The Influence of German Cinema on Newly Established Croatian Cinematography, 1941–45

Daniel Rafaelić

Historical background

Space constraints do not allow me to set out in detail the historical background of the Independent State of Croatia (*Nezavisna Država Hrvatska* – NDH) which lasted from 1941–45. The Kingdom of Yugoslavia, which for decades had been torn apart from within by Croatian–Serbian antagonisms, collapsed on 6 April 1941 when Germany and its allies invaded. The only part of Yugoslavia that survived in its own right was the Independent State of Croatia. Right-winged political extremists, the Ustasha, seized power as a result of a political deal between Benito Mussolini and Ante Pavelić, soon to become Croatian *Poglavnik* (leader). The deal was sanctioned by Hitler, who received a friendly satellite in return. Laws were immediately introduced that discriminated against Jews, Gypsies and all political non-sympathisers. It quickly became clear that the new NDH would follow the laws laid down by Nazi Germany.[1]

For the purpose of this chapter, the most interesting new law was the one with reference to cinematography. It was issued on 4 June 1941, under the name Legal Provision for Protection of People's and Aryan Culture of Croatian People (*Zakonska odredba o zaštiti narodne i arijske kulture hrvatskog naroda*) and it forbade Jews from 'any participation in labour, organisations and the facilities of social, youthful, sports and cultural life of Croatian people in general, especially in literature, journalism, visual and music arts, urbanism, theatre and film'.[2] The Croatian Government was clearly determined to follow Nazi film policy. But before charting the German influence on cinematography in NDH, it is important to understand the film industry that had exited before the Balkan Peninsula was intertwined with military conquest.

Cinematic background

Aside from neighbouring countries, film production in Croatia before the Second World War was virtually non-existent. Film production was mostly left to professionals and amateurs alike, using only their own capital. The government had no interest whatsoever in helping and financing domestic film production. Although films were shown in Croatia from 8 October 1896, feature (silent) films were produced by private production companies from 1917, and various educational films proved popular in Croatian villages. Private investment in film was always destined to fail. The domination of American (at first) and subsequently German films resulted in decreasing investing in any form of cinematography, with the exception of film distribution. Despite the grim situation, there were enough enthusiasts who filmed despite the lack of commercial opportunities, leaving for posterity a number of wonderful artefacts. Josip Karaman, Arnošt Grund, Joza Ivakić, Aleksandar Gerasimov, Franjo Ledić, Oktavijan Miletić and the others did what they thought was necessary – they were creating from a non-existent cinematography tradition. However, on the eve of the Second World War, film exhibitors decided to close their cinemas. It is not surprising therefore that the period just before the Second World War was referred to as 'cinematography without films'.[3]

New cinematography: Legal background

Only a few days after the installation of NDH, on 23 April 1941, the *Film Directorship* (*Ravnateljstvo za film*) was formed as part of the National Secretary for Public Enlightenment (*Državno tajništvo za narodno prosvjećivanje*, DTNP).[4] Marijan Mikac was appointed Director.[5] The Film Directorship started organising film production, distribution and screenings. It also apprehended all non-Croatian film companies, and appointed to them special supervisors,[6] while the cinemas owned by Serbs and/or Jews were confiscated.[7]

In accordance with the above-mentioned Legal Provision for Protection of People's and Aryan Culture of Croatian People, films produced in the countries to whom NDH had declared war (or countries that had not joined the Tripartite Pact) were immediately forbidden. After 14 December 1941,[8] when NDH declared war on the United States, American films were also banned. This ban opened a wide gap that was happily filled by Germany and Italy. This marks the beginning of their cinematic influence in Croatia.

In order to control every part of the cinematographic process, now for the first time officially supported and controlled by the government, the Censorship Commission (*Povjerenstvo za ocjenu slikopisa*, POS) was established. It had the task of viewing films and issuing censor booklets, referring to a film's length, whether it had been approved for screening in full or whether it had been edited and it also set out the type of audience that would be allowed to see it. For example, a film may have been restricted to an adult audience and banned to youth. For the year 1941 the Commission saw 270 films, of which 14 were banned.[9] The Commission's data also provide a very important source for understanding the politics of the Film Directorship. It is clear that during the first 8 months of 1941, NDH imported (and screened) 154 German, 50 Italian, 24 French, 19 Hungarian, 3 Norwegian, 3 Czech, 2 Mexican and 1 Swedish film.[10] Obviously the ban on American films provided opportunities for other countries to export their films to Croatia. This trend lasted until the end of NDH in 1945, increasing the number of countries involved.[11]

Directions for the new Croatian cinematography were set out to journalists on 4 June 1941 by Marijan Mikac. From now on films were going to be completely in the service of Croatian state. Their task was 'to inform and educate Croatian people', and not 'to poison them with false film commercials'.[12] In practice, this meant that the Film Directorship would produce films that reflected the Croatian past and especially the present glory [sic]. Such propaganda would embrace all film formats: *Kulturfilme*, newsreels and feature films.

The first film (1941) produced in NDH was *From the great historical speech of Poglavnik dr. Ante Pavelić on the Square of Stjepan Radić in Zagreb on 21 May 1941* (*Iz velikog povijesnog govora Poglavnika dra. Ante Pavelića na trgu Stjepana Radića u Zagrebu 21. svibnja 1941*). This film marked the official beginning of film production in NDH. The film showed Ante Pavelić speaking to the masses interpolated with historical charts of Croatia through the centuries, intended to justify the reign of Poglavnik Ante Pavelić and his Ustasha in Croatia. This kind of film would become the preferred form of film production in Croatia (aside from newsreels), until the end of the Ustasha reign. NDH produced more than 20 of them.

The legal and financial background of new cinematography was completely stabilised when, on 19 January 1942,[13] the National Film Office 'Croatia Film' (*Hrvatski slikopis*) was formed.[14] Moreover, on 24 January 1942,[15] the National Information and Propaganda Office at Government Chairmanship (*Državni izvještajni i promidžbeni ured kod Predsjedništva Vlade*) was established and became the vehicle for all of propaganda activities, including press, radio, speeches and of course film. It is clear that this office reported directly to the Government Chairmanship. Eventually the Croatian Ministry for Propaganda and Public Enlightenment would unify all aspects under its patronage, in the same way as the *Reichsministerium für Volksaufklärung und Propaganda* (RMVP) did in Germany. Head of this new National Film Office (Croatia Film) was Marijan Mikac.

The first law concerning film (1942)[16] in NDH was based on the German model:

> The purpose and the scope of the Office is the production of national newsreels, educational, entertaining, propagandistic and commercial films; the promotion of Croatian, government and national, benefit by means of film; the establishment of comprehensive film screenings in the country and domestic films abroad; mediation at export of domestic and import of foreign film. Independent incomes derive from renting foreign and domestic films, from Office's own cinema theatres, commercial films and film magazine. If the income of the Office is not suffice, Government help is available. . . . "Croatia Film" is freed of all direct and indirect taxes, governmental and self managed fees and surtaxes.

According to this law, film in NDH would achieve economical stability, but direct Government patronage would allow the State to 'guide' Croatia Film to achieve its propaganda objectives.

Newsreels and the beginning of German influence

Short documentary films were typical propaganda vehicles for the time, but they did not reflect events as fast as newsreels. Although there had been several attempts to produce Croatian newsreels before the Second World War, only a few had succeeded – and with various quality and partial success.[17] Therefore the Film Directorship of NDH decided to produce newsreels of its own, but this time with assured financial backing. On 28 August 1941, the first issue of *Hrvatska u rieči i slici – HURIS* (Croatia in Word and Picture) was released.[18] This newsreel would immediately become very popular in NDH and would continue until the end of NDH, in May 1945, by which time HURIS had produced 175 editions. Initially it produced newsreels every 15 days, but from April of 1942 it became a weekly newsreel. Aside from HURIS, the German Ufa newsreel (Foreign Weekly Newsreel or *Auslandstonwoche*, ATW) and the Italian Luce newsreel (*Giornale Luce*) were the dominant newsreels. (They had been shown in cinemas before the Second World War, together with *Fox Movietone News*.) HURIS became their main competitor because it was showing events relevant to Croatia, while other two only included occasionally news from Croatia. Not surprisingly, a considerable amount of pressure was exerted on the Film Directorship and especially on Marijan Mikac. German films and newsreels were represented by Joseph Klement, Head of Super Film, direct importer of all Ufa films and newsreels in Croatia.[19] On the Italian side, the *Giornale Luce* newsreels were imported by the Esperia firm, headed by Giovanni Semeraro.[20] Although Italian newsreels in northern parts of Croatia were never popular, the German newsreels were. So, it was decided by German representatives that the newsreel HURIS must be suspended, because it was obvious that film-goers preferred movie theatres where domestic newsreels were being screened.[21] Eventually, after a minor diplomatic war, differences were resolved and Croatian and German newsreels were shown side by side. Of course, the *Deutsche Wochenschau GmbH* (German Newsreel Company, producer of the ATW) did their best to include news and stories from Croatia.[22] The turning point was December 1943. After 100 issues of HURIS, a new Croatian newsreel was formed. It was called *Hrvatski slikopisni tjednik* (Croatia Film Weekly, HST), but despite its new name and design, the serial number continued from the old HURIS editions. Thus the new newsreel started (or rather continued) from number 101. However, it was over twice as long as the HURIS editions[23] for simple reason that it consisted mainly of news from Croatia but, as a bonus, it also included various sections from the ATW.[24] This merger of the Croatian and the German newsreel was a clear evidence of the growing power of Croatia Film Directorship and, moreover, it signalled the end of German newsreels in Croatia. The Italian *Giornale Luce* on the other hand completely collapsed along with Mussolini's fascist regime in September 1943. Croatian newsreels had won a hard propagandistic battle. But the German propaganda machine had other means at its disposal.

People in the Storm (*Menschen im sturm*)

The biggest Nazi influence on the Croatian people was through feature films which proved extremely popular, while at the same time providing an opportunity for German propaganda.[25] It is not my intention to analyse in detail German films that were shown during this period. Rather, I intend to focus on a few representative examples in order to illustrate the wider situation.

Croatia, being a land of various landscapes, was popular with film-makers before the war. It was no surprise, therefore, that the German production company Tobis decided to shoot some parts of *People in the Storm* (*Menschen im Sturm*, 1941) on location in Hrvatsko Zagorje (near Zagreb).[26] Film shooting was undertaken during July 1941. Everybody who was somebody in NDH was present at the shooting. Marijan Mikac seized this opportunity to promote the power of new Croatian cinematography as well as to establish himself. So an extensive and extravagant photo shoot was arranged, together with lots of banquets.[27] The film was directed by Fritz Peter Buch and the stars included Olga Tschechowa, Gustav Diesel and Kurt Meisel. *People in the Storm* was premiered in Zagreb on 21 March 1942 in the 'Dubrovnik' cinema. Since it was an important film for Germany and Croatia alike, the premiere was attended by Croatian and German-visiting dignitaries.[28] The film was a typical example of German film propaganda: it justified the German occupation of Slovenian territory, because of the violent behaviour of local Serbs towards a small ethnic German community

Croatian poster for the Tobis production *People in the Storm* (*Menschen im Sturm*, 1941). In this propaganda film, situated in Yugoslavia, Vera Oswatic (Olga Tschechowa/Chekhova) helps protecting her fellow ethnic Germans (*Volksdeutschen*) against aggressive Serbs. The movie was instrumental in justifying the German attack on Yugoslavia in April 1941. *Source*: Croatian Cinematheque.

living there. *People in the Storm* portrays the Slovenian family of Aleksandar Osvatić and his German wife Vera, who, together with the daughter from her first marriage, move close to the border with Germany in the last days of the Kingdom of Yugoslavia, just before war started.[29] While the Serbian army is prosecuting *Volksdeutsche* (German ethnic minorities in Yugoslavia), captain Rakić is positioning his troops on Osvatić's property to prevent defectors. Vera uses Captain Rakić's infatuation with her to organise defections across the border. Under the threat of being discovered, Vera arranges for Marialouise's boyfriend, local teacher Hans, and his class, to flee across the border. To prevent Vera from being discovered, the local pharmacist Paulić, a Croat, sacrifices himself.[30] After the refugees successfully cross the border, Vera is discovered, and as she attempts to cross the border herself, captain Rakić shoots her.[31] It is interesting to note that this film was designated *für Jugendliche nicht zugelassen* – forbidden for the youth.[32]

This summary illustrates excellently the general guidelines of German propaganda in the Balkans. First there is the justification for the occupation of Slovenian territory. This was typical German propaganda: all German communities should be united into one Reich. After Austria had already been incorporated in German state, Slovenia was next. On the other hand, the very positive role of the Croatian pharmacist in *People in the Storm* signifies a German recognition of the existence of NDH – even though German forces could overrun Croatia at any time. The *Ustasha* and the Italians assured Germany NDH did not represent a threat to German plans in the region.[33] Finally, there is the role that the Germans assigned to the Serbs as the main arch-enemy. This was more than simply a political concession to the government of Ante Pavelić; it represented a real racial hatred between Germans and Serbs. This depiction of the Serbs as arch-enemies of everything good and righteous was the most important propaganda theme in the other German film, but this time a documentary: *Smrt Jugoslavije/Rat na Balkanu* (*Death of Yugoslavia/War on the Balkans*).

Documentaries – *Kulturfilme*

The German invasion of Yugoslavia and Greece was filmed by the propaganda companies of the Wehrmacht that were responsible for supplying the German Ministry of Propaganda (RMVP) with battle footage. This film material was later assembled in the 50-min documentary *Death of Yugoslavia/War on the Balkans* (*Smrt Jugoslavije/Rat na Balkanu*). Just as in *People in the Storm*, once again the German army acted as a saviour of its allies. The Serbs, reportedly implementing British policy, are shown terrorising Croats, Slovenians and, of course, the German minorities. Germans then act as liberators, confining only Serbs from the Yugoslav army – and liberating others, who had been 'kept there against their will'. This film is probably the best example of the power of German propaganda machine – since it

Cover of a Croatian leaflet about the anti-British propaganda film *Uncle Krüger* (*Ohm Krüger*, 1941), loosely based on the life of Paul Krueger and his role in the Boer War. *Source*: Croatian Cinematheque.

created illusions of heavy fighting over difficult terrain which the victorious German troop overcome in only 12 days in order to destroy the Serbian eagle (*Die Serbische Adler*).[34] Of course, this is not true, because the Yugoslav army capitulated almost immediately. The *Death of Yugoslavia*, aside from propaganda value, is also very important for it recorded the establishment of NDH, at a time when the Croatian film industry did not exist. The film was exhibited as early as end of May 1941 and it proved to be a great success.

It is little known that Oktavijan Miletić, one of the pioneers of Croatian film, had, in 1940–44, directed several films for the German Ufa and Tobis film companies. Because of his involvement with German film producers, Miletić declined an offer of the Film Directorship of NDH, in order to direct the first film produced in NDH, the above-mentioned *From the great historical speech of Poglavnik dr. Ante Pavelić on the Square of Stjepan Radić in Zagreb on 21 May 1941*.[35] But his influence and knowledge was so immense that as soon as he was done with the Germans, he received various offers from the National Film Office 'Croatia Film' (*Hrvatski slikopis*), all of which he eagerly accepted. In 1944, he was the first Croatian film director to make a Croatian feature length film, *Lisinski*. The cooperation between Miletić and Tobis film started in 1940, when he filmed, edited and directed *Sculpting in Croatia* (*Bildhauerkunst in Kroatien*, 1940). Today, this film is presumed lost.[36]

In September 1941, Joseph Eckardt, Director of the *Kulturfilm* Department at Tobis, arrived in Zagreb[37] to organise the *Festwoche des Deutschen Kulturfilms* (*The Week of German Kulturfilme*) that was held on 9–16 December 1941. This manifestation was another platform for German cinema to show off its cinematographic supremacy.[38] Dr Eckard announced the next two films that Oktavijan Miletić would direct for the Germans: *Agram* and *The Life of Croatian Peasants* (*Kroatisches Bauernleben*).[39] *The Life of Croatian Peasants* was premiered at *The Week of German Kulturfilme* in Munich, in November 1942. Miletić attended as a special guest of Dr Goebbels, who introduced the film. It is not clear why it took almost a year before the film was shown in Croatian cinemas, where it finally premiered in November 1943.[40] It has remained virtually unknown in Croatia.[41] This wonderful, short film (a real treasure for ethnologists) shows the daily life and routine of a Croatian peasant and his struggle to overcome nature's obstacles in order to enjoy fruits of his labour. The film ends with the peasant's wedding. It is very important here to note that Oktavijan Miletić, inspite of his collaboration with Goebbels, refused to compromise his principles or his film art. This is probably why Miletić was able to continue his cinematographic work after the war ended.

Film stars, magazines, books

Film was not the only means of German propaganda in Croatia.[42] Everything surrounding the film industry was fertile ground for propagandistic actions.

In NDH only one film magazine in the Croatian language existed. It was called *Hrvatski slikopis* (Croatia Film). It was issued monthly, from May 1942 until April 1945. Although it was meant to be the main source of information for Croatian films, German film productions dominated its pages – as they had dominated the cinema screens. As a result, it remains one of the main sources for studying German cinematography in NDH. It featured photographs, various descriptions of films, mini-biographies of the stars and directors as well as numerous anecdotes from their lives.

In the early days of NDH, SUPER Film was the main importer of Ufa films. It published *Njemačke slikopisne novosti* (German Film News), which started as bimonthly magazine, and then continued to be published monthly. Of course, it was completely dedicated to German film production, portraying films currently in cinemas, and as a result, this was an important propagandistic tool for German film companies. Although other journals and newspapers brought news from the world of cinema, several magazines such as *Hrvatski krugoval* (Croatian Radio) and *Signal* also dedicated much of their space to film. In various details they followed everything related to popular films. For example, during the Easter of 1943, when 25th anniversary of Ufa was being celebrated, popular German actors Marte Harrel and Wolf Albach-Retty visited Zagreb. They came to promote their new film, Géza von Bolváry's *The Secret Countess* (*Die Heimliche Gräfin*, 1942),[43] and the press followed them everywhere.[44] To illustrate their popularity, HURIS included their visit in its newsreel (issue 70). They also travelled to Zagreb's surroundings, and signed autographs for the crowds eagerly waiting to see their new film.[45]

It soon became apparent that despite the grim war situation in NDH, film and its bi-products could actually be profitable. Film, books and magazines, which had been scarce before the war, flourished during NDH. The first national film history was written by Mirko Cerovac (*Slikopis*, 1943), but translations of the original books upon which popular films had been based were also proving popular. Such is the case of the book *Židov Süss – slikopisni roman* (a film novel based on Veit Harlan's *Jew Süss* (*Jud Süss*, 1940)) by J. R. George.[46] The notorious anti-Semitic film was first shown to the Croatian public in May 1941, but in the following year (May–June 1942) in *Umjentički paviljon* (Art pavilion) in Zagreb, an exhibition *Židovi* (Jews) was organised.[47] It was accompanied by the Croatian documentary film *How the Anti-Jewish Exhibition Arose* (*Kako je nastala protužidovska izložba*, 1942) which showed why the exhibition had been put together and how the 'Jewish question' was being dealt with in NDH.[48] This was the only racist and anti-Semitic film ever produced by *Hrvatski slikopis* (Croatia Film). As an incentive to visit the exhibition, three free cinema tickets were issued for special screenings of the Nazi anti-Semitic films: Fritz Hippler's 'documentary' *The Wandering/Eternal Jew* (*Der Ewige Jude*, 1940) and the feature films *The Rothschilds' Shares in Waterloo* (*Die Rotschilds. Aktien auf Waterloo*, 1940) by Erich Waschneck and, of course, *Jud Süss*. Obviously the Nazis were determined to use every conceivable means to disseminate their ideology. In conclusion, however, it is fair to say that the Germans encountered little resistance from Croatian cinema-goers.

Notes

1. For more details about these Legal provisions, as well about history of Kingdom of Yugoslavia, refer to H. Matković, *Povijest Nezavisne Države Hrvatske* (Zagreb: Naklada P.I.P. Pavičić, 2002), pp. 175–6.
2. 'Zakonska odredba o zaštiti narodne i arijske kulture hrvatskog naroda', *Hrvatski narod* (5 June 1941), p. 1.
3. I. Škrabalo, *101 godina filma u Hrvatskoj* (Zagreb: Globus, 1998), pp. 99–111.
4. M. Mikac, *Tri godine rada Hrvatskog slikopisa* (Zagreb: Državni slikopisni zavod «Hrvatski slikopis», 1944), p. 23.
5. Marijan Mikac (1903–72) had before the war worked in 20th Century Fox and Paramont distribution offices in Zagreb, but his popularity was due to his 1937 novel *Doživljaji Morica Švarca u Hitlerovoj Njemačkoj: satirični roman* (*The Adventures of Moritz Schwartz in Hitler's Germany: Satirical Novel*). This political satire caused him great trouble with the Gestapo in 1941, only a few days after his appointment as Director of Film Directorship. He continued writing, but with far less success. Among his other works, he wrote an overview of cinematography in NDH: *Film u Nezavisnoj Državi Hrvatskoj* (Madrid: Drinina knjižnica, 1971). For more about Mikac see B. Donat, 'Nepoznati i zaboravljeni Marijan Mikac', *Kolo Matice Hrvatske: časopis za kulturu, umjetnost i društvena pitanja*, Obnovljeni tečaj, 3(151): 9/10 (1993), pp. 711–37.
6. M. Cerovac, *Slikopis (Film)* (Zagreb: Državni slikopisni zavod «Hrvatski slikopis», 1943), p. 90.
7. Hrvatski državni arhiv (*Croatian National Archive*) in a box 27, 237 of *Odsjek za tisak i slikopis* (*Department for press and film*), documents reveal that some cinemas were sold, for example, to *Ustaška mladež* (*Ustasha youth*), but it is obvious that this was done under coercion.
8. Matković (2002), p. 173.
9. Cerovac (1943), p. 94.
10. E. Bauer, *Die entwicklung der Publizistik in Kroatien* (Zagreb: Europa Verlag, 1942), pp. 60–2, 80–1. Interestingly, Bauer mentions that the Commission banned only six films: four French and two Hungarian.
11. Films from countries that were members and/or supporters of the Tripartite Pact.
12. *Spomen-knjiga prve obljetnice Nezavisne Države Hrvatske 10.4.1941–10.4.1942* (Zagreb: Državni izvještajni i promičbeni zavod, 1942), p. 42.
13. According to *Zakonska odredba broj* (*Legal provision No.*) XXIII-154-Z-1942. Mikac (1944), p. 32.
14. Cerovac (1943), p. 95. Unfortunately, the office title when translated in English is quite misleading.
15. *Zakonska odredba broj* (*Legal provision No.*) XXXIII-231-Z-1942. Mikac (1944), p. 27.
16. *Legal provision No.* XXIII-154-Z-1942.
17. The most notable were *Zvono newsreel* by Franjo Ledić and *Zora newsreel*, both from 1930s – for more about early Croatian newsreels see V. Majcen, 'Tradicija filmskih žurnala u hrvatskoj kinematografiji', *Kinoteka*, 4:4 (1989), pp. 35–6; V. Majcen,

'Tradicija filmskih žurnala u hrvatskoj kinematografiji (2)', *Kinoteka*, 5:5 (1989), pp. 33–5; V. Majcen, 'Filmski žurnal: pojava zvuka', *Kinoteka*, 6:6 (1989), pp. 34–5.

18. The title itself was taken from Austrian newsreel *Österreich in Bild und Ton* (Austria in Picture and Sound) which was produced until the 1938 Anschluss and the implementation of *Deutsche Wochenschau*. For more on Austrian newsreels see M. Achenbach and K. Moser (eds), *Österreich in Bild und Ton/Die Filmwochenschau des Austrofaschistischen Ständestaates* (Wien: Filmarchiv Austria, 2002).
19. Mikac (1944), pp. 28–9.
20. Ibid., p. 40.
21. Ibid., pp. 55–7.
22. The best guide for *Deutsche Wochenschau* is P. Bucher, *Wochenschauen und Dokumentarfilme 1895–1950 im Bundesarchiv-Filmarchiv* (Berlin: Bundesarchiv Koblenz, 2000) – for NDH look in the index for references to *Kroatien*, *Agram* (Zagreb), *Pavelic* and so on.
23. HURIS newsreels were on average 200 m (7 min.), while HST was about 500 m (18 min.).
24. Kulturno značenje slikopisnog rada 'Hrvatska u rieči i slici' br. 100!, *Nova Hrvatska* (28 November 1943), p. 6.
25. So did Croatian filmmakers, who were sent on a regular basis to study in the Babelsberg studios in Berlin.
26. *Hrvatski narod* 132 (26 June 1941), p. 4 contains extensive details about the shooting.
27. I recently discovered original negatives of this photo shoot in the vaults of the Croatian History Museum, and currently they are being digitalised for archiving in the Croatian Cinematheque. Some of the photos were published in Mikac (1971), p. 38.
28. *Hrvatski narod* 383 (22 March 1942), p. 2 contains a report from the film premiere.
29. Of course, before the *Anschluss* this was Yugoslav–Austrian border.
30. It is interesting to note that in the Croatian promotional material for *People in the Storm*, which I uncovered in a private owner's possession, the role of Croatian pharmacist was given much greater prominence.
31. The Croatian promotional material suggests that although Vera is shot, she had successfully crossed the border.
32. *Paimann's Filmlisten Wochenschrift für Lichtbild – Betrachtung*, Wien (27 January 1942), p. 4.
33. Just like the Independent State of Slovakia, at that time.
34. The crest of Kingdom of Yugoslavia has two eagles on it. Destroying of this crest in Zagreb has prominent role in the film.
35. Marijan Mikac, *Film u NDH* (Madrid, 1971), p. 30.
36. A. Peterlić and V. Majcen, *Oktavijan Miletić* (Zagreb: Hrvatski državni arhiv-Hrvatska kinoteka, 2000), p. 167.
37. *Hrvatski narod* 200 (2 September 1941).
38. *Himmelstürmer, Jugend fliege, Tiergarten Südamerika, Flösser, Melder durch Beton und Stahl, Schnelle Truppen, U boote, Fallschirmspringer, Die erde singt, Deutsche in der Zips, Die Insel der Dämonen, Fliegende Früchte, Bergbauernjahr, Schlacht im Osten* and *Steinmetz am Werk* were shown and were well received – see programme booklet in Stampata collection of Croatian National Archive no. 80/120.
39. *Hrvatski narod* 205 (7 September 1941). *Agram*, like *Sculpting in Croatia*, was considered lost; however, there is a wonderfully preserved 16 mm copy of *The Life of a Croatian Peasant* that I uncovered in Filmarchiv Austria in January 2004.

40. *Hrvatski slikopis,* 11 (1943), p. 10 and *Hrvatski krugoval,* 40 (1943).
41. The film was screened, for the first time after 62 years, on 30 May 2005 in cinema Tuškanac in Zagreb, and 23 July 2005 at the Pula film Festival. See also, *Borci za Hrvatsku* (Fighters for Croatia, 1944) a combination of documentary and fiction, portraying a group of Croatian soldiers who are sent to Stockerau, near Vienna, for military education.
42. For the other forms of German propaganda, see M. Jareb, Njemačka promičba u Nezavisnoj Državi Hrvatskoj od 1941. do 1945. godine, *Godišnjak Njemačke narodne zajednice VDG Jahrbuch* (2001), pp. 171–97.
43. The film was directed by Géza von Bolváry in 1942.
44. *Nova Hrvatska* 106 (4 May 1943).
45. It is interesting to note that Marte Harel and Wolf Albach Retty were not the first choice of the Film Directorship of NDH. It was originally intended that director Veit Harlan and his wife, the actress Kristina Söderbaum, would arrive in Zagreb to promote their new film *Die goldene Stadt* (golden City) – Dolazak njemačkih slikopisnih umjetnika u Zagreb, *Hrvatski narod* 613 (22 December 1941), p. 2.
46. Židov Süss – slikopisni roman (Zagreb: NZ Hrvatska knjiga, 1944.). The original version was published by Ufa's own publishing company: J. R. George, *Jud Süß* (Berlin: Ufa-Buchverlag, 1941).
47. For detailed description of the exhibition, see *Hrvatski narod,* 400 (14 April 1942), p. 7.
48. The film is 310 m long.

8
A Dangerous Neighbourhood: German Cinema in the Czechoslovak Region, 1933–45

Ivan Klimeš

The democratic Republic of Czechoslovakia was created at the end of the First World War (1918), as one of the succession states of the Austro-Hungarian Empire. The new state was politically and economically dominated by the Czechs but had large German and Slovak ethnic minorities as well as smaller Hungarian, Ukrainian and Polish minorities. Centuries of sharing Central European territory had created numerous economic, political and cultural ties between the Bohemian Lands and the German Reich. Following the creation of Czechoslovakia these ties intensified. This trend, which was already noticeable under Austrian rule, manifested itself among other things in the entertainment industry.

The Czechoslovak film market (1918–38) and its ties with the German film industry

The German population of Czechoslovakia, the 'Sudeten Germans', were to adapt most readily to the rapid industrialisation of cinema. This was particularly true for the inhabitants of the industrial region of North Bohemia, who had ties both to Vienna and to the great industrial centres in Germany. Nevertheless, it was the tendency of the Czech population to live in constant contact with German culture that, despite the rhetoric of the Czech national movement, contributed to the establishment of German cinema as the second-ranking national cinema on the Czechoslovak market in the 1920s. Tensions between the German minority and the ruling ethnic Czech majority rose repeatedly, manifesting, for instance, in the famous Prague demonstrations where extremist groups protested against the presentation of German films.[1] Nonetheless, the viewing behaviour of the Czech public indicates that even after the advent of sound film the trend was in quite the opposite direction. German films took second place in terms of viewer preference, ranking right after Czech films, not only with regard to the number of films on the Czechoslovak market, but with respect to the popularity of country of film origin as well.[2]

By the time Hitler came to power in Nazi Germany, early disputes associated with the advent of sound had already taken shape, involving both the reaction of the public and the patent issue, some even resulting in lawsuits. Under the 'Paris Agreement' of 1930, Czechoslovakia was part of the patent zone of Tobis-Klangfilm, a supra-national group of companies. After some initial disputes, Tobis-Klangfilm finally reached an agreement with the professional organisations of the Czechoslovak film industry, led by the Central Union of Cinematographers (*Ústřední svaz kinematografů*), settling for a flat licensing fee for patent infringing equipment.[3] In 1933, the Czechoslovak film industry was embroiled in another big issue – the introduction of the quota system. In 1932 – relatively late in comparison to other European countries – Czechoslovakia started protecting its domestic film market by regulating film imports and supporting domestic film production. Modelling its legislation after the British Cinematograph Films Act (1927), the Czech Ministry of Industry, Trade and Crafts made the issue of import licenses conditional to the production of domestic films. It also introduced standards regulating the number of foreign films that could be imported to Czechoslovakia in a given year (and hence, *de facto*, how many domestic films would be produced).[4]

The Ministry of Trade had already attempted earlier, in the late 1920s, to introduce such a model to support domestic film. The proposed act got bogged down during inter-ministerial negotiations about the model as a whole, but one reason that the earlier attempt had failed was that the big American companies had threatened a boycott of the Czechoslovak market.[5] When the quota system was finally introduced in 1932, the American companies actually did resort to this extreme measure. The Motion Picture Producers and Distributors of America did not accept the terms of the Czechoslovak quota system. Prague subsidiaries of the American companies Fox, MGM, Paramount, United Artists and Universal refused to produce Czech films and stopped the import of American films into Czechoslovakia. This event dramatically transformed the landscape of distribution offerings in very short order. What had until then been the dominant share of American cinema in the Czechoslovak market fell to fourth place over the course of 1932. The American's privileged position was taken over by German cinema – just as Adolf Hitler was coming into power in Germany.[6] The Prague subsidiary of the German company Ufa ended up reacting in precisely the opposite fashion. Ufa decided to accept the new conditions and began producing its own Czech films. The first of them, *The Little Window* (*Okénko*), directed by Vladimír Slavínský and featuring rising stars Hugo Haas (who would be dismissed from the National Theatre in 1938 because of his Jewish origins) and Lída Baarová, premiered in early March of 1933.[7] Even after the domestic film production requirement for importers was eliminated in 1934, the Prague branch of Ufa continued producing films in the country. In total, Ufa produced 15 Czech films between 1933 and 1940.[8]

Although the Ministry of Trade was satisfied with the economic effect of the quota system, the new situation provoked considerable tension in film circles. Cinema owners complained of a shortage of new films, and more nationalist-oriented journalists attacked the influx of German films. The Ministry of Foreign Affairs expressed considerable unease as well: Jindřich Elbl, the foreign ministry's cinema desk officer, who would be one of the eight authorised representatives of nationalised cinema from 1945 to 1948 (responsible for import and export) characterised the overall situation in a special memorandum to the minister as follows: '. . . the film import policy of the Ministry of Trade has led, though perhaps unintentionally, to a situation in which, for the past 2 years, cinematograph theatre has been systematically promoting a trend and influences in cinema that are undesirable and, in part, even antagonistic to the Czechoslovak state government'.[9] Under pressure from other government offices and the public, after complicated negotiations with the Americans, the Ministry of Trade did finally abandon the quota system in November 1934, and the relative strengths of key national cinemas in the Czechoslovak market returned to their original proportions, although with a significantly lower total volume of films.[10]

After the abandonment of the quota system, the Ministry of Trade suggested to representatives of the domestic film industry that they should regulate the import of foreign films themselves. This lead to the establishment of the Cartel of Film Importers (Kartel filmových dovozců) in September 1935. The cartel established general rules for film imports, even including price ceilings which were intended to prevent inflated prices for films due to intra-market competition. Germany, as the second strongest national cinema represented on the Czechoslovak market, contributed to a large degree to the general implementation and acceptance of this price regulation. In January 1936, representatives of the Reich Film Chamber signed an agreement with representatives of Czech cinema governing conditions for the import of German films into Czechoslovakia. From the Czech perspective the agreement's major benefit lay in the acceptance of the price conditions set by the cartel: the agreement essentially legitimised these terms for international commerce. Parallel negotiations with representatives of the Austrian film industry towards a Czechoslovak–Austrian cinema agreement broke down over those same terms, for that very reason. Pointing to the newly reached agreement with Germany, the Czechoslovak side rejected the Austrian proposals, which were based on specific features of the Austrian film industry (for example, the fact that in Austria, 90 per cent profits from the exploitation of feature films came from exports). The Czechoslovak–German film agreement of 1936 spontaneously became a sort of unofficial standard.[11]

February 1937 saw the ratification of a new bilateral film agreement, this time including the export of Czechoslovak films to Germany.[12] The agreement guaranteed the exchange of films between the two countries in the ratio of 1:15, with the stipulation that no more than five Czech films in a German version would be exported to Germany per year. Under the agreement, these films were to be imported into Germany without quota sheets and would be treated in the approval procedure like films produced in Germany. Imported films not covered by this agreement would be subject to the standard regime for foreign films.[13] The text of the agreement does not make clear what is meant by German versions of Czech films, whether that meant a 'multiple language version' (MLV) or a dubbed version (apparently either). At any rate, it is noteworthy that the ratio stipulated reflected actual practice: Czechoslovakia produced around five multiple language versions of Czech films annually from 1931 to 1938, the vast majority of them in German, aiming at German-speaking countries, and imported around 80 German films every year.[14] The agreement was advantageous for the Czechoslovak side, as the possibility of bypassing the German quota system while exporting Czech films to the German market benefited Czech exporters. The Germans, for their part, had a guarantee of the regular acceptance of the stated number of German films, and with it a permanent presence on the Czechoslovak market not vulnerable to the increasingly dramatic situation in bilateral relations at the political level.[15] Hence the Reich's strategy towards the Czechoslovak film industry was a fairly obliging one, for the sake of ensuring that German cinema maintained the favourable position it had been holding in the Czechoslovak market.

In defence of democratic values, the Czechoslovak government (through the Film Advisory Council (*Filmový poradní sbor*) at the Ministry of Trade) issued guidelines that set the certain conditions on film imports. Under these guidelines, films that did any of the following were not admissible:

1. Jeopardise or harm state interests
2. Jeopardise public law and order (regulations)
3. Might lead to disturbances in the national, religious or political tolerance
4. Jeopardise our political – democratic – system either directly or indirectly through the propaganda of other governments or non-critical praise of monarchies, aristocratic societiesand so on
5. Evoke and glorify the former politic constellation in Central Europe
6. Mar or contravene the relations of Czechoslovakia towards other nations, especially towards such as are in agreement with the concepts of Czechoslovak foreign policy
7. Defame persons of other nations

   [. . .][16]

The state also furthered its interests by placing geographic restrictions on the use of the language of the German minority. Films dubbed into German could only be shown in municipalities where over half the population was ethnically German; if a company showed such a film anywhere else, it was required to pay a fee of 20 000 crowns into the 'registration fund' (a fund for the promotion of cinema).[17]

While the state may have retained certain wariness in its relations with Germany, in cinematic circles the German neighbour was viewed with considerable admiration. Certainly, they were impressed by the interest that the German government took in cinema. In late April of 1935 there was an international film congress held in Berlin on behalf of the International Film Chamber.[18] The 40-member delegation sent to the Berlin congress from Czechoslovakia came back bearing powerful impressions. Germany could boast the recently established film academy and the brand new Reich Film Archive (*Reichsfilmarchiv*); up to 2500 congress participants were able to see Leni Riefenstahl's *Triumph of the Will* (*Triumph des Willens*, 1935); a 50-member delegation was even given an audience with Adolf Hitler.[19] The International Film Chamber and the International Federation of Film Critics (*Fédération Internationale de la Presse Cinématographique*, FIPRESCI) were both established at the congress, which also advocated the establishment of national film archives, while representatives of the Reich Film Chamber also appealed for the organisation of national film chambers. Although they denied that it was a source of inspiration, Czech cinematic circles were also clearly interested in the institution of the *Reichsfilmdramaturg*:[20] that same year, 1935, Julius Schmitt, the leading Czech producer, suggested that some kind of 'official Czech cinema dramaturge office' might one day emerge from the current thoughts about film dramaturgy.[21]

After Hitler's accession to power, Czechoslovakia became one of the destination countries for emigrants fleeing Germany. Several Jewish producers, directors and actors found work in the film industry there, despite protests from the film unions. Directors Max Neufeld, Walter Kolm-Veltée, Jakob and Luise Fleck, and Robert Land, and actor Hans Jaray and others were involved in the production of multiple language versions of Czech films. Czechoslovakia was also one of the major customers for what were known as 'independent films' from Austria, that is, productions by Jewish emigrants who were attempting to establish themselves in the Austrian film industry, which had no chance of being exported into Germany.[22]

German influence on the (Czech) film market of the 'Second Republic' and the 'Protectorate of Bohemia and Moravia' (1938–44/45)

The Munich Agreement (September 1938) resulted in the dismemberment of the state of Czechoslovakia. In the west, Sudetenland was incorporated into Nazi Germany. In the east, Slovakia was turned into an 'independent' satellite state of Nazi Germany while Poland and Hungary acquired pieces inhabited by 'their' ethnic minorities. The remainder of Czechoslovakia, the so-called 'Second Republic' or 'rump' Republic, only existed from October 1938 until 15 March 1939. On that date, the Republic was invaded and occupied by the German Wehrmacht. Czechoslovakia ceased to exist and was turned into a German 'protectorate'. The Protectorate of Bohemia and Moravia, as it was henceforth called, still had a Czech government but was in reality governed by the administration of a German Reich Protector.[23]

The signing of the Munich agreement and the creation of the 'Second Republic' had an immediate impact on the film sector through the marked reduction in the size of the cinema theatre network. With the severance of Sudetenland and additional territories a total of 545 cinemas (almost 30 per cent of the original network, of which only 354 had been German) were suddenly outside of the newly demarcated borders.[24] A xenophobic mood accompanied the oppressive atmosphere in the 'rump' republic. Nationalist rhetoric was heard mingled with the rhetoric of anti-Semitism, even in the film sector. Particularly enterprising in this respect was the Czechoslovak Film Union (*Čs. filmová unie*), under the leadership of director Václav Binovec, as well as the Central Union of Cinematographers, which deliberately played the anti-Semitic card in its attack on film rental operations, and on local subsidiaries of American companies in particular.[25]

The establishment of the Protectorate fuelled extensive changes in the entire film sector. Shock at the collapse of the Republic fed a spontaneous desire towards internal integration of the sector. In response to the country's occupation, as early as May 1939, the Centre of Film Branche (*Ústředí filmového oboru*) was set up, associating the individual representatives of the Central Union of Cinematographers, the Film Production Union (*Svaz filmové výroby*), the Film Industry and Commerce Union (*Svaz filmového průmyslu a obchodu*), the Film Import Association (*Sdružení filmového dovozu*) and the Czech Film Union (*Česká filmová unie*). The new central organisation underwent several transformations over the following months. As of July it was subject to the supervision of Hermann Glessgen, film commissioner of the Office of the Reich Protector. The aim of this centralised union institution, which gradually took on the character of a film chamber, was to create more stable internal organisation on the one hand and to protect it from the outside on the other. At the same time, of course, its very existence made it easier for the Germans to implement occupation policies in the film sector and to regulate domestic cinema securely.[26]

In the end, the plan of creating a film chamber came to fruition under German direction. By decree of the Reich Protector, dated 26 October 1940, on 15 February 1941 the Bohemian–Moravian Film Center (*Českomoravské filmové ústředí – Böhmisch-mährische Filmzentrale*, ČMFÚ/BMFZ) was created, a Czech–German public corporation with mandatory membership for all business owners, merchants and artistic film employees engaged in film-making (formally this obligation extended to German subjects of the Protectorate[27]). The chairman (a Czech) and vice-chairman (a German) were appointed by

Joseph Goebbels (front) visits the Barrandov Studios in Prague on 5 November 1940. On the left: state secretary Karl Hermann Frank. *Source*: Czech News Agency, CTK Photo Desk.

the Reich Protector and the Protectorate government had three representatives in the organisations management. The state delegated several of its powers to this highest-level body of corporate self-government, including that of granting concessions for the operation of cinemas. The mission of the ČMFÚ was to promote cinema within the framework of the overall economy, set binding regulations for internal transactions within the sector, represent the interests of individual groups, and resolve any conflicts arising among members of the chamber. All professional cinematic activities within Protectorate territory fell under its jurisdiction. As the ruling body in the sector, the ČMFÚ acted with great enterprise and regulated with directives the everyday activities in the film sector down to a high level of detail. In addition to a wide range of lower level directives, it introduced the mandatory registration of film subjects (December 1941), the approval of programmes produced (December 1941), an obligatory sequence for the information in the introductory credits and a maximum length for them of 50 m (July 1942), and monitoring of correct Czech usage by Czech language experts. It also set a maximum length of 2600 m for a feature film (August 1941) and imposed a compulsory film programme: cultural short (*Kulturfilm*), newsreel and feature film (July 1941). ČMFÚ clearly ruled the Czech film industry and continued to so right up until May 1945, when it ceded its duties to the National Committee of Czech Film Workers (*Národní výbor českých filmových pracovníků*). Through ČMFÚ, Czech film workers gained considerable experience with the central direction of the sector as a whole and in that sense it represents a significant developmental phase on the path towards the post-war introduction of the state monopoly in film commerce, when many former ČMFÚ representatives found employment in the ruling bodies of nationalised cinema. The establishment of the ČMFÚ brought with it a fundamental change in the overall legal framework in the film sector, as it *de facto* revoked the effectiveness of Ministerial Act No. 191 of 18 September 1912, which had until then been the key legal standard in the sector.[28]

Before the Munich Agreement dismembered Czechoslovakia's so-called 'First Republic' (1918–38), two central authorities shared jurisdiction over the film sector. The Ministry of the Interior was responsible for film censorship and the issue of cinema theatre licenses whereas the Ministry of Trade took care of everything else, for example allocating state funds for film production and foreign currency for film imports, awarding of film prizes and so on. The Germans took over film censorship on 1 September 1939 – the responsibility went to the Office of the Reich Protector, where later on a film inspection office (*Filmprüfstelle*) was set up based on the German model. The Ministry of the Interior lost its second area of competence (licenses for cinema theatre operations) with the establishment of the ČMFÚ. Following dismantlement of the Ministry of Trade in a wider reorganisation of central authorities, cinema (now more or less limited to decisions regarding funds for Czech film production) came into the purview of the Ministry of Public Enlightenment (*Ministerstvo lidové osvěty*) in January 1942.

Two events symbolised the approaching fate of the Czech film industry under the Protectorate. On 16 March 1939, the name of Osvald Kosek, the only member of Jewish descent of the AB Company's board of directors, was struck from Commerce Register. That same day also saw an unsuccessful attempt by Czech fascists to occupy the studios at Barrandov. Right from the start, the fundamental objective of the German occupiers in the film arena was to take control of the production base of Czech cinema. Their main instrument in this, as in other sectors of the Czech economy, was the Reich Protector's Decree on Jewish Property of 21 July 1936, which set off the 'Aryanisation' process.

In July 1939, an 'Aryanisation office' for the entire film sector was created in Prague. A registry of family origin (the so-called 'Aryan registry') was set up at this office; this was the office that registered the confirmations of 'Aryan' descent (*Ariernachweis*) that were a prerequisite for continuing in the field. The requirement to submit such a document to the director of the Aryanisation office by 30 September 1930 extended to all company owners, all board members (boards of directors and management boards), authorised agents, directors and signatories, as well as to licensees, operators, and directors of cinema theatres, and to artistic film-workers involved in film production (including director's assistants, production heads, sound technicians, etc.). Jewish staff had to be dismissed by 15 August 1939, so that Czech cinema would enter the 1939/1940 with no Jewish employees.

In July and November 1939, the German 'trustee' (Treuhänder) Karl Schulz took over respectively the modern studios of Barrandov with its experienced and high-quality staff and the Host studios in Prague. Largely through his efforts, all three Prague studios gradually fell into German hands. The majority stakeholder in AB Company, Miloš Havel, was forced to sell his shares to Germans in the spring of 1940; Bat'a Film Studios (*Filmové ateliéry Bat'a*, FAB) had to give up their lease on the studio in Hostivař, and finally, Karl Schulz manoeuvred the owner of Prague's third studios, Foja in Radlice, into selling them in March 1942. Only a few days earlier the Bat'a studios in Zlín had succumbed to pressure from the German Tobis group of companies – which set up the subsidiary company Bohemian–Moravian Small Film Company (*Böhmisch-mährische Schmalfilmgesellschaft*) which specialised particularly in animated and puppet film too.[29]

Control of the production base of Czech cinema represented the first step along the path to the planned liquidation of Czech film production.[30] This end was never actually fully achieved, but nevertheless the indicators for domestic production from the Protectorate years are alarming. Annual production of feature live-action films fell from 41 in 1939 to 9 in 1944. From 1943 to 1945 only two Czech firms were allowed to produce films: National film and the Havel family's Lucernafilm. In the new environment, Czech producers had to rely completely on production capacity allotted by Prag-Film; only rarely and with difficulty could they get access to the most modern studios, those at Barrandov. Only 23 Czech films were made at Barrandov in the years of the Protectorate (only 11 between 1941 and 1945), while 42 German films were produced there in the same period. The majority of the Czech films that were made were filmed in the smaller and less well equipped studios in Hostivař and Radlice. In total, 124 feature live-action films and 1230 other films were made in Czech production from 1939 to 1945. Although the effect on the production volume of documentary and news films was relatively small, the number of producers was reduced by half. German film production developed alongside Czech film production in the territory of the Protectorate, with using Czech directors, cameramen, composers, actors and other professions, including the Czech technical staff at the Barrandov studios.

In late 1941, the Germans transformed the AB Company into the stock-company Prag-Film for this purpose; the company then became part of the

Reich's Ufa group of film companies (and, later on, of the Ufi Trust). Prague and its Barrandov studios evidently played a key role in the plans made by the Germans for cinema: a new studio was constructed at Barrandov at Goebbels' instigation; there was major renovation of the film laboratories, as well as the introduction of colour film production; the establishment of the animated film studios; and the founding of the Prag-Film Orchestra in 1943, which was transformed into the Film Symphony Orchestra (*Filmový symfonický orchestra*, FYSIO) after liberation.[31]

Film commerce was also subjected to extensive changes during the Protectorate years. After 15 March 1939, a whole raft of Czech, American and French films were banned, and as were all Soviet films. With the onset of the war in September 1939, all remaining English and French films were banned and there was a further reduction in American films. The last remaining American films stayed on the Czechoslovak market to a limited extent right up until the United States entered the war. Although the import of nearly the entire German production partially 'compensated' for this loss, the statistics reveal a relatively dramatic recession in film commerce. By 1944 the number of premiers had fallen by nearly 65 per cent (from 242 in 1939 to 87 in 1944). Germany had an unrivalled hegemony on the market: German films represented 55–69 per cent of new annual offerings in the years 1940–44. Of all German films, only certain propaganda films were not made available to Czech audiences, those which might provoke negative feelings in the Czech population against the protectorate (for example, Veit Harlan's *The golden City* (*Die goldene Stadt*, 1942), portraying, in *Heimatideologie* spirit, the tragic fate of a German girl from the countryside who is destroyed by her association with a Czech waiter from Prague).[32] Local Czech production had a share ranging from 10 to 17 per cent of annual offerings.

Clearly, Czech films enjoyed the greatest popularity with the public during the Protectorate: public demand regularly kept Czech films in Prague premiere cinemas two to three times longer than German films. German films were by no means the subject of any boycott, though one indication for which is the steep rise in audience attendance numbers against the background of the domination of German films in the Protectorate market. But it was rare for German films to be as popular with cinema audiences as their Czech counterparts – with the exception, it would seem, of Willy Forst's *Operetta* (*Operette*, 1940), the 'Austrian' musical 'retro' film with its multiple star cast, and Ufa's spectacular German colour film, *Münchhausen* (1943), fourth in the series.

The decline in film commerce was accompanied by a reduction in the number of operations doing business in the sector. In the 1930s, approximately 40 film distributors rented out films in Czechoslovakia. There were still 20 such operations active in 1939; however, with the concentration took place within the film commerce sector, by 1943 there were only 7 (9 in 1944).[33] A considerable change in the legal status of such operations also played a role. Film commerce had always been 'free', but from 1941 one required permission from the ČMFÚ to engage in it.

At the start of the Protectorate, there were four newsreels in the Czech Lands – the domestically produced *Aktualita* in two editions, Ufa's *Auslandstonwoche* (Foreign Weekly Newsreel ATW, in Czech and German versions) and two American productions, *Fox* (Czech) and *Paramount* (Czech and German). Production of the American newsreels was stopped in 1939, so for the remaining period only the *Aktualita* and Ufa newsreels were shown in cinema theatres in Protectorate territory: both completely in the service of German war propaganda.

For the period of 1 year, beginning in late July of 1937, the original Czechoslovakian newsreel *Aktualita*, issued by the company of the same name (in which the state had a partial interest), was issued in a German version as well, targeting the German minority in Czechoslovakia. In August of 1938, the German edition was cancelled due to lack of interest on the part of Sudeten German cinemas – or to be more precise, it was replaced by a second Czech version (B).[34] *Aktualita* continued to operate after the Protectorate began – with one of the company's co-founders, Karel Pečený, as its head. In February 1942, *Aktualita* received a new owner: the *Deutsche Wochenschau GmbH*, responsible within the system of the German film industry for film news reporting within the Reich and the newly acquired territories. *Aktualita* continued to bring out A and B versions, with the new addition of German subtitles. A newsreel consisted of six to seven items, more than half of which were taken over from the ATW or German Weekly Newsreel (*Deutsche Wochenschau*) – generally with a week's delay. The final two items were always connected with the situation on the front.[35] Showing them was mandatory in cinemas and there were even controls set up to ensure that audience admission genuinely took place prior to the newsreel screening rather than just before the main feature. The period of their circulation was also gradually decreased from 28 to 16 weeks in 1940 and then to 10 weeks in 1941, for reasons of relevancy. In view of the fact that 55 copies of *Aktualita* were produced in contrast to only 16 copies the *Deutsche Wochenschau GmbH* made in the final period of the Protectorate, it is clear that *Aktualita* was competently fulfilling the propaganda aims of the German occupying powers. The *Aktualita* crew also received certain special assignments – for example, recording Joseph Goebbels' 3-day visit to Prague in November 1940; portraying the destroyed town of Lidice in the post-Heydrich era; and making propaganda film about Terezín.[36]

Cinemas were fairly evenly distributed around Bohemia and Moravia (in contrast to a much lower density in Slovakia, let alone Ruthenia). With the severance of the Sudetenland under the Munich Agreement, the number of cinemas on the territory of the Republic had fallen from 1850 to 1279, and the dissolution of the Republic saw the further loss of the cinemas in Slovakia and (Hungarian-occupied) Ruthenia. When the Protectorate was formed there were a total of 1115 cinemas in the Bohemian Lands. While the number of cinemas in Czechoslovakia had already been essentially stagnating from 1933 to September 1938, numbers in the territory of the Protectorate actually rose by almost 12 per cent, during the period of 1939–44, to 1244 cinemas. As in the territory of the Third Reich, the construction of permanent cinemas for narrow film was typical for the period: 77 such cinemas were built from 1941 on. It is also interesting to note a new shift associated with the long-term decrease in the numbers of travelling cinemas, whose historical role had appeared to be drawing to a close in the 1930s. In the Protectorate period the number of travelling cinemas returned to the levels of the first half of the 1930s, although their economic significance was negligible on the whole, and their cultural significance was of secondary importance.[37]

Legal conditions for operating cinemas were fundamentally changed. The license system that dated back to 1 January 1913 was eliminated as of 31 July 1941 and replaced at first with the requirement of ČMFÚ membership and then, as of 30 July 1943, with the introduction of cinema concessions, this time tied to professional eligibility as determined by the ČMFÚ, and not by Ministry of the Interior as it had been prior to 1941. So, paradoxically, it was under the Protectorate – although under distorted circumstances – that film-makers finally got what they had been striving for since the early years of the century's second decade. In the early days of occupation, Aryanisation had a marked effect on the structure of cinema ownership.[38] Another fundamental transformation of the structure of cinema operators took place when activities of the Sokol gymnastic organisation, the most significant operator, accounting for more than half of cinemas, were halted in the spring of 1941.[39] In 1942, the Bohemian–Moravian Cinematographic Company (*Českomoravská kinematografická společnost*) was established in order to operate the Sokol cinemas (and those of the Legionnaires), under German administration and management. A similar fate caught up with the Orel cinemas, after the Catholic gymnastic organisation's activities were stopped in 1942: its cinemas were thenceforth administered by a special 'trustee' (*Treuhänder des beschlagnahmten Orel-Vermögens*).

Cinema attendance rates during the Protectorate show a continual increase – over 127 million viewers for 1944 – an incredible 132 per cent increase compared with 1939. No single factor was responsible for this abrupt rise. Most European countries saw steep increases in attendance during the war years. In addition, this increase is a sign that Czech society accepted cinema as an autonomous cultural phenomenon and turned to it at a time of upheaval in cultural life with corresponding interest. It is quite clear that a significant role was played by the maintenance and even improved quality of Czech production, which enjoyed truly exceptional popularity. Cinema's position was also strengthened by the gradual reduction in other types of entertainment available, culminating in the closure of theatres in 1944.

According to contemporary witnesses, in late 1939 a major discussion took place at the Prague's cultural centre *Mánes* in which several dozen writers, film-makers and actors attempted to find an answer to the essential question of whether to attempt to keep maintaining and further developing Czech cinema amidst the restrictions and lack of freedom, or to stop working in protest at the situation and wait for the post-war period. The assembly came to the conclusion (influenced by the remarks of Vladislav Vančura, among others) that it was crucial to preserve every opportunity of contact between artists and the public. Three basic principles for Protectorate film-making were formulated at the meeting: films (particularly those with contemporary subject matter) must not come across as collaborationist; they should foster a mood of resistance in the Czech population (specifically, by strengthening national feeling through references to cultural and historical tradition); and the ultimate end should be an overall improvement in the quality of domestic production.[40] In the field of the fiction film, film-makers in the main managed to keep these resolutions; the area of news and documentary films, however, was a more problematic one.

The attempt to stiffen resistance in the public by accentuating national cultural and historical tradition was typical of film-making in the years of the Protectorate, and the 1939–41 period in particular. Films based on the works of a whole raft of classic Czech writers were produced, while Czech national music and the local musical tradition in general were also much in the foreground. Films of this kind could be relied on to resonate with the public, without giving the censors any grounds for objection. František Čáp's scrupulous adaptation of the Božena Němcová novel *Babička* (Grandmother, 1940), culminating in the 'national oath' of loyalty to the Czech land, and Vladimír Slavínský's film *That Was a Czech Musician* (*To byl český muzikant*, 1940) about bandleader František Kmoch, the author of a long series of popularised songs, were both cited in a Gestapo report on Czech cultural efforts in 1940 as examples of films that had inspired spontaneous national demonstrations in cinemas.[41]

Along with the films taking up the symbolic material of national themes, of course, production of films that were purely entertaining and frequently not of the best quality continued unabated in the early years of the Protectorate. But shrinking opportunities for domestic film production stimulated increased interest in the quality of Czech cinema in both producers and state authorities, who hoped to demonstrate Czech cultural maturity, even in this young, modern medium. Urgency born of external pressure led essentially to a 'natural' selection of artists according to their talent or solid technical mastery. On the creative side, the dominating personalities among directors in Czech Protectorate cinema were primarily Otakar Vávra and Martin Frič, František Čáp for the youngest generation. The attention of film circles and state authorities was also concentrated on attention to the literary groundwork of a film, resulting in the increasing role of film dramaturgy. In 1940, initiated by the Minister of Trade, the Council of Film Lectors (*Sbor filmových lektorů*) was established to assess screenplays and original material for films, with some of the leading Czech writers as members.[42] In 1940 and 1941, as a flamboyant manifestation of Czech cinema culture, the first screenings of the year's new Czech films were held at an event held in Zlín funded by the Ministry of Trade called the 'Film Harvest' (*Filmové žně*). (Preparations for the next year were thwarted by the Germans.)

Cinema in 'independent' Slovakia (1938–44/45)

Despite the exceptional circumstances and repressive pressure, the Czech film industry demonstrated a marked ability to survive and a clear stability that were the products of its sophistication, its popularity with Czech audiences and its low level of economic dependence on exports. Paradoxically, not even as shocking an experience as the dissolution of the state, which had a severe impact on many sectors, had a very great immediate impact on the film sector. In the interwar years, from the internal perspective, Czechoslovak cinema and Czech cinema were one and the same: all production capacity was in Bohemia and Moravia; Prague, Brno and Zlín had become the major film centres. Regular production did not develop in Slovakia until the late 1930s; only one-off, occasional activity went on there. In the same period, attempts to build up the regional film distributing operations tended to be of short duration, due to the sparse nature of the cinema network. After the establishment of the independent Slovakian state, the Slovakian government decided to address this situation. Act No. 14 of 18 January 1940 established that 'a company to be appointed by the Ministry of the Economy shall attend to domestic film production, building up of cinemas, and the import, export and commerce in films in the territory of the Republic of Slovakia'.[43] The Ministry appointed the company Nástup, the establishment of which the government itself had arranged in the previous months. Nástup was a limited share company, with 51 per cent state participation. The act guaranteed this company a monopoly position in the area of film commerce, import and export. Nástup took over (with German assistance[44]) production of the newsreel of the same name, *Nástup*, which had been produced since November 1938. In addition to film news reporting, it engaged to a limited extent in the production of documentary films.

The establishment of an independent Slovakian state also brought a change in the structure of the owners and operators of cinemas with regard to nation of origin. By law, only Slovakian citizens could apply for a cinema-operating license. As a result, corporations based in Prague and Brno lost their cinemas, as did Jewish operators, whose enterprises were swallowed up by the fascist 'Hlinkova garda'. By 1945, that organisation owned 131 of a total of 254 cinemas.[45]

Slovakian cinema, forming rather belatedly and, to some extent, at the state's behest, did not have adequate technical foundations for film production and was also confronted with serious deficits of personnel. Both of these factors were remembered when plans for the post-war organisation of the sector were made illegally by Czech and Slovak film workers working together. Their views were influenced by recent experience with the exceptional significance of culture in times of oppression. Film professionals from a range of political persuasions made plans for the nationalisation of the sector from around 1941, in the conviction that as cinema was, in the first rank, a cultural phenomenon the state ought to take over its care. State officials came to share the opinion that the role of the state in cinema should be strengthened, as evidenced by the draft for a directive on the nationalisation of cinemas drawn up by the government-in-exile in London.[46] Cinema was ultimately nationalised as a whole, by Decree of the President of the Republic No. 50/45 of 11 August 1945, the first sector of the national economy in the liberated Republic of Czechoslovakia to be so.

Notes

1. N. M. Wingfield, 'When Film Became National: "Talkies" and the Anti-German Demonstrations of 1930 in Prague', *Austrian History Yearbook*, 29:1 (1998), pp. 113–38; D. Moravcová, *Československo, Německo a evropská hnutí 1929–1932* (Praha: Institut pro středoevropskou kulturu a politiku, 2001), pp. 198–216.
2. P. Szczepanik, 'Poněmčený Hollywood v Praze: Recepce "německých verzí" a popularita zahraničních filmů v pražských kinech počátkem 30. let', *Iluminace*, 18:1 (2006), pp. 59–84.
3. The one-off fee for use of patent infringing equipment ranged from 4000 to 9000 crowns depending on the size of the cinema.
4. For details of the quota system, see G. Heiss and I. Klimeš, 'Kulturindustrie und Politik: Die Filmwirtschaft der Tschechoslowakei und Österreichs in der politischen Krise der dreißiger Jahre', in G. Heiss and I. Klimeš (eds), *Obrazy času: Český a rakouský film 30. let/Bilder der Zeit: Tschechischer und österreichischer Film der 30er Jahre* (Praha – Brno: NFA – OSI Brno, 2003), pp. 408–10, 457.
5. I. Klimeš, 'Stát a filmová výroba ve dvacátých letech', *Iluminace*, 9:4 (1997), pp. 141–9; 'Osnova zákona k podpoře domácí filmové výroby', *Iluminace*, 9:4 (1997), pp. 161–75.
6. The issue is not that simple of course. Even imports of German films registered a huge drop (from 171 films in 1931–84 in 1932). This was a reflection of the Ministry of Trade's drastic overall restriction of imports in 1932 – imports overall were down by a factor of 56 per cent relative to 1931.
7. Baarová eventually left Prague for Berlin. She starred in several German productions but was forced to leave the country in 1938, when Hitler ordered the break-up of her love affair with Joseph Goebbels. H. Fraenkel and R. Manvell, *Goebbels der Verführer* (München, 1960), pp. 240–8.
8. 1933: *Okénko* (*The Little Window*, dir. Vladimír Slavínský), *Její lékař* (*Her Doctor*, dir. Vladimír Slavínský), *Madla z cihelny* (*Madla from the Brickworks*, dir. Vladimír Slavínský); 1934: *Zlatá Kateřina* (*Golden Catherine*, dir. Vladimír Slavínský), *Dokud máš maminku* (*While You Have a Mother*, dir. Jan Sviták), *Grandhotel Nevada*

(*Grandhotel Nevada*, dir. Jan Sviták); 1935: *Pan otec Karafiát* (*Father Karafiát*, dir. Jan Sviták); 1936: *Komediantská princezna* (*The Comedian's Princess*, dir. Miroslav Cikán), *Švadlenka* (*The Seamstress*, dir. Martin Frič); 1937: *Advokátka Věra* (*Lawyer Věra*, dir. Martin Frič), *Lidé na kře* (*People on the Iceberg*, dir. Martin Frič); 1938: *Škola základ života* (*School Is the Foundation of Life*, dir. Martin Frič); 1939: *Jiný vzduch* (*Changing Wind*, dir. Martin Frič), *Tulák Macoun* (*Macoun the Tramp*, dir. Ladislav Brom); 1940: *Katakomby* (*The Catacombs*, dir. Martin Frič). But no multiple language version was produced for any of these films.

9. Archives of the Ministry of Foreign Affairs, III. section 1918–39, box 400, vol. Osvěta, no. 13.602/1934; Foreign ministry to interior ministry, Prague, 27 January 1934.
10. In the years of the quota system, that is 1932–34, new German films accounted for 37.9 per cent of total film premieres (the formerly dominant United States accounted in the same period for only 15.5 per cent), from 1935–37 it was 24.3 per cent (42.3 per cent for American films). Nevertheless, the principle of the approval procedures for film imports introduced in Czechoslovakia in 1931 was retained and was reflected in the decrease of the total volume of newly released films – in the final years of the 1920s there were 500–600 new films annually, from 1932 to 1934 the state cut that number to 219, 215 and 216, respectively. From 1935 to 1937, the average number of new films reached 328. According to the experts of the time, the capacity of the Czechoslovak cinema network (with, on the average, 1925 cinemas in the years 1931–37) amounted in fact to around 300 new films.
11. Heiss and Klimeš (2003), pp. 440–52, 475–83. For Czech and German-language versions of the agreement, see *Národní filmový archiv* (National Film Archive, NFA), file 'Kartel filmových dovozců'.
12. The Reichsfilmkammer represented Germany; representatives of the three major professional associations (Film Industry and Commerce Union of Czechoslovakia, Film Production Unions in Czechoslovakia and Central Union of Cinematographers in Czechoslovakia) signed for Czechoslovakia. The Czechoslovak Ministry of Foreign Affairs viewed activities of this sort with considerable disquiet, as they were not subject to any state controls although there could be no doubt about their foreign policy implications. There was no appropriate counterpart to the Reichsfilmkammer either in the Czechoslovak film industry or in the structures of the state administration, which both complicated negotiations for the agreement and somewhat reduced its significance. Nazi Germany was very interested in seeing other countries establish film chambers, viewing such chambers as an institutional instrument for furthering German influence. That is why the Germany was so involved in the activities of the International Film Chamber.
13. Czech version of the agreement: J. Havelka, *Čs. filmové hospodářství IV: Rok 1937* (Praha: Nakladatelství Knihovny Filmového kurýru, 1938), pp. 15–16; German version of the agreement: 'Filmabkommen bereits in Kraft: Der offizielle Wortlaut der deutsch-čsl. Filmvereinbarungen', *Filmwoche* [Aussig], 17:10 (1937), p. 1.
14. I. Klimeš, 'Multiple-language versions of Czech films and the film industry in Czechoslovakia in the 1930s', *Cinema & Cie*, 4 (Spring 2004), pp. 89–101.
15. The conclusion of bilateral film agreements became practically standard practice in the second half of the 1930s. Germany was at the forefront of this, trying to regain the ground in the European markets that it had lost following the Nazis' accession to power. Czechoslovakia entered such an agreement with the United

States (in the form of an exchange of note) in June 1938. For a list of signed agreements, see Heiss and Klimeš (2003), p. 445.

16. J. Havelka, *Čs. filmové hospodářství III. Rok 1936* (Praha: Nakladatelství Knihovny Filmového kurýru, 1937), p. 19.
17. Ibid.
18. See Chapter 2.
19. The Czech delegates at this audience were Ernst Hollmann, chairman of the Svaz německých kin v ČSR (Union of German Cinemas in Czechoslovakia), and the chairman of the Central Union of Cinematographers, Vladimír Wokoun, who later represented Czechoslovakia at the International Film Chamber.
20. See the introductory chapter by Welch & Vande Winkel.
21. J. Schmitt, 'Filmová situace optimisticky', *Přítomnost*, 12:24 (1935), p. 377.
22. A. Loacker and M. Prucha (eds), *Unerwünschtes Kino: Der deutschsprachige Emigrantenfilm 1934–1937* (Wien: Filmarchiv Austria, 2000).
23. Hitler initially appointed Konstantin von Neurath. Von Neurath was gradually replaced by Reinhard Heydrich. After Heydrich's assassination, Colonel Kurt Daluege became Reich Protector.
24. J. Havelka, *Filmové hospodářství V: 1938* (Praha: Nakladatelství Knihovny Filmového kurýru, 1939), p. 41.
25. I. Klimeš, 'Die "Entjudung" der tschechischen Filmindustrie', in Loacker and Prucha (2000), pp. 77–84.
26. J. Doležal, *Česká kultura za protektorátu: Školství, písemnictví, kinematografie* (Praha: NFA, 1996); T. Fauth, *Deutsche Kulturpolitik im Protektorat Böhmen und Mähren 1939 bis 1941* (Göttingen: V&R unipress, 2004).
27. This regulation brought the Office of the Reich Protector into conflict with the Berlin leadership of the *Nationalsozialische Deutsche Arbeiterpartei* (NSDAP), which immediately protested against having a Czech head up the ČMFÚ. But the Office of the Reich Protector considered it important that the many unpopular measures that the ČMFÚ was to introduce be brought in under Czech auspices. See the correspondence between the propaganda office, *Reichspropagandaleitung*, of the NSDAP and the Office of the Reich Protector [Amt des Reichsprotektors] of 1941, Bundesarchiv (BA), NS/18 (Reichspropagandaleitung der NSDAP), vol. 361.
28. J. Hora, *Filmové právo* (Praha: Právnické knihkupectví a nakladatelství V. Linhart, 1937); K. Knap, *Přehled práva filmového* ([Praha]: Knihovna Filmového kurýru, 1945). The official press organ of the ČMFÚ was the bilingual *Věstník Českomoravského filmového ústředí/Mitteilungen böhmisch-mährischen Filmzentrale* (1941–45).
29. P. Bednařík, *Arizace české kinematografie* (Praha: Karolinum, 2003).
30. T. Dvořáková, 'Německá dohoda o budoucnosti kinematografie protektorátu', *Iluminace* 14:4 (2002), pp. 101–5.
31. T. Dvořáková, 'Prag-Film (1941–1945): V průniku protektorátní a říšské kinematografie', MA thesis, Dept. of film studies, Faculty of Arts and Philosophy, Charles University in Prague, Praha, 2002; Fauth (2004), pp. 21–2.
32. These propaganda films were shown in selected cinemas that only Wehrmacht and NSDAP members could attend.
33. J. Havelka, *Filmové hospodářství v českých zemích a na Slovensku 1939 až 1945* (Praha: Čs. filmové nakladatelství, 1946), p. 38.
34. I. Klimeš and P. Zeman, 'Aktualita 1937–1938: Československý zvukový týdeník/Tschechoslowakische Tonbildschau/Slovenský zvukový týždenník', *Cinema & Cie* [Bologna], No. 4 (Spring 2005), pp. 62–70.

35. K. Margry, 'Newsreels in Nazi-Occupied Czechoslovakia: Karel Peceny and his Newsreel Company Aktualita', *Historical Journal of Film, Radio and Television*, 24:1 (2004), pp. 69–117.
36. K. Margry, 'Theresienstadt (1944–45): the Nazi propaganda film depicting the concentration camp as paradise', *Historical Journal of Film, Radio and Television*, 12:2 (1992), pp. 145–62.
37. L. Pištora, 'Filmoví návštěvníci a kina na území České republiky: Od vzniku filmu do roku 1945', *Iluminace*, 8:4 (1996), pp. 35–60.
38. T. Dvořáková, 'Funkce treuhändera v protektorátním filmovnictví', *Iluminace*, 16:1 (2004), pp. 11113; 'Práva a povinnosti treuhändera', ibid., pp. 115–25.
39. There were 692 Sokol cinemas as of 1 January 1945. The cinemas continued to operate, but revenues flowed into the account of the 'Finance Office' (Vermögensamt). Havelka (1946), p. 51.
40. E. Klos, *Dramaturgie je když... Filmový průvodce pro začátečníky i pokročilé* (Praha: ČSFÚ, 1987), pp. 41–2.
41. F. Springer, 'Důvěrná zpráva gestapa o českém kulturním úsilí v roce 1940', *Svobodný zítřek*, 2:3 (1946), p. 8.
42. I. Klimeš, 'Stát a filmová kultura', *Iluminace*, 11:2 (1999), pp. 125–36.
43. V. Macek and J. Paštéková, *Dejiny slovenskej kinematografie* (Martin: Osveta, 1997), p. 83.
44. See Chapter 18.
45. Ibid., pp. 74–6.
46. K. Jech and K. Kaplan, *Dekrety prezidenta republiky 1940–1945: Dokumenty I* (Brno: ÚSD AV ČR in Doplněk, 1995), pp. 390–2f.

9

The Attempted Nazification of French Cinema, 1934–44

Brett Bowles

The decade between the formation of the Popular Front in February 1934 and the liberation of Paris in August 1944 was among the most turbulent in French history.[1] Plagued by persistent economic hardships linked to the Great Depression and increasingly bitter ideological divisions, France struggled to maintain its international status. The economic vitality, growing cultural prowess, and socio-political unity of authoritarian regimes in Germany, Italy, and the Soviet Union seemed to highlight French cultural decadence and the deficiencies of liberal democracy vis-à-vis Fascism and Communism. France's shocking defeat in the Second World War and the ensuing German occupation devastated an already weakened nation economically and psychologically.

Cinema played a crucial role in shaping Franco-German relations throughout the 1930s and the Occupation, drawing an annual total of between 220 and 300 million French spectators.[2] Historiographically speaking, the study of film (both fiction and documentary) as a tool of commerce, cultural influence, and ideology not only provides a basis for evaluating the Nazis' success in subjugating a hereditary rival; it also offers fresh insight into the dynamics of French national identity during a seminal period whose impact is still felt today. In general terms, the French attitude towards German cinema can best be characterised as repulsion-attraction. While French cinema professionals envied the Reich's enormous investment of material resources in the industry, admired the high technical polish of its productions, and feared the systematised efficiency of its film production and distribution, they deplored tight state controls (especially censorship) restricting freedom of expression and the appropriation of art as a tool of National-Socialist ideology. During the 1930s, German cinema served as a foil against which the French industry defined itself in order to assert its own distinct national character predicated on small-scale craft skills, high quality, creative improvisation, and independence from governmental interference. Under the Occupation the Nazis' efforts to control French cinema intensified, but achieved only mixed results commercially and ideologically. In fact, German-inspired institutional support structures and the psychological tensions of the so-called 'dark years' added new aesthetic depth to French cinema and cured the industry of long-standing organisational flaws.

Disgusted envy: French views of Nazi cinema in the 1930s

By the time Hitler took power in January 1933, French cinema was just beginning to suffer the effects of the Great Depression, which accelerated a long-term economic decline initiated by the cataclysm of the First World War. The loss of over 2 million men from the work force, combined with systemic under-mechanisation and a collective cult of mourning that stifled adaptation to changing needs, undermined French industry throughout the 1920s and the 1930s. Output in many sectors, including cinema, dropped below pre-war levels. Until 1918, France produced approximately 80 per cent of all feature films in circulation worldwide. However, in the 1920s its international market share declined sharply under competition from American and German studios whose efficiency in production and distribution was far superior to the French model of small-scale, improvisational film-making.

France also lagged behind technologically for several years after the arrival of sound cinema. Thanks to securing the first patents on sound recording and reproduction equipment, a trio of American and German companies (Western Electric, RCA, and Tobis Klangfilm) exercised a virtual monopoly over the world market. By early 1930, Tobis had already established a sound studio in Epinay just outside Paris and put René Clair under contract for *Under the Roofs of Paris* (*Sous les toits de Paris*, 1930) and *Give Us Liberty* (*A nous la liberté*, 1931). Shortly thereafter Paramount began churning out multiple-language cinematic adaptations of popular plays at its Joinville studio complex. Yet many French critics and directors resisted the new medium for fear that it would transform the 'seventh art' into vulgar 'canned theatre'.[3] This initial delay cost French cinema dearly by reducing its visibility in the world market and making it dependent on imported films and equipment to satisfy growing demand for talkies. From 1929 until 1932, a total of 400 German feature films were shown in France, but only 62 French pictures were distributed in Germany. The trend continued throughout the decade, with foreign productions representing up to 75 per cent of all feature films shown annually in France. The United States led the way with an average market share of 50 per cent, while Germany consistently placed second at around 10 per cent.

French cinema officials deplored the disproportion, but remained powerless to resist because of systemic organisational and economic deficiencies. The onset of the Great Depression sparked a wave of bankruptcies among French production companies – 58 in 1933, 88 in 1934, 55 in 1935, and 64 in 1936. Among those ruined were the country's two largest firms: Gaumont, which closed its doors in July 1934, and Pathé, which succumbed in February 1936, bought out by Kodak. During the same period the French film industry operated at an enormous deficit, losing between 50 and 90 million francs annually. To make matters worse, cinema was the most heavily taxed of all France's entertainment industries. In 1936, state deductions alone reached 21 per cent, compared to 15 per cent for music halls and 11 per cent for cabarets. With the additional weight of local fiscal deductions, nearly half of all gross box-office receipts were consumed by taxes which grew heavier as economic conditions worsened.

The financial crisis exposed the profession's other congenital handicaps, the most pernicious of which was an almost total absence of institutional structure and state support. Between 1932 and 1938 seven different initiatives to remedy the situation fell through, undermined by ongoing political divisions and rapid turnover of governments. A special governmental commission formed in 1934 following Gaumont's demise estimated that restructuring and refinancing the industry would require a state investment of 200 million francs, an exorbitant figure rejected by a succession of finance ministers. Moreover, the sharing of administrative responsibility for cinema among three different ministries (Education, Foreign Affairs, and Commerce) facilitated fraud among producers, distributors, and theatre owners. The bankruptcy of Pathé in 1936 was the direct result of double-dealing by its director Bernard Natan, whose fall also brought down 35 other companies. Such scandals undermined investors' confidence, causing a marked dispersion and decline in finance capital. Between 1935 and 1937 the number of production companies rose from 158 to 170 while their total net worth fell from 17 million to 12 million francs. Of the 202 production firms registered in 1937, 80 per cent had a total capital value of less than 50 000 francs. Because feature films typically required an initial investment of 2 million francs, most French producers faced ruin each time they undertook a new project.[4]

While French cinema foundered, German film-making was a model of discipline and efficiency under the Nazis, who immediately moved to exploit their weaker neighbour. Ufa and Tobis, both placed under tight state control by Goebbels in 1933 and generously financed by the Film Credit Bank,[5] realised an economy of scale unmatched in France. Shortly thereafter the Reich also reorganised the Alliance Cinématographique Européenne (ACE), a Paris-based subsidiary of Ufa originally founded in 1926. In its original incarnation, ACE Paris had been a relatively minor player in French cinema, serving primarily as an export conduit for Ufa movies. However, after receiving a huge injection of fresh capital and being handed over to Alfred Greven, an ambitious producer and personal friend of Göring's, the firm expanded rapidly by distributing French-made films, investing in several major Parisian studios, and purchasing theatres in key metropolitan areas throughout the country. As for Tobis, it continued to operate the

Epinay studio complex in suburban Paris. By the end of 1934, the three German juggernauts provided an estimated 15 per cent of the French film industry's total finance capital, a figure that held steady until 1938.

Though the Nazis had the means to saturate the French market with dubbed films rented at fees substantially lower than those charged by domestic distributors, there was little hope of competing with American imports. Cultural taste was also a dissuading factor. During the Weimar years, French audiences had shown little enthusiasm for Expressionism, the horror genre, and the *Strassefilm*, preferring dialogue-rich melodramas and comedies derived from popular theatre and music hall performance, as in René Clair's hits *The Million* (*Le Million*, 1931) and *Bastille Day* (*Quatorze Juillet*, 1932), both produced and distributed by Tobis. Goebbels abandoned the high-volume 'dumping' practiced by Ufa and Tobis during the first years of the sound era in favour of a selective film export policy sensitive to differences in national style. Between 1933 and 1938, Germany sent an average of 35 feature films annually across the Rhine packaged with a roughly equal number of *Kulturfilme*. In both genres the strategy was to choose technically polished, ideologically non-threatening productions focusing on German cultural heritage, achievements in the fields of science, technology and art, social reforms promoting health and hygiene, and the high quality of life enjoyed by workers. While these themes often implicitly promoted National-Socialism, direct references to the regime and its leaders were kept to a minimum. Whenever possible, Nazi exports stressed commonalities with French culture such as the organic link between national identity and rural patrimony. *Heimat* films exemplified by *The Prodigal Son* (*Der verlorene Sohn*, 1934), *The Lost Valley* (*Das verlorene Tal*, 1934), and *The Mountain Call* (*Der Berg Ruft*, 1938) received special export priority because their portrayal of return to the earth as an antidote to the ills of urban modernity echoed Marcel Pagnol's hit ethnographic melodramas *Heartbeat* (*Angèle*, 1934) and *Harvest* (*Regain*, 1937).

By projecting the appearance of a peaceful, modern, and progressive nation firmly rooted in tradition, Goebbels hoped to counteract negative media coverage of the Nazis' expansionist, increasingly aggressive agenda and to quell residual anti-German sentiments from the First World War. Transparent propaganda such as *Hitler Youth Quex* (*Hitlerjunge Quex*, 1933), Riefenstahl's *Day of Freedom: Our Armed Forces* (*Tag der Freiheit: unsere Wehrmacht*, 1935), and *The Eternal Forest* (*Ewiger Wald*, 1936) were scrupulously withheld from the French market. However, the caution that initially characterised Nazi film export policy dissipated progressively as the regime consolidated its power. The most notable example is Riefenstahl's lyrical tour-de-force *Triumph of the Will* (*Triumph des Willens*, 1935), which was not distributed internationally for more than 2 years after its domestic premiere in March 1935. Its first foreign screening in July 1937 at the Paris World's Fair sparked widespread Communist and Socialist protests, but the film enthralled critics of virtually all political colours and won the gold medal for best documentary. Despite ongoing calls to ban Riefenstahl's work in France, a specially edited cut of *Olympiad* (1938) arrived the following summer thanks to the intervention of the *Comité France-Allemagne*, a privately funded, pro-fascist organism of cultural exchange headed by Fernand de Brinon and Otto Abetz.[6]

Despite solid distribution and marketing, dubbed and subtitled German productions drew a relatively limited audience and only minimal profit in France. Ufa and Tobis thus chose to focus on convincing French personnel to work on French-language films shot in Berlin. In late 1933, Goebbels negotiated an exchange agreement which allowed each country to make and export up to 20 movies annually in the other's language. The accord, which guaranteed certain financial advantages including special tax rates, constituted a one-sided victory for the Nazis since the French were unable to invest scarce resources in pictures intended solely for the German market. Lured by cutting-edge technology, high salaries, unmatched production efficiency, and comfortable working conditions, a growing stream of French talent flowed across the Rhine as the financial crisis in Paris deepened. In addition to signing respected directors such as Jacques Feyder, Jean Grémillon, Yves Mirande, Jacques de Baroncelli, and Marc Allégret, the Nazis attracted an even more impressive pool of stars featuring Jean Gabin, Pierre Blanchar, Danielle Darrieux, Arletty, Charles Vanel, Jules Berry, Michèle Morgan, Mireille Balin, Raimu, and Michel Simon.

In all, Ufa and Tobis made a total of 64 French-language films between 1933 and 1938. At first most were slightly modified versions of German-language pictures shot simultaneously, but towards the end of the decade original productions came to dominate.[7] The latter were especially popular with French spectators, generating the top-15 hits *Carnival in Flanders* (*La Kermesse héroïque*, 1935), *Baccarat* (*Baccara*, 1936), *Loverboy* (*Gueule d'amour*, 1937), *Heart of Paris* (*Gribouille*, 1937), and *Coral Reef* (*Le Récif de corail*, 1938).[8] That success hinged in large part on ACE Paris' deft marketing strategies which vigilantly depublicised the Nazi money at work behind the scenes. For French intellectuals committed to stopping the spread of fascism and preventing the economic colonisation of their country, the situation was nothing short of treasonous. In June 1938, Henri Jeanson openly denounced the Ufa-produced picture *Strange Mr. Victor* (*L'Etrange Monsieur Victor*) as a betrayal of French national interests: 'Like so many other so-called 'French' films today, Jean Grémillon's latest work allows Germany to drain from France the foreign currency required to fuel intensive production in its war factories.'[9] His assessment was alarmist but essentially accurate. Between January 1937 and August 1938, German films earned 33 million francs in France, while French films grossed only 7 million francs in the Reich.

The depth of France's cinematic inferiority complex vis-à-vis Germany is perhaps best dramatised in *The Dark Side of German Cinema* (*Les Dessous du cinéma allemand*, 1934), a pamphlet secretly financed by the French Army's counter-intelligence service and published by Marcel Colin-Reval, editor-in-chief of the corporate journal *La Cinématographie française*. Its stated goal was to 'unmask the workings of Hitler's propaganda in France' by combining the prose of Charles-Robert Dumas, author of the popular Captain Benoît spy novel series, with a series of cartoons by political caricaturist Ralph Soupault. The cover drawing shows Hitler bombarding France with film canisters while factory chimneys belch smoke in the background. A second, disturbingly prophetic image depicts France lulled into complacency by Nazi propaganda as storm troopers race towards Paris in an all-out *Blitzkrieg*. For all its sensationalism, the pamphlet had little effect. French spectators continued to flock to German-financed films as government officials remained deadlocked on how to reform their industry.

Even the Popular Front government did not effectively address the issue. Between December 1936 and April 1937, a multi-party commission of National Assembly deputies and senators conducted an inquiry emphasising yet again the urgent need for reform. In 1938, Minister of Education Jean Zay finally created a special emergency panel to draft a national cinema statute, but it did not take effect until March 1939, only months before the outbreak of war and too late to do any good.[10] French cinema managed to remain solvent only thanks to a massive injection of capital by Lloyd's of London, which financed 75 per cent of all French production during the 1937–38 season. Even the Popular Front's most loyal supporters showed frustration at its failure to reorganise French cinema. In December 1937, Jean Renoir, whose *The Great Illusion* (*La Grande Illusion*, 1937) had just been banned in Germany and Italy, published an acerbic open letter which read in part:

> If dictatorships show no compunction about banning films, at least in exchange they have the clarity of vision to support national film production financially. I do not know what role our government will play in the future, but I believe that its most crucial duty is to show confidence in our cultural genius and to resuscitate a great industry, a source of national wealth that bad French capitalists are letting die.[11]

The impotence of French cinema fuelled not only recriminations against the government, but xenophobia and anti-Semitism as well. During the 1920s and the early 1930s, France welcomed a large number of film professionals from eastern and central Europe whose talents significantly enhanced the technical quality and stylistic range of French national production.[12] Among the most influential were immigrants from Germany fleeing Nazi persecution: directors Max Ophüls, Fritz Lang, Robert Siodmak, and Anatole Litvak; cinematographer Kurt Courant; producer Erich Pommer. Yet French hospitality quickly evaporated amidst rising unemployment and financial scandals involving Alexandre Stavisky and Bernard Natan. Echoing the justifications used by Hitler in 1933 to exclude Jews and other 'undesirable' foreigners from German cinema, French commentators of all political colours demanded the 'sanitisation' of their industry as a necessary step towards recovering economic stability and national grandeur.

By mid-1934, French officials had established quotas stipulating that non-citizens could not exceed 10 per cent of the major artistic personnel or 25 per cent of the total crew on any given production. Yet appeals for more severe measures flourished, often using the explicitly racist and violent language exemplified in a May 1938 article calling for a 'new Saint Bartholomew's Day [the state-sponsored murder of several thousand French Protestants by Catholics in 1572] which this time will not be a massacre of innocents, but an act of self-defence to rid our industry of its wogs [*métèques*]'.[13] In November a French labour union conducted a census of foreigners employed in Parisian studios and, concluding that the industry was still 'overrun', called for the immediate revocation of all work visas granted during the previous 3 years, limiting foreigners to 10 per cent of the total cinema work force, and forbidding them from Gallicising their names to escape detection.[14] Following closely behind a new series of Nazi laws restricting Jewish professional opportunities, the Munich Agreement, and the *Kristallnacht* pogrom, such proposals marked the culmination of France's long-term inferiority complex vis-à-vis its powerful neighbour and set the stage for even more virulent anti-Semitism under the Occupation.

Uneasy alliance: Franco-German film policy during the Occupation, 1940–44

The defeat of 1940 was the worst catastrophe in modern French history, displacing millions from their homes, irreparably damaging the nation's honour, and confirming the sense of decadence that had plagued the country throughout the 1930s. The armistice agreement, signed in July, divided France into two primary geo-political entities: a northern 'occupied' zone administered by the German military and a southern 'free' zone governed by a newly formed French state under Marshal Philippe Pétain. By German design the Vichy regime remained strong enough to suppress internal dissent but too weak to mount a serious military threat, thereby freeing Wehrmacht forces to attack Great Britain and, beginning in June 1941, the Soviet Union. Though Vichy enjoyed substantial autonomy until late 1942, it willingly collaborated with the Reich from October 1940 onwards and progressively abandoned traditionalist, authoritarian values in favour of fascism. In addition to serving as the main foreign supplier of resources for the Nazi war machine, the French played an active role in the persecution of Jews and Communists. While conforming to this overall trend, Franco-German cinema relations reveal the tensions and conflicts that existed within the framework of state collaboration. Both sides used cinema to promote their own agendas, which often diverged during the first 2 years of the Occupation.

In August 1940, the Germans established a quasi-monopoly in the northern zone by banning all Anglo-American movies, as well as all French pictures released after 1 October 1937, and granting ACE Paris exclusive distribution rights over all films. In so doing they addressed several complementary goals: to foster admiration among French spectators for German style, technical quality, and stars; to entertain and thereby pacify a country deeply wounded by the war; to present a favourable impression of National-Socialism and German cultural achievements while demonising the Reich's enemies (especially Jews and British 'plutocrats'); finally, and perhaps most important, to frame French participation in building a 'New Europe' as an imperative of national survival.

Feature films and documentaries participated equally in the task of economic and ideological colonisation. Though most of the former were star vehicles featuring the likes of Marika Rökk, Emil Jannings, Heinrich George, Zarah Leander, and Ilse Werner, several heavily publicised historical dramas – *Robert Koch* (1939, about the Nobel Prize-winning German doctor's efforts to cure tuberculosis), Hans Steinhoff's *Uncle Krüger* (*Ohm Krüger*, 1940) an Anglophobic account of the Boer War, Veit Harlan's anti-Semitic *Jew Süss* (*Jud Süss*, 1940), and Carl Froelich's *The Heart of a Queen* (*Das Herz der Königin*, 1940) – attempted to weave Nazi values into the affective fabric of entertainment. Each new release was distributed with two mandatory 'programme complements': a short Ufa or Tobis documentary (*Kulturfilm*) and *Les Actualités Mondiales* (*World News*) a weekly French-language version of Ufa's Foreign Weekly Newsreel (*Auslandstonwoche*, ATW) made in Paris by a production team of the *Deutsche Wochenschau GmbH*. Whereas the stand-alone documentaries tended to treat ideologically anodyne topics from the fields of science and nature, the newsreels articulated overtly pro-Nazi, anti-Semitic, and Anglophobic propaganda. Irrespective of their content differences, all German films were supported by newspaper advertisements, favourable reviews in collaborationist French newspapers, mural posters whose print runs often exceeded 100 000 copies, the closely censored corporate journal *Le Film*, and a lavishly illustrated, Ufa-financed colour fanzine titled *Ciné-Mondial*.[15]

While flooding northern France with their work, the Germans began efforts to build a pan-European cinema empire capable of competing with Hollywood on the world market. Responsibility for the project fell to a new Paris-based firm called Continental Films under the direction of long-time Ufa producer Alfred Greven. Greven believed that future success hinged on combining German organisational, financial, and technical prowess with French creativity and cultural refinement, qualities which in the 1930s had maintained French cinema's international prestige despite its declining market share. Moreover, Greven was convinced that limiting France to the role of captive consumer and servile production partner would undermine the fusion of Franco-German talent and undermine Nazis' long-term cultural and economic interests.[16] On this point he disagreed with Goebbels, who favoured ruthless hegemony rather than cross-cultural cooperation.[17] In his diary the Propaganda Minister characterised his subordinate's approach as 'entirely wrong':

> It is not our task to supply the French with good pictures or to give them movies that conform to their nationalistic mentalities. If the French are satisfied with shallow, frivolous junk, we ought to make it our business to produce such cheap trash. We must proceed as the Americans do in North and South America. We must become the dominant filmmaking power on the European continent. It would be mad for us to encourage competition against ourselves. Insofar as pictures are produced in other countries, they must be only of a local character. It must be our aim to prevent as much as possible the founding of any new national film industry, if necessary by hiring stars and technicians to work in Berlin, Vienna, or Munich.[18]

In practice, Nazi film policy used a mix of draconian force and more subtle means of coercion. A series of decrees issued in October and November 1940 excluded Jews from the profession and seized their assets, which represented a substantial portion of pre-war French finance capital. The stolen money was then reinvested in new German-controlled companies with French names and administrators. Shortly after founding Continental, Greven took control of three theatre chains in the occupied zone expropriated from Jewish owners: *Paris Exploitation Cinémas, La Société des Cinémas de l'Est,* and *La Société de Gestion et d'Exploitation de Cinémas*. Together they formed a network of 70 theatres worth 1.6 million francs.[19] In addition, between August 1940 and April 1941 the Germans suspended all independent French production in the northern zone and banned imports from the south so that Greven could pressure French talent into signing with Continental. Virtually unlimited resources allowed Continental to offer unmatched salaries, comfortable working conditions, and guaranteed distribution to virtually every functioning cinema in the country. Cinema personnel unable or unwilling to escape abroad faced a difficult choice: accommodate the Germans or face unemployment during a period of increasing material hardship.

These tactics yielded mixed results. By mid-1941, Continental had hired an A-list of actors including Danielle Darrieux, Pierre Fresnay, Fernandel, Harry Baur, and Raimu. Yet Greven was less successful in attracting top directors, his entreaties having prompted Jean Renoir and René Clair to leave for the United States. Marcel Pagnol, who owned his own studios in Marseille, also refused repeated invitations to come and work in Paris. Marcel Carné signed but subsequently refused to honour his contract after discovering that Greven had lied to him about the willingness of others to join Continental. Despite his extensive pre-war experience working in Berlin, even Jean Grémillon avoided Greven, preferring to make his wartime films in the southern zone out of German reach. Tobis did eventually manage to appropriate northern-zone distribution rights for Grémillon's hit *Stormy Waters* (*Remorques*, 1941) featuring Jean Gabin and Michèle Morgan, but that was small consolation for the fact that both stars had immigrated to Hollywood.

During the first 8 months of the Occupation, French moviegoers did not respond well to German imports, which accounted for 40 (68 per cent) of the 59 new feature films released in the occupied zone.[20] Box-office receipts for the first quarter of 1941 fell 44 per cent below comparable to 1938 figures.[21] Although *Filmprüfstelle* (Censorship Office) officials found the solid performance of *Jud Süss* encouraging, response to *Les Actualités Mondiales* was tepid at best. French police surveillance revealed that Parisian spectators were openly hostile towards the newsreel. In addition to coughing, sneezing, and stamping their feet in unison to drown out the voice-over commentary, they whistled at the sight of Wehrmacht soldiers on screen and applauded images of German homes destroyed by English bombing raids. Pro-collaborationist clips, especially those featuring French leaders, drew equally negative reactions; other propagandistic documentaries did not fare much better. *Campaign in Poland* (*Feldzug in Polen*, 1940), a newsreel montage depicting the 1939 blitzkrieg through Warsaw and Danzig, evoked only 'quiet anguish and stupor'.[22] In late 1940 and early 1941, audience dissent was sufficiently widespread to necessitate projection with the lights half on, dozens of arrests, and temporary closure of theatres where repeat offences occurred. Though such measures had a preventative impact, changes to the newsreel's content proved more effective. The inclusion of reports devoted specifically to French cultural topics and the activities of the Vichy government, followed in April 1941 by the decision to allow occupied-zone distribution of films made in the south, eliminated virtually all audience dissent. The Germans subsequently adopted a more liberal approach to economic and political colonisation which depended on the participation of French partners.

In August 1940, the Vichy government's first priority was to establish its credibility with French citizens by stressing its independence vis-à-vis the Nazis and commitment to fostering national recovery through a programme of social and cultural reforms known collectively as the National Revolution. This political imperative, combined with German pressure to allow distribution of *Les Actualités Mondiales* and Ufa/Tobis fiction films in the unoccupied zone, prompted Vichy to create a department within its Ministry of Information devoted specifically to cinema and radio. Reacting to army intelligence reports that Greven had successfully purchased a theatre in Toulouse and Lyon through French intermediaries and established rental contracts with

ACE Paris, Vichy administrators cleverly blocked encroachment on their territory by bartering newsreel footage of the British attack on Mers-el-Kébir from 3 July 1940. Because the film depicted in graphic detail the sinking of the French Mediterranean fleet and death of 1300 sailors, its propaganda value for the Germans was inestimable. Using a negative print (which the *Propaganda-Abteilung Frankreich* subsequently reedited to make even more Anglophobic than the original French montage) and exclusive northern-zone distribution rights granted to ACE Paris as collateral, Vichy cinema head Jean–Louis Tixier–Vignancour and inter-zone cinema liaison officer Guy de Carmoy bought the time needed to organise film production in the south.[23]

In the 3 months between the first negotiations and the Mers-el-Kébir film's premier in late October, Tixier–Vignancour and de Carmoy founded *France-Actualités Pathé-Gaumont* (*Pathé-Gaumont French News*, FAPG), a weekly newsreel supporting Vichy's ideological agenda, as well as a bimonthly documentary series called *La France en Marche* (*France on the March*, FM). Both started in early November, thereby filling the cinema vacuum in the unoccupied zone and temporarily thwarting Greven's plans to expand southwards. Distributed only in the southern zone and in French North Africa, Vichy filmed news did not compete directly with *Les Actualités Mondiales*, but their content contrasted sharply. Whereas the *Actualités Mondiales* (AM) engaged in aggressive promotion of Franco-German collaboration and denunciation of the Reich's adversaries, FAPG and FM crafted an integrationist discourse of renewal, strength, and solidarity based on the National Revolution, the cult of personality surrounding Pétain, the activities of the French Armistice Army, and the continuing prosperity of France's colonial empire. Moreover, FAPG contained virtually no pro-German, anti-Semitic, or anti-British clips and was not required viewing in unoccupied-zone theatres. During the first year of the Occupation these differences invited moviegoers to believe in the myth of a pro-Resistance, anti-German Vichy which was gathering strength to re-enter the war behind the smokescreen of state collaboration.[24]

While using newsreels to rally support for its tendentious politics, Vichy prioritised feature film-making as a tool of economic recovery and buoying public morale. For the first time in the nation's history, a French government directly subsidised cinema and provided the industry with a coherent organisational infrastructure. The centrepiece was the *Comité d'Organisation de l'Industrie Cinématographique* (COIC), an umbrella organism founded in December 1940 with sub-committees devoted to production, distribution, technological support, artistic development, and the collection of statistics. Vichy also set up a national film censorship board composed of representatives from various governmental ministries. Efficiency and high quality were essential because of the government's precarious financial situation, which worsened over time as a result of the Germans' pillage of resources and the precipitous devaluation of the franc. French film-makers in the south faced an increasingly severe shortage of equipment and basic raw materials, particularly development chemicals, film stock, and printing machines. Most important, only two sites in the unoccupied zone featured studios and laboratory facilities: Marcel Pagnol's small complex in Marseille and La Victorine in Nice. Though Vichy never fully resolved the systemic deficiencies that had plagued French cinema throughout the inter-war years and never amortised its investment, it did succeed in reviving film production. By August 1941 the situation was sufficiently stable to found a national cinema school in Nice known as the *Centre Artistique et Technique des Jeunes du Cinéma* (CATJC).

Paradoxically, the mutual suspicion that characterised Franco-German film relations at the outset of the Occupation inaugurated a process of uneasy accommodation in which each side pursued its own distinct interests. Two exchange agreements, the first governing newsreel footage and the second inter-zone feature film distribution, were crucial. Beginning in November 1940, the Germans began integrating clips from FAPG (which were often edited to remove overly nationalistic content) into the their own newsreel (*Actualités Mondiales*) as a way of managing spectator dissent. For its part Vichy welcomed the opportunity, limited though it was, to extend its message to the occupied north. At the same time, FAPG started incorporating carefully filtered AM footage, including the infamous handshake between Pétain and Hitler at Montoire, to downplay the appearance of state collaboration. Angered by the initial success of FAPG and the exclusion of ACE Paris from the unoccupied zone, by February 1941 Greven and the German Armistice Commission successfully initiated negotiations with Vichy to create a jointly produced newsreel that would be distributed throughout France in place of the ACE Paris and FAPG. Yet hammering out the exact modalities of that proposal proved contentious because of ongoing economic and ideological competition.[25]

The poor box-office performance of dubbed German films during the last quarter of 1940 and the first quarter of 1941 motivated the *Filmprüfstelle* to allow imports from the southern zone. One of the most popular was Marcel Pagnol's *The Well Digger's Daughter* (*La Fille du puisatier*, 1940), a rural melodrama set in 1939–40 about a French fighter pilot and his peasant sweetheart. Though the Germans carefully excised references to the invasion of Poland and aerial battles involving the Luftwaffe, the film retained a nationalist flavour, thanks to inclusion of Pétain's sorrowful radio address announcing the armistice. Already a smash hit in the south, the film enjoyed even greater success in Paris, where its exclusive run lasted 16 weeks and amassed 4.5 million francs in receipts.[26] In April 1941, Vichy censors also began allowing unoccupied-zone distribution of certain German-made films, but just prior to Christmas rescinded the screening visa for Willy Forst's *Bel Ami* (1939), adapted from a Guy de Maupassant novella mocking the

A new offensive weapon unforeseen by Geneva. *Source*: Ralph Soupault, *Les Dessous du cinéma allemand* (1934).

decadence of late nineteenth-century bourgeois society. Surprisingly, the government simultaneously pulled *Jew Süss* and *Uncle Krüger* from circulation in French North Africa. The decision was ideologically motivated, but not because Vichy objected to the latter films' anti-Semitism and Anglophobia. Indeed, both had drawn good crowds in the preceding months and complemented the regime's own policies. However, *Bel Ami*'s depiction of a venal and morally corrupt France threatened Vichy's public credibility by undermining the image of renewed strength and unity that the regime wanted to project to its citizens. In several southern cities spectators protested the film and demanded its prohibition, thereby forcing a response.[27] Once the news reached Paris the Germans retaliated by banning *The Well Digger's Daughter* and a lesser French-made success titled *Strange Suzy* (*L'Etrange Suzy*, 1941) throughout the occupied zone. The censorship deadlock would last a full year, ending only when Vichy agreed to reauthorise an edited version of *Bel Ami*.[28]

This incident was only one of many conflicts in an ongoing tug-of-war that was equal parts political and economic. In the summer of 1941, French police reported that Greven was aggressively purchasing theatres south of the demarcation line through a newly founded front corporation.[29] According to German documents, the initiative encompassed 13 theatres worth 45 million francs across the unoccupied zone and 35 more worth 30 million francs in North Africa.[30] In so doing, Greven sought to maximise distribution of forthcoming Continental productions, which began to appear in September, while simultaneously weakening the market position of French-made films. Given its limited financial resources, there was little Vichy could do to respond. More important, in late 1941 and early 1942, French officials' will to defend their

Advertising posters for *The Fantastic Adventures of Baron Münchhausen* (1943), Ufa's first full-length feature to employ Agfacolor technology. Despite a massive production budget of 6.5 million Reichsmarks and equally lavish marketing, the film's French release in February 1944 generated hostility rather than enthusiasm, as the mutilated version of the poster attests. In addition to the swastikas, note the addition of a moustache transforming Hans Albers/Münchhausen into Hitler, the noose drawn around his neck, and the inscription 'Film boche, n'allez pas' ('Kraut film, don't go') *Source*: Bowles Collection.

political independence dissipated steadily under new Minister of Information Paul Marion and Prime Minister Pierre Laval. Following the invasion of the Soviet Union, German-made anti-Bolshevik clips became a regular part of FAPG, which was made mandatory in all cinemas. The joint newsreel agreement finally came to fruition in August 1941, leading to the release of *France-Actualités* (FA) exactly a year later. The subsequent invasion of the southern zone in November 1942 marked a definitive turning point in Franco-German relations, which shifted rapidly from self-interested accommodation to ever-closer ideological collaboration. Public support for Vichy eroded rapidly thereafter, as did the popularity of FA. Despite an auspicious debut thanks to the recycling of nationalistic French themes, by mid-1943 the newsreel's producers acknowledged that the newsreel's anti-Allied, pro-collaborationist message was largely ineffective. During the last 2 years of the war, Vichy 'censors' occasionally banned German-produced films that violated the moral tenets of the National Revolution, but was no longer able to sell the illusion of its sovereignty to moviegoers.

For all its intensity early in the Occupation, underlying political tensions between Vichy and the Germans never seriously hampered the fusion of creative talent that Greven coveted. The unique circumstances of collaborative film-making during the Occupation enriched French cinema not only technically by demonstrating the potential of rationally organised, state-financed production using cutting-edge equipment (especially panchromatic film stock capable of capturing more nuanced lighting effects) and marketing techniques; the ethical ambiguities and psychological pressures inherent in the process added a new level of aesthetic depth to the French national style by expanding the conventions of 1930s poetic realism. The doomed working-class heroes and complacent melancholy of pre-war dramas gave way to a darker, more disturbing moral universe where the boundary between good and evil is constantly shifting and rarely perceptible. These traits made Continental's pictures among the most successful of the period. Today cinema historians credit *Strangers in the House* (*Les Inconnus dans la Maison*, 1942), *The Murderer Lives at Number 21* (*L'Assassin habite au 21*, 1942), *The Devil's Hand* (*La Main du diable*, 1943) and *The Raven* (*Le Corbeau*, 1943) with pioneering French film noir.

Directors who avoided contact with the Germans also contributed to the movement, but in a slightly different register. Whereas Continental specialised in suspenseful thrillers set in the present, independent French film-makers avoided the contemporary context in favour of historical costume dramas and adaptations of age-old legends. This clever strategy ensured that films such as *The Devil's Envoys* (*Les Visiteurs du soir*, 1942), *The Eternal Return* (*L'Eternel Retour*, 1943), and *Children of Paradise* (*Les Enfants du Paradis*, 1945) not only avoided censorship entanglements and secured nationwide distribution, it also allowed directors to combine the escapism and fantasy that audiences craved with obliquely allegorical commentary on the emotional and moral conflicts that characterised life during the dark years. In that sense Jean Cocteau's *Beauty and the Beast* (*La Belle et la bête*, 1946), originally scheduled to begin shooting in mid-1944 but postponed by the Normandy invasion, exemplifies the mood and style of the era.

During the Occupation, documentary film-making also enjoyed an improbable renaissance and became a major force in French cinema. Vichy and the Germans both placed special emphasis on documentaries, making them a mandatory part of cinema programs in both zones and generously funding their production. Excluding newsreels, there were approximately 400–450 non-fiction films made in France from 1940 to 1944. Among the many made specifically as propaganda vehicles, there were also a significant number of disinterested productions devoted to cultural and scientific topics. The driving force behind the latter variety was the 'Arts–Sciences–Voyages' series organised by André Robert in Paris. His overarching goal, beyond paying obligatory homage to Marshal Pétain, was to raise the technical and the aesthetic level of French documentary by using Ufa *Kulturfilme* as a model. Thanks to generous production support from both Vichy and the Germans, the initiative yielded good results. Robert held public screenings of 65 films (57 French and 8 German) between March 1941 and November 1943, culminating in the country's first non-fiction film festival. By publicising the high-quality work of rising directors such as Georges Rouquier, who began making his classic *Farrebique* (1946) during the war, Art–Sciences–Voyages brought the documentary genre increased public visibility and critical respect, thereby establishing a national affinity for documentary which survives today.[31]

In the end, the Nazis' attempted colonisation of French cinema must be regarded as a qualified failure ideologically and economically. Despite their tacit acceptance of state collaboration, the vast majority of spectators never supported fascist values or the German war effort. To Goebbels' lasting chagrin, only 121 (35 per cent) of the 348 films released in France during the war were made in Germany, and only one French actor, Harry Baur, worked in Berlin. Even with virtually unlimited resources at its disposal, Continental managed to finish only 30 pictures by early mid-1944 and was just beginning to reap the financial dividends of Greven's cooperative, inter-cultural approach to film-making. Ironically, the Occupation had a beneficial, long-lasting impact on French cinema by forcing the government to address the financial and organisational problems that had long plagued the industry. Despite scrupulous post-war efforts to erase all traces of Vichy, the cinema infrastructure it created survived with minimal modifications: the COIC evolved into the *Centre National de la Cinématographie* (CNC) and the CATJC was refounded as the *Institut des Hautes Etudes Cinématographiques* (IDHEC). Today these institutions still constitute the backbone of French cinema. Indeed, French film policy since 1945 has been predicated on a principle adopted from the Nazis through Vichy: that cinema is a uniquely powerful expression of national identity and international influence which deserves special state funding support and protection from foreign competition. Known in France under the rubric of *exception culturelle*, over the past decade this view has grown stronger than ever in response to globalisation and Hollywood's ever-growing European market share. In a further echo of the war, French producers and directors have shown a renewed interest in collaborative film-making that combines technological expertise, aesthetics, and capital across national boundaries. Though a decade proved insufficient for the Nazis to build a worldwide cinema empire, the foundation they laid still stands today. Thankfully, it now supports a humanistic mode of cultural production dedicated to mutual enrichment and diversity rather than exploitation and persecution.

Notes

1. For a concise overview of the period, see N. Atkin, *The French at War, 1934–1944* (London: Longman, 2001).

2. Unless otherwise noted, all statistics cited in this chapter are taken from *La Cinématographie française*, France's largest weekly corporate film journal.
3. C. O'Brien, *Cinema's Conversion to Sound: Technology and Film Style in France and the U.S.* (Bloomington: Indiana University Press, 2005).
4. J.-M. Renaitour, *Où va le cinéma français?* (Paris: Editions Baudinière, 1937), pp. 56–7.
5. See the introductory chapter by Welch and Vande Winkel.
6. L. Kinkel, *Die Scheinwerferin: Leni Riefenstahl und das Dritte Reich* (Hamburg: Europa Verlag, 2002), pp. 86–7.
7. Of the 39 films made from 1933 to 1935, 33 (85 per cent) were alternate versions, but that figure dropped to 32 per cent (8 of 25) between 1936 and 1938. Statistics compiled from M. Bessy and R. Chirat, *Histoire du cinéma français: encyclopédie de films, 1929–1939*, 2 vols (Paris: Pygmalion, 1995).
8. Rankings tabulated in C. Crisp, *Genre, Myth, and Convention in the French Cinema, 1929–1939* (Bloomington: Indiana University Press, 2002), pp. 319–31.
9. H. Jeanson, '*L'Etrange Monsieur Victor* de Jean Grémillion', *Paris-Spectacles*, 24 June 1938, p. 5.
10. P. Leglise, *Histoire de la politique du cinéma*, vol. 1 (Paris: Librairie Générale de Droit et de Jurisprudence, 1970), pp. 179–98.
11. J. Renoir, 'Le cinéma et l'état', *Vendredi*, 24 December 1937, p. 1.
12. A. Phillips, *City of Darkness, City of Light: émigré Filmmakers in Paris, 1929–1939* (Amsterdam: Amsterdam University Press, 2003).
13. H. Revol, 'Sur quelques projets de chambardement', *Cinéma-Spectacles*, 6 May 1938, p. 1.
14. '4040 étrangers dans le cinéma français: ce que demande le Syndicat Professionnel Français', *La Cinématographie française*, 25 November 1938, p. 12.
15. On the marketing of feature films during the war, see R. Chateau, *Le Cinéma français sous l'Occupation, 1940–44* (Paris: La Mémoire du Cinéma, 1995).
16. K. Engel, *Deutsche Kulturpolitik im besetzten Paris, 1940–1944: film und theater* (Munich: R. Oldenbourg Verlag, 2003), pp. 138–53; and E. Ehrlich, *Cinema of Paradox: French filmmaking under the German Occupation* (New York: Columbia University Press, 1985), pp. 39–55.
17. Ehrlich (1985), pp. 135–57.
18. E. Fröhlich (ed.), *Die Tagebücher von Joseph Goebbels*, vol. 4 (Munich: K.G. Saur Verlag, 1995), p. 317, entry for 19 May 1942.
19. B. Drewniak, *Der deutsche Film, 1938–1945* (Dusseldorf: Droste Verlag, 1987), pp. 728–9.
20. Figures compiled from *Le Tout-cinéma: annuaire professionnel du monde cinématographique* (Paris, 1942), pp. 533–52.
21. Figures printed in *Le Film*, 20 May 1944, p. 8.
22. Report dated 11 October 1940, BA 2097, 'Situation de Paris' series, Archives of the Paris Police Prefecture. For further details, see B. Bowles, 'German Newsreel Propaganda in France, 1940–1944', *Historical Journal of Film, Radio, and Television*, 24:1 (2004), pp. 45–67.
23. For details, see B. Bowles, '*La Tragédie de Mers-el-Kébir* and the Politics of Filmed News in France, 1940–1944', *Journal of Modern History*, 76:2 (2004), pp. 347–88.
24. B. Bowles, 'Newsreels, Ideology, and Public Opinion under Vichy: The Case of *La France en Marche*', *French Historical Studies*, 27:2 (2004), pp. 419–63.

25. For a detailed account of Franco-German film politics, see J.-P. Bertin-Maghit, *Le cinéma français sous l'Occupation: le monde du cinéma français de 1940 à 1946* (Paris: Perrin, 2002).
26. '*La Fille du puisatier* a battu tous les records', *Le Film* (11 October 1941), p. 66.
27. Report by the Inspection Générale des Services des Renseignements Généraux, 5 July 1941, French Archives Nationales (hereafter An), AN/F 7/15293.
28. Note from Prime Minister Darlan to Minister of Information, dated 20 December 1941, French Archives Nationales (hereafter AN), F 60/300; weekly reports by Referat Film, 2 January 1942 and 9 September 1942, Bundesarchiv-Militärarchiv Freiburg, RW 35/224.
29. Reports by the Inspection Générale des Services des Renseignements Généraux, 31 July 1941 and 8 September 1941, AN/F 7/15293.
30. Drewniak (1987), p. 725.
31. On the politically motivated documentaries, see J.-P. Bertin-Maghit, *Les Documenteurs des années noires: les documentaires de propaganda en France, 1940–1944* (Paris: Nouveau Monde Editions, 2004); on Arts–Sciences–Voyages, see S. Wharton, *Screening Reality: French Documentary under German Occupation* (Bern: Peter Lang, forthcoming).

10

Cinema Goes to War: The German Film Policy in Greece During the Occupation, 1941–44

Eirini Sifaki

When the Second World War broke out in 1939, Greece remained neutral. General Metaxas had created a Greek version of the Third Reich (a fascist dictatorship) in 1936 but was opposed to German or Italian domination and refused to allow Italian troops to enter Greece in 1940. In October 1940, after a farcical ultimatum, Italy invaded Greece from Albanian territory. Greek resistance proved stronger than expected and when the Italian troops were driven back into Albania, Nazi Germany came to Mussolini's rescue in April 1941. The ensuing occupation of Greece, in which Bulgarian troops also took part, plunged the country into abject misery, the conditions of which included an acute food shortage.[1] Until the Italian armistice of September 1943, Italian troops remained the principal occupying power in Greece, although the Germans controlled the key economic areas. The German Wehrmacht took over the occupation of Greece after the Italian withdrawal. One year later, in October 1944, Germany 'strategically retreated' from Greece.[2]

It is against this complicated political, military and economic background that one must understand why Nazi Germany heavily influenced Greek cinema, but, unlike other occupied countries it never fully colonised the indigenous film industry which partly explains why Italian films remained relatively popular. This chapter seeks to contribute to a better understanding of the impact of Third Reich cinema by looking at the German film policy in occupied Greece. The main archival source of this research is the Greek film magazine *Kinimatographikos Astir*, which became a forum for dialogue between professionals of the film industry. Even though the Greek press was subjected to strict censorship, this publication enables us to analyse the commercial relations that the representatives of the Propaganda Ministry held with domestic film companies.

The Second World War represents a considerable break through regarding film consumption, as films were imposed by the German authorities. In order to be able to continue their activities, the film world was prepared to cooperate obediently with the German authorities and with the film representatives of the German Ministry of Propaganda (RMVP).[3] By contrast, this was not the case for theatre, which became a considerable means of resistance during the war. The impact of German films and their relationship to other films will also elucidate the limits and the nature of cinema-going and the ongoing competition from Hollywood.

The Greek film market during the Second World War

Before the Second World War, Greek cinematography had produced few films. Production was not organised on a stable basis, while the infrastructure was very limited in relation to the needs of the market.[4] The war had a profound effect on every market sector including the cinema industry. Even the transportation of films into Greece became much more complicated as, for example, American films now had to be transported via the Pacific, India, Iraq, crossing by rail Baghdad and Turkey.[5] The declaration of war in Europe seriously worried the distributors, who predicted a reduction in their imports. Local production being almost non-existent, the Greek cinema market depended completely on foreign imports, a *sine qua non* condition for the operation of cinemas and by extension for the entire cinematographic sector. On 9 April 1940, the Germans entered Thessaloniki. One of the first orders given by the occupation forces was for the cinemas to open, in order to show that life continued peacefully under their exalted protection. Previously, due to fear of bomb alerts, cinemas operated sporadically, opening at irregular hours.[6]

With the occupation of Greece, the first cinematic measures taken by the German authorities concerned the prohibition of American films and the requisition of the majority of the American subsidiaries offices as well as the Greek distribution firms. In addition, as in all the occupied countries, the German authorities also requisitioned several movie theatres which were called *Soldatenkinos* and were intended for the sole entertainment and leisure of the soldiers. With the entry of the Germans there were no other changes in the operation of cinemas, apart from the banning of films which came from countries hostile to the Axis Forces, the obligatory screening of German propaganda newsreels, and the adaptation of screening times to the curfew and the necessity of saving electricity.[7] The German government also sent out German film industry representatives who were responsible for defining and enforcing the Reich's cinematographic policy, thus, for example, Eugene Shen, in 1941, replaced in 1943 by a certain Schmidt.[8]

From 1941, the only films shown in Greece came then from Germany, Italy and Hungary. Furthermore, Ufa created a Greek subsidiary[9] that was given a local flavour by the name of *Hellas Films*. Hellas Films distributed exclusively German films, while exploiting *Pallas*, one of the most prestigious central cinemas in Athens. During the same year, the Italians founded

Esperia Film, using Italian capital, and distributing Italian films.[10] Contrary to *Esperia*, which did not possess the monopoly of the Italian productions, *Hellas Films* had a total monopoly of German films. And while with Italian films most distributors managed to stay in business and continue their activities, all the German films were gathered, seized, by the company *Hellas Films* even before its official foundation. Greek companies suffered a great deal from these measures and were literally forced out of business. The most serious damage caused by this practice was suffered by the *Hellenic Cinematographic Union* (EKE) and by the *Anzervos* Company. Their films were withdrawn without any legal and financial redress. Moreover, the EKE was forced not only to sell its offices at a price fixed by the Germans themselves, but also to sign over the movie-theatre *Pallas* free of charge.

Film audiences and spectatorship during the war

The collective behaviour of wartime audiences is a complex issue that merits special attention. My primary concern here is to approach the historical audience from the point of view of the changing rules and regulations in film exhibition. The coordination of the film industry profoundly affected the conditions of movie-going in various ways, beginning with the dramatic changes in distribution and the new regulations pertaining to exhibition. Cinema-going during the war entirely fulfilled the escapist function of cinema. Going to the movies allows individuals to withdraw from the pressures of everyday life and to seek distraction in other experiences. The war generated many types of price increases, including the price of cinema tickets. In addition, as is often mentioned in the film magazines of the period, apart from the concern to ensure food – which was a vital priority – people did not have great deal to do, other than going to the cinema in order to escape their misery. 'After all, cinema remains the least expensive spectacle. A ticket in a central first run cinema costs the same price as a package of cigarettes.'[11] Cinema undoubtedly remained the least expensive form of entertainment; if we compare it, for example, with the theatre – which cost at least four times more. On the other hand, an important part of the audience now consisted of the occupying forces. Certain cinemas were requisitioned and used for the entertainment of the German soldiers. In Thessaloniki, the cinema Dionysia was transformed into a *Soldatenkino*, the Pathé into the *Germania Kino* and the Pallas into the *Frontbühne*. The Ilyssia was signed over to the Italians. In Athens, the Attikon became the *Soldatenkino Victoria*, the Apollon was turned into the *Kino Apollo*, while the other cinemas were obliged to announce the titles of films in German and Italian, in addition to Greek. These measures were extended throughout Greece.[12]

The German authorities were also entitled to pay a special reduced price at cinemas. Cinema owners were always obliged to place at the disposal of the German army a tenth of their seats, at a special price – one-tenth of the normal price. An unlimited number of seats had to be reserved for officers, who paid 500 Dr. instead of 4000 Dr. Italian officers were entitled to pay a military price only if they had a German identity card.[13]

Even in 1942–43 when the bombing of the cities and the collapse of the economy turned everyday life into a constant struggle for survival, cinema attendance remained buoyant. Greek cinemas presented specific characteristics according to the season and constituted another important parameter of cinema-going. Open-air cinemas operated from May to October and were more numerous (in every neighbourhood), given the low cost of their installation. So in spite of the war, we can observe an increase in film attendance, even in the summers of 1942 and 1943. This can be explained by the lack of other entertainment venues and the risks of public transport that obliged people to be cautious and not to move away from their district.[14] It should be added that open air cinemas represented a social practice rather than a cultural practice.[15] Very often spectators had already seen films in the winter and went to summer cinemas simply in order to spend a pleasant evening with friends and forget the misery of war.

At the time of the German occupation, people were especially interested in the newsreels. Four cinemas in Athens (Asty, Cineak, Cosmopolit, and Cine News) – compared to two in the pre-war period – screened exclusively war newsreels, accompanied by short-length films. It is a measure of their importance that the largest advertisements in the press came from these cinemas. It must be underlined that the mandatory newsreels shown at other cinema's also attracted people's attention. Cinema owner Lefteris Sklavos remembers that towards the end of the war, the screening of the Allied landings at Normandy attracted particularly high attendances. The audiences wanted images that suggested an end to war, even though the newsreels came from the German propaganda machine.[16]

However, German film policy in Greece was not just based on intimidation and coercion. On the contrary, public relations played an important role. Goebbels' initial goal was to promote German cinema and to build his film empire with long-term and far-reaching political and economical effects in mind. Private screenings, official-receptions, cocktail parties and dinners in chic restaurants were held on the occasion of Ufa's silver jubilee in Athens.[17] The guest lists included not only prominent film professionals and cinema owners, but also newspaper directors, the diplomatic corps and political representatives of the country.[18]

Other strategies used to promote German production included regular articles in the specialist press usually drawn from the foreign press (Swiss[19] or German[20]), on the German newsreels and on *Kulturfilme*. Germany was portrayed as the most significant national producer and exporter of the weekly newsreels whilst German *Kulturfilme* offered a cultural oasis worldwide. Indeed, the cinema in the Third Reich remained one of the strongest

European producers after the onset of the war in 1939 with an average of 80 feature-length films per year as well as documentaries, shorts and newsreels. Production standards were also measured favourably against American studio models.[21] As in other occupied countries the German authorities tolerated Greek production under certain conditions. Confident that Germany would be victorious, its leaders planned to create a 'New Europe' under German control which would also break the American domination of world markets. To this end, European ideals and values were emphasised and contrasted with Hollywood's film hegemony.[22]

Before the German occupation, American domination of the Greek film market was strongly established and American films proved the most popular with Greek audiences. Until 1940–41, the German films screened in Greece barely amounted to 8–12 per cent of the total admissions, while American and French productions accounted, respectively, for 60–70 per cent and 15–25 per cent of the market.[23] As a result of the occupation, German films began to dominate the Greek box office for the first time. Some German films had already been available before the war. For example, the German musical *Enchanted Evening* (*Es war eine rauschende Ballnacht*, 1939), directed by Carl Froehlich and starring Marika Rökk and Zarah Leander,[24] can be found in fifth place in the Greek box-office returns for the season 1939–40. In addition, in 15th place for the same year was Hans Steinhoff's historical film *Robert Koch* (1939), directed by Hans Steinhoff and produced by Tobis. The biopic, representing Koch as a great German hero for propaganda purposes, had been distributed by the Greek company Anzervos. (As mentioned above, during the occupation, companies like Anzervos lost all rights to exploit German films to the Ufa subsidiary, Hellas Films.)

During the same period, the Greek public showed its preference for some European films, like the French *Beating Heart* (*Battement de cœur*, 1940 – 10th place) and *She Returned at Dawn* (*Retour à l'aube*, 1938 – 11th), both directed by Henri Decoin, or *L'Entente Cordiale* by Marcel L'Herbier (1939 – 12th place). There was, in the 1930s already, a considerable German investment in France's film industry. This investment was increased by the formation in 1940 of the German 'French' company Continental Films.[25] Thus, we find that many of the French films screened in Greece were dubbed into German and subtitled in Greek – like *Her First Affair* (*Premier Rendez-vous*, 1941) a comedy by Henri Decoin produced by Continental. Also in 1940, only one Greek film, *Song of the Depart* (*Το τραγούδι του χωρισμού,*), the first talking film directed by Filopimin Finos (who was to become the most important figure of the Greek commercial cinema in the late 1950s), is classified among the top 20 (at the 17th place).

However, this changed radically after the occupation of Greece by the Nazis in 1941. The winter season 1940–41 ends with the occupation and its tragic consequences. In the Table 10.1, we can clearly see the impact that this had on the number of films distributed in Greece.

Table 10.1 Number of films released according to the country's origin in 1940–41 and 1941–42

Winter season	German films	Italian films	Hungarian films	Spanish films	French films	Turkish films	Anglo-American films
1940–41	17	0	3	2	22	0	94
1941–42	83	28	11	3	1	1	0

Source: *Kinimatographicos Astir*, No. 6 (493), Athens, 7 June 1942.

After the ban on imports of American films by the German authorities, the only films projected on the Greek screens from the 1941–42 season onwards came from Germany, Italy and Hungary. Thus as early as 1940–41, we can already see three German productions including Leni Riefenstahl's *Olympia* (1938) in the 8th place.

The war documentary *Victory in the West* (*Sieg im Westen*, 1941) was screened in Athens during the winter season of 1940–41, in the cinemas *Titania* and *Pallas*, and reached 43 187 admissions, which placed it 7th in the box-office. As Hans Richter points out, this film served throughout Europe as a diplomatic weapon, an instrument of political demagogy. 'When Germany set out to occupy Greece and Yugoslavia in 1941, it used the film *Sieg im Western*, about the war in France, as a threat and means of extortion.'[26] However, the Greek public prefered other foreign films. This is confirmed by the extraordinary success of the Hungarian film *Dankó Pista* (1940), directed by Làslo Kalmàr and produced by Hunnia – Mester Film[27] – which can be found in the second place in 1940–41 and first in 1941–42. In the years 1940–41 no Greek films were produced. At the end of 1942, Dimitris Ioannopoulos, a new film director, produced *The Voice of the Heart* (*Η φωνή της καρδιάς*, 1942). This sentimental comedy surprised cinema audiences and was applauded and praised by both critics and the public.[28] Marcos Zervas provides us with some very significant details on the impact this film had at the time: 'During the first release of the film, which was held at the cinema Rex, spectators burned newspapers and went to express their enthusiasm in the Omonia place. The Germans chased them with weapons. Fortunately they calmed down when they realised that it was only a demonstration of enthusiasm for a Greek film. Naturally they did not understand the importance of this for occupied Athens. For people of that time, it constituted a declaration of life, the proof that we continued to exist and create, in spite of the conquerors.'[29] Screened in the cinemas *Rex* and *Esperos*, the film was the most popular one during the period 1942–43, with 102 287 tickets sold. It nearest rival sold only 50 740 tickets. The next five box-office hits were Italian films, followed by Hungarian, German and French films. One contemporary critic claimed: 'In spite of the hatred of the Greeks for everything that was Italian, the public seemingly found more in common with Italian films and less propaganda and more elements of racial resemblance. Consequently German films were squeezed during the first two years of the occupation.'[30]

Towards the end of the war (late 1943) German production accounted for at least 70 per cent of the films shown in cinemas while *Hellas Films* monopolised the distribution network. Moreover, on 25 October 1943 (following the Italian armistice) the occupation authorities prohibited the screening of all Italian films in Greek cinemas.[31] During the cinematographic season 1943–44, we find the German film *Münchhausen* (1943) in first place at the box office. Directed by Josef von Baky for the 25th anniversary celebrations of Ufa, the production, filmed in Agfacolor and pioneering many cinematic special effects, was considered a 'masterpiece of fantasy' that Ufa permitted itself in a massive 'act of denial' 2 years before its collapse.[32] In the same year, three Greek films appeared for the first time in the top 20 box-office receipts.

Conclusion

An examination of the Greek film market during occupation shows that German film policy attempted to directly influence the cinematographic sector, both ideologically and economically. An analysis of the Greek box-office illustrates that although Nazi film policy successfully exploited the conquered territories in terms of expanding its own film distribution, it ultimately failed in its wider cultural aims of manufacturing a lasting ideological influence on the subjugated populations.[34] Cinema audiences continued to acclaim Italian and Hungarian films together with the Greek film *The Voice of the Heart*. Table 10.2 also shows that it is only after having prohibited Italian films in 1943 that Germans managed to have 8 of their films among the top 20. Indeed, during the cinematographic season 1942–43, out of the 20 films of the box-office, only 4 were German productions (instead of 9 in 1941–42) while 13 came from Italy.

After the liberation (1944–45), Ufa and the German cinema were considered as the embodiment of the enemy, as illustrated in the following

Table 10.2 Origin of the 20 most popular films 1939–44[34]

Box office (20 films) by national origin										
SEASONS	US	GER	UK	FR	IT	ES	GR	HU	TU	Unknown
1939–40	11	2		4	1	1	1			
1940–41	11	3	1	1		1		3		
1941–42		9			5			5	1	
1942–43		4			13		1	2		
1943–44		9		2			4	1		4

Note: Country of origin – USA, US; Germany, GER; France, FR; Spain, ES; Russia, RU; Italy, IT; Greece, GR; Hungary, HU; England, UK; Turkey, TU.

Κινηματογραφικός Ἀστήρ

ΕΤΟΣ ΚΑ' — ΑΡΙΘ. 4 (531)

ΑΘΗΝΑΙ - 8 ΜΑΡΤΙΟΥ 1944

ΧΑΝΣ ΑΛΜΠΕΡΣ

Ὁ περίφημος γερμανὸς καλλιτέχνης ὁ ὁποῖος ὑπεδύθη ἐπιτυχῶς τὸν ρόλον τοῦ βαρώνου Ἰερωνύμου Μυνχάουζεν εἰς τὸ ὁμώνυμον ἔργον τὸ ὁποῖον προεβλήθη εἰς τὴν πόλιν μας.

Front page of the Greek film journal *Kinimatographikos Astir*, featuring Hans Albers: 'The famous German artist who played successfully the title role of Baron Münchhausen that was screened in our city.' Josef von Baky's *Münchhausen* (1943) was a prestige production, filmed in colour to celebrate the 25th anniversary of Ufa. *Source*: *Kinimatographikos Astir*, 8 March 1944.

Κινηματογραφικός Ἀστήρ

ΕΤΟΣ Κ' — ΑΡΙΘ. 2 (506)

ΑΘΗΝΑΙ 25 ΙΑΝΟΥΑΡΙΟΥ 1943

ΑΓΑΠΑ ΜΕ

ἡ ἀριστουργηματικὴ ταινία τῆς

ΜΑΡΙΚΑ ΡΕΚ

τὴν ὁποίαν ἡ U. F. A. διὰ τὸ

ΑΡΓΥΡΟΥΝ ΙΩΒΙΛΑΙΟΝ ΤΗΣ

ἐπεφύλαξε νὰ προσφέρῃ εἰς τὴν ἐν Ἑλλάδι πελατείαν της

ΕΚΜΕΤΑΛΛΕΥΣΙΣ

ΕΛΛΑΣ ΦΙΛΜ

Front page of the Greek film journal *Kinimatographikos Astir*, featuring Marika Rökk. Her latest Ufa picture, *Love me* (*Hab' mich Lieb*, 1942), was distributed by Hellas Film in early 1943. *Source*: *Kinimatographikos Astir*, 25 January 1943.

extract drawn from *Kinimatographicos Astir* : 'Nevertheless, our revenge on the German monopoly that we were forced to endure for three years, is already achieved, because the German studios closed following the general mobilisation of Goebbels and the German cinema is now nothing more than a bad dream.'[35] Not surprisingly, the Nazi cinema provoked strong feelings. Critics evoked censorship and coercion and reminded their readers that they had risked the firing squad if they dared to criticise German films. Nazi films were characterised by a critic as 'an interminable bunch fabricated by Ufa, Tobis, Berlin, Bavaria, where every biography, every historical film was transformed into anti-British, anti-allied, anti-democratic propaganda or in exaltation of the virtues of the German race, of the 'grandeur' of the Reich and the value of the German soldier. . . .[36] Yet not all German cinema reflected these stereotypical traits: *Münchhausen* proved otherwise, having achieved extraordinary success and popularity with Greek cinema audiences, reaching number one at the box office only a few weeks before the Liberation of Greece. The fascination with the cinema of the Third Reich remains; not only because of its powerful propaganda campaigns, but also because of its attempts to build a solid film industry and exercise enormous ideological influence over a mass audience.

Notes

1. For an overview of Greek history during the Second World War, see C. M. Woodhouse, *The struggle for Greece, 1941–1949* (London: Hurst & Company, 2002); M. Petrakis, *The Metaxis Myth: dictatorship and propaganda in Greece* (London: I. B.Tauris, 2005).
2. R. Clogg, 'Greece', in I. C. B. Dear and M. R. D. Foot (eds), *The Oxford companion to World War II* (Oxford: Oxford University Press, 2001), pp. 398–403.
3. E. Sifaki, *Jalons pour une histoire du cinéma en Grèce (1939–1954): pratiques culturelles, logiques commerciales et stratégies d'acteurs d'après la revue Kinimatographikos Astir*, thèse de doctorat, Université Paris 3 – Sorbonne nouvelle 2004, p. 226.
4. Ch. Sotiropoulou, *Diaspora in Greek cinema. Effects and influences in the thematic development of films during the period 1945–1986* (Athens: Themelio, 1995), p. 35 (in Greek).
5. G. Georgopoulos, 'The past guides the future. An historical review of the cinema decade 1937–1946', *Kinimatographicos Astir* (December 1948), p. 3 (in Greek).
6. N. Theodosiou, *War and cinema, Giant film posters* (Athens: Kalamata International Documentary Film Festival, 2002), p. 45 (in Greek).
7. Sifaki (2004), pp. 242–50.
8. *Kinimatographikos Astir*, N. 1 (505) (10 January 1943), p. 15.
9. B. Drewniak, *Der deutsche Film 1938–1945* (Düsseldorf: Droste Verlag, 1987), p. 791.
10. *Kinimatographikos Astir*, N. 1 (488) (January 1942).
11. *Kinimatographikos Astir*, N. 3 (490) (March 1942).
12. N. Theodosiou (2002), p. 45 (in Greek).
13. *Kinimatographikos Astir*, N. 20 (524) (31 October 1943).
14. *Kinimatographikos Astir*, N. 4 (491) (April 1942).

15. E. Sifaki, 'Global strategies and local practices in film consumption', *Journal for Cultural Research*, 7:3 (2003), pp. 243–57.
16. Theodosiou (2002), p. 50.
17. *Kinimatographikos Astir*, N. 5 (509) (7 March 1943).
18. *Kinimatographikos Astir*, N. 8 (512) (mid-April 1943).
19. J. Landry, 'War and cinema. German War newsreels', *Les mois suisse (may 1942)*, in *Kinimatographikos Astir*, N. 13 (500) (25 October 1942), pp. 6–7 (in Greek).
20. G. Bagier, 'Colour *Kulturfilm*: science, nature and art on the screen', *Das Reich* (16 January 1943) in *7th Art Magazine*, Athens, No. 1 (March 1944), pp. 14–15; 'On the occasion of the 25th anniversary UFA's *Kulturfilm*', *Kinimatographikos Astir*, N. 5 (509), Athens (7 March 1943), pp. 14–15 (in Greek).
21. M. Silberman, *German cinema, texts in context* (Detroit : Wayne State University Press, 1995), p. 53.
22. 'The production of German films. Europe to Europeans', *Kinimatographikos Astir*, N. 4 (508) (22 February 1943) (in Greek).
23. M. Ploritis, 'Assessment of three dead years', *Kinimatographikos Astir*, N. 16 (543) (30 November 1944), pp. 4–7 (in Greek).
24. K. Kreimeier, *The Ufa story. A history of Germany's greatest film company 1918–1945* (New York: Hill and Wang, 1996), p. 301.
25. See the contribution by Bowles elsewhere in this book.
26. H. Richter, 'Der politische Film', in W. Karsten (ed.), *Theorie des Kinos: Ideologiekritik der Traumfabrik* (Francofort/Main, 1972), p. 71. Cited in Kreimeier (1996), pp. 305–6.
27. See Frey's and Kirk's contributions elsewhere in this book.
28. A. Mitropoulos, *Découverte du cinéma grec* (Paris: Seghers, 1968), pp. 36–7.
29. M. Zervas, *Finos Film. Myth and Reality* (Athens: Agira, 2003), p. 141 (in Greek).
30. Ploritis (1944), p. 6.
31. *Kinimatographikos Astir* N. 20 (524), Athens (31 October 1943).
32. Kreimeier (1996), p. 330.
33. Ibid., p. 499.
34. Data collected from the Greek film magazine *Kinimatographicos Astir*, which at the end of each summer summarised the box-office results for films screened in the Athenian cinemas the previous year. *Kinimatographicos Astir* specifically published the Greek title of the films, the cinemas where they played, and the admissions carried out for each film. The tables were devised by juxtaposing several sources in order to find the initial title of each film, the genre, the country of origin, the production company, and the distributor in Greece, for the first 20 films that dominated the public's preferences.
35. Ploritis (1944), p. 7.
36. Ibid., pp. 4–7.

11

Competitor or Compatriot? Hungarian Film in the Shadow of the Swastika, 1933–44

David S. Frey

Writing to Reich Minister Joseph Goebbels in late 1933, Hungary's Interior Minister József Széll detailed an understanding he believed Hungarian and German political elites shared. Both groups agreed that they must fashion their film industries from a 'national point of view' and eliminate the artifice of cosmopolitan 'internationalism'. 'Film must suit each *Volk*', preached the Interior Minister, 'and each *Volk's* film must assume a characteristic place in the market'. As a minor, linguistically isolated European power of less than 9 million inhabitants, however, Hungary faced a dilemma: it had neither the resources nor the internal market to sustain the 'national' niche industry it desired. 'Profit', Széll admitted, 'was impossible on production of Hungarian version films for Hungary only.' The solution, suggested Széll, was access to the German movie market. The Interior Minister assured his German counterpart that his nation's films would not compete directly with German films since they would be 'Hungarian' products, culturally and perhaps racially distinct from those made by Germans. These features, naturally, would attract new audiences, and all sides would benefit from greater trade and mutual cultural understanding.[1]

Széll's note raised many of the key issues that shaped film relations between Hungary and Germany from the time of the Nazi seizure of power to the German occupation of Hungary in March 1944. Rhetoric about the 'national point of view' abounded, but defining a national film and organising an industry to create an explicitly national product proved a divisive enterprise. Thus, the nature of Hungary's filmic relationship with Germany was constantly in flux. Should Hungary primarily be a consumer, contributor, compatriot or competitor – a consumer of German film, a contributor of distinctly Hungarian film to the German film trade, a compatriot in the campaigns to rid Jews and Americans from all facets of the continental motion picture business or a competitor for foreign markets? Frequently, contradictory ideological, commercial and geopolitical currents bounced Hungary between these competing objectives. Undoubtedly, Hungary's phoenix-like feature film-making revival, from moribund in 1929 to the continent's third rank in 1942, behind only Germany and Italy, owes much to the extension of Nazi German domination in Europe. Yet Hungary, the only Central European state with a developed indigenous sound film industry that continued production through the Second World War, proved far less docile, far more fractious and far more independent than German officials hoped.[2] As a result, German and Hungarian film elites frequently found their aims conflicted, and Széll's dream of symbiotic national industries never materialised. Clash and competition, rather than cooperation, proved the relational norm.

The early sound era and the growing din of conflict

When sound arrived in Hungary in 1929, film-making was virtually non-existent. Hungary's vibrant silent film industry had been destroyed by post-First World War political and economic turmoil. German nationalist and early Nazi legislation paradoxically served as a catalyst for the rejuvenation of Hungarian film production. Between 1930 and 1933, Germany adopted a series of laws designed to foster a national film industry and protect the jobs of ethnic Germans. This legislation forced several hundred Hungarian film professionals out of Berlin and Munich, many of whom fled to Budapest.[3] Suddenly, the stagnant Hungarian industry possessed the critical supply of human capital necessary to both create quality film and attract crucial domestic and international capital. Géza von Bolváry, a well-known Hungarian director who continued to work in Germany, wrote in February 1932 of the impact of these changes: 'The biggest surprise... is that Hungarian film is sensational business.... It is worthwhile for every... producer to work in Budapest.'[4] The expulsion of Hungarian film-makers from Germany also created tensions between the leading exponents of Hungarian film, most of whom were Jewish, and Germany. In response to this 'pogrom against Hungarians', these cinema elites called for retaliation, including boycotts of German films.[5] This strange and strained dynamic was to have long-term consequences for Hungarian–German film relations.

When the Nazis passed a fourth film order in June 1933 it became almost impossible for Hungarians, particularly Hungarian Jews, to choose German citizenship and thus remain in Germany. Internationally known Hungarian film directors, writers and producers such as István Székely, Béla Gaál, Károly Nóti, Ferenc Molnár and Joe Pasternak, all of whom had flitted among European film cities and occasionally Hollywood and all of whom were born in the Jewish faith, now found themselves unwelcome in Berlin. This second wave of expulsions engendered a sea change in the Hungarian–German film trade, particularly in regard to film exchange. During the second half of 1932, German film comprised nearly 60 per cent of the Hungarian feature film market.[6] In 1933, renewed calls for trade restrictions or outright avoidance of German movies came from a variety of cultural and business circles, and this time, the result was seismic. Hungarian distributors unofficially, yet significantly, slashed imports of German film. Some segments of the movie-going public, particularly the Jews of Budapest, mounted low-key boycotts, while other spectators became repulsed by the qualitative decline in German film production. In a period of 18 months, between January 1933 and mid-1934, even in the absence of official government action, Germany's share of the Hungarian feature film market collapsed, dropping from 60 per cent to less than 19 per cent.[7] Domestic Hungarian production remained minimal and could not fill the void left by the declining German market share. To maintain its film culture and to continue to provide its theatres with material, Hungary turned to the United States.

From 1933 through the beginning of the 1940s, Hollywood-made film dominated the Hungarian market, while the German share grew progressively smaller.[8] As a result, German *Filmpolitik* towards Hungary became focused on diminishing Hollywood's share, expanding the possibilities for exhibition of German film and convincing Hungary to enact domestic reform in order to reduce or eliminate the influence of its 'film Jews'. In Hungary, the cinema world was divided between a powerful but frequently split anti-German element, in which a number of Jewish producers, distributors and cinema owners were influential; a faction headed by government bureaucrats and film elites which viewed cooperation with Germany as desirable; and an increasingly raucous anti-Jewish, but not necessarily pro-German, Hungarian nationalist wing. The splits were hardly consistent or purely ideological. Anti-German Jewish producers coveted access to the German market. Pro-German Hungarian officials called for an increase in imports of German film, but not so much that it might force Hungarian film off the market. Hungarian right-wing nationalists called for state control of the film industry, modelled on the German Reich Film Chamber, yet did not favour greater numbers of German film screenings, fearing that this might incite Hungary's German minority. However, by the latter half of the 1930s, Hungary seemed to be moving inexorably into the Nazi orbit, its leaders driven by the desire to revise the universally hated Treaty of Trianon, the 1920 treaty which had stripped Hungary of nearly 70 per cent of its pre-First World War territory and almost 60 per cent of its inhabitants.

This desire to regain lands and influence, coupled with the massive attraction of the German market, led Hungary's political elites to make continued attempts to curry the favour of Nazi cultural officials. The conundrum for Hungary was that its film industry's creations, those it wished to sell in Germany, were 'precisely that Hungarian-packaged film culture which they [the Nazis] so radically endeavoured to root out at home [in Germany]'.[9]

In a 1935 speech reproduced in the Nazi periodical *NSK*, Hans Hinkel, one of Goebbels' top aides, stated in no uncertain terms that Germany had no interest in importing 'destructive' films made by Jewish artists in foreign lands, precisely those men and women Germany had so recently expelled. Hinkel specifically targeted Hungary, along with Austria, Poland, France and the United States. Germany wished to strengthen its cinematic ties with Hungary, Hinkel noted, but only if Hungary understood that Germany would not accept films that were 'damaging to the Volk'.[10] Convinced that the Hungarian film creations had become, in the words of Hungary's Ambassador to Berlin Szilárd Masirevich, 'Jewified [*elzsidósodik*]' and divested of their *völkisch* character, German officials actively hindered the screening of Hungarian features.[11] Through the late 1930s, despite the continued publication of articles in Germany and Hungary touting the 'natural and historical' ties between the two countries and their shared 'union of fate' [*Schicksalsgemeinschaft*], Nazi officials continued to employ a purposeful diplomatic schizophrenia.[12] They frequently agreed to accept Hungarian films only to deny most of them the requisite exhibition licenses. These actions occurred despite the conclusion of a bilateral German–Hungarian cultural accord in 1936 and a specific film accord in 1938. In the latter treaty, German authorities agreed to grant permission for exhibition of up to eight Hungarian films each year and promised that German companies would make an unspecified number of features in Hungary and distribute them globally. Despite these paper commitments, film relations between the two states remained icy. It was not until mid-1938, when the geopolitical context had been radically altered and the Hungarians themselves addressed the fundamental question of Jewish involvement in Hungarian film that German–Hungarian film relations began to warm.

Hungary's place in the Nazi 'New Order'

That the Jewish question was central to Hungarian–German film relations was clear to all concerned. The sole reason Hungarian film exhibitions had been stymied by Germany was Hungary's failure to consent to incorporate an 'Aryan paragraph' for films it wished to export, agreed both the American Ambassador to Hungary and the Hungarian Ambassador to Germany.[13] Hungary's diplomats consented to a secret protocol for exports to Germany – the Aryan paragraph – in 1936 negotiations.[14] However, in spite of growing right-wing pressure to do so, government bureaucrats made few efforts to impose the burden of the Aryan paragraph on the rapidly growing, and largely Jewish, film industry until 1938. In February 1938, the Lower House of the Hungarian parliament approved the Film Agreement with Germany, including the Aryan paragraph. Only 3 months later, Hungarian legislators passed law XV/1938, known as the First Jewish Law. This legislation empowered Hungarian officials to build institutions intended to severely curtail the numbers and influence of Jews in Hungarian society. Within the film industry, government bureaucrats and Christian cultural elites spent months negotiating the organisation and function of the Hungarian Theater and Film Arts Chamber and the National Film Committee, the two main bodies designed to insure the nurturing of a 'Christian national spirit' in the Hungarian film industry. Meanwhile, Jewish investment in film production plummeted and the industry descended into crisis. The chaos continued through mid-1939, until passage of the Second Jewish Law more concretely defined the uppermost limits of Jewish involvement in Hungarian culture and society.[15]

During this crisis, which was exacerbated by the Nazi annexation of Austria and dismantling of Czechoslovakia, Nazi authorities stepped up their efforts to engineer change in the Hungarian film world, efforts which continued through the early 1940s. As the German and Hungarian economies and militaries became progressively more intertwined, particularly after Hungary joined the Axis invasion of Yugoslavia in April 1941, the Hungarian film world became more heavily influenced by the whims of its neighbours to the West. German officials now directly intervened in Hungarian film-making, exhibition, distribution and even continental export through a variety of coercive as well as cooperative means.

Significant segments in Hungarian film found elements of the Nazi campaign to exert a more direct influence over their industry quite palatable. The Nazis bankrolled the establishment of new 'Christian' Hungarian film production companies, such as Mester Film.[16] They purchased one of Budapest's 13 largest premier theatres, the Corvin theatre, and bought licenses for other smaller theatres. These efforts were intrusive, yet mutually beneficial, particularly in the eyes of the anti-Semitic nationalists and pro-Nazi ethnic Germans.[17] Other enterprises received rapturous approval even in anti-German Hungarian circles. In late 1940, Hungary's largest film studio, the quasi-state-owned Hunnia studio, was searching for an excuse to expand its film production capacity. Its quest received a great boost from the German government in early February 1941, when the German–Hungarian Culture Committee (*Deutsch-Ungarische Kulturausschuss*), a bilateral committee of government officials and film luminaries, determined that Germany should immediately begin filming four features in Budapest.[18] In return for German investment, Hungary consented to make the necessary studio space available by renovating the defunct Star studio, one of Hungary's greatest silent studios. Hungarian film figures hoped this contract would be the breakthrough they had long desired, the means of encouraging cooperation and goodwill in Hungarian–German film relations. State authorities ordered the army, which had converted the Star site into a truck repair depot, to turn over the studio to Hunnia for refurbishing and reconstruction. The four co-productions completed between late 1941 and 1942 marked the high point of Hungarian–German relations.[19]

This crest was brief, however, as Hungary's desire to maintain a degree of cultural sovereignty clashed with Germany's goal of continental domination. An unintended consequence of the Nazis' shocking subjugation of Europe between 1939 and 1940 was that it created conditions that allowed Hungarian film production to flourish. The destruction of Czechoslovakia not only eliminated a significant source of film in Central Europe, it also broke up the Little Entente, the political–military alliance between Czechoslovakia, Romania and Yugoslavia. This development permitted Hungarian–Yugoslav relations to improve, just as the onset of war was to radically reshape the European political and cinematic maps. Nazi victories ended Polish production, drastically reduced and eventually stopped French and British film from reaching Central and South-eastern Europe, and eventually resulted in the expulsion of Hollywood products from the continent. In the light of this paucity of film and warmer relations with its northern neighbour, Yugoslav authorities ended their prohibition on Hungarian features in late 1939. The success of Hungarian film in the Yugoslav market in 1940 convinced importers in other countries – from Bulgaria to Turkey to Finland – to contract for Hungarian-made film. Hungarian pictures did so well in these new markets, particularly in Yugoslavia, that by mid-1940, Hungarian motion pictures in Yugoslavia ranked first in overall receipts and second, behind only Hollywood, in the number of films screened.[20] In a matter of months, Hungary had transformed from a consumer of German films to a *bona fide* competitor in several markets. This prompted the head of the Cultural Section of the German Foreign Ministry to order his country's embassy in Budapest to endeavour to limit Hungarian film exports, as they represented commercial and ideological threats to 'German film' and more broadly, 'German *Kulturpolitik*'. In the Balkans, he warned, the entire public, particularly Yugoslavia's ethnic Germans, were under threat from 'Jewish distributed Hungarian film' because Hungarian 'film-Jews' were the 'chief carriers' of anti-German propaganda in South-eastern Europe.[21] German authorities did win preferential treatment for their films in late 1940, but not before Hungary had screened over 140 films in Yugoslav theatres and earned unprecedented returns.

The surprising success of these Hungarian products led not only to a sharp rise in Hungarian motion picture exports, but a boom in domestic production. Axis-imposed border alterations from 1938 to 1941 allowed Hungary to incorporate well over 150 new theatres and 4 million potential spectators.[22] By the 1942/43 film year, Hungarian studios were churning out over 50 films annually, their works were making headway in many European markets and Hungarian film officials were boasting of Hungary's regained cultural and political clout in Central Europe. A Hungarian film, *People on the High Mountains* (*Emberek a havason*), claimed one of the top awards at the 1942 Venice Film Biennial. 'Every [exported] Hungarian film takes the place of a German film', bragged Nándor Jenes, a top employee in the

Hungarian Film Office, the country's second most prolific studio. Apparently, Nazi bureaucrats, much to their chagrin, reached the same conclusion. This was the reason that Nazi film officials felt the need to suppress Hungarian film, suggested Jenes.[23] In addition to making screening more difficult in the Balkans, the Germans exerted their power in the International Film Chamber (*Internationale Filmkammer*, IFK) to restrict Hungarian access to export markets throughout Europe.[24] The IFK, despite Italian and Hungarian opposition, placed quotas on the numbers of Hungarian films its members could import annually and required that all international film trade go through the German Transit Film company.[25]

Perhaps the most egregious and effective German actions aimed at curtailing the growth of Hungarian film were Nazi threats to severely limit shipments of raw film if Hungary did not abide by various IFK decisions. Hungary lacked any indigenous capability to produce raw film, the material needed to make movies as well as copies of imported film. It imported over three-fifths of its raw film from Germany as of 1942, and, as a result, was susceptible to Nazi extortion.[26] When Hungarian officials resisted German plans for European export quotas, and soon after specifically adopted a policy of procrastination in regards to the German plans to eliminate all American features from the European continent,[27] German officials lost patience and threatened to stop all shipments of raw film. It was not until a German delivery scheduled for October 1942 did not occur and Hungarian production nearly ground to a halt that Hungary consented to Nazi demands that all imports and screenings of American film be outlawed by the close of the year.[28]

Raw film limits, export quotas, the elimination of American film, strong-arming via the IFK were some of the tools the Nazis utilised 'to subdue Hungarian production', wrote Nandor Jenes.[29] Yet constraining production was only one of the German aims. By purchasing theatres and exhibitions licenses, the Nazis hoped they would be able to assure the wider distribution of their media products in Hungary and better influence Hungarian public opinion. Perhaps the most influential step they took to implement this strategy was to found *Descheg* (*Deutsche Schmalfilm Exportgesellschaft*) and its Hungarian offshoot, *Kefifor* (*Keskényfilm Forgalmi Kft.*) in 1941. Both Hungarian and German film elites believed narrow film, which included features, *Kulturfilme* and advertisements, to have important persuasive power. *Kulturfilme*, educational films, news reports, tourism films and advertisements in particular offered what authorities on both sides believed to be 'real' glimpses of their cultures.[30] They were a means of glorifying national or racial achievement, of visualising and promoting national characters, ways of life and ideologies.[31] Nazi bureaucrats also believed narrow film, because it was much smaller and lighter, offered a number of additional advantages that suited it for use abroad. Nearly any political or social organisation could afford a relatively inexpensive 16 mm projector. Narrow format feature films could be distributed throughout Europe, avoiding licensing fees and circumventing Jewish-owned cinemas, making them much easier to screen in areas of German settlement outside the Reich.

In 1941, *Kefifor* received the largest outlay of cash from *Descheg* compared to all other European *Descheg* branches, and *Descheg* also awarded it a monopoly over all German narrow film in Hungary.[32] Simultaneously German diplomats negotiated an agreement with Hungary that in effect mandated that one-third of all narrow film exhibitions in Hungary be comprised of Nazi products. In 1942, Nazi film officials attempted to convince their Hungarian counterparts that there should be a 1:1 ratio of German to Hungarian narrow film in every showing, but this motion was rebuffed by Hungary's Interior Minister Ferenc Keresztes-Fischer.[33]

An additional element of Nazi film strategy in Hungary was the use of mobile sound film trucks (*Tonfilmwagen*), fully equipped cinemas on wheels that could travel to remote areas for propaganda purposes or to serve troops. In the first three months of 1943, for example, sound film trucks held 118 showings which attracted nearly 70 000 residents of Hungary.[34] The *Auslandsstelle des Lichtbilddienstes der Filmabteilung* (Auli), the department of

A night in Transylvania (*Egy éjszaka Erdélyben*) was a German–Hungarian co-production filmed in Hungary in 1941. The Hungarian version, starring Zita Szeleczky, was directed by Frigyes Bán. The German version, *Tanz mit dem Kaiser* (*Dance with the Emperor*, 1941), was directed by Georg Jacoby. It starred Marika Rökk and was distributed all over Europe. Left: the original Hungarian poster of *A night in Transylvania*. Right: the Belgian poster of *Dance with the Emperor*. *Sources*: Hungarian poster: National Széchényi Library; Belgian poster: Vande Winkel/Warie Collection.

Das Ufa-Theater „Urania" in Budapest bei der Uraufführung des Ufa-Films „U-Boote westwärts!"

Premiere of the Ufa film *U-boats, go west* (*U-Boote Westwärts*, 1941), a propaganda film about the blockade and the Battle for Britain, at the Urania theatre in Budapest. The Urania was, like the Urania in Berlin, a very luxurious premiere theatre. *Source*: H. Traub, *Die Ufa. Ein Beitrag zur Entwicklungsgeschichte des deutschen Filmschaffens* (Berlin: Ufa-Buchverlag, 1943), p. 255.

Goebbels' Propaganda Ministry charged with film distribution and exhibition outside of the Reich, had planned to send nearly 40 sound film trucks to Hungary. The Hungarian government, however, thwarted these plans at an early stage. In November 1940, when Auli sent its second *Tonfilmwagen* to Hungary, the Hungarian Foreign Ministry registered its reservations.[35] When Germany tried to ship three more trucks into Hungary in September 1941, Hungary denied permission for any additional mobile cinemas to cross its borders. The importance here is less the number of sound film trucks Germany dispatched to Hungary than what they represented. Film trucks, narrow film distribution, the purchase of theatres and film companies, diplomatic encouragement to speed the expulsion of Jews from the Hungarian film industry – all were invasive attempts to manipulate the Hungarian film market. These efforts to alter the content of the material Hungarian audiences saw, where they saw it and how it was delivered, coupled with Nazi efforts to dictate how many features Hungary could make and where these films could be shown outside of Hungary, collectively represented a cohesive programme to control Hungarian cinema. Yet this relationship was not simply one of dominance and submission. At the same time, Hungary was seeing its cultural sovereignty restricted by increasingly bold German interventions, its newly 'Christianised' Hungarian film business experienced an unprecedented boom, culminating in Hungary's rise to prominence in the continental

European film community in the 1940s. This advance was largely attributable to the Nazi-wrought New Order and Hungary's participation in it. Neither did this symbiotic dynamic preclude Hungarian resistance to Nazi hegemony. Hungary's desire to nurture its own national film industry often placed it at loggerheads with Germany, whether it was over Jewish participation in the film trade or access to foreign markets.

Ultimately, it was the decision of Hungary's ruling oligarchs to act independently, exploring the possibility of a separate peace with the Allies in a poorly conceived and only semi-secret manner that convinced Nazi leaders to order the occupation of Hungary in March 1944. While the Hungarian film industry continued to function after the arrival of German troops, feature film production withered. The Germans and their Hungarian proxies purged those few Jews still active in the motion picture business. Few investors remained willing to risk their capital in film production, particularly as the Red Army approached from the East. When the Nazis ousted the Hungarian Regent Miklós Horthy in October 1944 after a failed attempt to withdraw Hungary from the war, feature film production had ceased and the imminent invasion of Budapest meant exhibition in a large section of the country was restricted. By the time the Nazis finally took complete control of the Hungarian film industry, the phoenix had once again turned to ash.

Notes

1. J. Széll to J. Goebbels, Nr.157 789/1933 (undated, likely 30 November 1933). *Hungarian National Archives (hereafter HNA) Óbuda,* Z 1124, 1 raktári sz., 20 dosszié sz., pp. 218–19.
2. Among Central European states, excluding Germany, only Austria, Czechoslovakia, Hungary and Poland had feature film production capacity in 1938. By January 1940, film production in Austria and the Czech lands had been absorbed by Nazi Germany, and Polish production had ceased, leaving Hungary the sole remaining independent feature film producer in Central Europe.
3. Wolfgang Mühl-Benninghaus suggests that German authorities specifically targeted the Hungarians and Austrians who participated in German film-making. W. Mühl-Benninghaus, *Das Ringen um den Tonfilm. Strategien der Elektro- und der Filmindustrie in den 20er und 30er Jahren* (Düsseldorf: Droste Verlag, 1999), pp. 351–2.
4. G. Bolváry, 'Ma mar nem lehet kételkedni a magyar filmgyártás lehetőségében', *Magyar Filmkurír,* VI: 4–5 (6 February 1932), p. 6.
5. *Auswärtiges Amt Archiv Bonn (hereafter AAA),* Gesandtschaft Budapest, Fach 218, Akt. VII, 16, Pressebericht, Nr.171, 8 August 1932. See also 'A német filmkontigens-rendelet', *Filmkultura,* V: 7–8 (July–August 1932), p. 1.
6. *HNA,* Országos Mozgóképvizsgáló Bizottság [OMB] elnöki iratok, K 158, 7 cs., 1936, pp. 188–9. Depending upon the source, statistics vary, but all agree that Germany held approximately 50 per cent of the annual features market, and nearly 60 per cent if one counts only the second half of 1932. See I. Langer, 'Fejezetek a filmgyár történetéből, I–II.rész, 1919–48', Hungarian Film Institute unpublished manuscript, Budapest, 1980, p. 120; and H. Castiglione, '1933/34

Grafikonja – Adatok a szézon mérlegéhez', *Filmkultura*, VII: 6 (1 June 1934), pp. 5–7.

7. Castiglione (1934), pp. 5–7; 'A magyar filmpiacon 1934. augusztus 1.-től 1935. julius 31.-ig 237 magyar és külföldi film jelent meg', *Filmkultura*, VIII: 11 (1 November 1935), pp. 10–11; *HNA*, OMB elnöki iratok, K 158, 6 cs., 1934–35, Alapszám 365/1934.
8. Statistics from 1932 to 37 are indicative of this change. H. Castiglione, 'Szinváltozások a magyar filmfogyasztás mozaikjában', *Filmkultura*, X: 4 (1 April 1937), pp. 2–4.
9. MKK Berlin (S. Masirevich) to Foreign Minister K. Kánya, 8759/1933. Berlin, 19 November 1933. *HNAiK* 66, 218 cs., 1933, III-6/c.
10. H. Hinkel, 'Schutz dem deutschen Kulturschaffen', *NSK*, 183 (8 August 1935). Hungarian diplomats in German communicated these exact sentiments to their cabinet-level superiors in Budapest. See MKK Berlin (Bóbrik) to Foreign Minister Kánya, 322/biz.-1935, Berlin, 30 October 1935. *HNA*, K 636, 605 cs., 1932–36, file pp. 278–82.
11. See Note 9.
12. 'Ungarische Kulturpolitik', *Germania*, 318 (17 November 1934); *Bundesarchiv Berlin* (hereafter *Barch)*, R 11, 1259 – 'Deutsch-Ungarische Handelskammer in Budapest – Jahresbericht 1938' (Budapest: February 1938), p. 3.
13. MKK Berlin (Sztójay) to Foreign Minister Kánya, 1014/1936, Berlin, 7 March 1936. *HNA*, K 66, 296 cs., 1936, III-6/c, Alapszám 911/1936. J. F. Montgomery to Secretary of State, No. 364, Budapest, 3 April 1936. *United States National Archives* (hereafter *USNA*), RG 59, M-1206, Roll 6, Decimal file 864.4061/Motion Pictures 57.
14. Interior Ministry memo, m.kir. BM 109412 sz., 1937, V. Kútfő, 22.tétel, Alapszám 108166. *HNA*, K 150, V.Kútfő, 15.tétel, Országos Mozgóképvizsgáló Bizottság ügyei.
15. Hungary's Second Jewish Law, Law IV/1939, adopted in May 1939, defined Jews by blood and further lowered the maximum percentage of Jews in all professions and institutions of higher learning to 6 per cent.
16. Mester Film received 300 000 pengő of investment from the German filmmaker Fritz Kreisle, likely at the behest of German authorities, to fund the production of four films. 5 July 1938 Hunnia Igazgatósági jegyzőkönyv. *HNA-Óbuda*, Z 1123, Raktári sz. 1, Dosszié sz.1, Igazgatósági jegyzökönyvek, 1938, file pp. 47–8. Nazi agents invested German capital in several other Hungarian companies in the early 1940s. See D. S. Frey, *National Cinema, World Stage: A History of Hungary's Sound Film Industry*, 1929–44 (New York: Columbia University (Unpublished Ph.D. Dissertation) 2003), pp. 393–7.
17. German and Hungarian sources indicate that Germany was interested in purchasing or controlling up to three premier theatres in Budapest. State Secretary Kálmán Tomcsányi, an assistant to Interior Minister Keresztes-Fischer in charge of cinema issues, claims to have thwarted German efforts to buy more than one theatre. See testimony of Tomcsányi in 'Tanúvallomási jegyzőkönyv', Magyar Államrendőrség Budapesti Főkapitányságának Politikai Rendészeti Osztálya, 21389 sz./1945, Budapest, 26 January 1946. Budapest Municipal Archives (*BpFL)*, People's Court documents related to the trial of Kálmán Tomcsányi, Nb. 839/1946, file p. 45
18. '21 November 1940 Jegyőkönyv – Hunnia Igazgatósági ülésről'. *HNA-Óbuda*, Z 1123, Raktári sz. 1, Dosszié sz.2. Igazgatósági jegyzőkönyvek, 1940–42, file p. 93

[1940]; 'Star Atelier', Aufzeichnung I, 16 April 1941, report on 10–13 February 1941 meeting of Deutsch-Ungarische Kulturausschuss. *AAA*, Gesandtschaft Budapest, Fach 27, Kult 12, Nr 4a, 'Filmwesen Ungarn'.

19. The films made were *Maske in Blau/Kék álarc* (1941), *Der Tanz mit dem Kaiser/Egy éjszaka Erdélyben* (1941), *Karnival der Liebe* (1942) and *Die heimliche Gräfin* (1942).
20. 'Jugoslawiens Filmeinfuhr', *Auslandsstimmen für die deutsche Wirtschaft*, 611 (21 August 1940).
21. Kolb to Gesandtschaft Budapest, 30 June 1940, Kult K 6753/40. *AAA*, Gesandtschaft Budapest, Fach 27, Kult 12, Nr 4a, 'Ungar. Filmpropaganda in Yugoslawien'.
22. H. Castiglione, 'A magyar mozipark új térfoglalása. A visszacsatolt Felvidék bekapcsolódása a magyar filmélet vérkeringésébe', *Magyar Film* I: 3 (4 March 1939), pp. 7–10; H. Castiglione, 'Ruszinszkó és a magyar mozipark', *Magyar Film* I: 19 (24 June 1939), p. 8; 'Hány mozi működik jelenleg Erdélyben?' *Magyar Film* II: 39 (28 September 1940), p. 4; 'A délvidéki mozgószinházak jegyzéke', *Magyar Film* III: 19 (10 May 1941), p. 3.
23. 'Jelentés a Jenes Nándor olaszországi utjáról', 3 November 1942. *HNA*, K 675, 3 cs., 16 tétel, 1942–43, file p. 47. Jenes was also an official in the Manufacturing Ministry.
24. In early 1942, the IFK granted Hungary permission to send four films to Italy, the same amount to Spain and 20 to Croatia; otherwise Hungary received no specific allotment for any other IFK member country. Hungarian officials were very bitter at this measly allotment of shares of foreign markets, rightly viewing it as an affront to their country, then the third leading producer of motion pictures on the continent. 'IFK. Tagungen der Internationalen Filmkammer' (IFK, 1942), see minutes, Berlin, 2–3 March 1942; Rome, 8–10 April 1942; and Florence, 10–11 May 1942.
25. By mid-1942, Hungarian authorities regarded the IFK as an 'imperialist' tool of the Germans designed merely to insure that German products were placed abroad and properly promoted. Vitéz P. Morvay, 'Jelentés a Nemzetközi Filmkamara 1942.ápr.római ülésről', 15 April 1942. *HNA*, K 150, V. Kútfő, 15.tétel, 3593 cs., file pp. 1–2
26. In 1942, three companies sold raw film to Hungary–Agfa (German), Ferrania (Italian) and Kodak (United States). The amount received from Kodak was minimal. See A. Lajta, *Filmművészeti Évkönyv* (1942), pp. 207–8. At the November 1942 IFK meeting in Budapest, Minister of Cults and Education J. Szinyei Merse declared the raw film question to be the most pressing issue plaguing Hungarian film. Quoted in *Magyarország Évkönyve – 1942*. IX (Budapest: Stádium Sajtóvállalat Rt, 1943), p. 104.
27. I. Kőszeghy to Minister of Cults and Education, 69.947/III sz. - 1942, Budapest, 26 May 1942. *HNA*, K 507, 91 cs., 12 tétel, 1937–41, Filmügyek.
28. Frey (2003), pp. 413–16.
29. 'Jelentés a Jenes Nándor olaszországi utjáról' (1942), file p. 47.
30. H. Hoffmann, *The Triumph of Propaganda. Film and National Socialism 1933–45*, Trans. J. A. Broadwin and V. R. Berghahn (Providence and Oxford: Berghahn Books, 1996), pp. 132ff.; F. Moeller, *Der Filmminister. Goebbels und der Film im Dritten Reich* (Berlin: Henschel Verlag, 1998), pp. 347–402; and R. Armes, 'Cinema of Paradox: French Film-making during the Occupation', in G. Hirschfeld and P. Marsh (eds), *Collaboration in France. Politics and Culture during the Nazi Occupation, 1940–44* (Oxford: Berg Publishers Ltd., 1989), pp. 126–9.

31. Géza Ágotai, for example, the second in command on the National Censorship Committee, wrote of narrow culture film as an influential *'Vorkämpfer der ungarischen Kultur'*. Géza Ágotai, '400 Schmalfilmtheater in fünf Jahren', *Interfilm. Blätter der internationalen Filmkammer* Heft 6 (August 1943), p. 76.
32. Deutscher Schmalfilm-Vertrieb GmbH 'Geschäftsübersicht ab Gründung bis einsschl. 31.Dezember 1941'. *Barch*, R 55/493, Fiche 2.
33. Although the German–Hungarian Cultural Committee agreed that the ratio of narrow films should be 1:1 at a June 1942 meeting, the Hungarian government refused to accept this decision, maintaining the 2:1 ratio. See handwritten notes on back of F. Inotay Interior Ministry memo, BÜM 116.833/1943, Budapest, 17 July 1943. *HNA*, K 150, V. Kútfő, 15.tétel, 3594 cs., 1942–43.
34. 'Tätigkeitsbericht des Reichspropgandaamtes Ausland für die Monate Januar, Februar, und März 1943'. Reichspropagandaamt Ausland, Pro 2005, Berlin, 30 April 1943, p. 23. *Barch*, NS 18/12. The majority of the audiences were ethnic German Hungarians.
35. Kolb to German Embassy Budapest, Kult K 11547/40, Berlin, 30 November 1940. *AAA*, Gesandtschaft Budapest, Fach 27, Kult 12, Nr 4b, 'Filmwesen ung. dt. Beziehungen, 1939–41'.

12
A War within the War: Italy, Film, Propaganda and the Quest for Cultural Hegemony in Europe (1933–43)

Aristotle A. Kallis

During the 1920s the Fascist regime in Italy transformed itself from a precarious experiment into a consolidated political system with both 'totalitarian' and universal ambitions. Benito Mussolini spoke in 1929 of fascism as an 'export product'; three years later, in the *Doctrine of Fascism,* he went even further, presenting Fascism as a viable alternative to both socialism and liberalism and proclaiming that the twentieth century would be 'the century of Fascism'.[1] By that time the regime had already developed a portfolio of activities that transcended the boundaries of Italy and ranged from financial assistance to ideological kindred movements (including the German *Nationalsozialische Deutsche Arbeiterpartei* (NSDAP), the Croat Ustasha and Macedonian separatists), diplomatic support to 'revisionist' governments and the active propagation of Fascism across Europe and beyond through establishing a network of organisations in a large number of countries.

The international activities of Italian Fascism, broadly conceived within the context of propaganda, expanded both quantitatively and qualitatively during the 1930s. Until 1935 the Fascist leadership had used foreign propaganda as a device of political influence and cultural hegemony. With the campaign against Ethiopia (1935–36) and Italy's involvement in the Spanish Civil War (1936–39), propaganda acquired a further dimension – this time as an extension of the regime's military activities. The need to use propaganda as a means of projecting a positive image for Italian Fascism, for presenting its own version of 'truth' and for supplying evidence of the alleged 'regeneration of the Italian nation under Fascism', was taken very seriously by the regime.[2] As a result, during the 1930s a significant organisational streamlining and expansion of propaganda activities took place, with institutional initiatives inside Italy and the systematic infiltration of foreign markets with Italian propaganda 'commodities'. This campaign embraced a wide spectrum of activities that after May 1937 fell under the institutional banner of the Ministry of Popular Culture (*Ministero della Cultura Popolare*, MinCulPop).[3]

Luigi Freddi and the General Directorate for Cinematography (DGC)

Cinema – alongside press, literature, radio and art – occupied a crucial position in the Fascist regime's efforts to exercise a form of cultural hegemony outside Italy.[4] As a modern medium with a relatively short history, cinema did not receive much attention by the Fascist authorities in the 1920s. During this period, the nascent Italian film industry continued to operate with relative autonomy and also with limited resources and fractional political assistance. Perhaps the most significant development in this domain during the first decade of Fascist rule was the establishment of *Luce* (*L'Unione Cinematografica Educativa*, Educational Cinematographic Union; the acronym also means 'light' in Italian) in 1923, whose function was primarily conceived as a medium of domestic information (newsreel, documentaries). Cinema's international political and cultural propaganda capital, however, was exploited far more systematically and expansively after 1933. The creation of the General Directorate for Cinematography (*Direzione Nazionale per la Cinematografia*, DGC) in 1934 constituted a significant gesture that reflected the regime's determination to invest in cinema production as a device of domestic and international hegemony. Under the leadership of Luigi Freddi, the DGC envisaged the future of Italian cinema as a mixed venture: centralised, generously funded by the state and serving the ideological goals of Fascism, but also with relative artistic autonomy and partly functioning within an internal market that was not oblivious to considerations of profit. Freddi identified the omnipotence of Hollywood as both a challenge to be overcome and a model for partial imitation. His pivotal role in the creation of the *Cinecittà* in 1937 – a magnificent studio to rival those in the United States – reflected the ambitious scope of his vision. He was also determined to support a healthy increase in domestic production with both high artistic quality and commercial potential for the domestic and the international market.

Freddi took over the supervision of Italian cinema at a crucial time, not just inside Italy but also in Europe. From January 1933 the National-Socialist regime in Germany emerged as a major radical force in European politics. The relations between the two regimes and leaders went through a series of phases – from an initial awkward rapprochement shrouded in mutual suspicion in 1933 to the near-conflict situation of July 1934 (Austrian coup), antagonism until 1936 and then the gradual convergence of the 'Axis' – again not without antagonisms, hesitation or misgivings – that culminated in the May 1939 alliance of the Pact of Steel.[5] The dynamism of the Nazi regime filled Mussolini with a blend of admiration, menace and disdain; this was a blend that – in different formats – would underpin Italian Fascist policy towards the regime's Axis ally until the very end. Freddi himself had criticised in no uncertain terms the handling of cinema by the Nazi authorities after his trip to Germany in 1936.[6] His corporatist vision of cooperation amongst the political, cultural and financial stakeholders of the film enterprise clashed with what he perceived as a 'violent' subjugation of cinema to the most rigid prerequisites of ideology in Hitler's Germany. His universalist perception of cinema as a device of indirect cultural hegemony diverged crucially from the far more interventionist handling of film production by Joseph Goebbels' Ministry of Popular Enlightenment and Propaganda (*Reichsministerium für Volksaufklärung und Propaganda*, RMVP). His refusal to authorise a complete ban on foreign (primarily American) imports in Italy contrasted sharply with the Nazi heavy-handed policy that revolved around strict censorship, anti-Americanism and anti-Semitism.

With the onset of war in 1939, Italian cinema was faced with new opportunities and challenges. The occupation of large parts of the European continent by the Axis troops opened up new markets for cultural infiltration. Practical considerations of production and distribution had to be measured against shifting military and material realities caused by the military conflict. At the same time, the need for intensifying propaganda activities in the context of the military campaign was taken up by both Axis partners. The result was an intriguing blending of coordination and cooperation, on the one hand, with antagonism and sometimes hostility, on the other. In this respect, cinema offers a significant case study for examining these patterns, as well as for assessing the relative success and failure of the Fascist attempts to use cinema as a device of propaganda influence and cultural domination across Europe.

Propaganda, film and the 'German factor': The Spanish Civil War

From the moment that Hitler came to power in 1933, the Fascist authorities in Italy showed great interest in the institutional innovations of the National-Socialist regime. The establishment of the RMVP in March 1933 and the creation of the Reich Culture Chamber with a separate Reich Film Chamber in its structure, in the following summer,[7] were studied carefully in Rome. The decision to incorporate cinema production in the Under-Secretariat for Press and Propaganda (*Sottosecretario per la Stampa e Propaganda*, SsSP) in 1934 (a responsibility previously belonging to the Interior Ministry and Ministry of Corporations), the subsequent institutional upgrading of the Under-Secretary to the status of ministry in June 1935 and the eventual creation of the MinCulPop in May 1937 under the leadership of Dino Alfieri with the law 752[8] reflected the elevated significance of propaganda both as domestic mechanism for consensus-building and as medium of foreign political and cultural influence. The intensifying activity in the domain of propaganda should be understood in three contexts – namely, the attempt to 'internationalise' Fascism, to fight against Bolshevism in what Mussolini himself called a 'European war of doctrines',[9] and to counter German National-Socialist influence in Europe after 1933.

The first real test for the new political function of Fascist propaganda on the international level came with the Spanish Civil War (1936–39). Although film propaganda abroad had become an integral part of the regime's Propaganda General Directorate (*Direzione Generale per I Servizi della Propaganda*, DGSP) ever since June 1934[10] and had played a crucial role in promoting the Fascist version of 'truth' during the campaign in Ethiopia (1935–36), it was in Spain that the opportunities for, and difficulties of the Fascist project of international political/cultural hegemony were put to the test. Whilst until the beginning of the Civil War the Italian penetration of the Spanish market was 'absolutely nil', especially compared to the overwhelming presence of Hollywood products, a more systematic approach by the DGC from 1937 onwards delivered a notable improvement.[11] The creation of the National Union for Film Export (*Unione Nazionale Esportazione Pellicula*, UNEP) facilitated the complex process of film selection, dubbing or subtitling and distribution. By February 1938, it was envisaged that more than 27 Italian films, a similar number of documentaries and specially prepared (dubbed) versions of the Luce newsreel were widely shown in nationalist-controlled Spain, through a series of formal agreements with local film organisations and distributors. Significantly, the number of films reached the figure of 35 by July and was expected to reach 70 in the near future.[12]

Nevertheless, the substantial rise of Italian film exports in Spain from 1937 onwards was both a complex and costly undertaking, fraught with anxieties and difficulties. In spite of the best efforts of the DGC and UNEP to establish normative processes of export and distribution, the operation continued to be conducted in a manner that was criticised as 'chaotic', 'discontinuous' and 'lacking in organisation'.[13] In particular, the considerable costs of dubbing and the financial risk of the unpredictable and unstable (not least due to the war) Spanish market threatened to render the whole enterprise 'unsustainable'.[14] In spite of formal agreements with distributors (such as Imperial Film of San Sebastian, Cifesa Seville and private entrepreneurs such as Lorenzo Fargas de Juny of San Sebastian),[15] there were substantial financial difficulties that troubled Freddi. According to his frequent reports throughout 1937–39, neither the (bad) state of the Spanish economy nor the complexities of the 'clearing' agreements augured well for the future of Italian film exports. In order to alleviate the situation, Freddi petitioned his superiors in the MinCulPop for generous state subsidies to cover the costs of dubbing and distribution. As a result, from February 1938, DGC (through UNEP) was authorised to contribute to production costs and public relations visits to Spain.[16] This initiative reflected accurately Freddi's conception of the propaganda role of Italian cinema as a centralised, state-subsidised enterprise but also alert to external commercial opportunities.

There was something else, however, that increasingly troubled the Fascist authorities in Rome with regard to the penetration of the Spanish market during the Spanish Civil War. The involvement of Nazi Germany in the conflict did not stop at diplomatic and military assistance; it also had a distinct political–ideological propaganda dimension that antagonised the similar Italian Fascist efforts. Of course, at that stage the relations between the two regimes were still cloaked in ambiguity and suspicion, in spite of their common lip service to the wider ideological significance of the confrontation in Spain and their gradual rapprochement after 1935.[17] Even so, a complex pattern of relations that oscillated between cooperation and antagonism came to characterise Italian–German relations during the Spanish Civil War that outlived the conclusion of the Pact of Steel in 1939 and extended into the Second World War. Already during 1937 the DGC and the UNEP were noting with alarm the aggressive infiltration techniques used by German propaganda authorities in Spain. The German newsreel (*Auslandstonwoche* or Foreign Weekly Newsreel, ATW) prepared by the Ufa giant had been made available to audiences in Nationalist-controlled Spain long before the Italian authorities were alerted to the political and commercial potential of the Spanish market.[18] During 1937, the DGC and the UNEP repeatedly alerted the regime's propaganda apparatus in Rome to the very real threat of a German monopoly through the distribution of films and the systematic infiltration of Spain by Nazi propaganda material. Agonising calls to match the level of German involvement in film activities and emulate the Nazi aggressive penetration technique continued to inundate the Ministry of Press and Propaganda. It was primarily this threat of German domination that galvanised the Italian propaganda machinery and resulted in the noticeable improvement of the situation from mid-1937 onwards. As a result, by early 1939, Freddi could boast that the DGC had done 'a good job' in Spain, especially considering the chaotic start of Italian involvement two years earlier.[19]

Italian film in the Axis 'New Order' (1939–43)

The 'German factor' remained a crucial determinant of Fascist propaganda activities after General Franco's victory in the Civil War in Spain. Since its creation the MinCulPop provided a more assertive and systematic framework for exporting Italian film products across Europe. With the formalisation of the Italian–German Axis alliance in the spring of 1939, contacts between official of the two regimes intensified, culminating in the comprehensive framework agreement (Accord) for the coordination of propaganda activities that was concluded in mid-August. This initiated a pattern of more formal and frequent visits between the RMVP and the MinCulPop with a view to streamlining a joint Axis propaganda venture and increasing the cultural penetration of the European market at the expense of United States and 'western' influence in this field.[20]

Yet, once again the Italian Fascist regime found itself at a disadvantage vis-à-vis its German partner. During the summer of 1939 the Italian Ambassador in Berlin monitored and reported back to his superiors in Rome the far-reaching changes in the Nazi propaganda structures put forward by Goebbels. Only days after the conclusion of the August 1939 Accord the Italian Foreign Minister (and former head of the Fascist propaganda until 1936), Galeazzo Ciano, found out about the German plans to invade Poland.[21] After long deliberations in Rome, Mussolini decided to adopt a policy of 'non-belligerence' and stay out of the European conflict for the foreseeable future. Consequently, with the onset of the Second World War in September 1939, Fascist Italy again found itself at odds with its primary ally.[22] Even more importantly, however, it was unprepared to compete with the Germans and thus take advantage of the new opportunities for penetrating the European market with its own cinema production. At a time that the (by then centralised) newsreel production in Germany was about to flood the occupied and neutral countries,[23] Mussolini was still struggling with limited resources, an awkward diplomatic position and an institutional apparatus that was not geared to a pan-European military conflict.

This does not mean that film propaganda activities had been neglected by the Fascist authorities prior to 1939. As early as 1937 the DGSP had – in addition to Spain – established networks in Greece, Yugoslavia, Poland and also Latin America. A total of 874 film products, totalling 536 000 m, were exported abroad during that year.[24] Contacts with studios and producers across Europe intensified after 1936; these included even Britain, which the ministry authorities considered a promising and lucrative market until well into 1939![25] In organisational terms, the upgrading of the SsSP into Ministry in 1935 also introduced a wider reorganisation of film activities. *Uffizio 4* of the new institution dealt specifically with cinema and 'artistic' propaganda; in addition, *Uffizio 2* (*Nuclei per la Propaganda all'interno e all'estero*, Centres for domestic and foreign propaganda, NUPIE) engaged in anti-Bolshevik propaganda abroad, facilitating the distribution of relevant visual material such as newsreel and documentaries.[26] As for the state, the increasing emphasis on propaganda from the mid-1930s onwards resulted in a number of legislative and financial measures that had a positive impact on the domestic film production and distribution abroad.[27] The 1938 'Alfieri laws' brought the export and import of films firmly under the control of the state (through *Ente Nazionale Industrie Cinematografiche*, National Agency for Cinema Industry, ENIC), introducing quotas for US imports and providing more decisive financial help to domestic producers (from 18 million lire in 1934 to more than 70 in 1937). As a result, the number of Italian films rose from the 30–40 level (1933–38) to 75–85 (1939–41). State pressure for increasing production (initially, towards 'quota 80', then to the far more ambitious 'quota 140'[28]) was also aimed to expand the volume and quality of exports. This goal was perfectly in line with Freddi's vision, even if at times the latter found his cooperation with the Minculpop minister Alfieri rather frustrating.[29]

The period between the outbreak of the Second World War in September 1939 and Italy's entry into the conflict in June 1940 gave some breathing space to the Fascist regime to digest the implications and prepare for a more expansive film policy in Europe. In October 1939, Alessandro Pavolini replaced Alfieri at the top of Minculpop; a few months earlier Freddi himself gave his place at the DGC to Vezio Orazi.[30] A series of amendments to the 1938 law were passed, designed to increase state involvement in all aspects of film production. But the penetration of foreign markets continued to show a slight, unremarkable expansion. The increasing co-operation with the German propaganda/cinema authorities in 1938–39 had already given Freddi the opportunity to review the situation in the Italian film industry and outline new priorities for the future. Abandoning his former criticism of the Nazi management of film in Germany, he now seemed alert to the political and financial implications of the Italian-German alliance. Co-production, sharing of good practice, cooperation of actors and directors from the two countries, as well as coordination of subjects appeared to him to be the logical extension of the initial agreement. The former admirer of Hollywood practices had now become converted to the prospect of an Axis bloc to the US domination of European markets.[31] To that effect he underlined the need for a series of further agreements in order to add 'a practical dimension of utility and efficiency' to the initial accord.[32]

Pavolini himself, as well as Freddi's successors at the DGC – Orazi and (from 1941) Eitel Monaco – shared this conviction and worked hard to take advantage of the opportunities provided by the Axis alliance. The minister of Popular Culture made a series of visits to Germany and negotiated a more comprehensive agreement about film imports–exports in October 1940. The new framework allowed for the increase of film exports from each Axis partner and for measures to facilitate their wide distribution, both inside the two countries and in occupied Europe. Between 1940 and 1943, Italian penetration of the German market increased dramatically. Germany continued to top the list of Italian exports throughout the war, eclipsing Spain as the most lucrative market: from 15 films totalling 5.7 m (1940) to 23 and 6.3 m (1941) to an impressive 38 and 32.8 m respectively (1942).[33] In the summer of 1940, emphasis was also placed on the need for joint action in 'bringing about a new economic and cultural order in the domain of cinematography in Europe'.[34] A year later, Pavolini and Goebbels agreed on a wider framework of Italo-German cooperation that involved substantial increases in exporting films to each other through the upgrading of the *Deutsche Italienische Film Union* (German–Italian Film Union, DIFU), in technical collaborations and in promoting the 'coordination' of cinema in Axis-occupied Europe under the auspices of an International Film Chamber.[35] The joint promotion of Axis cinema had also been incorporated into the planning for the Venice Film Festival, which from 1939 onwards featured only films from Axis countries/satellites and awarded the prizes primarily on the basis of political/ideological merit rather than quality.[36] The preferential treatment of German films at Venice was evident in the distribution of awards for best foreign film after 1938: Leni Riefenstahl's *Olympia* (1938), Gustav Ucicky's *The Postmaster* (*Der Postmeister*, 1940), Hans Steinhoff's *Uncle Krüger* (*Ohm Krüger*, 1941) and Veit Harlan's *The Great King* (*Der grosse König*, 1942).

However, the determination of the two regimes' propaganda authorities to promote political and cultural cooperation soon ran into many difficulties. In spite of reassurances by the RMVP officials (not least, of Goebbels personally) with regard to an increase in the import and distribution of Italian films in the Reich, the results continued to fall below expectations until well into 1941. DIFU did ensure that the number of imported films from Italy increased throughout 1940 and 1941 (reaching 17 in the first half of 1941 and projected to climb to above 20 by the end of that year) but the production and distribution companies in Germany proved rather lethargic in promoting them.[37] Even after the complete nationalisation of film industry in the Third Reich in 1941 the new giant Ufi appeared incapable or unwilling to distribute the necessary number of Italian films that would bring their number to the level agreed by Pavolini and Goebbels, namely 30 or above.[38] Furthermore, the continuous requests of Italian authorities for cooperation between studios in the two countries and for co-production of films in 'double version' (*doppia versione*) went largely unheeded by the German film industry.[39]

But there was a more troubling problem facing the Italian film and propaganda authorities in their dealings with their Axis ally. In spite of an expressed commitment of the two sides to jointly manage cinema in occupied Europe, the German authorities proved far less accommodating in practice. In June 1941, Eitel Monaco noted with alarm that the prior agreement for the distribution of Italian film products to Axis-controlled areas in Europe through Berlin was not being fully implemented by the Nazi authorities. In particular, he informed Pavolini that Italian films were distributed to occupied France with a 6-month delay; by contrast the German equivalent products were despatched without any attention to those formalities that were invoked by the Germans in order to explain the hold-up of Italian films.[40] More broadly, throughout 1940–41 Italian propaganda authorities continued to accuse Germans of showing 'hesitation and lack of uniformity' when dealing with the implementation of the Italo-German film agreements.[41] For their part, the Germans frequently expressed disapproval of Italian film import practices, particularly with regard to two thorny issues: first, the lack of an outright ban on American products in Italy (the Fascist regime never followed its German counterpart in effecting a full embargo, choosing instead to make the choice and distribution of foreign films the exclusive preserve of the state-controlled ENIC[42]); and, second, the Italian policy of actively favouring the distribution of domestic film products at the expense of imported (even German) ones.[43] The Italian authorities resisted German pressures on both these issues, reassuring instead their Axis interlocutors about their commitment to minimising any possible disruption caused by them. Furthermore, they showed good will in heeding early Nazi demands for avoiding separate contacts with authorities in occupied countries, thus leaving the initiative to the Germans in negotiating an 'Axis' agreement for the distribution of German *and* Italian films.

The result of the ambiguities surrounding Italo-German relations in the domain of film and propaganda was a mixed pattern of cooperation and competition that reflected the wider state of affairs between the two Axis partners. In fact, after an initial short period of exploring opportunities for comprehensive coordination, each partner chose to design policy in rather autonomous terms. The geo-political agreement between Hitler and Mussolini about 'spheres of influence' in Axis-occupied Europe[44] provided the Italian authorities with a *de facto* primary area of domination – namely the Danubian basin and the Balkan peninsula. This explains why Romania, Yugoslavia, Greece, Hungary and Bulgaria (along with Germany and Spain) became favoured markets of Italian film exports after 1941: the relevant revenue from these activities increased from around 4 m lire in 1941 to almost 25 m lire in 1942.[45] Italian authorities used the Luce newsreel and documentary products to promote the goal of ideological and cultural domination abroad; and it was often the threat of German penetration of these same markets that prompted the MinCulPop to increase spending in promoting film activities, which was estimated at 3.6 m lire in 1943 – far above spending in any other propaganda activity abroad.[46] Separate arrangements with authorities in the occupied countries within the above 'sphere of influence' resulted in an exponential increase in despatches of the Luce newsreels and magazines (*Telegiornali, Notiziari, Attualità*) and documentaries. The volume of such products rose from less than 500 000 m in 1938 to 1.1 m in 1942.[47] Similar independent arrangements regarding the sale of films were also concluded, particularly after the beginning of 1942, when a new law provided state financial incentives for the 'diffusion of Italian culture abroad'.[48] Revenue from the sale of films reached 35 m lire in the first 5 months of 1943, showing steady increase in spite of mounting production and distribution difficulties due to the deteriorating military situation.[49]

The Italo-German competition and mutual suspicion also extended beyond matters of distribution to the sphere of film content and presentation. The stereotypical image of Italy and the Italians had always suffered from low esteem inside Nazi Germany – initially because of theories suggesting their alleged 'racial' inferiority (not 'Aryans' but belonging to the 'Mediterranean race') and after 1939 due to Italy's poor military performance.[50] This helps us understand why the 1940 German film *In Blue Life* (*Ins blaue Leben*) provoked negative comments from audiences in showing a German girl falling in love with and marrying an Italian.[51] Nazi clichés about the Italians were sometimes also implicit in entertainment films: for example, the 1942 German blockbuster *The Great Love* (*Die grosse Liebe*) upset the Italian authorities with the way in which it portrayed Italians and life in the country. This latent German–Italian antagonism and suspicion extended to documentary/historical films as well. In 1942 the Italians produced the documentary-style film *Bengasi* that chronicled the occupation of the north African city of Benghazi by the Axis forces in 1941. The film premiered at the Venice Biennale (where it received awards for best Italian film – the prestigious *Coppa Mussolini* – and best male actor) but enraged Goebbels who refused to give authorisation for its distribution in the Reich. The reason he used to justify his decision was that the film (rather counter-factually) depicted the Axis victory as a predominantly Italian achievement, with very little credit given to the Germans. The Reich Propaganda minister thought that this 'falsification of history' would upset German audiences and exacerbate their already negative feelings towards the Italians.[52] A similar accusation of 'falsification' was raised by the Eitel Monaco in 1941 concerning the Ufa production of a film on the history of the Suez canal. The script that came to the attention of the Director of the DGC portrayed the engineer Alois Negrelli (who produced the first plan for the project) as German when, according to him, he was of 'Italian–Tyrolese' descent. Monaco continued to press the German authorities – through Pavolini – in the direction of emphasising that Negrelli was 'Italo-German' (!) and of ensuring an Italian–German co-production of the film.[53] As it became evident in 1942 that the film was not a priority for Ufa and cooperation was not forthcoming, Pavolini endeavoured to get Italian producers (Atesia Film) to produce the film[54] but the plan was eventually dropped.

Conclusions

Freddi's successors in the DGC continued to promote the vision of an Italian cinema as a device of both political/ideological influence and cultural hegemony over Axis-occupied Europe. They shared his determination to maintain high qualitative standards of production, a mixed pattern of state intervention and relative artistic freedom that remained far less intrusive than the equivalent in Nazi Germany or Soviet Russia, and his internationalist vision of cultural penetration. During the Second World War, Italian cinema experienced considerable growth in terms of output, revenue and diffusion alike. Only part of this growth, however, should be attributed to the opportunities provided by the new situation in Europe resulting from Nazi conquest. Although revenue from film activities exceeded one billion lire in 1942 (a rather impressive 50 per cent increase from the preceding year), income from exports represented less than 8 per cent of the above figure (89 m lire). The financial benefits of the rather successful diffusion of Italian newsreel and documentaries – particularly in Germany, the Balkan countries and Spain – were partly offset by the increasing costs of dubbing and distribution.

In this context, the initially ambitious Italo-German plans for a joint re-organisation of the European film market proved little more than

In the Second World War, Nazi Germany allowed Italy only to export a limited number of films to countries that were German-occupied. One of the happy few, of which this is a Belgian poster, was Amleto Palermi's *The Sinner* (*La Peccatrice*, 1940). The film starred Vittorio De Sicca, who after the war wrote film history with *The Bicycle Thief* (*Il Ladri di biciclette*, 1948). *Source*: Vande Winkel/Warie Collection.

wishful thinking. The Nazi authorities did re-organise the International Film Chamber and used it as a medium to promote their vision of a pan-European cultural space. They even agreed to the Italian request to appoint Giuseppe Volpi as president – a move that was defended by the Italian authorities on the basis of the planned 1942 Universal Exposition in Rome.[55] Yet, from the outset the Italo-German partnership was a rather strained affair and this ambiguous situation continued well after the consolidation of the Axis and the outbreak of the war.[56] Elements of competition and antagonism that characterised Italo-German relations during the period of the Spanish Civil War were partly alleviated or suppressed under the guise of the fascist alliance, but they were never resolved in favour of an actual cultural partnership. This was partly due to the rather limited resources available to Italian cinema when compared to Nazi Germany. It might also have a lot to do with the general discrepancy in dynamics between Italian and German cinema, the latter having already developed a momentum and acquired an international status of its own long before Nazi intervention in the 1930s and the Second World War.[57] Furthermore, the deterioration of the military situation facing Italy in 1942–43 caused severe logistical problems to the country's film industry (e.g., reduction of production to 'quota 80'[58]), disrupted distribution networks and led to a *de facto* marginalisation of its cultural input in the European 'new order'.

However, the eventual failure of the Italian Fascist project of cultural domination was not simply a matter of material, logistical and structural weaknesses in the indigenous film production. The Nazis never conceived of the Axis project as a genuine condominium – and this was as true of military matters as it was on cultural and political ones. As a result, Italian Fascist film authorities found their relation with their Axis partner exciting on paper and in discussions but increasingly frustrating in practice. The increase of the penetration of Italian film products in occupied Europe owed less to joint adventures and more to the determination of the authorities in Rome to match or at least approximate the German input in this domain. Even the seemingly preferential treatment of Italian production in Nazi Germany was hampered by distribution limitations and the general attitude of deprecation that the Nazi authorities and the general public held for their Axis partners. Frustrated by the lack of cooperation and thwarted by the Germans' attempts to ensure their primary cultural position in the new European market, Italians promoted their own vision of cinema culture through independent arrangements, often in direct competition with their military and ideological allies. In the end, however, the fate of this vision in the European 'new order' was subverted and then crushed under the weight of the same problems and realities that defeated all other Fascist ambitious wartime projects.

Notes

1. On the international-universalist ambitions of Mussolini, see M. Ledeen, *Universal Fascism. The Theory and Practice of the Fascist International, 1928–1936* (New York: H. Fertig, 1972). The quote is from B. Mussolini, 'Political and Social Doctrine of Fascism', in M. Oakeshott (ed.), *The Social and Political Doctrines of Contemporary Europe* (New York: Cambridge University Press, 1949), pp. 167–74.
2. *Archivio Centrale di Stato (ACS), Ministero della Cultura Popolare* (hereafter *MCP*), Gab(inetto) 86, 'Appunto', Freddi to Alfieri, 4 January 1938. All subsequent document references are to the ACS collection.
3. Generally on the propaganda apparatus of the Italian Fascist regime, see P. Ferrara, 'Il Ministero della Cultural Popolare', in Ferrara (ed.), *Il Ministero della Cultura Popolare e il Ministero delle Poste e Telegrafi* (Bologna: Il Mulino, 1992); P. V. Cannistraro, *La fabbrica del consenso: fascismo e mass media* (Bari: Laterza, 1975).
4. See in general G. P. Brunetta, *Storia del cinema italiano,* 4 vols (Rome: Editori Riuniti, 1993); G. Aristarco, *Il cinema fascista. Il prima e il dopo* (Bari: Dedalo, 1996); C. Carabba, *Il cinema del ventennio nero* (Florence: Vallecchi, 1974); L. Freddi, *Il cinema,* 2 vols (Rome: l'Arnia, 1949); J. A. Gili, *Stato fascista e cinematografia. Repressione e promozione* (Rome: Bulzoni, 1981); C. Lizzani, *Storia del cinema italiano. 1895–1961* (Florence: Parenti, 1961); M. Verdone, *Storia del cinema italiano* (Rome: Newton Compton, 1995).
5. For the development of Italo-German relations and the two regimes' foreign policy, see M. Knox, 'Conquest, Domestic and Foreign, in Fascist Italy and Nazi Germany', *Journal of Modern History,* 56:1 (1984), pp. 1–57; Ibid., 'Expansionist Zeal, Fighting Power, and Staying Power in the Italian and German Dictatorships', in R. Bessel (ed.), *Fascist Italy and Nazi Germany* (Cambridge: Cambridge University Press, 1996), pp. 113–33; A. Kallis, *Fascist Ideology. Territory and Expansionism in Italy and Germany, 1919–1945* (London: Routledge, 2000), Chapters 4–5.
6. Cannistraro (1975), pp. 459–62; G. P. Brunetta, *Storia del cinema italiano,* vol 2: *Il cinema del regime, 1929–1945* (Rome: Editori Riuniti, 2001, new ed.), pp. 15–16.
7. On the structures of Nazi propaganda, see D. Welch, *The Third Reich. Politics and Propaganda,* 2nd ed. (London: Routledge, 2002); A. Kallis, *National Socialist Propaganda in the Second World War* (Basingstoke: Palgrave, 2006), Chapters 1–2.
8. *Archivio Centrale dello Stato: Guida Generale degli Archivi di Stato Italiani* (Rome: Uffizio Centrale per I Beni Archivistici, 1981), pp. 106ff.
9. B. Mussolini, 'I volontari e Londra', in Edoardo e Duilio Susmel (ed.), *Opera Omnia di Benito Mussolini,* vol. XXVIII (Florence/Rome: La Fenice, 1959), pp. 218–20.
10. MCP, Gab 86, 'Appunto', Freddi to Alfieri, 4 January 1938.
11. MCP, Gab 84, 'Appunto', Freddi to Alfieri, 1938 (no specific date).
12. MCP, Gab 68, 'Appunto', Freddi to Alfieri, 18 February 1938; 'Appunto', Freddi to Alfieri, 27 Februay 1938; cf. MCP, Gab 83, 'Elenco film veduti per la Spagna Nazionale', Report by Giulio Santangelo (UNEP), 15 July 1938.
13. MCP, Gab 68, 'Propaganda cinematografica in Spagna', DGC Report, 13 November 1937.
14. MCP, Gab 68, UNEP to Alfieri, 15 July 1938.
15. MCP, Gab 83, 'Appunto', MinCulPop (illegible signature) to Alfieri, 9 August 1938.
16. Freddi, 'Appunto per la DG per il Servizio della Propaganda a al Gabinetto', 23 February 1939.

17. M. Funke, *Sanktionen und Kanonen. Hitler Mussolini und der internationale Abessinienkonflikt 1934–36* (Düsseldorf: Droste, 1970); Kallis (2000) Chapter 5.
18. See Chapter 19.
19. MCP Gab 86, 'Appunto', Freddi to Alfieri, 1938 (n.d.).
20. MCP, Gab 168, 'Accordo cinematografico italo-tedesco', 13 August 1939.
21. F. Siebert, *Italiens Weg in den Zweiten Weltkrieg* (Bonn: Athenäum, 1962), Chapter 7; C. J. Lowe and F. Marzari, *Italian Foreign Policy 1870–1940* (London and Boston: Routledge & Kegan Paul, 1975), pp. 338ff.; G. Ciano, *Europa verso il catastrofe* (Milan: Mondadori, 1948), pp. 449–59; *Documenti Diplomatici Italiani*, 8th Series, vol. XIII, nos 1/4/21.
22. Kallis (2000), Chapter 6.
23. R. Vande Winkel, 'Nazi Newsreels in the New Order, 1939–1945: The Many Faces of Ufa's Foreign Weekly Newsreel (Auslandstonwoche) versus the German Weekly Newsreel (*Deutsche Wochenschau*)', *Historical Journal of Film, Radio and Television* 24:1 (2004), pp. 5–34; Kallis (2006), Chapter 7.
24. MCP, Gab 168, Direzione Generale per I Servizi della Propaganda, Report for film activities for the year 1937 (no specific date).
25. MCP, Gab 168, Report of Ambassador in London to DGSP, 27.4.1936; cf. *Atti Consiglio dei Ministri* (ACM), 1939–40, MCP, 'Disegno di legge con quale si autorizza l'Ente Nazionale Industrie Cinematografiche (ENIC) ad assumere del conto per lo Stato partezipazioni azionarie in società di produzione cinematografiche', 3 October 1939.
26. MCP, Gab 168, Ministry of Press and Propaganda, Annual Report for year 1936, February 1937. For NUPIE activities see MCP, NUPIE, 33, folder: 'Propaganda all'estero', Report on NUPIE activities, 28 March 1940.
27. Brunetta (2001), pp. 13–25.
28. A. Pavolini, 'Rapporto sul cinema', in *Cinema italiano* (Rome: Direzione Generale per la Cinematografia, 1941), pp. 2–3.
29. MCP, Gab 168, Freddi to Alfieri, 1937 (no specific date), concerning a disagreement between the two about preventive censorship.
30. ACM 1938–39, MCP, Appointment of Dr Vezio Orazi to the DGC, 4 April 1939.
31. M. Argentieri, *L'asse cinematografico Roma-Berlino* (Rome: Libreria Sapere, 1986), pp. 35–45, 59.
32. MCP, Gab 168, 'Appunto', Freddi to Pavolini, 18 August 1939.
33. MCP, Gab 143, 'Esportazioni film', DGC to Minister of Popular Culture, May 1943.
34. MCP, Gab 69, 'Viaggi Pavolini in Germania', Report by Orazi on Pavolini's visit to Germany (20–25 June 1940), 25 June 1940.
35. MCP, Gab 68, 'Viaggi Pavolini in Germania', Monaco to Pavolini, 19 June 1941.
36. Brunetta (2001), pp. 41–4. See also the conscious promotion of Axis cinema through the institution of 'Italo-German Film Week' at Venice, starting in August 1940, in MCP, Gab 69, Report by Orazi on Pavolini's visit to Germany, 25 June 1940.
37. MCP, Gab 68, 'Viaggi Pavolini in Germania', Monaco to Pavolini, 16 June 1941.
38. MCP, Gab 68, 'Viaggi Pavolini in Germania', Pavolini, Report on his trip to Germany, 22 June 1941; MCP, Gab 74, Monaco to Pavolini, 29 April 1942.
39. MCP, Gab 68, 'Viaggio Pavolini, 16–18 marzio 1942 a Monaco', Monaco to Pavolini, 13 March 1942.

40. MCP, Gab 63, Monaco to Pavolini, 15 June 1941.
41. MCP, Gab 74, Monaco to Pavolini, 29 April 1942.
42. L. Solaroli and L. Bizzarri, *L'industria cinematografica italiana* (Milan: Parenti, 1958), pp. 30–5; Brunetta (2001), pp. 22–3.
43. MCP, Gab 68, 'Viaggi Pavolini in Germania', Monaco to Pavolini, 19 June 1941.
44. M. Funke, 'Die deutsche-italienische Beziehungen: Anti-bolschevismus und aussenpolitische Interessenkonkurrenz als Strukturprinzip der "Achse"', in M. Funke (ed.), *Hitler, Deutschland und die Mächte. Materialien zur Aussenpolitik des Dritten Reiches* (Düsseldorf: Droste, 1977), pp. 828–30.
45. MCP, Gab 95, DG per I Scambi Culturali to Pavolini, 30 June 1943; cf. MCP, Gab 68, 'Promemoria', meeting between Under-Secretary of Ministry of Foreign Affairs Woermann and representatives of DG Stampa e Propaganda, no date (1941).
46. MCP, Gab 95, Rapporto DG per I Scambi Culturali to Polverelli, 29 May 1943.
47. MCP, Gab 95, DG per I Scambi Culturali to Pavolini, 26 August 1942.
48. ACM 1942–43, MCP, 'Legge n 129 per la diffusione della cultura italiana all'estero', 29 January 1942.
49. MCP, Gab 109, Monaco to Polverelli, 16 July 1943, Report on sales of films for 1943.
50. On German/Nazi theories about the 'racial' derivation of the Italians, see A. Gillette, *Racial Theories in Fascist Italy* (New York: Routledge, 2002), Chapter 1.
51. BArchiv, NS 18, 347, Doc 39 (Partei Kanzlei, Bericht aus Madgeburg-Anhalt, 9 December 1941).
52. W. Boelcke (ed.), *The Secret Conferences of Dr Goebbels: The Nazi Propaganda War, 1939–43* (New York: E. P. Dutton and Co, 1970), pp. 203–4.
53. MCP, Gab 68, Monaco to Pavolini, 17 June 1941.
54. MCP, Gab 68, Riassunto degli argumenti trattati nell'incontro di Monaco tra Goebbels e Pavolini, 17 March 1942.
55. MCP, Gab 68, Monaco to Pavolini, 19 June 1941.
56. M. Argentieri, *Il cinema in guerra. Arte, comunicazione e propaganda in Italia 1940–1944* (Rome: Editori Riuniti, 1998). See also B. Martin's contribution elsewhere in this volume.
57. See generally, E. Rentschler, *The Ministry of Illusion. Nazi Cinema and Its Afterlife* (Cambridge, MA and London: Harvard University Press, 1996), Introduction; D. Welch, *Propaganda and the German Cinema, 1933–45* (London & New York: IB Tauris, 2001, rev. ed.); S. Deren, *The Cradle of Modernity: Politics and Art in Weimar Republic (1918–1933)*, unpublished MSc thesis, Middle East Technical University, Ankara, 1997, pp. 129–63; T. G. Plummer (ed.), *Film and Politics in the Weimar Republic* (New York: Holmes and Meier, 1982).
58. MCP, Gab 83, Monaco to Polverelli, 4 January 1943.

13
Celluloid Competition: German–Japanese Film Relations, 1929–45

Janine Hansen

From 1929, the Ufa Company in Berlin regularly received visits from one representative of the Japanese film industry. Nagamasa Kawakita, Japanese film pioneer and founder of film import company Tôwa Shôji Gôshi Kaisha, invariably came to Germany once a year and bought the previous year's feature films and some *Kulturfilme* to screen in Japan. For the Ufa, this trade represented a steady flow of convertible currency, if not exactly a huge income. Ufa's international department was under permanent pressure to yield profits, but because it concentrated on the European markets, Japan was never high on its agenda. In this context the Ufa board was reluctant to consider proposals that strayed from the usual business lines. For example, in 1934, Koichi Kishi, a Japanese who sometimes worked for the company's *Kulturfilm* and marketing departments, suggested the founding of a German–Japanese film production company offering 1 million Reichsmark as funds to be supplied by the Japanese government. The board was not interested.[1]

Japanese–German film exchange: The framework

Despite the strategic alliance between the Axis partners that began with the Anti-Comintern Pact in November 1936, neither Ufa nor any other German film company regarded the Japanese market as a field of expansion worth pursuing. This included Joseph Goebbels, the German Propaganda Minister. In a speech delivered before film experts on 28 February 1942, Goebbels said that after the war the whole earth would undoubtedly be divided into spheres of interest and that the modern technical methods of mass leadership, film and radio, would then have an even greater importance: 'We have to give the film a purpose and a mission and then conquer the world with it, too.' In the same speech he praised the Japanese for their 'religious enthusiasm' that allows them to topple empires much bigger and richer than their own and concluded that if the Germans were one day filled by this kind of enthusiasm and still had the right leadership, the world would belong to them.[2] However, there is no hint that the German film was meant to have a mission in Asia, too. By this time, the Japanese controlled much of mainland China and South-East Asia, and were busy setting up cinemas and distributing Japanese films in these territories – a fact the Ufa intermediary in Tokyo, Johannes Barth, urgently advised his bosses in Germany to consider: 'Without or against the Japanese film industry, there is nothing with regard to film anybody can do in East Asia anymore.'[3] But the board had other priorities and was content to carry on as before while the war made business in and outside Germany more and more difficult.

Film imports from the West to Japan had been no easy task even before the beginning of the Second World War. Ever since the introduction of the talkies there was the language problem to overcome, together with bureaucratic and economic obstacles and the tight currency control imposed by the Japanese government in 1937.[4] Strict censorship meant, for example, that every kissing scene had to be cut. But what hindered the film import business most was the fact that Japan had been at war with its neighbour China since 1931, a war that escalated in the following years until Japan entered the Second World War with its attack on Pearl Harbor on 7 December 1941. The economy was subject to wartime regulations long before the Second World War began in Europe. Among the first to be affected by this were the American film companies. In 1936, before the Japanese government banned US films for about a year in 1937, a total of 268 American films were shown in Japan, as compared to 25 from Germany, 23 from France, 14 from Great Britain, and 3 from Austria. The big Hollywood studios like Paramount, MGM, Universal Pictures, Warner Bros., and 20th Century Fox all had offices in Tokyo equipped with American staff watching the local market and promoting their films. European film companies were represented by small Japanese import firms like Tôwa Shôji. After the ban the market share of US films was still 8 per cent in 1938 (as compared to 12 per cent in 1934) while the European share remained at 3 per cent in both years.[5] After Pearl Harbor the import of American films was banned again, and after 1942 the import of all foreign films became virtually impossible because the shipment routes via the Trans-Siberian railway or aboard trade vessels by sea could not be used anymore.

Before the war, the greatest obstacle to importing films to Japan was the Japanese film industry itself. The annual production amounted to about 500 films (more than Hollywood) – most of them being 'period films', tales of samurai set in Japan's feudal past. Movies were an affordable mass entertainment. In 1933, there were 1065 film theatres in the country, most of them located in Tokyo and other big cities. In 1937, the number went up to 2003. The vast majority screened only domestic films and were affiliated with one of the big studios Toho, Shochiku, and Nikkatsu. These majors pushed their products into the cinemas and film theatre owners had little choice but to accept what was offered. Film programmes changed often and quickly; usually a film would only stay on screen for about 2 or 3 weeks. Only 47 cinemas in Japan showed foreign films at all.[6] Nevertheless, American, French, and German films, in particular, were an important part of the Japanese urban culture. This can be seen from an enormous amount of reviews, comments, and other articles published in newspapers and the numerous film magazines. Critics often cited foreign films to lament the shortcomings of the Japanese product, and film-makers sometimes used foreign avant-garde films as foils for their own work. Apart from this, Japan was a proud film nation and eager to export their films to the West. Newspapers and film magazines featured a heated debate on the subject of how to get the national movie output onto Western screens and how to make Japanese films compatible with world market – a debate that had to do as much with national pride as with economic ambitions.

Japanese films in Germany

A key figure in this realm was Kawakita, Ufa's business partner since 1929. He had lived in Germany from 1923–24. After going back to Japan he founded the film import company Tôwa Shôji in 1928. Kawakita and his wife Kashiko were entrepreneurs with a vision. Importing foreign films was only one aspect of their work, another goal being the export of Japanese films to the West. After the first failure in 1929 with *Nippon*, an omnibus film containing pieces by three directors, Kawakita decided to try a different approach. In 1935, he went to Berlin and hired director Arnold Fanck for what was to be the first German–Japanese co-production.[7] Fanck's mountaineering films were known in Japan for their scenic beauty. Even though his films were box office hits in Germany, film companies hesitated to employ this eccentric film-maker because his insistence on extensive outdoor shooting caused production costs to soar. Fanck was therefore happy to strike a deal with Kawakita, and together they embarked on a project that was meant to please Japanese and German audiences alike. The story evolves around Teruo, a young man torn between duty and loyalty towards his family and tradition (embodied by his Japanese fiancée) and his search for individual freedom and independence (embodied by Gerda, his German friend and soul mate). In the end, the wild young man is tamed, marries, and takes his wife from overcrowded Japan to the vast plains of Manchuria where they live as settlers protected by the Japanese army. The film, *The New Earth* (*Atarashiki tsuchi*), premiered in Tokyo on 4 February 1937 just 3 months after Germany and Japan had become partners in the Anti-Comintern Pact. Seven weeks later, on 23 March 1937, it had another glamorous premiere in Berlin with Nazi dignitaries including Goebbels and other ministers as well as senior

Nationalsozialische Deutsche Arbeiterpartei (NSDAP) representatives present. In Germany, the film title was *A Daughter of the Samurai* (*Die Tochter des Samurai*). Even though Goebbels ordered the press to praise the film lavishly he criticised it in private saying it should be cut rigorously. Reviewers in Germany dutifully lauded *A Daughter of the Samurai* and very often stressed the common trait between Germans and Japanese – both being a *Volk ohne Raum* (people without living space). Reviews in Japan were much less favourable but the film proved to be a box office success in both countries.

Kawakita accompanied the film and its Japanese lead actress Setsuko Hara to Germany, and their tour of the Reich received a considerable press coverage. The *Lichtbildbühne* magazine featured an interview with Kawakita on its front page entitled 'Will the Japanese film secure itself a position in the West?'[8] Actually, *A Daughter of the Samurai* remained the only such success for a Japanese film and for Kawakita. There was only one more co-production, *The Holy Goal* (*Das Heilige Ziel*, 1939), a semi-documentary on the Olympic preparation two Japanese ski jump athletes undergo with their German coach. The film was completed in 1939 but was not screened before 1942, and it received less than enthusiastic reviews. Other Japanese films released in Germany were *Ine and her Horse* (*Ine und ihr Pferd*, 1941) and the air force film *Nippon's Wild Eagles* (*Nippons wilde Adler*, 1942), a film about the training of young pilots and their sorties in China. A German advisor supported the production of this film, and it was commissioned and in part financed by the Japanese military who dedicated it to Adolf Hitler and the German people. During its solemn premiere in Berlin on 5 June 1942, the Japanese ambassador and many representatives from the Nazi and *Wehrmacht* elite were present.[9] The *Filmkurier* called the film an 'epic song of the Japanese pilots' spirit' and characterises it by two quotes from the film itself: 'Your life does not belong to you, it belongs to Nippon' and 'For us, to die decently means the same as to live decently.'[10] Even though film magazines like *Filmkurier* and *Lichtbildbühne* regularly ran articles on the situation of the Japanese film industry, on Japanese films shown in Tokyo, or on how German films fared in Japan, Japanese films remained more or less unknown in the Reich.

German films in Japan

In comparison, quite a number of German films made it to the screens in Japan. Between 1933 and 1942, when government regulations forced all film-importing companies to merge into one and at the same time film import more or less came to a halt altogether, Tôwa Shôji brought nearly a hundred German films into the cinemas. These included *Girls in Uniform* (*Mädchen in Uniform*, 1931) and the leftist workers film *Kuhle Wampe* (1932), political and propaganda films like *Hitler Youth Quex* (*Hitlerjunge Quex*, 1933), *Dawn* (*Morgenrot*, 1933), *Refugees* (*Flüchtlinge*, 1933), *Operation Michael* (*Unternehmen Michael*, 1937), *Campaign in Poland* (*Feldzug in Polen*, 1940) and *Victory in*

Nagamasa Kawakita, Japanese film pioneer, founder of film import company Tôwa Shôji Gôshi Kaisha and producer of Arnold Fanck's *The Daughter of the Samurai* (1936). *Source*: Kawakita Memorial Film Institute.

the West (*Sieg im Westen*, 1941), many musical films like *Lover Divine* (*Leise flehen meine Lieder*, 1933), *Waltz War* (*Walzerkrieg*, 1933), and *Masquerade in Vienna* (*Maskerade*, 1934), the Leni Riefenstahl documentaries *Triumph of the Will* (*Triumph des Willens*, 1935) and *Olympia* (1938) and Zarah Leander vehicles like *La Habanera* (1937) and *To New Shores* (*Zu neuen Ufern*, 1937) among many others.[11]

Each year the leading Japanese film journal *Kinema Junpô* asked critics to select the Best Ten domestic and foreign films. In 1933, *Girls in Uniform* was voted the best foreign film and in 1934 *The Congress Dances* (*Der Kongress tanzt*, 1931) came second. Until 1939 nearly all the German and Austrian films appearing on this list were music or melodramatic films like *Farewell Waltz* (*Abschiedswalzer*, 1934), *Vienna Burgtheater* (*Burgtheater*, 1936), *The Girl Irene* (*Das Mädchen Irene*, 1936), and *The Real Big Follies* (*Die ganz grossen Torheiten*, 1937). The emigrated German film-makers Ernst Lubitsch, Fritz Lang, and G. W. Pabst who were working in the United States and in France also feature prominently, with six films to their credit among the Best Ten between 1933 and 1939. The year 1940 sticks out as an exception. It was an especially successful year for German films in Japan, and it also

Propaganda Minister Joseph Goebbels at the Japanese Embassy in Berlin, to celebrate the German premiere of Arnold Fanck's *The Daughter of the Samurai* (1936), in April 1937. From left to right: German lead actress Ruth Eweler, Goebbels, Japanese lead actress Setsuko Hara and the Japanese envoy, Viscount Kintomo Mushakoji. *Source*: Ullstein-Bild.

shows how the critics' appreciation of foreign films changed as the Second World War drew closer: *Olympia Festival of the Nations* (the first part of Riefenstahl's *Olympia*) was voted number one, *Operation Michael* came in at number three and *Olympia Festival of Beauty* (second part) was voted number five.[12]

During the 1930s, critics and journalists in Japan were still relatively free to express their opinions. One of the leading critics was Akira Iwasaki, a well-known leftist who often wrote about German politics, culture and films in various magazines. In the 1936 *Film Yearbook*, he published an article critical of the Nazi film policy.[13] The quality of German films had declined, he wrote, because film was now completely subjected to the aim of Nazi propaganda. He then explains that many artists who had made Berlin the centre of the European film before the Nazis came to power had now been forced out of their jobs and often also out of the country. Today, he concludes, Germany has lost its former position to France or Great Britain. Now, one had to lower the expectations one cherished towards German films because the Nazis were using all aspects of German culture in their destructive way, and film was no exception.

Torn between two countries. Teruo in a scene from *The Daughter of the Samurai* (1936). *Source*: Matthias Fanck.

In his book *Hitler and Film* published after the war, Iwasaki analyzes *Operation Michael* which had been a box office hit in Japan. The film tells the story of a German army battalion surrounded by enemy troops in the First World War. They cannot break out, so the major asks his general to attack the enemy even though this would mean certain death for his own battalion, too. The film glorifies the soldiers' desperate fighting spirit in a hopeless situation and their heroic deaths. Iwasaki sees this concept of *Heldentod* (heroic death), a concept he traces back to the medieval German culture, the Nibelungen legend, as one of the reasons for the film's success in Japan. The idea that the 'value of a soldier lies more in the depth of his sacrifice than in the size of his victory', as Heinrich George, playing the general says in the film, also existed in Japan but was introduced much later in the Meiji period (1868–1912). This underlying principle of heroic death that defines Karl Ritter's films *Operation Michael* and *Leave on Word of Honour* (*Urlaub auf Ehrenwort*, 1938) is what Japanese audiences could relate to according to Iwasaki.[14] *Operation Michael* is also one of the very few films where one can trace a direct influence from a German upon a Japanese film: *General, Staff, and Soldiers* (*Shôgun to sanbô to hei*, 1942) was based on *Operation Michael*. Apparently, the film company Nikkatsu made it only after an officer from the Army Information Section – an army section in charge of censorship – asked all Japanese film companies why they did not produce war films as sophisticated and effective as *Operation Michael*. Ironically, it was this same army section that later ordered a number of changes to *General, Staff, and Soldiers*.[15] In July 1945, only a few weeks before the war ended with the bombs on Hiroshima and Nagasaki, *The Last Visit Home* (*Saigo no kikyô*) was released. It follows a squadron of future kamikaze pilots on leave before they are to haul themselves into enemy strongholds and into their own deaths. The plot resembles another Ritter film, *Leave on Word of Honour*.[16]

One more film that made an impact in Japan was *Request Concert* (*Wunschkonzert*, 1940). The film tells the story of two lovers who are separated when the young man, a pilot, has to go off to war on a secret mission. His lover realises he still cares when she hears his requested song on the radio programme, the *Wehrmacht Request Concert*. Thanks to the radio they can meet again. When the film opened in Japan the *Filmkurier* proudly noted on its front page that *Request Concert* was received with great enthusiasm by the Japanese press for its sense of humour and its entertaining treatment of a serious war topic.[17] One of the Japanese articles on *Request Concert* was written by well-known critic Hideo Tsumura. In his six-page review in the leading literary magazine *Chûô Kôron*, he calls it a new type of war film because it is not set in the past or on the battleground like most Japanese war films but based on the daily life of civilians and soldiers during wartime. He complained that the sound quality of many domestic films was so bad one could hardly grasp the dialogue much less enjoy any of the music. About 10 years after the introduction of the talkie in Japan now here was a film that made use of the modern techniques talkie and radio as no other film had before. Tsumura wants *Request Concert* to be an inspiration for Japanese film-makers: 'The Japanese have been fighting [in this war] for more than 5 years, but is there any Japanese film depicting the daily life of the people as beautifully?' The question is a rhetorical one, and so he concludes his text with an appeal to the Japanese film world to push into a new era of war film production.[18]

Another genre that enjoyed huge popularity in Japan was the music film. It seemed only natural that musical films and film operettas should come from the country of Beethoven, Liszt, and Schubert, and it made little difference to a great part of the audience that this would be Austria as much as Germany. Willi Forst's films *Unfinished Symphony* (1934, an Austrian–British coproduction) and *Vienna Burgtheater* were well liked by critics – both were among the *Kinema Junpô* Best Ten in the respective years of their Japanese release – and audiences alike. Critic Murao Nakamura called *Unfinished Symphony* a film as beautiful and charming as the melodies of Franz Schubert and predicted that people around the world would probably love the film with all their hearts just as they loved Schubert's melodies.[19]

In 1936 the magazine *Germania* printed a travel account by a journalist from Dairen in Manchuria. He relates how the Japanese audience as much as the expatriate Germans felt entertained by German comedies and music films. What interested audiences abroad most were comical films and film operettas on the one hand and military–technical films on the other hand, he noted.[20] The popularity of musical films inside and outside the Reich was well known in the *Reichsministerium für Volksaufklärung und Propaganda* (RMVP), and Goebbels was not exactly pleased with this reputation of the German film.

German newsreels and the so-called *bunka eiga* (culture film, a literal translation of the German word *Kulturfilm*) were shown in Japanese cinemas on a regular basis. Since 1940, cinemas were required to show culture films with every entertainment programme.[21] Kawakita's Tôwa Shôji imported dozens of educational *Kulturfilme*, many of them directed by Nicholas Kaufmann, Ulrich K. T. Schulz, Wolfram Junghans, or Oskar Fischinger.[22] Cinemas regularly screened the foreign news digest *Nichiei Overseas News* (*Nichiei kaigai nyûsu*).[23] The style of these foreign newsreels which included material from the *Deutsche Wochenschau* (German Weekly Newsreel, DW – images that probably reached Japan through the *Auslandstonwoche* or Foreign Weekly Newsreel, ATW) notably influenced camerawork in Japan.[24] They also had an impact on Japanese politicians who were reluctant to grant shooting permits until they realised how they could make use of the medium when they saw Hitler's performances in German newsreels. But among Japanese news cameramen there were also voices critical of German newsreels. In an article published by the film magazine *Eiga Hyôron* in April 1941, cameraman Shuji Taguchi wrote, 'I believe German newsreels aren't news but government propaganda films. [. . .] I don't want to speak badly of Germany but if these newsreels are shown in a Japanese cinema for a week or two viewers will lose confidence.'[25]

Apart from the influence that individual German films and newsreels may have had on certain Japanese productions there was one more field in which the impact of Nazi Germany became apparent; namely in the overall regulation of the film world. In October 1939, a new film law was enacted, a law that put great emphasis on control and censorship. About the only contemporary who dared to openly criticise the film law was Iwasaki, and this led to his imprisonment in 1940.[26] He called the film law the Japanese version of the German *Lichtspielgesetz* (Reich Cinema Law).[27] Some of its regulations resembled the German law. All persons working in the film industry had to obtain a state licence, a pre-production censorship of all dramatic scripts was imposed, film theatre owners could be compelled to screen educational films, films could be banned despite having passed inspection, the screening of films 'necessary for enlightenment and propaganda' could be ordered, the Home Ministry was enabled to dictate what kind and how many foreign films could be imported, and on top of this there were clauses enabling the Ministry to regulate production and distribution whenever they thought this was 'necessary for public good'.[28]

Conclusion

Some German films together with Nazi film control undeniably made an impact in Japan. When it comes to war films, concepts like heroic death and self-sacrifice for the nation seem to be a common staple and a narrative necessity more than anything else. On the whole, German films made up a minuscule part of the body of films screened in Japan between 1939 and 1945. To the general audience, a German film seemed as Western as any French or American movie. The same can be said of the censors who were trying hard to eliminate from the screens all signs of Western decadence endangering traditional and moral values. During the Second World War they reduced the influx of foreign films – including those from Germany – to a faint trickle. By that time, the Ufa board had other things to worry about. In their meetings they now discussed how to continue film projects with staff drafted into the *Wehrmacht*, killed on the battlefield, and cinemas destroyed in air raids. Even in this ghostly situation, the Ufa board protocols still note that whenever they heard anything from Japan at all it seemed like business as usual.[29] The German film conquering the world thus remains a chimera with regard to Japan and much of East and South East Asia.

Notes

1. See Bundesarchiv (hereafter BArch) R 109 I/1029a, p. 10.
2. See speech in G. Albrecht, *Der Film im Dritten Reich. Eine Dokumentation* (Karlsruhe: Schauburg, Fricker & Co, 1979), pp. 484–500.
3. 'Bericht über die Filmwirtschaftliche Lage in Japan und den von ihm beherrschten Gebieten', 7 October 1941, BArch R 109 I/1612, p. 12.
4. For a general survey of the situation in Japan, see P. B. High, *The Imperial Screen. Japanese Film Culture in the Fifteen Years' War, 1931–1945* (Madison, WI: The University of Wisconsin Press, 2003).
5. All figures from T. Ramsaye (ed.), *The International Motion Picture Almanac* (New York: Quigley Publishing Company, 1934–40); vol. 6 (1934–35), p. 991; vol. 10 (1938–39), p. 1042; vol. 11 (1939–40), p. 930.
6. Figures from *The International Motion Picture Almanac* (1938–39), p. 1041.
7. For a more detailed analysis, see my '*The New Earth* (1936/37) – A German–Japanese Misalliance in Film', in A. Gerow and A. M. Nornes (eds), *In Praise of Film Studies. Essay Collection in Honor of Makino Mamoru* (Yokohama/Ann Arbor: Kinema Club, 2001), pp. 184–98.
8. *Lichtbildbühne* (30 March 1937), p. 1.
9. G. Haasch (ed.), *Die Deutsch-Japanischen Gesellschaften von 1888–1996* (Berlin: Edition Colloquium, 1996), pp. 255–62.
10. *Filmkurier* (6 June 1942), pp. 1–2.
11. Tôwa Shôji also distributed films from other countries, mainly France and Great Britain. See list of films in A. Kabasawa *et al.* (eds), *Towa no hanseki. 50 Years of TOWA: 1928–1978* (Tokyo: Tôhô Tôwa, 1978), pp. 11–22.
12. Listings in M. Takeuchi (ed.), *Sengo Kinema Junpô Best Ten zenshi 1946–1996* (Tokyo: Kinema Junpôsha, 1997), pp. 380–1. After 1940, only Japanese films were awarded.

13. K. Iwamoto and M. Makino (eds), *Eiga nenkan. Shôwa hen I. Shôwa 11nen-ban. Dai 6 maki* (Tokyo: Nihon Tosho Sentâ, 1994), pp. 57–60.
14. A. Iwasaki, *Hitorâ to eiga* (Tokyo: Asahi Shinbunsha, 1975), pp. 184–5.
15. Ibid., p. 177.
16. High (2003), pp. 486–7.
17. *Filmkurier* (26 October 1942), p. 1.
18. H. Tsumura 'Sensô eiga to shite no *Kibô Ongakukai*', in *Chûô Kôron* 12/1942, pp. 194–9.
19. Iwamoto and Makino (1994), p. 73.
20. *Germania* (12 March 1936), quoted from BArch R 8034/2804, p. 148.
21. A. M. Nornes, *Japanese Documentary Film. The Meiji Era Through Hiroshima* (Minneapolis: University of Minnesota Press, 2003), p. 63.
22. See the complete list in Kabasawa *et al.* (1978), pp. 65–70.
23. M. Okumura 'Über den Einfluß der *Deutschen Wochenschau* auf die japanischen *Nihon Nyûsu* während des zweiten Weltkrieges', *Iconics* (May 2000), p. 60.
24. High notes in his analysis of the 1942 feature film *General, Staff, and Soldiers* how the filmic style is influenced by the director's awareness of Nazi war documentaries, comparing it to *Campaign in Poland* and *Victory in the West*, see High (2003), pp. 301–5.
25. Quoted from Okumura (2000), pp. 67–8.
26. A. Shimizu, 'War and Cinema in Japan', in A. M. Nornes and Y. Fukushima (eds), *The Japan/America Film Wars. World War II Propaganda and Its Cultural Contexts* (Chur: Harwood Publishers, 1994), pp. 30–1.
27. This German law is discussed in the first chapter (Welch and Vande Winkel) of this book.
28. For a critical study of the Japanese film law, see G. J. Kasza, *The State and the Mass Media in Japan, 1918–1945* (Berkeley: University of California Press, 1988), pp. 234–42.
29. BArch R 109 I/1716a, p. 90.

14

From *Dawn* to *Young Eagles:* The (Failed) Attempt of Germanisation and Nazification of Luxembourg through Cinema, 1933–44

Paul Lesch

With the emergence of talking pictures in the early 1930s, French films went into decline – at least temporarily – on account of the greater linguistic accessibility of German cinema to Luxembourgish audiences. Luxembourgers are more or less proficient in German as well as French, as a result of their schooling; however, they have but one mother tongue, to wit Luxembourgish. Few would deny that Luxembourg is a decidedly multilingual country. However, there are limits to this multilingualism, given the Luxembourgers' uneven mastery of the three national languages. Despite a deeply ingrained francophilia, the majority of Luxembourgers have a better command of German, largely owing to the affinities between Luxembourgish and the German language. The decline of the French cinema was lamented by many contemporary intellectuals anxious to redress the balance between French and German influences in Luxembourg.

German films in the Grand Duchy of Luxembourg of the 1930s

In a general fashion, non-political German entertainment pictures, such as comedies, musical and adventure films, were very popular in Luxembourg. Particularly successful productions included *The Unwitting Angel* (*Der ahnungslose Engel,* 1936), *Ball at the Metropol* (*Ball im Metropol,* 1937) and *Talking about Jacqueline* (*Man spricht über Jacqueline,* 1937). This success is not simply to be explained by the above-mentioned linguistic empathy, but also a highly ingenious promotion strategy on the part of the German studios, which, unlike French producers, provided both Luxembourg cinema owners and the press with a wealth of publicity material, most notably articles, stills, star biographies, caricatures, sketches and so on.

Cinema with an overtly political stance was rather less appreciated in the Grand Duchy and, in 1934, *Dawn* (*Morgenrot*, 1933) was banned by the Luxembourg government after noisy protests from liberal students and the political left. This decision had a long-term impact, and, henceforth, cinema-owners largely chose to avoid German films liable to give rise to fresh outbursts and suffer the same fate as Ucicky's work. Therefore, very few Nazi propaganda films, or films apt to be perceived as such, found their way into Luxembourgish theatres.[1] In October 1938, the screening of a German newsreel featuring a very subjective report on the Sudeten crisis in Czechoslovakia sparked a spontaneous demonstration among part of the audience, which, in turn, led to its prohibition by ministerial decree. After the outbreak of the war in September 1939, the anti-Semitic musical comedy *Robert and Bertram* (*Robert und Bertram*, 1939) was banned, as were political and/or militarist films such as *Tumult in Damascus* (*Aufruhr in Damaskus*, 1939), *Escape into the Dark* (*Flucht ins Dunkel*, 1939) and *Goal in the Clouds* (*Ziel in den Wolken*, 1939). Altogether, the Luxembourg government banned 10 German productions with a political agenda.

If, subsequent to the advent of talking pictures, non-political German cinema enjoyed a certain degree of success in Luxembourg, the situation changed towards the end of the decade. The pan-Germanic rhetoric of Nazi Germany, as well as the exacerbation of international tensions, was perceived by many Luxembourgers as a growing threat to the country's independence. The ensuing 'anti-German sentiment'[2] also manifested itself in a certain dislike of German films.[3]

In 1937, the Luxembourg Minister of Justice, René Blum, had the pacifist American picture *The Road Back* (1937, a James Whale picture about the First World War) banned, thus yielding to pressure exerted on the Luxembourg government by the German Legation. Cowed by the pan-Germanic aims of certain German circles eager to assimilate Luxembourg into the Reich, the Luxembourg government did not want to antagonise diplomatic relations with Germany. Fearful of being reproached by the Germans with any breach of neutrality, Luxembourg was extremely circumspect in her foreign affairs, seeking by all means to eschew whatever might provide 'the Germans with a pretext for a possible political or military intervention in the Grand Duchy'.[4] Between 1938 and 1940, at least 10 films were forbidden after being denounced by Berlin on the grounds of their so-called 'anti-German'[5] leanings.

The Nazi occupation, 1940–44

On 10 May 1940, German troops invaded Belgium, the Netherlands and Luxembourg. Grand Duchess Charlotte and the government chose exile and left the country prior to the arrival of the German army. The country fell under the control of Gauleiter Gustav Simon, Chief of Civil Administration, who was directly subordinate to Hitler. He lost no time in implementing an aggressive policy of assimilation and Germanisation. His main endeavour was to eradicate any trace of French linguistic or cultural influence in Luxembourg. In the eyes of the occupier, Luxembourg was German territory. Just like Alsace and Lorraine, the Grand Duchy and its population (about 293 000 in 1940) were to be reclaimed by the Fatherland. Luxembourg was to disappear and dissolve into the Reich. Everything was ready for the official appropriation of the Grand Duchy by Germany. All political parties and unions were prohibited; institutions like Parliament or the Council of State were abolished. Symbols of national sovereignty and independence, such as patriotic monuments, flags, portraits of the Grand Duchess, vanished from the public realm. The law, administration, education and the press were brought into line with the Nazi regime.

From August 1940, the German authorities also advocated a radical restructuring of cinema operating. The propaganda machine condemned Jewish distributors and their alleged dishonest practices, the fierce competition that had existed among the various cinema operators since the late 1930s, and the prevailing publicity strategies. They likewise objected to the double-feature programme, which offered two films per screening. From May 1940, sessions were limited to one fiction film, accompanied instead by newsreels, and *Kulturfilme* deemed to be of the highest cultural and political importance by the German authorities. Luxembourg, being considered a part of Germany, was shown the same version of the *Deutsche Wochenschau* (German Weekly Newsreel, DW) as was screened all over the Reich, and not the customised Foreign Weekly Newsreel (*Auslandstonwoche*, ATW) destined for occupied regions.

The Germans claimed to have improved the artistic and above all moral qualities of the choice of films on offer, implying that Luxembourg film operators had been concerned only with profits. The German occupier thus wished to reclaim the 'cultured' public from the 'trash and kitsch business' of the 1930s. Propaganda continued to insist on the cultural value of German films. All of a sudden, cinema operators were regarded as cultural agents with a mission: 'To be a cultural agent is to be committed to society. It is therefore incumbent on theatre owners to fulfil their task in the only possible way: a national socialist spirit.'[6]

Within the context of the Germanisation of Luxembourg, the names of film theatres changed in September 1940. In Luxembourg City, the *Marivaux* became the *Metropol*, the *Capitole* was shorn of its final 'e', while the *Cinéma de la Cour* (Court Cinema) was re-named *Kammer-Lichtspiele* (Chamber Light-Plays), and the *L'Ecran* (Screen) became the *Corso*.

Thereafter, film fare consisted for the most part of productions of German origin. American films, which, before May 1940, had made up a major percentage of pictures shown in Luxembourg, were banned from screens, as were French films, which had also been well represented in the country's cinemas. The panoply of pictures available to Luxembourg cinema-goers was thus conspicuously narrowed. The new scheduling comprised a very large number of re-runs and old films, more than half of the German works shown predating the war. Still, not every picture that passed muster was German-made. Out of the 763 films screened between May 1940 and September 1944, 94 (or 14 per cent) had a non-German pedigree. Yet virtually all of these 'foreign' pictures, which were duly dubbed into German, came from countries that were neutral, occupied, or on friendly terms with Germany. The nation that figured most prominently in Luxembourg film theatres was Italy, with 40 films, followed by Austria (28), all of which were pre-1938, Spain (7), Hungary (4), Sweden (4), Finland (2), Czechoslovakia (2), Japan (1), Egypt (1) and France (1). Although non-German films were, as a rule, less popular than those from Germany and Austria, a few foreign stars, like Italian actor-singer Beniamino Gigli and Spanish actress Imperio Argentina were popular with Luxembourg audiences.

In the first months of the occupation, cinema audiences were almost exclusively composed of German soldiers and citizens; Luxembourgers shunned the German films, which included belligerent and militaristic pieces such as *Pour le Mérite* (1938). The Security Service (*Sicherheitsdienst* SD) estimated in one of its regular reports on the situation in the besieged Grand Duchy that the offer of films in the aftermath of the invasion was not truly adapted to the specific requirements of the country: 'What few Luxembourgish cinemagoers there were had a hostile attitude. It stands to reason that what with their previous influencing, Luxembourgers are unable to understand these films, creating a need for a period of transition.'[7]

In order to increase the attractiveness of cinema, the occupier implemented a price policy that maintained low-ticket prices that was both ideological and commercial. As the German Mayor of Luxembourg City wrote in 1943, 'the fixing of prices is based on the assumption that this will promote interest in the pictures on offer, thereby acquainting people from all walks of life with German cinema, and in a cultural and propagandist sense, curbing their predilection for French and American films'.[8] These initiatives bore fruit as the boycott mood progressively weakened and Luxembourg audiences began, once more, to flock to film theatres on a regular basis. This renewed interest showed no signs of flagging between January 1941 and August 1944.

It was entertainment cinema that benefited most from this surge in popularity. In the grim context of war and occupation, films became a rare source of distraction and escape for a public eager for the comedies, love stories and great spectacles. According to Secret Police (SD) reports, productions like *The Immortal Heart* (*Das unsterbliche Herz*, 1939) and *The Heart of the Queen* (*Das Herz der Königin*, 1940) were resounding popular triumphs in the very circles judged as not friendly to the German cause. The actors best loved by Luxembourg audiences were mostly comedians such as Hans

Moser, Theo Lingen, Jenny Jugo, Hans Söhnker, Lucie Englisch, Elisabeth Markus, Heinz Rühmann and Brigitte Horney, or the stars of the so-called *Revue-Filme* (musical films), including Marika Rökk and Zarah Leander.

The uncontested favourite, however, was Veit Harlan's *The golden City* (*Die goldene Stadt,* 1942). Other notable successes included *Love Me* (*Hab' mich lieb,* 1942), *The Great Love* (*Die grosse Liebe,* 1942) starring Zarah Leander, *Münchhausen* (1943), *The Big Number* (*Die grosse Nummer,* 1942), the comedy *I Entrust my Wife to You* (*Ich vertraue Dir meine Frau an,* 1943) and the Mozart biography *Whom the Gods Love* (*Wen die Götter lieben,* 1942).

In spite of the popularity of the entertainment film, the German authorities felt that cinema was not sufficiently utilised in Luxembourg as 'a tool for political influence and popular education'.[9] They deplored the fact that it was basically the comedies that went down well, as opposed to the artistically and ideologically more ambitious pictures. For Germans, the Luxembourg public was 'utterly incapable of grasping the value of film as art'.[10]

Cinema as a political propaganda weapon

Security Service reports describe Luxembourgers as frequently displaying a downright hostile attitude towards the weekly newsreels.

> In Esch-upon-Alzette, they are doggedly presented as fictitious to the point where a significant part of the audience leaves the theatre before the newsreel has even begun, whenever the main feature precedes the newsreel. Last weekend, an incident occurred in Luxembourg City that would seem to confirm, partly at least, the observations made in Esch. Footage of German and Italian planes discharging bombs was greeted with spontaneous laughter by some spectators, a response that permits one to gauge the unsympathetic and provocative mind-set one finds in certain circles in Luxemburg.[11]

On some occasions, screenings of these newsreels even led to 'anti-German incidents'.[12]

From 1940, the Security Service maintained that film schedulers had to make allowances for the peculiar place, which was the Grand Duchy. A selection of propaganda films, programmed by Luxembourgish cinema owners, was actually withdrawn by the German authorities for political reasons.

> The picture *Feuerteufel* [Luis Trenker's *The Fire-Devil* (1940)], which famously dramatises the oppression of the people of Kärnten at the hands of the Napoleonic army, as well as the liberation struggle of the former, is not suitable viewing for German-occupied Luxemburg, seeing as the Luxemburgish population largely regards the *Wehrmacht* as intruders, and is not at all shy of saying so in public. This is likely to have negative repercussions on the country's future disposition.[13]

The same explanation was put forward to justify the cancellation of *The Fox of Glenarvon* (*Der Fuchs von Glenarvon*, 1940), one of several German propaganda anti-British films dealing with the struggle of the Irish against England.

For all that, the German occupiers did not altogether scheduling political propaganda films. In addition to the newsreels, numerous military nationalist, anti-British and anti-Semitic pictures could be seen on Luxembourg's screens. All these films benefited from massive press endorsement in the national media and from countless newspaper articles calling attention to their historical and ideological importance. Some works hailed as being 'valuable to state affairs' such as *Bismarck* (1940), *Homecoming* (*Heimkehr*, 1941), *The Great King* (*Der grosse König*, 1942), *Uncle Krüger* (*Ohm Krüger*, 1941) and *Victory in the West* (*Sieg im Westen*, 1941) were ceremonially released with formal premieres, so as to achieve maximum effect. These films, intended to extol German genius, glorify heroic deaths, promote a fighting-spirit, stigmatise the enemies of Germany, call for unconditional obedience, and convince the Luxembourgers that their future was German, were fêted by the press through glowing reviews.

The Nazi propaganda film to be released amidst the greatest publicity campaign in the history of the occupied Grand Duchy was Hans Steinhoff's *Uncle Krüger*, being itself one of most lavish productions in Nazi cinema. The German authorities had invested much hope that the film would undermine the pro-British sentiments of a high percentage of the Luxembourg public. However, this optimism was soon to be dashed. A Security Service report reveals that the response given to the film in several towns did not correspond to the high expectations of the Germans or the Movement of the German People (*Volksdeutsche Bewegung*, VDB), an association of Luxembourgish collaborators:

> Whereas the Germans among the spectators showed the most vivid interest in the screening, a vast majority of Luxemburgers declined to go and watch the film in spite of all the media publicity. Word-of-mouth from anti-German circles labelling the film as a vehicle for German propaganda did its worst.... So far *Uncle Krüger* has achieved nothing in the way of ascertainable positive propaganda.[14]

This critical, not so say overtly hostile, attitude of sections of the Luxembourg public towards anti-British productions seemed to 'melt into thin air' on the occasion of the release of the famous anti-Semitic picture *Jew Süss* (*Jud Süss*, 1940). Heralded by press articles and explicit commentaries, the film opened at the Marivaux in November 1940, at a point in time when Luxembourgers were once more beginning to attend screenings regularly after months of hesitation and boycott. As for the film's reception in Luxembourg, one Security Service report stated,

> Scheduling *Jew Süss* has been a success. The film is being seen by viewers from all sorts of backgrounds, and screenings are punctuated by the odd anti-Jewish exclamation. It is moreover much talked about in public, whereby special emphasis is placed on the extent to which the clarity of the plot makes it easily accessible.[15]

This early success, notwithstanding, the film did not enjoy an extended run.

The cinematic seduction of the nation's young

The Nazi authorities would not allow themselves to be fooled by the apparent impact of their propaganda upon wide sections of the population. The young were regarded as more amenable to Nazi ideology and as a result, their indoctrination became a pivotal element in German cinematic propaganda in Luxembourg.

The Germans looked upon the *Jugendfilmstunden* (Youth Film Hours) organised by the Hitler Youth (*Hitlerjugend*) as 'a crucial factor in the total education of German Lützelburg'.[16] Cinema was used with the express view of acquainting young Luxembourgers with the 'German spirit'. In order to reach an even wider target-audience, the German authorities proceeded to make cinema a regular component of primary and secondary education. November 1941 saw the creation of the National Film Service Luxembourg (*Landesbildstelle Luxemburg*), which was to foster and improve the pedagogical use of film within the framework of education. Entire collections of didactic films were thus placed at the disposal of primary and secondary teachers for use in their classes. However, the Germans were never entirely satisfied with this initiative and continued to deplore the teachers' lack of interest in ideological films.

It is difficult to measure the impact that educational films had with youth audiences. A Security Service report on the reception in Luxembourg of *Uncle Krüger* nonetheless permits a telling insight. The report mentions that more than half the students at a vocational school in Esch-sur-Alzette, when asked to write an essay on the film, were negative in their appraisal: '15 pupils, no doubt under the anti-German influence of their parents, dismissed it for being exaggerated and deliberately untruthful.'[17] The report concludes that these essays were representative of working-class opinion in Luxembourg.

More pertinent information as to the reception given by Luxembourgish youngsters to German films, particularly propagandist ones, comes from the headmasters of eight grammar schools in answer to a questionnaire on students' cinematic habits drawn up by the Chief of Civil Administration. The replies unanimously revealed that cinema-going was becoming increasingly popular, although, if one is to believe the various statements, the youngsters were, as a rule, less taken with the films classified suitable for minors. A point in case was Alfred Weidenmann's *Hands Up* (*Hände hoch*, 1942), a picture in praise of the *Hitlerjugend*, which students widely rejected.

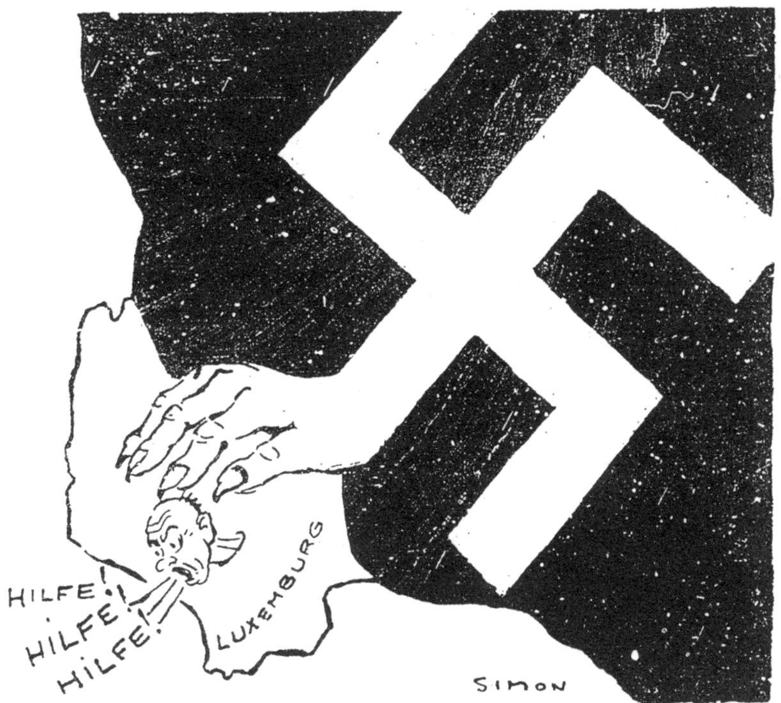

The Grand Duchy of Luxembourg cries for help against Germany. *Source*: Albert Simon, *Tageblatt*, 8 May 1934.

Teachers generally noted opposition to any blatant ideological propaganda. Several reports observed that 'such influencing' through films was very limited. 'The spectator usually goes to the pictures to be entertained. He therefore distrusts any discernible attempts at edification.'[18] The questionnaire of the Luxembourg Grammar School for Young Girls was scarcely more positive: 'Pupils' attitude towards contemporary issues is not noticeably affected by film. War-related affairs are invariably considered from a "Luxembourgish" viewpoint. The only development that could possibly qualify as progress is that the girls attend the entire show these days, unlike in 1941, when they only arrived after the newsreel.'[19]

Conclusion

Throughout the years of occupation, cinema was genuinely popular with the people of Luxembourg. After a brief period of boycott, the darkened cinemas became welcome places of diversion in an excruciatingly difficult time, thanks mainly to the countless entertainment films screened in cinemas across the country. Unlike other spectacles provided by the occupier, such as plays, concerts or literary readings, cinema was not felt to be explicitly German, despite the overwhelmingly German origin of most of the pictures shown. Nor was the consumption of German entertainment films perceived as a pledge of allegiance to Nazi Germany or Germanness.

The Luxembourg public may not always have been capable of discerning the ideological subtext of seemingly innocuous entertainment pictures. However, by and large, they rejected all overt propaganda films. In most cases, tendentious productions did not succeed beyond reaching those already converted to the Nazi cause. Ideological conditioning through propaganda films does not appear to have had any lasting effect on the majority of Luxembourgers.[20]

Notes

1. Rare exceptions included *Hangmen, Women and Soldiers* (*Henker, Frauen und Soldaten*, 1935), *White Slaves* (*Weisse Sklaven*, 1936), *Covered Tracks* (*Verwehte Spuren*, 1938) and *Robert Koch* (1939).
2. See E. Krier, *Deutsche Kultur- und Volkstumspolitik, Deutsche Kultur- und Volkstumspolitik von 1933–1940 in Luxemburg* (Bonn: Krier, 1978), p. 608.
3. Politisches Archiv des Auswärtigen Amts, Berlin, Akten der Gesandschaft in Luxemburg, Kult12 Nr 4, Filmwesen in Luxemburg, Report of 19 September 1938. Incidentally, this evolution ran parallel to a gradual revival of French cinema, whose popularity soared once more.
4. E. Haag and E. Krier, *La Grande-Duchesse et son gouvernement pendant la Deuxième Guerre mondiale* (Luxembourg: RTL Editions, 1987).
5. See also P. Lesch, 'Film and Politics in Luxembourg: Censorship and Controversy', *Film History*, 16:4 (2004), pp. 437–46.
6. *Luxemburger Wort* (29 July 1943).
7. Archives Nationales Luxembourg (hereafter ANLux), Chef der Zivilverwaltung (hereafter CdZ) SD 033 (24 May 1940).
8. Archives de la Ville de Luxembourg, NS LU 432 (3 August 1943).
9. ANLux, CdZ SD 029 (19 November 1940).
10. ANLux, CdZ SD 029 (14 November 1940).
11. ANLux, CdZ SD 026 (21 October 1940).
12. Centre National de Recherche Archives (hereafter CNR Archives), File 023 (5 November 1940). See also P. Lesch, 'The Reception of the Deutsche Wochenschau in Luxembourg during the German Occupation', *Historical Journal of Film, Radio and Television*, 24:1 (2004), pp. 35–44.
13. ANLux, CdZ SD 027 (1 October 1940).
14. CNR Archives, File 023 (15 July 1941).
15. CNR Archives, File 023 (5 November 1940).
16. *Nationalblatt* (5 April 1943).
17. CNR Archives, File 023 (15 July 1941).
18. ANLux, CdZ, A-2-1, 283, p. 0121.
19. ANLux, CdZ, A-2-1, 283, p. 0125.
20. For further information on the subject, see P. Lesch, *Heim ins Ufa-Reich? NS-Filmpolitik und die Rezeption deutscher Filme in Luxemburg 1933–1944* (Trier: Wissenschaftlicher Verlag Trier, 2002).

15
Dutch–German Film Relations under German Pressure and Nazi Occupation, 1933–45

Ingo Schiweck

During the First World War, imperial Germany respected the neutrality of the Netherlands. In the 1930s, as the outbreak of another war became more and more likely, the Dutch government was determined to stay out of the conflict again. Throughout the interwar years the Netherlands were, just like Belgium and Luxembourg, concerned with remaining as neutral as possible. Nevertheless, this attitude, which also influenced official policies vis-à-vis film censorship and exhibition,[1] did not stop Nazi Germany from invading all three countries on 10 May 1940. During the ensuing occupation of the Netherlands (1940–45), the Dutch film industry was completely orientated towards Germany.

Dutch–German film relations before the Nazi occupation

In the interwar years, the Netherlands had only a limited domestic film production. In the 1930s, Dutch film professionals disposed of two studio complexes in Amsterdam (*Cinetone*, established in 1933) and The Hague (*Filmstad Wassenaar*, established in 1935). Although more productive than its Belgian neighbour, the Dutch film industry remained relatively small. Dutch investors played a crucial role in the 1928 creation of *Tobis*, but this company (renamed *Internationale Tobismaatschappij* or *Intertobis* in 1932) acted internationally and did not boost Dutch film production. (In 1935, Max Winkler's *Cautio-Treuhandgesellschaft*, at the behest of the German Propaganda Ministry (*Reichsministerium für Volksaufklärung und Propaganda*, RMVP) in 1933, took over the majority of shares of *Intertobis*.)[2] As was the case in many other European countries, Dutch cinemas mainly screened films that were imported.

In the 1920s, German films occupied a rather strong market position in the Netherlands. The import of German films even increased when sound arrived, because the techniques of film subtitling or dubbing were initially inadequate. This resulted in many cinemas playing foreign-language films without subtitles, a practice that favoured the Germany film industry, as Dutch audiences had strong cultural ties with Germany and preferred German-language films. However, this advantage proved short-lived. From 1932 onwards, the improved technique of subtitling made the language the actors spoke far less important.[3] The number of German and American-imported films was still equal (approximately 160 each) in 1932 but Germany's market position considerably weakened in the following years.[4] In 1938, the Dutch film production only covered 0.4 per cent of the domestic market (2 of 471 movies). In 1939 this was 0.7 per cent (3 of 463). Clearly leading the field of imported movies and therefore also the total market were the United States with 62.6 per cent (295 of 471 movies) and 60.9 per cent (282 of 463) respectively. The German Reich followed (15.5 per cent or 73 movies in 1938, 15 per cent or 70 movies in 1939) and preceded respectively France (11 per cent or 52 movies in 1938, 14.9 per cent or 69 movies in 1939) and Great Britain (4.1 per cent or 19 movies in 1938, 5.7 per cent or 26 movies in 1939).

Dutch cinemagoers were for the first time introduced to National-Socialist film-making when *Dawn* (*Morgenrot*, 1933) was approved by Dutch film censors.[5] *Dawn* had been produced in the Weimar Republic, but premiered in Nazi Germany and overnight became a 'key-film of Third Reich cinema'.[6] On 2 February 1933, only a few days after President von Hindenburg had appointed him Reich Chancellor, Adolf Hitler attended the Berlin premiere of *Dawn*. The movie became very successful all over Germany. In the Netherlands, however, leftist protests against the film made the *League of Dutch Cinema* (*Nederlandsche Bioscoop Bond*, NBB) withdraw *Dawn* from all cinemas. In the following years the German envoy repeatedly consulted the Dutch Ministry of Foreign Affairs about the advisability of releasing German films that were likely to meet a similar boycott. For this reason, German propaganda films such as *Hitler Youth Quex* (*Hitlerjunge Quex*, 1933) and *Triumph of the Will* (*Triumph des Willens*, 1935) remained unreleased. Propagandistic films that were nevertheless submitted for censorship, such as *Campaign in Poland* (*Feldzug im Polen*, 1940), were rejected. The German envoy naturally also complained when movies with an anti-German or anti-Nazi tendency, such as *Confessions of a Nazi Spy* (1939), were (likely to be) approved by Dutch censors. The envoy knew all too well that his complaints would not fall on deaf ears, for the Netherlands did not want to harm relations with Germany.

Meanwhile, German-speaking film-makers – mainly emigrants from Nazi Germany and Austria – exercised an increasing influence on the Dutch movie business, in spite of Dutch hostilities and infrastructural and legal restrictions against emigrants. Moreover, the German film industry experienced a (relative) heyday under this influence. From 1934 to 1940 a total of 37 Dutch movies premiered in the Netherlands; 36 of which German-language immigrants occupied important functions. For example, Max Ophüls shot his *The Trouble with Money* (*Komedie om Geld*, 1936) in the Netherlands. Meanwhile, the German film director Detlef Sierck, who later became known as Douglas Sirk, also worked for the Dutch film industry.[7]

The new authorities

The German Wehrmacht invaded the Netherlands on 10 May 1940. The queen and her government went into exile in Great Britain and the Dutch Commander-in-Chief capitulated on 15 May. The Netherlands initially received a German military administration, which by the end of May 1940 was already replaced by a civil one. The 'Germanic' Netherlands, the final destination of which in the European National-Socialist new order remained undefined by Hitler,[8] was henceforth administered as a dependent province of the Third Reich. The German administration was headed by *Reichskommissar* (Reich Commissioner) Arthur Seyss-Inquart, who had played a key role in the annexation of Austria and also had been instrumental in the setting up of a General Government in occupied Poland. Seyss-Inquart stood directly under Hitler's command and had the highest civil governmental power. An SS-officer but not a puppet of SS-leader Heinrich Himmler, Seyss-Inquart initially strived for the 'self-Nazification' of the Netherlands: an unforced adhesion of the Dutch population to National-Socialism and the greater German Reich.[9] As time went by and it became clearer and clearer that most Dutchmen were not going to Nazify, the occupying regime became less lenient.

After the capitulation the Dutch film industry was 'reorganised' in order to serve German interests. A range of authorities was established to control and direct the Dutch movie system as well as to grant (at least formally) the Dutch National-Socialist Movement (*Nationaal-Socialistische Beweeging*, NSB) some participation. For these Dutch Nazis the occupation regime must have meant disillusionment. Admittedly, NSB members were prominently present in the newly established Dutch Ministry of Popular Enlightenment and Arts (*Departement van Volksvoorlichting en Kunsten*, DVK) that was modelled on Goebbels' Ministry of Propaganda (RMVP). The DVK was competent in the field of cinema but saw its powers limited by the Reich Commissioner's Department of Popular Enlightenment and Propaganda (*Hauptabteilung Volksaufklärung und Propaganda*, HAVP), which was also structured like the RMVP. The NSB soon discovered that the movie business being nominally declared a 'national' competence was of little value. The DVK's influence was restricted and German demands (demands of the HAVP in particular) were prioritised.

It is well known that the rivalries that existed between different authorities in Nazi Germany were exported to occupied territories. The Netherlands were no exception to this rule. The main two 'rival enterprises' in the sphere of Dutch culture – an area of crucial importance to propagandists – were on the one hand the Reich Commissioner, whose concept of 'self-Nazification' called for greater Dutch participation, and on the other Goebbels' propaganda ministry, which, like the SS, insisted that the Netherlands should be radically orientated towards the Reich.[10] The Dutch adoption of the Reich Culture Chamber model was, for instance, slowed down by these rivalries. The Dutch Culture Chamber (*Nederlandsche Kultuurkamer*, NKK) was therefore only established in late 1941. However, such rivalries seem to have hardly surfaced in the HAVP Film Department.[11] Although not necessarily for the same reasons, all German parties involved seem to have agreed that increasing German film imports was more important than stimulating Dutch feature film production.

The institutional reorganisation of the Dutch film World

On 19 July 1940, the Ministries of Justice and Internal Affairs issued a Decree on the Screening of Films[12] that was clearly drawn up by German instances and consolidated a policy that was already practiced. According to this decree, the Dutch Central Commission for Film Censorship (*Centrale Commissie voor de Filmkeuring*) could only authorise (new) productions that had already been authorised by the German propaganda ministry, in other words films that were also distributed in Germany. Also allowed for public screening were Dutch movies that had been (re-)censored after 14May 1940 and movies produced in the German Reich that had been certified after 31 December 1936. As mentioned in an internal memo of the DVK, this decree was promulgated without consulting Dutch film professionals. It boiled down to an embargo against most non-German foreign films that were screening in Dutch cinemas before the invasion. The decree initially allowed for the distribution of (authorised) American and even British (!) films, for the availability of German film prints was too low to answer the needs of all cinemas. These supply problems were eventually solved and from January 1941 onwards, British or American films were no longer accepted.

The decree of 19 July 1940 was obviously to the advantage of German feature film distribution, particularly the local branches of Ufa and Tobis, which were, in the spring of 1942, when the Ufi Concern was established, regrouped in the joint *Ufa-Tobis Filmverhuurkantoor*. Many competitors – not just 'Jewish' distribution companies that were erased or 'Aryanised' anyway – were forced to close down because their distribution catalogue had become redundant. Although a limited number of films from France (mainly Continental productions), Italy, Spain, the Protectorate of Bohemia and Moravia were released in 1940–45, the overwhelming majority of the available films remained German.

The occupation authorities were of course also determined to control the conditions under which authorised films reached Dutch audiences. Dutch cinemas were to be obligated to adopt a standard film programme (newsreel,

Kulturfilm and feature film) and to deny access to Jews. The HAVP Film Department found an excellent instrument for implementing such measures as well as for reorganising the entire film business in the above-mentioned League of Dutch Cinemas (NBB). The NBB was quickly turned into an umbrella organisation, membership of which was obligatory for anyone working in the film sector. In late 1941 the NBB was transformed into the Film Gilde (Film Guild) of the Dutch Culture Chamber. Its leadership was put in the hands of the Dutch editor and director Gerd Jan Teunissen, who as an NSB member also headed the film section of that organisation.[13] The actual leadership of the Film Guild was, however, not exercised by Teunissen or the NSB, but by the HAVP Film Department.

The above-mentioned *Central Commission for Film Censorship* (renamed *Rijksfilmkeuring* or *Reich Film Censorship* in August 1941) was another Dutch body that got its wings cut before it was indirectly handed over to the NSB. (Leadership of the *Reich Film Censorship* was, in line with the Führer principle, also given to Film Guild leader Gerd Jan Teunissen.) Officially, this Dutch state film censorship had greater influence during than before the German occupation, because the Nazis forbade Catholic censorship. This form of 'private' censorship had been quite strong in the interwar years (particularly in the south of the Netherlands) and was, not without reason, viewed by the Germans as an obstacle to the proliferation of German movies. The powers Teunissen and his censors could actually exercise were, however, limited. On the one hand, the Decree of July 1940 allowed the Dutch censors only to censor movies that had already been allowed by the German propaganda ministry. On the other, if Dutch censors objected to particular films or scenes, German instances could always exercise their right to overrule such decisions.

During the occupation, Alfred Greven, whom Joseph Goebbels had appointed *Reichsbeauftragter* (Reich Appointee) for the reorganisation of the French, Belgian and Dutch film business,[14] took over 11 Dutch cinemas on behalf of the Dutch Ufa branch, which had aready acquired three cinemas before the war. These takeovers – mostly from Jewish owners – were very much 'facilitated' by the pressures that came with the German occupation. Many other cinemas were subjugated to the Head of the HVAP Film Department, Peter Zimmer, and sometimes 'Aryanised', meaning that they were confiscated from their legitimate (Jewish) owners and sold to German or Dutch entrepreneurs who were more agreeable to the regime.

Film production

The *Cinetone* and *Filmstad* film studios, which the Dutch Ufa branch bought in April and May 1942 respectively (through its *Ufa Filmstad* subsidiary), were during the occupation intensively used by German companies. From autumn 1941 until autumn 1944, 18 German feature films were (partially) produced in these studios: 4 by Terra and 14 by Berlin-Film. (In early 1942, both companies became part of the Ufi Concern that was dominated by Ufa.) Among these 14 productions were Arthur Maria Rabenalt's *Fronttheater* (1941), Hans Steinhoff's *Rembrandt* (1942) and Fritz Peter Buch's *The Black Robe* (*Die Schwarze Robe*, 1943). German producers and directors came with their own staff. Nevertheless the production of these films created job and learning opportunities for Dutch film personnel too.

After the war, the Dutch film industry benefited from the knowledge local film people had accumulated under the German occupation. In most cases, the wartime cooperation with German film producers was not considered a direct form of collaborationism. The case of Dutch actor/singer Johan(nes) Heesters, who evidently benefited from the new state of things and became very popular while working in Nazi Germany from 1935 on, was viewed differently. Whereas his popularity in Germany endured after 1945, Dutchmen grew to resent his work in the country of the occupier – which they, too, had enjoyed before the liberation. His visit to Dachau concentration camp in May 1941, which became public knowledge in 1978, made Heesters *persona non grata* in his native country. In the last couple of years, however, the Dutch view of Heesters has mellowed, as the nation has taken to reappraise the role of individuals under occupation.[15] (After the war, little attention was paid to Ilse Werner, who, for commercial reasons, had also been presented as a 'Dutch' actress during the occupation. To the minds of most Dutchmen, however, Werner, the daughter of a Dutch businessman and a German woman, born in the Dutch Indies, had never been as 'Dutch' as Heesters was.)

While Dutch film studios and personnel were welcome to assist the production of German films, the Germans showed no interest whatsoever in the promotion of Dutch film production. As in other Nazi-occupied territories, the German film industry was interested in acquiring assets, obtaining production facilities and strengthening market positions, but not in supporting local competition. During the entire occupation, only one Dutch feature film was (officially) made.[16] *Butler for Three Weeks* (*Drie Weken Huisknecht*, 1943) was released almost a year and a half (March 1944) after its completion. It was, in comparison to German productions, of mediocre quality, which made it rather unsuccessful.[17] German-friendly organisations such as the NSB were allowed to produce propagandistic documentary shorts (*Kulturfilme*) and news films, but these were mainly screened within party circles and did not enter the commercial cinema networks.[18]

The only kind of Dutch film production that was truly supported during the occupation was the production of newsreels and animated films. During the first 4 years of the occupation, the German Ufa and its *Deutsche Wochenschau GmbH* subsidiary failed to obtain a monopoly position for their *Foreign Weekly Newsreel* (*Auslandstonwoche*, ATW). During those years the Dutch-language ATW version, *Ufa World News* (*Ufa Wereldnieuws*), only rarely featured Dutch items. Moreover, it had to compete with *Tobis Dutch News* (*Tobis Hollandsch Nieuws*), a newsreel distributed by the local Tobis branch but produced by the Dutch companies Polygoon and Profilti, which had produced Dutch newsreels since the 1930s. *Tobis Dutch News* only rarely featured German items and instead focused on the Netherlands. Within that framework it dedicated much attention to the activities of Seyss-Inquart. It was probably the Reich Commissioner and his entourage who granted the Tobis newsreel this unique position. To stimulate 'self-Nazification' and to promote his own activities, the Reich Commissioner undoubtedly preferred a domestic newsreel his services controlled themselves above a newsreel controlled by the RMVP.[19] Only in May 1944 were *Ufa World News* and *Tobis Dutch News* replaced by *Dutch News* (*Nederlandsch Nieuws*), a locally produced Dutch ATW version.

The Nazi's ban on American film distribution and therefore also on American cartoons created new perspectives for Dutch animators.[20] Some became involved in the whole or partial production of German cartoons, either in Dutch studios (*Bavaria Filmkunst* and *Fischerkoesen Film Produktion*, both established studios in The Hague) or in the German studios of the *Deutsche Zeichenfilm GmbH*. Others produced animation films or animated scenes that were later integrated in commercials. The Dutch animators Marten Toonder and Joop Geesink, who became famous after the war, learned the tricks of the trade in these war years. Also noteworthy is the anti-Semitic animation film *Reynaerde the Fox* (*Van den Vos Reynaerde*, 1943) that was, however, never shown publicly during the war.[21]

Film reception

The German invasion, the disappearance of many non-German imported productions and the NBB ban on Jewish access to cinemas (which the Germans initiated in January 1941) initially contributed to rather low cinema attendances. But this was soon to change profoundly. Dutch cinemagoers adapted to the new situation and the occupation years eventually turned out a golden era in terms of cinema attendance. With 42.9 million tickets sold in 1942, the level of the last pre-war year 1939 (40.4 million) was surpassed.[22] In 1943 the number of sold tickets even reached 55.4 million, a quantity Dutch cinema had never seen before. Those record attendance figures are even more surprising if one takes into account the restrictions imposed by the Nazis such as early curfews or the closure of cinemas. The year 1944 was also a profitable one, at least until the autumn, when many cinemas had to close down. Nevertheless not all cinemas were closed in late 1944. Audiences in occupied Netherlands continued to go to the movies until the last weeks of the war.

Of all the countries Ufa had branches in, only the Protectorate of Bohemia and Moravia reached higher distribution revenues than the Netherlands.[23]

In 1942–43 there was no other country in which Ufa had a market share that was as high as in the Netherlands, where it attained 86 per cent.[24] In this year and at least during the first 5 months of the business year 1943–44, one in five Reich marks made by the foreign activities of Ufa came from the Netherlands.[25]

Some members of Dutch resistance groups protested against the attendance of German films. Illegally published newspapers and pamphlets called for a boycott. *Trouw* wrote in mid-October of 1943: 'We feel deeply ashamed of the attitude of our people towards the cinema.'[26] According to such publications 'good' Dutchmen should not visit cinemas which were 'poisoned' by the occupants with their propaganda and entertainment products. Especially young people, keen on movies, seemed to have disregarded such requests. The connection between 'harmless' German entertainment movies and the hated occupation regime was in the eyes of many Dutchmen vague or non-existent. Movie-going was above all seen as an innocent pastime that offered escape from the grey reality of everyday life in an occupied country. Or as someone put it: 'We would rather be in the cinema than in sackcloth and ashes.'[27]

As secret reports indicate, the huge cinema attendance figures did not mean that everyone took in all parts of the film programme without criticism. The DVK sent out up to 500 controllers, most of them NSB 'comrades', who anonymously visited cinemas and submitted reports to the ministry. According to these reports, 'undesirable' audience reactions (verbal and non-verbal) were mainly heard or seen during the screening of newsreels, *Kulturfilme* and advertisements. One English-speaking (!) informant noted in 1940: 'As a matter of fact, most of the Dutch cinema-public prefers to come a quarter of an hour after the beginning of the programme hoping, that they will miss the Ufa newsreel.'[28] The newsreels proved so unpopular that, in February 1942, it was forbidden to mention starting and ending times of certain parts of the cinema programme in advertisements and other announcements.[29] Further, the reports testify of quiet and uncritical consumption of the feature films.

The *HAVP* published *Cinema & Theater* to promote new movies. *Cinema & Theater* was allowed to criticise – which was rare for a Dutch publication – particular German movies without openly challenging the dominance of the German feature film. The writers praised movies from other countries in particular because they could serve as an example for establishing a Dutch movie production. One of the magazine's eager readers was Anne Frank, who decorated the wall of her hideout with pictures of German movie stars.[30] In January 1944 she noted in her diary:

> Mister Kugler makes me happy every Monday when he brings along the *Cinema & Theater*: although this indulging is often referred to as a waste of money by the non-sophisticated inmates, they are astonished every time

> about my accuracy when naming exactly the participants of a certain movie after a year. Bep, who often spends her days off with her boyfriend at the movies, informs me about the title of the scheduled movie on Saturdays and I rattle through both the principal performers and the criticism at a single blow. It's not long since Mans told me I wouldn't need to go to the cinema later on because I knew the contents, stars and criticism so well.[31]

Very popular during the German occupation were the big budget movies Veit Harlan directed (starring Kristina Söderbaum) and also productions starring Heinz Rühmann, Zarah Leander and Willi Forst. Harlan's infamous *Jew Süss* (*Jud Süss*, 1940) was less successful.[32] Other big productions which had a very obvious anti-Semitic attitude failed as well. By contrast, the Harlan/Söderbaum production *The golden City* (*Die goldene Stadt*, 1942) was, as in other European countries, the biggest success ever released in 1940–45. From December 1942 to October 1943, some 1.7 million tickets were sold for this colour movie in the Netherlands.[33] Former visitors still remember its colours, plot and (by the standards of that era) erotic atmosphere. Other elements such as the underlying 'blood and soil' ideology and anti-Semitism

The Ufa Rembrandt Theatre in Amsterdam (left picture photographed around 1937) burned down on 26 January 1943 (right picture). In the background of the ruins: an advertisement for the 5th week of Veit Harlan's *The golden City* (*Die goldene Stadt*, 1942). It was rumoured that the theatre had been arsoned by members of the Dutch resistance to protest against the success of German films like *The golden City*. *Sources*: Left – H. Traub, *Die Ufa. Ein Beitrag zur Entwicklungsgeschichte des deutschen Filmschaffens* (Berlin: Ufa-Buchverlag, 1943), p. 252. Right – NIOD, Netherlands Institute for War Documentation.

The box office of a cinema in the occupied Netherlands. The sign on the left (below) is there just for the occasion and says, in Dutch, 'Tonight only accessible for the German Wehrmacht.' The sign on the right (below), which is always there, mentions, in German, that Wehrmacht members get a 50 per cent reduction. The sign on the right above, which is also always there, says, in Dutch, 'Jews cannot be allowed.' *Source*: NIOD, Netherlands Institute for War Documentation.

went apparently unnoticed. Many years later, Dutch actor Rijk de Gooyer reminisced:

> If you hadn't seen it, you could not join the talk at school anymore. What was so special about this movie? They were having sex!!! [. . .] At the time this was unique and as far as I remember even the first time in cinematography. I absolutely wanted to go there. There was however one obstacle: It was rated over 18.[34]

Another film that shaped the collective film memory of that era was *Quax, the Crash Pilot* (*Quax der Bruchpilot*, 1941) and its star Heinz Rühmann.

Epilogue

The efforts of German authorities to make the Netherlands part of a new National-Socialist order ultimately failed. Nevertheless, the Dutch film business had, under the German occupation, for almost 5 years been run quite efficiently as a well-oiled part of Joseph Goebbels' movie empire. After the liberation of May 1945, the Dutch film industry was, like all economic sectors, 'cleansed'. Gerd Jan Teunissen and his likes were put on trial and sentenced to imprisonment. Twenty-five NSB members and 'notorious collaborationists' were removed from the NBB, which had retaken its pre-war position.[35] However, this did not stop several of them from working in the film business again a couple of years later. German films were temporarily banned from Dutch screens, but welcomed back in 1949. The 'reactivated' movie makers of the 'Third Reich' and some new faces filled Dutch film theatres again.

Notes

This chapter is mainly based on I. Schiweck, *[...] weil wir lieber im Kino sitzen als in Sack und Asche. Der deutsche Spielfilm in den besetzten Niederlanden 1940–1945* (Münster–New York–Munich a. o.: Waxmann, 2002). Thanks very much to Karin and Boris Boden, Recklinghausen/Munich, for their help with the English translation.

1. See Chapters 1 and 14.
2. In 1937, *Cautio-Treuhandgesellschaft mbH* also acquired 26.49 per cent of the shares from Warner Bros. Pictures Inc. At the end of the war (1945), over 98 per cent of the shares were in German hands. Schiweck (2002), pp. 111–14. K. Dibbets, 'Tobis Made in Holland', in J. Distelmeyer (ed.) *Tonfilmfrieden/Tonfilmkrieg* (München: Edition text+kritik, 2003), pp. 25–33.
3. K. Dibbets, *Sprekende films. De komst van de geluidsfilm in Nederland 1928–1933* (Amsterdam: Cramwinckel, 1993), p. 330.
4. J. Th. van Taalingen, *Nederlandse Bioscoopbond 60 Jaar. Een Documentaire over de Nederlandse Bioscoopbond en het daarin Georganiseerde Film- en Bioscoopbedrijf* (Amsterdam: s.n., 1978), p. 61. It is interesting that the *HAVP* started in early 1941 with creating an index of all movies which were distributed in the Netherlands since 1933 (cf. Reichskommissar für die besetzten niederländischen Gebiete, GKzbV, HAVP [Fink], to the Beauftragter des Reichskommissars für die Provinzen, 'W o c h e n s p i e g e l', Nr. 5, 13/1/1941, p. 15, Nederlands Instituut voor Oorlogsdocumentatie (hereafter NIOD) 61–76, 19c). It is noteworthy that the decline of German film import, which began in 1933, was not linked to the coming to power of Hitler.
5. This paragraph on (German reactions to) Dutch film censorship in 1933–39 is based on J. van der Burg, 'Dit is niet in het belang ener goede internationale verstandhouding'. De Duitse politieke druk op de Nederlandse filmkeuring in de jaren dertig', *NRC Handelsblad* (28 January 1988), p. 8.
6. E. Hampicke, 'Auf Feindfahrt: "Morgenrot" von Gustav Ucicky', in H.-M. Bock and M. Töteberg (eds), *Das Ufa-Buch* (Frankfurt am Main: Zweitausendeins, 1992), pp. 320–3.
7. K. Dittrich van Weringh, *Der niederländische Spielfilm der dreißiger Jahre und die deutsche Filmemigration* (Amsterdam: Rodopi, 1987) (Amsterdamer Publikationen zur Sprache und Literatur; vol. 69), especially pp. 21/22 and 82; A. van Beusekom, 'Komedie om Geld, The Trouble with Money. Max Ophüls, The Netherlands, 1936', in E. Mathijs (ed.), *The Cinema of the Low Countries* (London: Wallflower Press, 2004), pp. 61–7, here pp. 64/65.
8. Cf. K. Kwiet, *Reichskommissariat Niederlande. Versuch und Scheitern nationalsozialistischer Neuordnung* (Stuttgart: Deutsche Verlags-Anstalt, 1968) (Schriftenreihe

der Vierteljahrshefte für Zeitgeschichte, no. 17); G. Hirschfeld, *Fremdherrschaft und Kollaboration. Die Niederlande unter deutscher Besatzung* (Stuttgart: Deutsche Verlags-Anstalt, 1984) (Studien zur Zeitgeschichte, vol. 25), pp. 22–40.

9. G. Hirschfeld, 'Nazi Propaganda in Occupied Western Europe: The Case of the Netherlands', in D. Welch (ed.), *Nazi Propaganda. The Power and the Limitations* (USA: Croom Helm, 1983), p. 144.
10. G. Hirschfeld (1983), p. 154.
11. G. Hoffmann, *NS-Propaganda in den Niederlanden. Organisation und Lenkung der Publizistik unter deutscher Besatzung 1940–1945* (Munich–Pullach–Berlin: Verlag Dokumentation, 1972) (Kommunikation und Politik, vol. 5), pp. 98–100, 105–107 and 128/129.
12. Verordnung der Generalsekretäre in den Ministerien für Inneres und für Justiz über die Vorführung von Filmen. Vom 19. Juli 1940/Besluit van de Secretarissen-Generaal van de Departementen van Binnenlandsche Zaken en van Justitie betreffende het vertoonen van films. Van 19 Juli 1940=Verordnung Nr. 57/1940/Besluit No. 57/1940 (VOBl. Niederlande 1940, pp. 196/197/VOBl. Nederland 1940, pp. 196/197). See also, for example, Th. Leeflang, *De Bioscoop in de Oorlog* (Amsterdam: De Arbeiderspers, 1990), p. 110.
13. A. Vermeer, *NSB-films. Propaganda of vermaak?* (Beetsterzwaag: AMA, n. d. [1987]).
14. See Chapters 1 and 9.
15. I. Schiweck, *'Laß dich überraschen . . . ' Niederländische Unterhaltungskünstler in Deutschland nach 1945* (Münster: agenda Verlag, 2005), pp. 15–49.
16. The amateurish *Murder at the Fasion House* (*Moord in het Modehuis*) was made illegally in 1943 by Alfred Mazure and was only shown after the war to journalists. For this and for other Dutch productions, see R. Bishoff, 'De Nederlandse Film in de Oorlog', *Filmfan* no. 33 (May 1981), pp. 24–7.
17. A. Pollé, 'Drie Weken Huisknecht', in R. Albers, J. Baeke and R. Zeeman (eds), *Film in Nederland* (Amsterdam–Gent: Ludion, 2004), pp. 84/85.
18. A. Vermeer (1987).
19. This is argued in R. Vande Winkel, 'Nazi Newsreels in Europe, 1939–1945: The Many Faces of Ufa's Foreign Weekly Newsreel (Auslandstonwoche) versus German's Weekly Newsreel (Deutsche Wochenschau)', *Historical Journal of Film, Radio and Television*, 24:1 (2004), pp. 21–5 and R. Vande Winkel, 'Filmjournaals in bezet Nederland (1940–1944): de Nederlandse nieuwsfilmoorlog in internationaal perspectief', *Tijdschrift voor Mediageschiedenis*, 6:1 (2003), pp. 72–92.
20. For a detailed analysis of the Duch animation industry during the Second World War, see E. Barten and M. Peters, *Meestal in 't Verborgene. Animatiefilm in Nederland 1940–1945* (Abcoude: Uitgeverij Uniepers, 2000).
21. E. Barten and G. Groeneveld, ' "Van den vos Reynaerde" (1943): How a Medieval Fable became a Dutch Anti-Semitic Animation Film', *Historical Journal of Film, Radio and Television*, 14:2 (1994), pp. 199–214.
22. The year 1939 was the first year the Central Office of Statistics, *CBS*, had figures for all municipalities.
23. Bundesarchiv (hereafter Barch) R 109 III/23, Niederschrift Nr. 1574 über die Ufa-Vorstandssitzung vom 4. Oktober 1944 in Berlin, pp. 9/10.
24. Barch, R 109 I/5507, Erster Bericht über das Auslandsgeschäft der Ufa-Auslandsabteilung für die Zeit vom 1. Juni – 31. Oktober 1942.
25. Barch, R 109 I/2152, Ufa Auslands-Abteilung, Situationsbericht über die Entwicklung des Auslands-Vertriebs 1942/43, 20 November 1943, attachments I and II.

26. *Trouw* from mid-October 1943, p. 8.
27. I. Schiweck (2002).
28. Politisches Archiv des Auswärtigen Amtes (PA), R 60686 (=Kult Pol-Geheim 90 [Niederlande. Berichte des Ges.-R. Wickel aus den [sic!] Haag. Berichte v. Vertrauensleuten betr. Stimmung der Bevölkerung, 1940, vol. 1]), 'The Situation in the Netherlands (V)', undated, p. 9
29. NIOD 104, 25c, DVK, Dienst Bioscoopcontrole, 'Rondschrijven Nr. 56', 5/2/1942, NIOD 102, 116Ac; NBB, Voorzitter, Voorschrift no. 14, 3/2/1942.
30. J. van Maarsen, *Ik heet Anne, zei ze, Anne Frank* (Amsterdam: Cossee, 2003), p. 108.
31. Rijksinstituut voor Oorlogsdocumentatie (ed.), *De Dagboeken van Anne Frank* (The Hague–Amsterdam: Staatsuitgeverij, Bert Bakker, 1986), p. 486 (28 January 1944).
32. The reception of the anti-Semitic films *Die Rothschilds* (1940), *Jew Süss* and *Der ewige Jude* (*The Wandering Jew*, 1940 – a Dutch version of which was produced, inserting footage of Dutch Jews) is analysed in E. Barten, 'Negentieneenen-veertig. De ontvangst van Duitse antisemitische films in Nederland tijdens de bezetting', in H. Wijfjes (ed.), *Jaarboek Mediageschiedenis* (Amsterdam: Stichting Mediageschiedenis, 1989), pp. 183–215. See also I. Schiweck (2002), p. 298.
33. *Cinema & Theater*, no. 44, 15 October 1943, p. 12.
34. R. de Gooyer, *Gereformeerd, en andere Verhalen* (Amsterdam–Brussels: Elsevier, 1981), p. 27. De Gooyer, who had just turned 17, got in anyway!
35. B. Hogenkamp, 'Het grote stilzwijgen: de filmzuivering in Nederland', in *GBG-Nieuws*, no. 34 (1995), p. 34.

16

From Will to Reality – Norwegian Film during the Nazi Occupation, 1940–45

Bjørn Sørenssen[1]

Norway was invaded by Nazi Germany on 9 April 1940.[2] The Norwegian National-Socialist Vidkun Quisling, leader of the small *Nasjonal Samling* party, immediately attempted a coup d'état by forming a 'government of national unity'. He was briefly recognised by Hitler as Norway's legitimate new ruler. Lack of Norwegian support for Quisling made Hitler change his mind and the country would, until the end of the occupation (May 1945), be governed by Reich Commissioner Josef Terboven. Final attempts were made to establish Quisling as a national figure with a semblance of independence. On 1 February 1942, Quisling was appointed Minister President. The real power remained, however, in German hands.

During these occupation years, an attempt was made at adapting Norwegian film to the social and economic 'new orientation' ('nyordning') that *Nasjonal Samling* and Vidkun Quisling tried to impose on Norwegian society. In the unevenly developed Norwegian film and cinema establishment, this led to a series of dramatic changes. In this chapter, I will attempt to highlight these activities and make an assessment of its implications at the time and in a wider perspective.

Two factors characterised Norwegian film before the outbreak of the Second World War: the absence of an indigenous industry and secondly, the existence of a municipal cinema system. Unlike its neighbours, Denmark and Sweden, both of whom could boast of national film industries of international renown (Denmark in the years before the First World War and Sweden in the years immediately after), the Norwegian film industry was virtually non-existent. Film production was sparse and sporadic, and although one could point to a few national romantic silents in the 1920s, Norwegian film production as a whole was negligible. Film directors appeared and disappeared and there were no organised companies until the mid-1930s and no film studio until 1935. The cinema exhibition system, on the other hand, was well organised and Norway was unique in the fact that the majority of motion picture theatres were municipally owned and administered – as they still are. This led to a short-lived boycott of Norwegian cinema theatres by the American film industry in the 1920s. The film legislation of 1913 made the exhibition of motion pictures dependent on licensing from the municipalities, and in the case of most of the urban municipalities, they decided to license themselves. The justification for this was that film was a new and potentially dangerously influential medium that should not be left to the control of a profit-hungry private enterprise. In reality, the exhibition of motion pictures became a welcome revenue for municipal as well as state authorities.

In the 1930s the organisation of municipal cinemas set up what eventually would become the nucleus of a film industry – the production company, Norsk Film A/S – a company still in existence. However, production was still as erratic as in the 1920s in spite of the establishment of the first (and so far, the only) Norwegian film studio in Oslo in 1935.[3]

German controllers and Norwegian collaborators

This was the situation confronting the German commissar for film and theatre matters, Wilhelm Müller-Scheld, when he arrived in Oslo in 1940 with the mandate to oversee and Nazify Norwegian film and theatre life. The Germans and the Norwegian collaborators, mainly people from Quisling's Nazi party, upheld a double administrative system for Norway, the consequences of which will become apparent from the following analysis. Müller-Scheld, who in the German *Reichskommissariat – Hauptabteiling für Volksaufklärung und Propaganda* functioned under the culture commissar, was in the spring of 1940 looking for a Norwegian accomplice to implement a National-Socialist strategy in the field of film and theatre. He first approached the only Norwegian film director who could be called a professional, Tancred Ibsen, who was the grandson of both Henrik Ibsen and literature Nobel Prize winner, Bjørnstjerne Bjørnson. Had Ibsen been persuaded to implement German policy, it would, of course, have been a great coup. (A son of Bjørnson would eventually come out in favour of the Nazis.) Ibsen was offered the positions of leader of a unified Norwegian film industry, as well as the position of leader of the national theatre, but turned both down.[4] Next, Müller-Scheld approached, or was approached by, one of the few veteran Norwegian film producers and directors, Leif Sinding. Sinding's motives for contacting and collaborating with the Nazis are unclear. Sigurd Evensmo suggests that Sinding was ideologically inclined to join the National Socialists, based on an earlier collaboration with the film-maker Lykke-Seest, who in the First World War made a couple of films clearly based on a strong anti-socialist ideology. At his post-war trial for collaboration, it was also maintained that he had held fascist views since encountering German National Socialists in the 1920s, and that he had been among the forces behind the creation of Quisling's Nasjonal Samling in 1933. None of these allegations were proved, but Evensmo[5] points to another motive that is considerably easier to substantiate: namely, Sinding's almost paranoid hatred of the Norwegian municipal cinema system, a system he thought was the main reason that Norway had never been able to establish a national film industry.

Müller-Scheld and Sinding formulated an organisation plan for Norwegian film within the newly created Department of Culture and Popular Enlightenment (*Kultur- og fokeopplysningsdepartementet*). This was led by a veteran in the Quisling movement, Gulbrand Lunde. Here, the State Film Directorate (*Statens Filmdirektorat*) was established with Sinding as its first leader. Sinding strongly pressed for the municipal cinema organisation to be placed under the Directorate, but it was decided to locate it in the Interior Department, which dealt numerous municipal matters. The Interior Department was led by Albert Hagelin, a former Norwegian businessman in Germany, who had been instrumental in connecting Quisling with Hitler in the late 1930s. During the years that Sinding led the Directorate, there would be several clashes between the two departments over the municipal cinema organisation's role in film politics.

As for the Film and Theater Commissar, Müller-Scheld, he appears to have played an open and visible role in the direction of Norwegian film policy only during the initial stage in 1940. That is not to say that he was of no importance after this, but it seems clear that the way the State Film Directorate was handling film matters generally was accepted as adequate by the German control instance. However, Müller-Scheld and his office would play a substantial role as a censorship institution and all proposed film projects would have to be accepted by him. In addition, the Germans played an important role in 'cleansing' the films already in distribution in Norway of anti-German tendencies. In December 1940, a ban on British films was introduced and during 1940 all of the American distribution companies in Oslo were closed.[6]

'The New Order' – Institutional reorganisation

The State Film Directorate was formally established on 1 January 1941 with Sinding as its Director and immediately set about reorganising the Norwegian film industry. In April, Sinding issued a decree for the exhibition of cinematographic images. The main content of this decree was the abolishment of the Norwegian film control – a censorship panel that had been in effect since 1913. From now on the Directorate would decide which films to show. This ignored the fact that the German film Commissariat had already set out that no films of 'enemy' origin were to be shown, German films should be given preference.

But another point in the decree was of a more radical kind, and was meant to be the first step in Sinding's ambitious plan to create a Norwegian national film industry partly financed by income from film distribution and exhibition. From now on film distributors and would-be producers would be dependent on recognition from the Directorate in order to distribute films for exhibition. This was followed in May and December by other decrees stating that only the Directorate would be allowed to import film, and the films would then be given to seven, later to be reduced to five, authorised film distributors. More important still: only these authorised companies would be allowed to produce films. In order to secure funding for this production, 50 per cent of profits from rentals should be set aside for production.

To his superiors in the department, the zealous Sinding hinted that this authorisation ought to be reserved to people who were representative of the 'new times': members of *Nasjonal Samling*. He also suggested that all leaders of municipal cinemas should be party members. This suggestion was turned down by the Interior Department, because they knew it would be impossible to find that many local party members willing to take on a job like this. Sinding also continued his fight against the municipal cinema system. Having lost the fight to privatise Norwegian film exhibition, he now turned to the municipally owned distribution and production companies with more success. The organisation of Norwegian municipal cinemas owned two import and distribution companies, *Kommunenes Filmcentral* and *Fotorama*. The latter was denied 'authorisation' and thus liquidated. Sinding would have liked the same to happen to Kommunenes Filmcentral (distributor of Ufa and Terra films[7]) but encountered resistance from the Interior Department who were not willing to see this source of income disappear, so all he could do was to bar Kommunenes Filmcentral from taking part in film production. His main target, however, was the municipally owned *Norsk Film A/S* with its brand new studio and production facilities at Jar, outside of Oslo. In August 1941, Sinding managed to press through a decision to transfer *Norsk Film* from the Interior Department to the State Film Directorate. At the same time it was decided that the company from now on only was to be regarded as a service organisation, providing production facilities to the productions of the Directorate and the authorised production companies.

Production of documentaries and propaganda films was organised directly under the Directorate and was located at the *Norsk Film* studios at Jar. This propaganda production unit was furnished with an ample budget from money raised by increasing the luxury tax on film exhibition, and from the summer of 1941 the unit started the first regular Norwegian national newsreel. The municipal cinema company of Oslo had a regular local newsreel during the last years before the war, but a newsreel with a national distribution was something new. The Germans were obviously positive to the idea, and provided a full documentary production outfit (an editioral board of the *Deutsche Wochenschau GmbH*) for the newsreel that was to be shown in connection with Ufa's Foreign Weekly Newsreel (*Auslandstonwoche*, ATW).[8]

The more openly propagandistic documentaries were mostly for in-house Nazi use. A series of films were made in order to recruit soldiers for the

Norwegian Legion, an outfit of Norwegian soldiers fighting for Hitler on the Russian front; other films glorified Quisling's home-grown version of SA, 'Hirden'. The best-known of these are Walter Fyrst's film *We Are Vidkun Quisling's Guardsmen* (*Vi er Vidkun Quislings hirdmenn*, 1942), which Leif Furhammar and Folke Isaksson have studied in their book *Politics and Film* and which Furhammar referred to as 'a *Triumph of the Will* - in clogs'![9] In addition to these propagandistic films, a number of documentaries dealing with various parts of Norway and aimed at disseminating traditional values were made.

By 1942 the reorganisation initiated by Sinding was finished – Norway had, for the first time, a national film policy and the organisational and economic possibilities to enforce it. In 1941, Sinding outlined a production of at least 12 films a year of high quality, films that would enable Norway to become an exporter of good entertainment to other countries in German-dominated Europe. In addition to this, the reorganisation would, according to Sinding, guarantee the production of 'films of great political and cultural importance'.

Further Activities of the State Film Directorate: Import and the International Film Chamber

After Sinding had retired from his position at the State Film Directorate in order to direct his energy into the production of films for the new age (see below), he was followed by Birger Rygh-Hallan, a lawyer, who, unlike Sinding, had no previous experiences from film or cinema. His period as a leader of the Directorate lasted a year and a half. During this time he faithfully implemented the policies established by Sinding, ending his career at the State Film Directorate in July 1944, with the creation of a new Norwegian film legislation built on the principles of Sinding's directive of 1941, supposedly replacing the law of 1913. After his retirement, Rygh-Hallan was 'rewarded' with the ownership of one of the five licensed import and distribution companies and it was left to a former business manager at the State Film Directorate to oversee the dwindling activities during the remaining 9 months of German occupation.

During Rygh-Hallan's time as leader of the Directorate, its activities became more international. In 1935 an International Film Chamber was established following an international congress in Berlin with the explicit aim to work as a counterweight to the American world domination in the film industry.[10] The initiative came from Germany, and as the activities of this organisation became increasingly more dominated by German interests and ideology during the next few years, the organisation withered away, to become completely dormant at the outbreak of the war in 1939. In 1941, however, at the height of German dominance over continental Europe, the International Film Chamber was revived, this time in order to 'coordinate' the film markets of occupied and neutral Europe.[11] An initial meeting was held in Berlin on 16 July 1941, with Leif Sinding as the official Norwegian representative. The primary aim of the conference was, according to Jan Olsson, to rid European screens of American film.[12] The congress reconstitued the International Film Chamber with a German (Karl Melzer) as its general secretary. Melzer visited both Oslo and Stockholm in this capacity in December 1941. A new meeting of the International Film Chamber was held in Venice in September of the same year and another congress in Rome in April 1942, this time with Rygh-Hallan as the Norwegian delegate.

Norway's participation in International Film Chamber was an important justification and legitimisation of the policies of the State Film Directorate and was used as an argument in the struggle for control of film import and distribution. In a joint letter from the State Film Directorate and the Department for Culture and People's Enlightenment to the Interior Department dated February 1942, the International Film Chamber was invoked to enforce the decision to levy a 5 per cent tax on box office income to be earmarked for newsreel production and 'cultural film' (*Kulturfilm*), a tax that, needless to say, was very unpopular with the municipal cinema managers.

The Norwegian State Film Directorate was also an enthusiastic supporter of the German demand that all American films should be banned from the countries represented in the International Film Chamber, an enthusiasm that was definitely not shared by countries like Italy, Spain, Portugal, Finland, Switzerland and Sweden. In an article in *Norsk Kinoblad* (the official press organ of the State Film Directorate) the author (most probably Sinding) maintained that countries that ignored the ban on American film did so at their peril – being dependent on the access of German raw film stock.[13]

The most important international contact was Sweden,[14] and in spite of the pro-German outburst referred to above, the State Film Directorate tried to maintain a good relationship with the Swedish film industry, the source of the some of the most lucrative films at Norwegian box offices. In addition, these connections served to maintain an appearance of legitimacy to *Nasjonal Samling* in the face of the considerable Norwegian emigrant community in Sweden. Rygh-Hallan made two visits to Stockholm, the last one to attend the annual congress of the Swedish Cinema Owners' Association in the spring of 1943. On this occasion, as on his earlier visit, in 1942, he was also required to report to the leader of intelligence for the Quisling government on the Norwegian exile community in Stockholm. In his report he emphasised the importance of the invitation from a Swedish organisation:

> [The fact] . . . that I was invited as a representative for the Norwegian film industry is to be considered extremely important in terms of propaganda, especially because this probably is the first official invitation to a branch of the new Norwegian government. . . . I was placed at an honorary table, together with representatives of the Swedish government.[15]

This reflects the isolation of the Norwegian Quisling government in its relationship to Sweden in 1943. By this time the Swedish government had re-established formal diplomatic relationship with the legal Norwegian government in exile in London and kept the Quisling government at arms length.

The relationship with Germany was more problematic for the State Film Directorate due to the pressure that Ufa applied in order to secure control over import and distribution of German film and film from other European countries in Norway. The State Film Directorate, both under Sinding and Rygh-Hallan, opposed this and eventually agreed a compromise whereby Ufa was allowed to set up a distribution company for German films in Norway. Eventually, Germany exported far more films to Norway than Sweden (115 German films versus an estimated number of 20 Swedish productions in 1941).[16] German officials were quite happy with the results of German film distribution: 'Film business in Norway has, apart from some insignificant boycott attempts, developed very satisfactory' (November 1944).[17]

The result in Norwegian fiction film production: 'The Lost Sausage-maker' and 'Young Wills'

So what did eventually come out of the major attempt at reorganising the Norwegian film industry in terms of 'films of great political and cultural importance'? The answer is 'very little'. In 1940 and 1941, eight films were produced, none of which could be said to be of any 'political or cultural importance', one of these films went on to become one of the most popular Norwegian films, the non-sensical Laurel-and-Hardy style comedy *The Lost Sausage-Maker* (*Den forsvunne pølsemaker*, 1941) featuring the escapist humour of Leif Juster and Ernst Diesen, two of the Oslo stage's most popular comedians. What is interesting with this and other comedies at the time is the glaring absence of wartime realities. The male love lead is seen munching chocolate out of an enormous box at a time when sugar, not to mention chocolate, was totally unavailable. In this and later comedies, characters are seen driving around in cars (fuel rationing was such that only buses and trucks were allowed on the roads, and then using wood-fueled gas generators instead of gasoline), drinking bottles of scotch whisky (a possible subversive political element overlooked by the censors) and smoking foreign cigarettes.

Popular comedies continued to dominate the five films produced in 1942; among them was the sequel to *The Lost Sausage-Maker* (a strong candidate for the title of the worst Norwegian film ever made) and a sophisticated comedy by Tancred Ibsen, who would be arrested and sent to Germany along with other Norwegian commissioned officers a little later. In spite of the new incentives being offered, the film community seemed to be dragging its feet, content to produce mediocre escapist entertainment.

The year 1943 saw the appearance of the politically oriented films that Sinding had promised. By this time he had retired from the position as 'Film-direktør' in order to produce and direct films for his own private company, *EFI-film* (distributor of Tobis productions[18]) which, not surprisingly, was among the five 'authorised' film companies. He turned to a play by the popular and conservative author Johan Bojer about an idyllic worker/boss relationship which comes under attack from evil capitalists. A lackluster affair, *The Song of Life* (*Sangen til livet*, 1943), was a far cry from the proclamations of Sinding a year earlier about the importance of political and culturally worthy film. In addition to directing this film, Sinding had spent considerable time and energy opposing the other, and far more interesting political film to appear in 1943 – Walter Fyrst's *Young Wills* (*Unge viljer*, 1943). Walter Fyrst had been one of the founders of Nasjonal Samling in 1933, but had fallen out with Quisling before the war. In 1940 he re-entered the party and 2 years later he came up with the idea for a feature film presenting the ideas of the Norwegian National-Socialist movement. Sinding was against the idea from the start; sensing that an overt manifestation of a movement deeply hated by a majority of Norwegians would cause trouble and perhaps destroy the box office possibilities of Norwegian films in the future.

However, Fyrst had secured the backing of Minister Gulbrand Lunde in 'The department of culture and popular enlightenment'. (Lunde was to die in a car accident later that year.) *Young Wills* is perhaps the most interesting Norwegian film to come out of the war in its attempt to propagandise Nasjonal Samling as a uniquely national phenomenon. In order to achieve this, Fyrst let the events in the film take place around the time Nasjonal Samling was established in 1933. The story is about the young couple: the daughter of the evil plutocrat Mr West and a worker's son, ostracised by his fellow proletarians because of his refusal to join the Marxist trade union is at times rather crude. Nevertheless, it provides an idea of the images that Nasjonal Samling wanted to project – that of a mass organisation mediating class struggle and making Norwegians aware of the values of their common national heritage. It was impossible to find a sufficient number of professional actors for this film, so in addition to a few Nasjonal Samling professional actors, the director had to rely on amateurs culled from the ranks of the Nasjonal Samling youth movement, deciding on two extremely blond youths for the romantic leads. The 18-year-old male lead was to die on the Russian front less than a year afterwards.

When the film was shown at municipal cinemas, it provoked exactly the sort of responses that Sinding had feared: massive demonstrations and attempted walk outs. On one occasion, in Fredrikstad, the unsuspecting audience was forced to sit through the movie at gunpoint! As a result, the film was withdrawn from general distribution and only shown

A contemporary photomontage from Walter Fyrst's *Young Wills* (*Unge viljer*, 1943), which propagandised the Norwegian National-Socialists of *Nasjonal Samling* as a uniquely national phenomenon. The blond hero and his equally blond sweetheart in Norwegian folk costume look toward a brighter future with Marxist class struggle and English-inspired decadence in the background. *Source*: Norsk Filminstitutt/Harald Hjort.

for 'internal use' at Nasjonal Samling meetings. This film, in addition to Fyrst's *We Are Vidkun Quisling's Guardsmen*, represented the apotheosis of the 'ideological' Norwegian film. In 1944, three non-ideological films were produced, while the films in production in 1945 were never released.

The legacy of Norwegian wartime cinema politics

With Liberation in 1945, the 'old order' of Norwegian cinema was re-established. The municipal exhibition and distribution organisations were freed of Nazi control and film production returned to the pre-war 'non'-policy, that is no state initiatives or incentives. *Norsk Film* was handed back to the municipalities' cinema organisation and the only lasting benefit from the occupation was the decision that *Norsk Film* should be given the newsreel studio equipped by the Germans as a wartime compensation. Workers on the Nasjonal Samling-controlled newsreel had been compiling film material in order to make a film about Liberation, and within 2 weeks after V-day (8 May 1945), a newsreel presenting the events of the German capitulation in Norway was screened all over the country. This newsreel became the beginning of the *Norsk Film Newsreel*, which was to run continuously until 1963.[19]

The other beneficial post-war effect of the Nasjonal Samling cinema policies was a film production fund founded on the 50 per cent profit cut on rental income earmarked for production introduced by Sinding. This policy of distribution taxation was discontinued, but, according to Evensmo, the fund of NOK 10.5 million was of vital importance to the establishment of film production after the war.

Sigurd Evensmo, film enthusiast and resistance fighter, who miraculously had escaped execution by the Nazis during the war, made this paradoxical statement when describing the legacy of Nasjonal Samling film policies as opposed to the total indifference of the pre-war democratic and social–democratic system to the plight of Norwegian film:

> Following the great upheaval of 1913 [i.e. the introduction of Norwegian cinema legislation opening up for municipal ownership of the cinema theatres] there had been no debate in Parliament about the functions of film and cinema in society, and the government had never attempted to contemplate whether this constituted a national cultural task. It was *Nasjonal Samling* which presented this as a national task from 1940, and which also saw to it that a film fund totalling 10.5 million Kroner was established from the taxation of rental income from the cinema theatres during the war.[20]

Notes

1. In addition to the sources presented below, the present article is mainly based on material made available from the post-war treason cases brought against the leading persons in Filmdirektoratet, particularly the cases against Leif Sinding, Birger Rygh-Hallan and Walter Fyrst. Papers from these cases include official documents from Filmdirektoratet, as well as affidavits from various persons connected with Norwegian film production, most notably the affidavit given by Gustav W. Boo, head of production at the Norsk Film studio. This material has been drawn from *Landssvikarkivet* (Archives of war treason cases) in the Norwegian national archive – *Riksarkivet.*
2. For a short introduction to the Norwegian experience of World War II, see O. Riste, 'Norway', in I. C. B. Dear and M. R. D. Foot (eds), *The Oxford Companion to World War II* (Oxford: Oxford University Press, 2001), pp. 638–43.
3. For a short English language presentation of Norwegian film history, see G. Iversen, 'Norway', in T. Soila, A. S. Widding, and G. Iversen (eds), *Nordic National Cinemas* (London–New York: Routledge, 1998), pp. 102–40.
4. T. Ibsen, *Tro det,eller ei!* (Oslo: Gyldendal, 1976), p. 199.
5. S. Evensmo, *Det store tivoli* (Oslo: Gyldendal, 1967), p. 228.
6. O. Hanche, 'Krig i kulissene – Filmpolitikk i Norge under andre verdenskrig', in G. Iversen (ed.), *Krigsbilder KUBE Skriftserie fra Institutt for kunst- og medievitenskap* 3 (2001), pp. 53–4.
7. B. Drewniak, *Der deutsche Film 1938–1945* (Düsseldorf: Droste Verlag, 1987), p. 748.
8. For a presentation of the Norwegian wartime newsreel, see T. Helseth, *Filmrevy som propaganda. Den norske filmrevyen 1941–45* (Oslo: Unipub Forlag, 2000); T. Helseth, 'Norwegian Newsreels under the Nazi Occupation', *Historical Journal of Film, Radio and Television*, 24:1 (2004), pp. 35–44.
9. L. Furhammar and F. Isaksson, *Politics and Film* (London: November Books, 1971).
10. See Chapter 2.
11. Jan Olsson gives an extensive description of the relationship between the Internationale Filmkammer and the Swedish film industry in J. Olsson, *Svensk spelfilm under andre världskriget* (Lund: LiberLäromedlelLund, 1984)
12. Ibid., p. 39.
13. Norsk kinoblad (1942), p. 1. The status of neutral Sweden in the Internationale Filmkammer was unclear, as pointed out in Olsson (1984).
14. See Wright's contribution elsewhere in this book.
15. Letter from Rygh-Hallan to Finn Støren in the Norwegian National Archive. Cited and translated from B. Sørenssen, 'Direktorat og direktiv:Kampen om filmen i den norske NS-administrasjonen', in Iversen (2001), pp. 53–4.
16. Drewniak (1987), p. 748.
17. Ibid., p. 749.
18. Ibid., p. 748.
19. For an English-language presentation of the post-war Norwegian newsreel, see B. Sørenssen, 'The Voice of Reconstruction: The Norwegian Post-war Newsreel', in R. Smither and W. Klaue (eds), *Newsreels in Film Archives* (Trowbridge: Flicks Books), pp. 44–56.
20. Evensmo (1967), p. 254.

17

Brown-red Shadows: The Influence of Third Reich and Soviet Cinema on Afrikaans Film, 1927–48

Keyan Tomaselli and Michael Eckardt

Afrikaners opposed the dominance of the Anglo-American cinema in the lead up to the Second World War by establishing an Afrikaner cinema. This initiative aimed to restore the nation's pastoral cultural integrity and to protect the *volk* (people) from the insidious influences of the 'city', dominated as it was by British imperialism. The Rescue Action League-Amateur Film Organisation (*Reddingsdaadbond-Amateur-Rolprent-Organisasie*, RARO) and a distribution arm, *Volks*-cinemas (*Volksbioskope*, VOBI) were established by Hans Rompel (1902–81) and various Nazi-supporting intellectuals in 1940. For these 'fathers' of Afrikaner film,[1] the state-controlled German film industry was the blueprint for organising Afrikaner film administration, production and distribution; Eisensteinian *mise-en-scene* and documentary realism comprised its aesthetic; and opposition to the Hollywood 'dream factory' was non-negotiable.

Theoretical underpinnings

Rompel was the son of Frederik Rompel (1871–1940), foreign news editor of the Afrikaans-language newspaper *Die Burger*. After studying psychiatry, Hans joined *Die Burger* as its photographer, later becoming its film critic. Rompel also wrote for *Huisgenoot* magazine and *The Afrikaner Amateur-Filmer* (*Die Afrikaanse Rolprentamateur*), contributing scholarly articles on film.[2] *The Cinema in Service of the Volk (Die bioskoop in diens van die volk)*[3] sketched his plans for film as a weapon to oppose *volksvreemde* (alien) and *volksgevaarlike* (threatening the *volk*) influences. One of Rompel's uncited but detectable sources[4] is *Under the Spell of Films* (*Im Banne des Films*, 1927).[5] This reactionary study regarded the film world as a struggle between American, Russian and other national industries. Impressed by the manner in which the German film industry had been reorganised by the Nazis, Rompel describes in detail the system of total state control as a desirable alternative to Hollywood.[6]

The American 'dream factory' in the service of 'large magnates' 'conceals a conscious goal'[7] in its apparent directionless nature; namely, the maintenance of the capitalist system and consumer subservience.[8] Rompel's analysis correlated with the Afrikaner perception of the workings of capital in South Africa at the time. Following the Anglo-Boer War (1899–1902), the economy was predominantly owned and controlled by English speakers representing imperial capital. Relegated to positions of subservience were the defeated Afrikaners whose unskilled labour underpinned primary industry, mainly mining. RARO aimed to inform Afrikaners, facing proletarianisation, on how Hollywood films legitimised the continuing anti-Afrikaner relations of production.

Opposition in Europe to American influence stemmed mainly from artists and intellectuals who mobilised the cultural maxim: 'People of Europe, protect your holy spiritual values.'[9] By 1932, these activists considered the German industry *leeg, doods en volksvreemd* (empty, dead and alienated).[10] This conflict was seen in terms of a *volkegevoel* (sentiment of the *volk*)[11] which resisted alien infiltration into *volkseie* (*volks* own) European film. The National-Socialist government rectified this by subjecting all film companies to financial examination by the Film Credit Bank, requiring membership of the Reich Film Chamber, while denying membership to Jewish-owned and 'politically unreliable' companies.[12] For Rompel, the fault lay not with the Jewish contribution itself, as much as it did with the inevitable cultural dilution which detracted from the purity of a *volkseie* portrayal.[13]

While the Nazi restructuring gave Rompel an indication as to how a South African industry should be managed, most of his ideas on form and content were gleaned from the Weimar Republic and Soviet cinema. Although hailing Soviet documentary realism,[14] he nevertheless criticises their obvious propaganda as being 'full of contradictions and generalisation'.[15] Instead he lauds German films from 1933 onwards, where the political tendency is artistically woven into the story without drawing attention to itself.[16] What Rompel valued most in the Soviet and German cinemas was their supposed closeness to everyday life, the dominance of the realistic rather than the fantastical, the simplicity and sincerity of setting and actors, avoiding sensationalism and striving for authentically strong emotional expression.[17] As an example, the silent *Fog over Mt.-aux-Sources* (*Newels oor Mt.-aux-Sources*, 1942), supervised by Rompel, was clearly influenced by German *Bergfilm* (mountain film) aesthetics.[18] Rompel defined film as the 'art of expressing ideas as visual and acoustical arranged motion into photographs'[19] and clearly favoured the silent film's elaborated modes of expression.[20] Approving the unchained camera in films of the Weimar Republic, giving the spectator the chance to replace the camera by the eye of the beholder, he criticised Hollywood's traditional repertoire of long shots, mid-shots and close ups.[21]

Rompel agreed with the South African censors in banning Soviet films. He feared a misunderstanding among the natives due to their 'lacking ability to consider the transmitted moral values carefully'.[22] Based on the revolutionary editing technique, *montage*, irreplaceably embedding the propaganda content into a films narrative, Rompel saw no chance for the censors to neutralise unwanted sequences. For Rompel, the Soviet film orchestrated the masses to great effect, executed by the film director using a psychological master plan based on communist ideology.[23]

Impressed with Lenin's use of cinema in spreading socialism, Rompel wrote, 'There aren't any dreams, but hard, stark reality; here are also no attempts to disguise the situation . . . '.[24] Of particular importance was the fact that Soviet production started with an amateur, Sergei Eisenstein, who meshed professionals and amateurs into a vibrant propaganda machine managed by the Commissar for Proletariat Culture.[25] The problem that Rompel faced in South Africa was similar to those experienced in Russia: insufficient capital for studios, sets and backlots meant that clips needed to be shot in the open, and in the absence of experienced actors, ordinary people had to suffice.[26] Most importantly, young, enthusiastic directors with a 'relatively limited experience of film were drawn from the ranks of the proletariat, the *volksiel* (the people's soul) and the *volksgevoel* (the people's emotion)'.[27]

Four production components in early Soviet film were considered crucial by Rompel for an Afrikaner cinema. First, other than major roles calling for trained actors, participants were to be selected from the masses: soldiers, farmers, workmen and so on. These people were simply to be themselves and behave naturally. Second was the use of crowds and the isolation, in close up, of one of its members to metonymically symbolise the emotions of the larger group. Third is the pursuit of realism. No make-up or ageing techniques were used. Players were chosen on the basis of their real age, appearance and occupation. Finally, the manner in which the subject matter was approached was recognised as being more important than the subject itself, for it is this which makes the film culture-specific and nationally pure.

Contrary to Eisenstein who set out to *create* and *manipulate* an ideological perspective, Rompel demanded that that Afrikaners *reflect* their true God-given orientation in film. Thus the link between Soviet cinema and the economic–administrative blueprint proposed by Rompel must be approached through an examination of his statement that emergent film experts can learn from the techniques of Soviet production, more so than from the intricate and illogical Soviet theory.[28] By ignoring the Soviet theoretical postulates, Rompel misinterpreted their goals and motivation. By emphasising the qualities of 'absolute realism', 'faithfulness to nature'[29] and the 'natural' status of the actor found in Soviet Cinema, while at the same time ignoring the theoretical derivation and discursive base, he also missed their connection between theory and practice. He was unaware of how dialectically derived film theory mediated ideological experiences in culturally specific ways through the principle of *montage*.

It was *montage* which obliterated the distinction between performer and the setting in which s/he performs by ideologically guiding the viewer's reaction along a closed chain of pre-determined responses. Where Eisenstein acknowledged that 'reality' could be filmed in any number of different ways, but with only one interpretation being valid, Rompel argues that there is only one reality – a God-given set of conditions, a pre-existent state of being, uncluttered by ideological interpretations that only amateurs in narrow contact with the Afrikaner soil could provide.[30]

The very creation of cities and the consequent capitalist structure they serve was an anathema. Dr P. Meyer, the then Secretary-General of the Federation of Afrikaans Cultural Associations (*Federasie van Afrikaanse Kultuurvereniginge*, FAK), describes the society that could have been, were it not for British imperialism:

> The Afrikaner created for himself a specific economic system which was given expression in the agricultural life on the farms. But the full development of this system was stopped by the British conquest of the country and replaced by a foreign imported system. The people of South Africa as a result had no opportunity to develop its own South African system on a Calvinist basis. If that had been the case, it would not have been a capitalistic system.[31]

This nostalgia for 'what might have been' underlies Rompel's objectives. It is not surprising that the recurring image of the evil city is endemic to nearly all Afrikaans cinema until the mid-1970s.[32] The 'Eden film' as espoused by Rompel was that Afrikaners be kept culturally pure and cleansed of alien influences that might have infected them in their learning of film craft from the foreigners who necessarily will have taught them.[33] The star system, dialogue, Hollywood and business methods, Jews or non-Afrikaners, or indeed professional technicians, were considered detrimental to retaining cultural purity.

Political economy

The establishment of the League for the Act of Rescue (*Reddingsdaadbond*, RDB) was sparked by the 1938 re-enactment of the Great Trek, which had occurred a hundred years earlier, in the form of the *ox wagon trek* (*Ossewa Trek*). Fifty per cent of the Reddingsdaad fund, earned from donations collected *en route* during the symbolic trek, was invested in a new finance house, Federal *Volk's* Investments (*Federale Volksbeleggings*). The remainder was placed under the control of the *Brothers League* (*Broederbond*), linked with the Economic Institute of the FAK which represented 2500 organisations. The FAK liaised with the *Ox Wagon Sentinel* (*Ossewabrandwag*), RDB, public service, Afrikaner churches and the *Purified National Party* (*Herenigde Nasionale Party*). FAK also had indirect influence with education departments, school boards and committees, Afrikaans parents and pupils.[34] Twenty per cent of the sum raised by the RDB was lodged with two Afrikaner insurance companies.[35]

The RARO films were distributed via VOBI, set up in 1940. This circuit included 300 schools, RDB-branches, commercial cinemas and cultural organisations. RARO, however, was unable to provide sufficient films of a reasonable standard. VOBI's slogan, 'Support Your Own Undertakings', neatly concealed the financial need to screen American movies deemed to have an insidious influence on Afrikaans audiences.[36] This uneasy marriage kept VOBI solvent during the War and for a short time after. Exhibition began in August 1940 at RDB-Bioskope on the Reef (Johannesburg). VOBI bought UTOLO Films of Africa, a production company, to produce films which would feed its outlets, and efforts were made to obtain further financial support from the RDB and one of its commercial offspring, *Federale Volksbeleggings*. These met with little success for VOBI could not offer profitable returns.[37]

Preparations for the establishment of VOBI were made as early as 1937 when it was realised that distribution should precede production.[38] Registered in 1941, it took over SA Commercial and Educational Services, which had supplied films, projectors and electrical apparatus to schools and other customers.[39] The aim was to service 'the implacable call of the *volk*' to produce 'indigenous pictures which breathe the Afrikaner spirit and country, pictures which are entirely our own'.[40] Costs should be kept to a minimum, warned Rompel: large-scale production requires studios, diversification and the use of outside organisations, all of which would vitiate the cultural identity which was the rationale behind the setting up of purely Afrikaner finance companies. RARO amateurs culturally cautioned commercial production which would be forced to stay on the beaten track. RARO was argued to be in a position to develop new directions – 'since not only are production costs unbelievably low, but the love that RARO's enthusiastic group of film amateurs have for their hobby, lends itself to a healthy quest for experimentation'.[41]

The RARO did not survive the war for it initially owed its existence to funding from the RDB and later its commercial activities through VOBI, which decreased substantially during hostilities.[42] Rompel also diverged from the primarily economic objectives of overarching Afrikaner resistance organisations which pragmatically engaged imperial capital in the cities, thus subjecting themselves to the very evils Rompel claimed were threats to Afrikaner identity.

Film and volksgevoel

The ideological divergence between RARO, on the one hand, and RDB and its Afrikaner and English-speaking allies, on the other, manifested in two different films on Afrikaner history. One was made by RARO, the other by the government. Impressed by the way film was used by Nazi Germany to project its national image, the Cabinet Minister of the SA Railways and Harbours, Oswald Pirow, sponsored *They Built a Nation* (*Die Bou van 'n Nasie*), produced by the English-speaking African Film Productions (AFP) during 1937–38. Pirow granted permission prior to its completion for its screening at the Voortrekker Centenary Celebrations to be held in Pretoria at the Monument in December 1938.[43] As early as 1934, Pirow had declared himself for a republic and dictatorship. In 1940, Pirow announced himself in favour of a 'New Order' which would consist of a strongly centralised white South African state in which home language would be unimportant. Its appeal was explicitly white, middle-class, anti-communist, and racist – rather than ethnic.[44]

Against this portrait it is possible to explain why the Afrikaans version of *They Built a Nation* was only considered as an afterthought and why AFP was subjected to attack from the Afrikaans press which alleged that the Afrikaans version was receiving less attention than the English edition.[45] Nevertheless, at its first invited screening on 12 December 1938 the film was 'accorded rapturous praise' by the Afrikaans press.[46] The English press was critical: whereas, in previous historical dramas, Briton and Boer had stood together.[47] The editor of *The Sunday Times* complained that *They Built a Nation* short-changed Great Britain's contribution to South Africa.[48] The film was not released until May 1939, 5 months after its preview, having also missed the Centenary Celebrations. While the English press complained about the omission of blacks and its overtly Afrikaner slant, the Afrikaans press considered it to have accurately portrayed the historical processes which would ultimately lead to the 'the free republic of South Africa'.[49] One commentator defended its 'spiritual cooperation', its avoidance of 'partisan sentiment' and how 'the English colonists and Afrikaners suffered and toiled together on the frontiers in the task of opening up the country'.[50] *The Cape Times*, on the other hand, noted 'its perfunctory treatment of Rhodes and Milner and its silence about the part played by South Africans of British descent in the building up of the nation'.[51]

Where *They Built a Nation* depicted a 400-year sweep, RARO's first film, *A Nation Maintains Direction* (*'n Nasie Hou Koers*, 1939), on the Voortrekker Centenary Celebrations, was, by 1940, screened on 285 occasions in 144 venues to about 50 000 viewers.[52] The Afrikaner support for both films was an indication of a movement which was to seize political power 10 years later in 1948. The cultural and ideological divisions which *They Built a Nation* identified were further exacerbated by *A Nation Maintains Direction*. It was shown a month before the outbreak of the Second World War and 'continued the emotionalising effect which *They Built a Nation* had begun'.[53]

The 1938 Voortrekker Celebrations fuelled the social, cultural and political movement, which was to direct the course of Afrikaner and South African history:

> It is difficult to find another single event which stirred Afrikaner emotion more between the Anglo-Boer War and the Second World War than the symbolic ox wagon trek of 1938. Not even the people who planned and organised it, the Afrikaner Broederbond, had the faintest idea it would be such an overwhelming success. It served to reunite Afrikaners in one nationalism and played a most significant role in the 1948 election victory.[54]

The cultural fervour stimulated by this symbolic trek rubbed off on the amateur cameramen who filmed the Celebrations. The ambience of the event was an important contributor to their later, more formal RARO operations where membership was restricted to Afrikaner cinematographers: what started out as a fairly inconspicuous attempt to celebrate the centenary of the Trek

> by sending a team of ox wagons from Cape Town to Pretoria became a rousing national movement. At the final celebrations 200,000 Afrikaners camped for days at Monument Koppie, the site chosen for the Voortrekker Monument to be completed 10 years later. Along the route to Pretoria thousands of Afrikaners (. . .) came to see the ox wagons, to touch them, to pray for them.[55]

Owned by the Voortrekkerbeweeging (Afrikaner Scout Movement),[56] the film is 5 h in duration, and was screened in two sections with an interval taking the form of a barbecue (*braaivleisaand*).[57]

While RARO's significance is of minimal importance in the history of Afrikanerdom and its bid to wrest power from dominant English capital, the influence of its parent body, the RDB cannot be underestimated. This ideological war was to be fought in the cities where 'protected jobs and higher wages for skilled non-whites equal with whites' and 'free competition between white and coloured and black' reduced wages overall.[58] One of the economic effects subordinated Afrikaners to blacks, who became known as 'poor whites'. Where the RDB, like the Broederbond which administered it, sought to mobilise the demoralised urban Afrikaner in the onslaught on English capitalist hegemony, RARO, in contrast, was still following Dr DF Malan's 1923 strictures where he urged urban Afrikaners to resettle on the *platteland* (rural areas).[59] By the early 1940s, however, Rompel's influence was on the wane. By 1945, RARO had only 200 members, and Rompel's association with the RDB weakened. His plea to colleagues to remain members of RARO indicates that they were disenchanted with RARO philosophy which, other than externalisation in *A Nation Maintains Direction*, had gained little proletarian support.

The RARO's refusal to use sound was self-defeating and Rompel became suspicious of VOBI when *Dark Traces* (*Donker Spore*, 1944) was made, apparently because VOBI interfered with their own plans for a RARO distribution network.[60] VOBI had pronounced a four-tiered programme:

1. The use of sound and 'absolutely pure' Afrikaans which would teach youth to trust their own language. The silent cinema advocated by Rompel was incapable of achieving this objective.
2. Films must be made on South African 'soil' reflecting Afrikaner morals, habits, history and life views which rest on a Christian foundation.
3. Afrikaans film should reflect literature and poetry and encourage a love of reading of indigenous literature. This cinema should identify volksmonumente (volk's monuments) and teach Afrikaners to protect what is theirs.
4. Afrikaans film must teach that patriots speak one language, have the same culture, are descendant from the same ancestors and are inspired by the same ideals and aspirations.

This programme compares favourably with Nazi attempts to disseminate covert propaganda in films carrying National-Socialist ideology. While Rompel neglected the advantages of commercial operations, VOBI, in contrast, intended producing on a large scale with the increased availability of material and apparatus after the War. Distribution would reach all areas previously isolated from Afrikaner cultural projects. Where suitable halls were absent or were contracted to 'alien companies', they were to be built with the help of allied organisations. The Churches' Afrikaans Film and Photographic Organisation (KARFO), established by Hein du Preez in 1947, stepped into the gap left by RARO: 'When we made *Dark Traces* we didn't even look at Rompel', explained du Preez who considered both RARO and VOBI as bumbling amateurish organisations. KARFO aimed to assist in the socialisation of urban Afrikaners while protecting cultural and spiritual heritage. Documentaries on mission work, and 13 features made from 1958 on, were used by KARFO as a means of enlightenment and information, using distribution strategies borrowed from John Grierson and the British Documentary Film Movement of the 1930s.[61] Where RARO was concerned with the pastoral, VOBI with heroes and martyrs, KARFO's pragmatism aimed to redress the stereotypical media image of Afrikaners created by RARO and others. Despite the lack of cooperation as far as Rompel was concerned, specific ideas gleaned from the Soviet directors lived on: according to du Preez, 'Eisenstein's *The Film Sense* was our Bible (. . .) *The Film Sense* opened up a whole new world to me.' Thus, RARO and VOBI differed not only in production techniques, but in theoretical emphasis as well. Where Rompel had dismissed Soviet aesthetics (but not the conditions of production), VOBI tried to adapt them to South African conditions, with the added complication of sound. Given the excitement of Afrikaans being accepted as a 'film language', this parallel development of a production language in Afrikaans was seen by Afrikaners as an important advance. The roles were played by a number of influential intellectuals, three of whom were later to head the South African Broadcasting Corporation under a Nationalist government after 1948.

The economic trends, which RARO resisted, were actively intercepted and used to advantage by the Broederbond, whose aims were primarily economic, with culture assuming a secondary importance and being coopted only in so far as it assisted with the capture of the English-dominated capitalist system. VOBI, in contrast, was sensitive to these processes,[62] and sought to deploy cinema in the economic class struggle as well. By the end of 1944, however, UTOLO had made little headway in attracting capital.

Hans Rompel, one of the 'fathers' of Afrikaner film, used the state-controlled German film industry as a blueprint for organising Afrikaner administration, production and distribution. *Source*: *Reddingsdaadbond 5 jaar, feesbrosjure* (anonymous leaflet, March 1945), p. 52.

At their third AGM in that year, UTOLO complained that the attitude of 'first show us what you can do before we invest' placed the company in an impossible financial position.[63] The VOBI–UTOLO partnership went into liquidation causing considerable financial loss to SASBANK which had underwritten the project.[64] Technically, UTOLO's films were a combination of poor sound, confused acting styles, stodgy camerawork and insufficient detail to the *mise en scene* – all of which vitiated whatever cultural sincerity had been encoded in its films. Summing up VOBI's failure, du Preez states,

> The [Afrikaner] public was enthusiastic (...) Unfortunately, the venture was tackled by persons who did not have the faintest notion of what they were doing (...) After the first flop which was an epic on the history of the church they repeated the performance twice (...) So complete was the failure that practically nothing was left over by which future film movements could benefit. (...) All they did was to create a disbelief in South Africa that Afrikaans pictures were at all possible (...) After the poor performance of many Afrikaans business ventures which were formed after 1938, it was realised that Afrikaner economic interests could only backed by financially sound ventures. VOBI was looking for endowments but SANLAM was interested in investments.[65]

Afrikaans films were not likely to be released in commercial cinemas which were tied up by the monopoly holders.

Rompel's strategy failed for many reasons: a Luddite attitude towards use of sound and especially dialogue; alienation from Afrikaner resistance movements and strategies which took the struggle to the cities; the elevation of the economic over the cultural as the mechanism of popular engagement; RARO and VOBI's lack of access to capital, commercial competition, and most importantly, the lack of political power prior to 1948. After 1948, RARO found itself in conflict with other producers and distributors like VOBI and KARFO, and indeed, with the political trajectory of Afrikaner Nationalism itself. Rompel's selective reading of Soviet film theory, his misunderstanding of the highly industrialised German political economy, and its need for huge-scale film production, could not be accommodated by amateur film. His attempt to find a path between amateur documentary realism and regulation of a national film industry was the ultimate contradiction.

Notes

1. P. Germishuys, 'Flickering Past', *South African Panorama*, 8:5 (1963), p. 7.
2. M. Eckardt, *Film Criticism in Cape Town 1928–1930* (Stellenbosch: SUN Press, 2005), p. 5.

3. H. Rompel, *Die bioskoop in diens van die volk (I+II)* (Bloemfontein: Nasionale Pers, 1942a resp. 1942b).
4. H. Rompel, 'Die Taak van die Rolprent', *Die Burger* (5 May 1930), p. 8.
5. H. Buchner, *Im Banne des Films* (München: Volksverlag E. Boepple, 1927).
6. Rompel (1942b), pp. 23–34.
7. Ibid., p. 13.
8. Ibid., p. 14.
9. Rompel (1942a), p. 104.
10. Rompel (1942b), p. 24.
11. Ibid., p. 24.
12. See Chapter 1.
13. Rompel (1942b), p. 33.
14. H. Rompel, 'Rolprente wat Ons nooit sal Sien nie', *Die Huisgenoot*, 14:432 (1930), pp. 20–3.
15. Rompel (1942b), p. 97.
16. Ibid., p. 24.
17. P. F. Wheeler, *Lokale Realisme in Speelprente van RARO en CARFO: 'n Inhoud-sontleding*, unpublished MA thesis, Bloemfontein, 1988, p. 32.
18. H. Rompel, 'Dokumentere Rolprente', *Die Huisgenoot*, 16:509 (1932), p. 47.
19. Rompel (1942a), p. 43.
20. H. Rompel, 'Klankprente, "Sterre" en Massa-produksie', *Die Huisgenoot*, 16:512 (1932), p. 49.
21. Ibid., p. 45.
22. Rompel (1930), p. 20.
23. Ibid., pp. 21ff.
24. Rompel (1942b), p. 15.
25. Ibid., pp. 15–18.
26. Rompel (1942a), p. 97.
27. Ibid., p. 103.
28. Ibid., p. 97.
29. Rompel (1942b), p. 20.
30. Rompel (1942a), pp. 45–6.
31. Quoted from *Die Volksblad* in P. Beukes, 'Dictatorship in Afrikaans Culture', *The Forum* (July 1938), p. 15.
32. K. G. Tomaselli, 'The Geography of Popular Memory in Post-Colonial South Africa: A Study of Afrikaans Cinema', in J. Eyles and D. M. Smith (eds), *Qualitative Methods in Human Geography* (London: Polity Press, 1988), pp. 136–56.
33. Rompel (1942b), p. 59.
34. J. H. P. Serfontein, *Brotherhood of Power: A Expose of the Secret Afrikaner Broederbond* (London: Rex Collings, 1974).
35. SANLAM (Suid-Afrikaanse Nasionale Lewensassuransie Maatskappy, South African National Life Assurers' Company) and SANTAM (Suid-Afrikaanse Nasionale Trust Assuransie Maatskappy, SA National Trust Assurers' Company); cf. T. D. Moodie, *The Rise of Afrikanerdom: Power, Apartheid and the Afrikaner Civil Religion* (Berkeley: University of California Press, 1980), p. 205.
36. H. du Preez, *Die Rolprent in Suid-Afrika,* unpublished manuscript, 1977, p. 41.
37. Ibid., pp. 41–2.
38. Rompel (1942b), pp. 47f.
39. 'Film Propaganda on the Platteland', *The Forum* (12 July 1942), p. 24.
40. Rompel (1942b), p. 48.

41. Ibid., p. 50.
42. The UTOLO 3rd AGM Report in *Kultuurfilma* (December 1944), p. 25.
43. *Sunday Express* (8 May 1938).
44. T. D. Moodie, *The Rise of Afrikanerdom: Power, Apartheid and the Afrikaner Civil Religion* (Berkeley: University of California Press, 1975), p. 210. See also O. Pirow, *Nuwe Orde vir Suid-Afrika* (Pretoria: Christelike Republiekeinse Suid-Afrikaanse Nasionale Socialistiese Studiekring, 1941).
45. *The Star* (25 February 1938).
46. T. Gutsche, *The History and Social Significance of Motion Pictures in South Africa* (Cape Town: Howard Timmins, 1972), p. 348.
47. K. G. Tomaselli, 'Capital and Culture in South African Cinema', *Wide Angle*, 8:2 (1986), pp. 33–44.
48. *Sunday Times* (25 December 1938).
49. *Die Transvaler* (26 May 1939).
50. T. J. Haarhof in *The Forum* (May 1939).
51. *The Cape Times* (29 May 1939).
52. *Die Transvaler* (8 August 1940).
53. Gutsche (1972), p. 351.
54. I. Wilkins and H. Strydom, *The Super-Afrikaners: Inside the Afrikaner Broederbond* (Johannesburg: Jonathan Ball, 1980), p. 95.
55. Ibid.
56. J. de V. Heese, 'Trimftog van die Voortrekker-rolprent', *Die Huisgenoot*, 24:944 (1940), p. 47.
57. Gutsche (1972), p. 345.
58. T. D. Moodie, *The Rise of Afrikanerdom: Power, Apartheid and the Afrikaner Civil Religion* (Berkeley: University of California Press, 1975), p. 199.
59. *Die Burger* (12 & 13 July 1923).
60. In the words of H. de Preez, 'by the time Rompel got RARO together, the Reddingsdaadbond was already on the wane. Promised funds were not forthcoming to RARO which consequently curtailed its operations'. All interviews with du Preez were conducted during April 1981.
61. K. G. Tomaselli, 'John Grierson in South Africa: Misunderstanding Apartheid', in J. Izod *et al.* (eds), *From Grierson to the docu-soap: Breaking the Boundaries* (Luton: Luton University Press, 2000), pp. 47–58.
62. E. Kohl, *Stel die Rolprent in Diens van die Volk* (Johannesburg: Volksbioskope, 1946), p. 21.
63. UTOLO 3rd AGM Report in *Kultuurfilma*, 1944 (December), p. 25.
64. du Preez (1977), p. 42.
65. H. du Preez, *KARFO Report submitted to Grierson*, unpublished manuscript, Part II, undated, ca. 1950, p. 2.

18
Film and Politics in South-east Europe: Germany as 'Leading Cultural Nation', 1933–45

Tim Kirk

'The new objective of European cinema is the national Film', wrote a Nazi cultural commentator in Vienna in 1942. 'National' films would enable the nations of Europe to present their lands and peoples to the outside world. Unfortunately many smaller countries – and this was particularly true of south-eastern Europe – lacked a native film production industry adequate to the task; and here the continent's 'leading cultural nations' must step in, and fill the gaps with appropriate films. The region had relied far too long on tawdry western imports, which people were now rejecting in favour of more serious, German films that addressed issues important to Europeans: *Jew Süss* (*Jud Süss*, 1940), for example, which had been shown in Balkan capitals the previous year. German cinema was faced with two tasks in south-eastern Europe, the commentary continued: First, to fill the gaps in the market created by the lack of 'national' films; and secondly, and more importantly, to disseminate German culture 'thereby continuing a tradition, and simultaneously awakening an understanding of the new developments now beginning in Europe'.[1]

German cultural imperialism in south-eastern Europe

The above-mentioned report, intended for internal circulation in the Reich and for distribution among Germany's diplomats and agents in the Balkans, reflects the unself-conscious assumptions and wishful thinking of German cultural imperialism in the region; and these in turn rested on a long-standing belief that this was Germany's political – and cultural – backyard. South-east central Europe and the northern Balkans had been dominated by the Habsburg Empire since the early eighteenth century, and there had been renewed German settlement in the region as the Ottoman empire had receded, notably in Transylvania during the reign of Maria Theresia. As a result there were substantial minorities of ethnic Germans (*Volksdeutsche*) in Romania, Hungary and Slovakia and smaller communities elsewhere.[2] In the perspective of many academic ethnographers in Austria and Germany it was from these 'bearers of culture' that any economic or cultural progress (in the broader, anthropological sense) was bound to have come: unlike the Germans, with their natural capacity for efficient organisation and hard work, the Slavs and other local ethnic groups were incapable of organising their own affairs, and for that reason might be considered to be under Germany's informal tutelage. In the new and deliberately inegalitarian Nazi language of international relations, the peoples of the region constituted (part of) a *Völkerfamilie* (family of nations) of which Germany was the natural *Führungsvolk* (leading nation). Accordingly, German cultural diplomats of the 1930s and the 1940s, mindful of the shortcomings of German propaganda during the First World War, not only set out to underpin the Third Reich's strong political presence in the region with a dense network of German-sponsored cultural activities, but also monitored local responses.[3]

Germany's 'external cultural policy' (*auswärtige Kulturpolitik*) in the region was conceived not least as a corrective to the baleful influence of western liberalism. With the defeat of the Central Powers in 1918, the collapse of the Habsburg Empire, the creation of successor states with – initially at least – liberal constitutions, and the construction of the 'little Entente', much of eastern Europe had been recreated in the West's image; and this political turning point had been reinforced by the influence of the burgeoning global commercial culture that was equated with 'Americanisation'. With the establishment of the Nazi regime, the decline of French influence in the region, and the development of unequal bilateral economic relationships with the Balkan states during the 1930s, Germany's presence had been reasserted in south-eastern Europe even before the outbreak of the Second World War. The extension of the Axis to encompass Hungary, Romania and Bulgaria, and the creation of dependent client states such as Slovakia (following the German occupation of Bohemia and Moravia in 1939) and Croatia (following the German invasion of Yugoslvia in 1941) had reinforced German influence in the region immeasurably. Although few territories were directly incorporated into the Reich, or directly occupied and administered by Germany, the whole region, from Bratislava to the Turkish border, was essentially a series of German (or nominally Italian) puppet states by the end of 1941, and Germany's presence was felt everywhere. It was a presence characterised by the same 'polycratic' rivalry between individuals, groups and institutions that characterised the Reich itself. Formal political arrangements, and the extent of German control, varied from country to country, but everywhere there was rivalry, competition and conflict: both between the various German interests in the region – the army, diplomats, police forces, Nazi functionaries and businessmen – and between Germans, local political and economic interests, and those of rival foreign powers in the region. Among this confusion the Balkans was being remade in anticipation of Germany's victory and post-war political hegemony: south-eastern Europe was to play a significant role in the construction of the Nazi new order. Borders were revised, old 'multi-national' states were broken up, and whole populations were to be 'resettled', all in the interests of 'racial' uniformity. Many of the region's inhabitants were drafted to work on farms or in factories under slave-labour conditions in Germany; but the most brutal displacement of all was the deportation and mass-murder of the Jewish population.

In the midst of this bloodthirsty context of war and 'ethnic cleansing', considerable effort was put into laying the foundations of German cultural hegemony: conferences and academic exchanges were organised, language courses were provided, and orchestras, theatre groups and art exhibitions toured; but the medium with most immediate impact, especially for popular audiences, was film. German films of all kinds were shown regularly in Balkan capitals, and their reception was closely monitored, particularly among the elites and intellectuals. Along with weekly digests of political developments and press commentary (*Wochenberichte Südosteuropa*) compiled in the press office of the *Gaugrenzlandamt* in Vienna, a parallel series of 'cultural reports' (*Kulturberichte Südosteuropa*) reviewed all aspects of the region's cultural activity.[4] This chapter seeks to assess the perceived impact of the 'new order' on cinema in the Balkans from the perspective of these analyses of the region's cultural development.[5]

Film in south-eastern Europe: An overview

The film business in south-eastern Europe began at the turn of the twentieth century, with demonstrations of the Lumière brothers' cinematograph in major towns and cities. Permanent picture-houses were quickly established, and these were supplemented by a network of itinerant cinemas bringing film-shows to the remotest villages, and these remained important in the Balkans until after the Second World War, bringing not only entertainment but also news and public information films to remote areas. In most countries short films were made depicting local scenes soon after the introduction of the cinematograph itself. In addition there were more ambitious attempts to produce feature-length narrative films of the kind that would achieve iconic status as pioneering documents of national cinema histories, as for example in the case of the 1912 film *War of Independence* (*Ražbouil independenţi*) by the Romanian director Grigore Brezaeanu. Film production industries of any significance were established only in Austria and Hungary however, and the latter in particular remained important as an exporter of films to the region as a whole.[6]

Hunnia, Hungary's leading film studio was established in Hungary 1911, and Pathé – then the most important distributor in the region – also produced films in Kolosvár (now Cluj in Romania) from 1913. There followed a boom in film production which saw the establishment of more than 30 such businesses by 1919, and a diversification from documentaries into narrative film even before the First World War. Film was taken seriously as an art form by Hungarian intellectuals, making possible the development of a film culture, with its associated press and star system. The early start, rapid development and supportive intelligentsia ensured that the indigenous film industry in inter-war Hungary was of a qualitatively different order from those elsewhere in south-eastern Europe; it was the only one that the Germans respected on something approaching equal terms. Hungarian and German film-makers had much in common, and Germans used the Hunnia studios to make a number of films.[7] Hungarian films were also clearly of interest to the sizeable German community in Budapest, and were reviewed regularly, and for the most part sympathetically, in the German-language newspapers *Pester Lloyd*, and *Deutsche Zeitung*. For their part the Hungarians took this respect for granted, asserted and – in a long article in *Nemzeti Ujsag* – even quantified Magyar cultural superiority, using statistics on literacy, health provision and professionalisation.[8] As far as German observers were concerned the only thing holding Hungary back was the perceived influence of the Jews, which was deemed to be extensive and detrimental. Jewish influence was held to be particularly deep-rooted in the entertainment industry and the role of Jews in Hungarian cinema was the subject of repeated and lengthy diatribes that invoked predictable stereotypes about the manipulative shallowness of Jewish culture and the sly dishonesty of Jewish business practices.[9] The occupation of Hungary and the deportation of Hungarian Jews in 1944 were accompanied by the 'retirement' of senior officials and their replacement by ideologically more reliable collaborators. Steps were taken to impose firmer central control on all aspects of the film industry in the last months remaining before the arrival of the Red Army, and plans to make explicitly anti-Semitic films were noted with approval. The *Deutsche Zeitung* commented favourably on preparations for a film of the Tiszaeszlár blood libel of 1882, when Jews had been accused (and acquitted) of the ritual murder of a Hungarian girl: 'one of the darkest chapters of the history of Hungarian Jewry', a 'tragedy from a bourgeois-liberal era', when the 'true' story had allegedly been suppressed by the Rothschild family and Jewish organisations at a cost of millions. (Another anti-Jewish film was planned, telling the story of a government official supposedly murdered by Jews for attempting to stop the spread of their influence in the Carpathians and their exploitation of the local Ruthene population.) The *Deutsche Zeitung* followed this up with an article entitled 'Order in the Hungarian Cinema' setting out the ostensible extent of Jewish control of the film business, and agitating for a review of contracts and cinema leases, and in July it was announced that a government commissioner would lead the reorganisation of Hungarian cinema. Even as the Red Army approached Budapest in the autumn of 1944 the Hunnia film concern was being re-staffed and restructured as a state-controlled institution and the principal vehicle of Hungarian film policy in the new cultural order.[10]

While German observers commented extensively on the content of Hungarian film, their interest elsewhere was largely restricted to the structure and development of the business in a region where local producers could be encouraged to draw on German technical assistance for the production of newsreels and documentaries (*Kulturfilme*), but where foreign imports would continue to cover the demand for feature films. A 'national' cinema was also encouraged where there was deemed to be a sufficient technical and creative basis, and for newly independent nations such as Slovakia and Croatia it was considered a symbol of cultural autonomy.

For the most part Germany's policy was to provide technical support, and to encourage bilateral contracts between institutions or companies in the Reich and local, largely state-owned organisations, such as Nástup in Slovakia[11] (in which the German ethnic community also had a small minority holding). In October 1939 the new organisation signed an agreement with the Reich Film Chamber, which enabled it to take any film produced in the Reich for distribution in Slovakia. In 1940 the majority of films showing in Slovak cinemas, including some two-thirds of feature films, were German, and Nástup worked closely with UFA on the production of newsreels. German commentators were pleased to note that showings of 'significant' films (such as *Uncle Krüger* (*Ohm Krüger*, 1941)), were preceded by introductory lectures to help cinema-goers understand the context. From March 1940, technical production of Slovak sound newsreels was moved from Prague to laboratories in Vienna, where Slovakia's own newsreel could be supplemented with German footage from the fronts, among other material. (The *Deutsche Wochenschau GmbH* had set up a newsreel board in Vienna for this purpose.[12]) With the help of the Reich Film Chamber and UFA, Nástup produced a series of propaganda films, starting with an 'educational' film about Slovaks abroad, and documentaries with an emphasis on great Slovaks, the country's natural beauty, customs and folklore, or neutral technological themes such as the development of artificial fibres, and the production of sugar – 'Slovakia's white gold'. Modern (German) technology supported the celebration of (local) tradition when Agfa colour was used for the first time in Slovakia in a 1944 documentary about marriage customs, bringing out the best in the colourful Slovak folk costumes. Slovak cinema's greatest achievement – from the German perspective – was a 1941 documentary filmed on the eastern front: *From the Tatra to the Sea of Azov*, which was successfully exported abroad – albeit only to Berlin, Vienna and Zagreb. Nástup's own film production was limited, but it also cooperated with government institutions such as the defence and interior ministries to films about military training and educational films about typhoid and diphtheria, diseases still common in Slovakia. In addition, Nástup also distributed foreign films: 128 feature films and 141 documentaries in 1943, the majority of them (73 and 98 respectively) German. Italian films accounted for a significant proportion of the rest (18 feature films and 36 documentaries). Not all sections of Slovak society welcomed German imports with the same degree of enthusiasm, however, and in 1942 a Catholic newspaper, *Katolicke Noviny*, produced a list of films dealing with subjects such as divorce, infidelity and 'free love' and declared them unsuitable for Catholics on grounds of immorality. The list included German titles such as Gerhard Lamprecht's *The Loved one* (*Die Geliebte*, 1939), Kurt Hoffmann's *Bachelor Paradise* (*Paradies der Junggesellen*, 1939) and Carl Boese's *Wedding Night* (*Hochzeitsnacht*, 1940).

Nástup encouraged aspiring writers and directors with prizes, and Slovakia's membership of the International Film Chamber provided scholarships in Germany or Italy. Above all, however, the development of film production was seen as an important dimension of nation-building, and its products frequently celebrated the Slovak people and landscape. Film festivals attracted both local worthies and German dignitaries alike, and in March 1944 celebrations for the fifth anniversary of the new state were accompanied by the premiere of a film about Slovakia's struggle for autonomy, and the beginnings of its history as a state. A German version of the film was shown at the same time, and a separate Croatian version had been made for Zagreb.[13]

Croatia[14] was in many ways in a similar position to Slovakia. It had not existed as an independent state before the German invasion of Yugoslavia in 1941, and had had no independent film production industry before then. 'Croatia-Film', which was founded after the establishment of the new state, specialised mainly in newsreel and documentaries. The first full-length feature film with sound, *Lisinski*, was produced in 1944, and dealt with the life of a nineteenth-century Croatian composer, a suitable celebration of the country's national cultural history. Croatia-Film was also a distributor, supplying both home-produced and German films to the Croatian market; and it owned some cinemas, the revenue from which went to subsidise its production work. Most cinemas, however, were dependent on German imports, which had already found a ready market in Croatia even before 1941, as the success of a German *Kulturfilm* week in Zagreb had demonstrated to the reported displeasure of the then rulers in Belgrade. Much of Croatia's own production was propaganda or documentary celebrating the emergent nation state, its landscape and its people. On the third anniversary of the state in 1944, the celebrations were accompanied by a short film entitled *The Poglavnik and the People*, and another short film entitled *Croatian Anton Day* celebrated three great Croatians with similar names: Ante Starčević, Antun Radic, and Ante Pavelić, the Poglavnik (leader) of the Ustaša movement.[15]

The centre of the Yugoslav film world before the war had been in Belgrade, and there had been several companies producing documentaries in the 1920s and the 1930s. Most feature films had come from abroad, however, and although Yugoslavia had been one of the principal importers of Hungarian films, the market had been dominated before the war by British and American imports: 'Only now are people in Serbia beginning to realise what little inner value these films actually have' a German reporter observed, 'and that their import in such large numbers was possible thanks only to the dominant position of the Jews and their helpers'. The film business in Yugoslavia retained something of the early days of cinema. Small towns and villages in Serbia were supplied by itinerant film shows. Banat-Film, for example, founded in 1942, had five mobile sound-film cinemas and 22 fixed picture houses suitable for showing small films (*Schmalfilm* – 16 mm prints). In April 1944, it was reported that the company had entertained 743 403 customers, and shown 92 feature films, 76 documentaries and 341 newsreels, and showings were regular, although only once or twice a month, in most of the 90 towns and villages where the company operated Films were also rented out to schools and other organisations.[16]

In addition to Brezeanu's historical epic, Romania had already produced newsreels before 1914. A number of directors had made their debut during the 1920s, including Jean Mihail and Jean Georgescu, but as was common in many parts of the Balkans the lack of career opportunities prompted many to emigrate to central Europe and America. German commentators of the 1940s looked back on the years between the wars as a benighted period characterised by patchy domestic production, the domination of western imports, and the almost total absence of any German films until the establishment of a German distributor in Bucharest in 1937, 'which had initially been greeted with indifference, one might even say it had been boycotted'. This situation was ascribed, in the usual way, to the Jewish domination of all aspects of the cinema business from film production and distribution to the ownership of cinemas and the specialist press. (The problem was supposedly exemplified by the film-making career of Horia Igiroşanu, who, it was argued, had been compelled to found his own film magazine, *Clipa Cinematographica*, to overcome the bias of the 'Jewish press', and established his own drama school to prepare young actors 'for the future Romanian national cinema'.)

From the perspective of German cultural commentators in the 1940s, true Romanian cinema was still in its infancy, and was associated with the promotion and support of the film business by the government from the mid-1930s, specifically from the establishment of the National Film Office (ONC) in 1938. Earlier 'attempts to make films privately' were dismissed as unsuccessful. Like similar organisations elsewhere in the region, the ONC produced mainly *Kulturfilme* and newsreels, the latter in collaboration with Wehrmacht propaganda companies (film units) from the beginning of the war, and then with the support of Ufa's *Deutsche Wochenschau GmbH*, which supplied material from Berlin. The emphasis of production shifted dramatically between 1938, when all 34 Romanian films were documentaries, and

1941, when 30 newsreels (or 'war reports' as they were now called) were produced, only two documentaries and a feature film. There were very few Romanian feature films, and most were made mainly with the support of Italian film enterprises.

Romanians had long spurned German film, so commentators were particularly interested in the shift from American to German imports since the late 1930s. In 1942 there were some 250 cinemas in Romania, 58 of them in Bucharest, mainly showing foreign films, and the overwhelming majority of these were now from Germany, although there had also been a sharp increase in the number of imported Italian feature films. The overall number of imports had fallen dramatically since the beginning of the war, however, above all the American films that had accounted for a third of all imports in 1938. Film distribution companies unable to comply with new government regulations intended to 'Romanise' the industry – and some had dealt only in American films – had simply been dissolved. The situation was very similar in Bulgaria, where there was also a very small domestic film industry that concentrated mainly on documentary, newsreel and educational film, and relied heavily on imports. In 1939, Bulgaria had still imported significant numbers of British and Soviet Films, but here German films were the most popular, even before the war and its attendant import restrictions.[17]

Of the countries on the periphery of the Balkan peninsula, Albania had no history of film production, and scarcely two dozen cinemas across the whole country. Turkey had produced a small number of its own films since the 1930s, but also imported a significant number of German films; and since Turkey was neutral this was a gratifying sign that the relative success of German film was not merely a consequence of restrictions on western imports. A film company was founded in Greece in 1944, but before that the needs of Greek cinemas[18] had been supplied almost entirely by foreign imports with subtitles. There had been some films made in the open air by amateurs, according to the *Donauzeitung*, successful less for the kitsch stories or backdrops – generally the Acropolis or another historical setting – than because audiences were finally hearing their own language on the screen.

Conclusion

The *Donauzeitung* reflected the paternalistic tone of much German commentary on the national cultures of the Balkans, but it also reflected a broader understanding of culture on the nationalist right within and beyond Germany that underpinned the Reich's cultural policy in the Balkans and as it related to the new European order generally. Cultural development would be directed by the state institutions on behalf of the community, not left to individuals and markets. Above all the shallow, commercial popular culture of the west would give way to a genuinely national cultural production (typified in the *Kulturfilm*), which would celebrate the diversity of local communities and the traditions and landscapes within which they were rooted. Higher forms of culture, however, from symphony orchestras and art exhibitions to serious cinema and literary translations would need to be imported from the continent's leading cultural nations, and above all Germany, as it shaped Europe's new cultural order.

Notes

1. Öesterreichisches Staatsarchiv, Archiv der Republik, Reichsstatthalterei Wien 41a/VI Kulturberichte Südosteuropa. Here Kulturbericht (AdR/Kb) 38, [DATE], p. iii, 'Betrachtungen zur kulturellen Lage: Der deutsche Film im Südosten'.
2. Valdis O. Lumans, *Himmler's Auxiliaries. The Volksdeutche Mittelstelle and the German National Minorities of Europe, 1933–1945* (Chapel Hill: University of North Carolina Press, 1993) pp. 10–22.
3. T. Kirk, 'Working Towards the Reich: The Reception of German Cultural Politics in South-Eastern Europe', in Anthony McElligott and Tim Kirk (eds), *Working Towards the Führer. Essays in Honour of Sir Ian Kershaw* (Manchester: Manchester University Press, 2003), pp. 205–23.
4. See P. Heinelt, 'Porträt eines Schreibtischtäters. Franz Ronneberger (1913–1999)', *Medien und Zeit* 2/3 (2002), pp. 92–111; P. Longerich, *Propagandisten im Krieg. Die Presseabteilung des Auswärtigen Amtes under Ribbentrop* (Munich, 1987), pp. 149ff. Here specifically pp. 244–5.
5. For the purposes of these reports south-eastern Europe comprised Slovakia, Hugary, and the entire Balkan peninsula beyond. There were also occasionally reports on Turley and the Middle East.
6. W. Fritz, *Kino in Österreich 1896–1930. Der Stummfilm* (Vienna: Österreichischer Bundesverlag, 1982); J. Cunninghan, *Hungarian Cinema from Coffee House to Multiplex* (London: Wallflower Press, 2004).
7. See also Chapter 11.
8. R63/353, 27. Kb 'Die ungarische Kulturüberlegenheit im Spiegel statistischer Daten'. *Nemzeti Ujsag* was an independent, progressive Catholic newspaper, and covertly pro-western.
9. See, for example, AdR, 23. Kb iii-v, 'Die Juden im ungarischen Filmwesen'.
10. R63/353, Kb.137, 8–14 May 1944; Kb 140, 29 May–14 June 1944; Kb 147, 17–23 July 1944; 150 Kb. 21 August–3 September 1944.
11. See also Chapter 8.
12. R. Vande Winkel, 'Nazi Newsreels in Europe, 1939–1945: The Many Faces of Ufa's Foreign Weekly Newsreel (Auslandstonwoche) versus the German Weekly Newsreel (Deutsche Wochenschau)', *Historical Journal of Film, Radio and Television*, 24:1 (2004), pp. 13–14.
13. Bundesarchiv (Barch), R63/352, p. 1ff. 126 Kulturbericht Südosteuropa (Kb), 14–20 February 1944, pp. i–ii, 'Betrachtungen zur kulturellen Lage: Das Slowakische Filmwesen'; Kb 125, p. 20; Kb 141, p12. AdR/Kb 38 vi; AdR, 35 Kb, pp. ii–iii, 'Slowakische Filme' (based on an article by Ivan J. Kovacevic in the Bukarester Tageblatt'.
14. See also Chapter 7.

15. R63/353, Kb, 136 1–7 May 1944; Kb 137, 8–14 May 1944; Adr/Kb 38, 'Der deutsche Film im Südosten', p. vi; R63/353 137. Kb., 8–14 May 1944.
16. Ibid., pp. v–vi; R63/353, Kb 135, 17–30 April 1944.
17. AdR, 21. und 22. Kb, pp. iii–v, 'Das Filmwesen Rumäniens'; 38 Kb., 'Der deutsche Film im Südosten'; 80. Kb, 8–14 March 1943.
18. See also Chapter 10.

19

German Films on the Spanish Market Before, During and After the Civil War, 1933–45

María A. Paz and Julio Montero

In the 1930s, Spain did not have a proper film industry. The film market of the politically and economically unstable nation was dominated by foreign, especially American, companies. As this chapter will demonstrate, the German film industry tried to expand its influence while and after Hitler helped General Franco win the Civil War (1936–39). However, this modest success proved short-lived.

The Presence of German films in the Second Spanish Republic (1933–36)

In 1931, the year in which King Alfonso XIII was deposed and the Second Spanish Republic was proclaimed, Spain produced only one feature film. The virtual non-existence of a domestic film industry held the doors wide open for foreign majors. Although, in the following years local film production increased significantly,[1] the Spanish film market continued to be dominated by American companies.

Before the Civil War (1936–39) heralded the end of the Second Republic, Germany and Spain did not have mutual agreements about film export or import. Official German–Spanish film diplomacy remained reduced to complaints, filed on behalf of the German Embassy against the screening of 'anti-German' films in Spanish cinemas. Negotiations usually did not proceed quickly. In October 1932, the prohibition of the French–British production *Under the Leather Helmet* (*Sous le Casque de Cuir*, 1932) was required. The German embassy protested in particular against the scene of a drunken German officer taking part in an orgy. The scene was not cut out until February 1934.

In March 1933, Rex Ingram's *The Four Horsemen of the Apocalypse* (1921) and *The Secret of the Submarine* (1915)[2] were prohibited. (As in many countries, smaller cinemas only slowly converted to sound, which allowed silent films to be around for quite some time.) The Germans felt that these films were 'rekindling resentment over the war', propagating an 'anti-German atmosphere',[3] offending their feelings and hurting the dignity and honour of their (former) army. With the Nazis in power, films referring to current German politics or to German anti-Semitism were requested to be prohibited too, such as an edition of the American screen magazine *The March of Time* (May 1936) that contained scenes of violence against German Jews. According to the German Ambassador, these scenes were obviously false and tried to turn viewers against the German nation.[4]

Meantime, the German Embassy organised propaganda activities for German residents in Spain, activities to which Spaniards feeling close to National-Socialism were also invited. In October 1934, the embassy started organising private screening of a series of eight films. In 1935, 27 more films were shown, including Leni Riefenstahl's *Triumph of the Will* (*Triumph des Willens*, 1935). In 1936, 13 more films were distributed before the outbreak of the Civil War put an end to this practice. All of these films were shown in Madrid and also distributed to Barcelona, Bilbao and Las Palmas, where important German colonies lived. As they were screened in private sessions, the Spanish government did not protest. But when attempts were made to show such films to larger audiences, during regular screenings for instance, the authorities stepped in and prohibited the film exhibition. This was the fate, for instance, of *Storm Trooper Brandt* (*SA Mann Brandt*, 1933) in 1934.[5] The propagandistic strategy behind these private screenings was twofold. On the one hand, adherence to National-Socialism, and on the other, the dissemination of a more positive image of Nazi Germany.

From May 1935 onwards, the German embassy also distributed documentary shorts (*Kulturfilme*). Some documented the German preparations for the Olympic Games,[6] others dealt with the typical customs, beauties and artistic treasures of German towns and regions.[7] Homage was also paid to events that were celebrated by the Nazis (like the *Wagnerfestspiele* in Bayreuth) and to all kinds of improvements instigated by Hitler's government. Like German feature films, these documentaries rarely made it to the regular cinemas.

However, German films were not totally absent from the mainstream cinema circuit. The introduction of sound films had, taking into account the Latin-American countries too, increased the commercial potential of Spanish-spoken or Spanish-dubbed films. German companies understood this too. By the end of 1932, Ufa started introducing its films through a local agent, the Spanish Film Alliance (*Alianza Cinematográfica Española*, ACE Madrid). From 1933 on, the activities of this company sparked off controversies in film magazines. Some film professionals spoke out against German films and Nazi film politics,[8] others spoke in favour.[9] Ufa (ACE Madrid) responded with a communiqué.[10]

The ACE Madrid promoted its Ufa films with extensive advertising campaigns. Magazines such as *Cinegramas* published extensive reports on actors, plots, directors and so on. Directors like Arnold Fanck were portrayed in a very positive light[11] and various German stars were promoted: Conrad Veidt, Emil Jannings, Brigitte Helm, Marlene Dietrich and Fanck's favourite, Leni Riefenstahl. Before 1933, German film exports to Spain had not been very successful. There had been some successes, such as Fritz Lang's *M – The Murderers are Among Us* (*M. Eine Stadt sucht einen Mörder*, 1931) and Josef von Sternberg's *The Blue Angel* (*Der Blaue Engel*, 1930).[12] Some comedies and operettas triumphed as well, such as *The Merry Wives of Vienna* (*Die Lustige Weiber von Wien*, 1931) and *The Madam's Secretary* (*Petit Officier... Adieu!*, 1930). It is, however, undeniable that the presence of German films on the Spanish market became much stronger after ACE Madrid started distributing Ufa productions on a regular basis. In 1934 and 1935, respectively, 117 and 107 films premiered in Spain. Each was shown averagely 4–5 weeks in Madrid. In the provinces too, German films became more successful than before. In Pamplona, for example, a progressive increase of German film screenings in local cinemas can be observed too. For instance, Karl Hartl's *Gold* (1934) and Erik Charell's *The Congress Dances* (*Der Kongress Tanzt*, 1931 – starring Lilian Harvey) were among the most successful films released in 1934. As the second example already demonstrates, many of the German films that were released in the Second Republic in or after 1933 had been produced in 1932 or before. Most recent productions that were distributed by ACE Madrid can hardly be described as National-Socialist propaganda films. (As explained above, such movies were rather distributed by the embassy and shown in private screenings.) Instead, ACE Madrid distributed escapist entertainment films such as *A Song for You* (*Ein Lied Für Dich*, 1933) with Jenny Jugo.

Along with these feature films, ACE Madrid distributed German documentaries (*Kulturfilme*) and newsreels. The documentaries and newsreels were apparently appreciated: 'Frequently (...) the public accepts documentaries with more enthusiasm than feature films.'[13] The newsreels ACE Madrid and Ufilms (a smaller company that released German films as well) distributed since December 1932 were subtitled versions of Ufa's *Auslandstonwoche* (Foreign Weekly Newsreel, ATW), which was the only German export newsreel since 1927.[14] These Spanish ATW versions, entitled *Actualidades Mundiales* (World News, also known as *Actualidades Ufa* or *Noticiario Ufa*), were entirely manufactured in Berlin, as was the usual procedure for each ATW.[15] The newsreel was shown in Spanish cinemas until the outbreak of the Civil War and represented almost 12 per cent of the newsreel market.[16] Although submitted to censorship, newsreels were never actually censored. Most of the German documentaries that were distributed simultaneously had an outright educational character and were for instance titled *Zoologic Varieties* (*Bunte Tierwelt*), *Flying Fish* (*Die fliegenden Fische*), *The World of Ants* (*Der Ameisenstaat*) or *Buildings of Imperial China* (*Die Bauten des Kaiserlichen Chinas*).

In June 1935, *Hispania-Tobis S. A. Madrid* (Tobis Madrid) was founded by the Amsterdam-based company *Intertobis* (*Internationale Tobis Cinema NV*). Until 1945, the company distributed Tobis and Ufa films too. Half of the company was owned by Spanish investors, the *Salgado y Cia SA*.[17]

German films in (both) Spain(s) during the Civil War (1936–39)

In July 1936, part of the regular army revolted against the government of the Republic. A Civil War broke out between the 'Republicans' and the 'Nationalists'. The conflict did not officially end until 1 April 1939. The power was eventually left in the hands of the 'Nationalist regime' that was lead by General Franco, who would exercise authoritarian powers until 1975. During the Civil War, Nazi Germany, like Mussolini's Italy, did not hesitate to support the Nationalist troops of Franco.[18] In November 1936, Germany, again like Italy, recognised the Nationalist regime as the government of Spain. Hitler appointed an official ambassador to the Nationalists, whose assistance to Franco became, especially from 1937, decisive in winning the war. The German ambassador also made efforts to strengthen economic ties between Germany and Franco's Spain. This also influenced German–Spanish collaborations in the field of cinema.

War means chaos and film distribution in a country divided by Civil War is anything but evident. Cinemas on both sides of the (moving) front lines were showing any print they could lay their hands on, sometimes exchanging films from one cinema to another.[19] Further away from the front lines, things were more organised. In the Republican zone, the activity of the 'German' distribution companies terminated immediately. After the mobilisation of trade unions and official entities, film distribution became strictly controlled. The Communists were distributing Soviet films through the *Film Popular* and Spanish films through the *Compañía Industrial Film Española* (Cifesa). Foreign majors continued to distribute their own productions and American films remained predominant in the cinemas of the Republican towns. The disappearance of 'German' film distributors did not put a full stop on the screening of German films in Republican regions. (No fees were paid and after the war, Germany would try to recover the revenues it lost.) In Madrid, which until early 1939 remained in Republican hands, 109 German productions were shown during the Civil War. In the Second Republic, 87 had been released before the Civil War broke out. The remaining 22 'new' films were new for the Spanish market but also belonged to the batch acquired for the 1935–36 season.

The 'German' film distribution companies moved to the Nationalist zone. These were ACE Madrid, Tobis Madrid and De Miguel, a private distributor who released Ufa entertainment films for a short period of time. However, film distribution in Franco's zone could only be re-established after the conquest of Bilbao (July 1937), the former distribution centre for the northern zone of Spain. The business profits of these companies were initially not very considerable. Films such as Willi Forst's *Mazurka* (1935) and Henry Koster's *Little Mother* (*Kleine Mutti*, 1934) were succesful in Nationalist as well as in Republican cinemas. But there were differences too: Gustav Ucicky's *Joan of Arc* (*Das Mädchen Johanna*, 1935) was successful in the Nationalist region (like the city of Pamplona) only – probably because of its nationalist and Catholic character.

German films were preferentially treated by film magazines published in the Nationalist zone, most likely because they were controlled by Falangists, the pro-Franco group closest to the Nazis. This trend increased since 1938, when the National Film Department (*Departamento Nacional de Cinematografía*) was founded. Riefenstahl's *Olympia* (1938) was very much admired.[20] Karl Ritter's *Pour le mérite* (1938) was being praised as a counterpoint to *All Quiet on the Western Front* (1930).[21]

The Spanish market remained relatively unimportant to the Germans until the Nationalists conquered the east of Spain (Barcelona was entered by Francoist troops on 26 January 1939) and Madrid (which fell on 28 March). When the conquest became imminent, the Reich Film Chamber (*Reichsfilmkammer*) initiated negotiations with Franco's film officials. The negotiations proved difficult for the (Hollywood-orientated) film preferences of the audience could not be changed overnight. It was also difficult to diminish the power of the American film companies that were – since the United States (like most countries) stuck to neutrality – doing business with both Spanish camps.[22]

The 'film negotiations' between Nazi Germany and Nationalist Spain started in May 1938,[23] nearly 1 year before the Civil War officially terminated. For the Germans, it was of crucial importance to have Ufa's newsreel (ATW) shown freely in Spanish cinema. Further, the Reich Film Chamber hoped to win the Spanish market for its fiction films and to obtain government protection for its films – protection that was not granted to American productions.[24] The Reich Film Chamber was represented at these negotiations by two German representatives (Schwarz and Lisenmeier) who apparently did not fully appreciate the complexity of the Spanish Nationalist politics. They talked to Spanish film propagandists and with officials of the Ministry of Trade – two groups that did not share the same views or hold the same objectives. For the Spanish propagandists, it was of utmost priority to improve the national and international image of the Nationalist regime. They therefore wished to impose the obligatory screening of a Spanish newsreel all over Spain. As far as commercial films were concerned, they only wanted to avoid foreign exchange costs. The Germans on the other hand did not want their Ufa newsreel (ATW) to disappear.

In June 1938, an agreement was reached. This allowed for the production, with German aid, of a Francoist weekly newsreel (*Noticiario Español*) and a monthly documentary. In reality, this Spanish newsreel would appear on a rather irregular basis and there would be no proper Spanish newsreel until 1943. More important, at least in German eyes, was the fact that the agreement allowed ACE Madrid to continue distribution of the ATW. As for feature films, the agreement allowed German companies to distribute 80 films in Spain without paying the corresponding taxes. For the German negotiators, this arrangement was economically not very important as long as the war continued. It was, however, hoped to become very advantageous after the war.

German films in Francoist Spain (1939–45)

Only 5 months after the official end of the Civil War (1 April 1939), Nazi Germany invaded Poland, thereby provoking the outbreak of the Second World War. The developments of that war, which Franco (unlike Mussolini) chose not to enter, would influence the relations between Nazi Germany and Franco's Spain for the following years. The presence of German films on the Spanish market was therefore also influenced by the developments in the war.

Nazi Germany and its film industry expected two rather different things from Spain and its film market. Economically, the German film industry wished to ensure that the debts, which Spain had built up in the last years would be paid off. It was also hoped that, now that Spain was again a stable state, Franco's government would guarantee the paying off of future debts. Politically, Germany wanted to make sure that Spain would not close its doors for documentaries and newsreels that represented Germany's view on the invasion of Poland, the Nazi-Soviet non-aggression pact and the imminent war in Western Europe. (It is significant that, from September 1939, the ATW newsreels distributed in Spain became Spanish-dubbed instead of subtitled.[25]) The Spanish government on the one hand did not want to jeopardise its good relations with Germany, on the other realised it needed German help to build up a film industry of its own. The German requests therefore did not fall on deaf ears, as the Spanish authorisation for the establishment of a German newsreel board (cfr. Infra) in Madrid illustrates. But Spain had aims of its own too. Apart from the wish to (re)construct the domestic film sector (production and distribution), Spanish film officials also wished to prevent all revenues made by German films returning to Germany.

In May 1939, negotiations were started to discuss the following:

1. The repayment, in foreign currency, of previous profits made from German films and the setting up of a system for future payments.
2. The definition of a quota of films that would be exempted from payments of rights.
3. The long-term assurance of the German newsreels and documentaries on the Spanish market.

The talks were concluded with a provisional agreement on 30 December 1939. The compromise was partly a success for the Spanish party. The transfer of profits made in previous seasons did not exceed the original amount suggested by the Spaniards (20.000 Reichsmark). With regards to the distribution of new films, Spain committed itself to start paying half of the profits in advance, but only 'if the trade balance with Germany allowed such'.[26] The established film quota was 80. No formal agreement was concluded on the distribution of German newsreels and documentaries, but it was provisionally agreed that these two categories together would not exceed 80, the same quota that had been introduced for films: 'No objections will be raised if each feature film is accompanied by a documentary or a newsreel, which, however, will not commit our party to transfer them and which, in any case, should be subject to a separate agreement on documentaries, cultural or educational, and newsreels.'[27]

In the following months, Germany repeatedly attempted to reach a definite agreement that would also include newsreels and documentaries. The great importance Germany attached to newsreels was a powerful weapon in the hands of the Spanish government, used to obtain benefits such as free unexposed film. A 'final' film agreement was signed in Berlin, on 26 April 1940, between representatives of the Reich Film Chamber and the film departments of the Spanish Ministry of Trade and the Spanish Ministry of Interior Affairs. The agreement prolonged earlier engagements and made sure that Spain would not object to further import of German newsreels. Spain refused, however, to grant those newsreels a monopoly and, to assert its 'independence' and 'neutrality', continued to import the American Fox newsreel. Spain also reduced its foreign currency expenditure, securing the raw film it needed as well as some investment money (half of the profits made by German films) to boost local film production. In short, the Germans sacrificed some of their economic aspirations in order to guarantee their propaganda objectives. The importance attached to newsreel propaganda is further demonstrated by the fact that an editorial board that was to produce a Spanish version of Ufa's Foreign Weekly Newsreel (ATW) in Madrid was set up on 15 November 1940. This board was a Spanish subsidiary of the German Newsreel Company (*Deutsche Wochenschau GmbH*). It was set up before its German parent company, had even officially been established.[28]

In the long run, the agreement of 26 April 1940 satisfied neither party. The Reich Film Chamber tried to negotiate a new agreement, the Spanish attempted to delay it by prolonging their answers.[29] Further, Spain started, in spite of the agreement, to limit the distribution of German films. To that end, they applied severe censorship. Documentaries with political messages were repeatedly cut.[30] Furthermore, 'moral grounds' were often invoked to censor German features.[31] The Germans complained that, on the level of national censorship, 'some highly spectacular films, mutilated by censorship, had become un-saleable'.[32] Furthermore, 'uncontrolled censorship of local and regional authorities'[33] was claimed to 'harm the interests of German film, which [in addition] was worsened by the understandable attitude of cinema entrepreneurs and exhibitors of that province who, based on the exhibited material, distanced themselves from German film productions for economic reasons'. From such complaints, it can also be deducted that German films were not appreciated in the Basque country and that exhibitors looked for easy excuses not to show them. The Spanish Association of Entertainment Entrepreneurs (*Sociedad Española de Empresarios de Espectáculos*) also protested against the disproportionate presence of German films. It confirmed that the audience preferred American films, which, in turn, were more profitable for them.[34]

All these films continued to be released by Spanish companies, most notably ACE Madrid and Tobis Madrid. In June 1941, the Spanish investors of *Salgado y Cia SA* increased their capital in Tobis Madrid. The Tobis parent company, by now almost completely German-owned and soon to be integrated in Ufa, was left with only 6.2 per cent of the shares. As Ufa was not interested in minority shares, the company sold the shares to the Salgado group (in December 1942) and, following an agreement with Salgado, kept on distributing films through Tobis Madrid.[35] ACE Madrid, in the offices of which Ufa had a representative,[36] also remained in Spanish hands.

Der Ufa-Film „Kora Terry" in Madrid

The Ufa production *Kora Terry* (1940), starring Marika Rökk, at the Palacio de La Musica, in Madrid around April 1941. Rökk played the virtuous Mara as well as her loose twin Kora. The second character, who died at the end of the film, allowed her to play rather risqué and un-National-Socialist scenes that increased the popularity of the film. *Source*: H. Traub, *Die Ufa. Ein Beitrag zur Entwicklungsgeschichte des deutschen Filmschaffens* (Berlin: Ufa-Buchverlag, 1943), p. 255.

In January 1943, the Spanish government started producing its own newsreel, the *Noticiarios y Documentales Cinematográficos* (No-Do) or 'Cinematographic Newsreels and Documentaries'. Its screening was compulsory and No-Do received a total monopoly, as the screening of other newsreels was no longer allowed.[37] This meant that the Spanish ATW as well as other foreign newsreels like the American *Noticiario Fox* were closed down. There is little doubt that the German propaganda ministry was not very happy about the disappearance of its Spanish ATW version, but it clearly did not have a choice. Although the editorial board of the ATW no longer existed, it was not really closed down. Through its subsidiary, the *Deutsche Wochenschau GmbH* supplied No-Do with equipment, raw film stock and German and international newsreel items derived from the ATW. No-Do, in its turn, supplied its German partner with local items, which secured the inclusion of Spanish items in the *Deutsche Wochenschau* (DW) and ATW.[38] The reverse was also true. No-Do also derived items from Allied newsreels: Allied and German newsreel items were sometimes edited into the same No-Do issue, which could lead to strange combinations.[39]

German–Spanish (film) relations deteriorated after 1942, as it became increasingly clearer that Germany would lose the war, and Spain distanced itself more and more from its former friend. The Spanish side was striving to avoid the drain of foreign currency by any means. The issue became so inflamed that the Germans preferred to reduce the number of authorised films in order to guarantee efficient conditions of payment (40 feature films and 40 documentaries). Contrary to the past, recoverable profit had become of greater interest than the presence of German films on the Spanish market. The last German protest on the subject of the film that we know of was a verbal note of the German Embassy in Madrid (6 December 1943). It required that American actions in Spain did not affect the Spanish–German trade of films. The reply of the Spanish Ministry[40] showed that this German weakness was known. Other pending issues, not related to film, remained unanswered.

In retrospect, proportionally not that many German feature films were shown in Franco' Spain. Old prints had been circulating for years and the outbreak of the Second World War had not facilitated the renewal of the film stock. The number of German film premieres in Francoist Spain was noticeably lower than in the Republican period. And the trend continued to go down. In 1939, 69 German films had premiered in Madrid, whereas it was only 51 in 1940, 21 in 1942 and 6 in 1945. The shortages of new productions led to the re-showing of older successes, such as Géza von Bolváry's *What Women Dream* (*Was Frauen Träumen*, 1933 – co-written by Billy Wilder) and Willi Forst's *Lover Divine* (*Leise Flehen Meine Lieder*, 1933). Among the most popular German films were comedies and musicals like *Hallo Janine* (1939) and *Don't Go to Bed without a Kiss* (*Ungekusst Soll Man nicht Schlafen Gehen*, 1936) in 1941; *The Desert Song* (*Das Lied der Wuste*, 1939) and *Kongo*

Express (1939) in 1942. In 1943, *The Great King* (*Der Grosse König*, 1942), *Bel Ami* (1939) and *Rembrandt* (1942) did relatively well. In 1944, *The golden City* (*Die goldene Stadt*, 1942) and *Quax, the Crash Pilot* (*Quax, der Bruchpilot*, 1941) stood out among the 13 films released that year. In 1945, *Titanic* (1943) and *Lake of Bees* (*Immensee*, 1943) did quite well. Censorship remained a great problem for German film plots conflicted with Spanish moral norms. In the first half of 1944, 19 German films were censored. Five were prohibited and nine rated for grown-ups only, which limited the audience.[41]

Conclusion

German films were mostly shown on Spanish screens during the Second Republic. Their presence declined during the Civil War and even more so during the years of Franco's rule. The audience preferred escapist films and most German films shown in Spain dated from before Hitler's rise to power. Musical comedies in particular were popular. Overt Nazi propaganda films were hardly shown. By the end of the war, having signed up the Bretton Woods Agreements, Spain stopped the distribution of German films altogether.[42]

Notes

This chapter is part of the research project funded by the Spanish Ministry of Science and Technology (BSO2001-1207 Cinema Going in Spain (1896–1939). Organisation of entertainment as a modernising factor).

1. J. M. Capparós Lera, 'Feature films in the Second Spanish Republic, 1931–1936', *Historical Journal of Film, Radio and Television*, 5:1 (1985), pp. 63–76.
2. *Boletín Oficial de la Provincia de la Coruña*, 27:3 (1933).
3. Archivo del Ministerio de Asuntos Exteriores Español (hereafter AMAE), R 852/77.
4. AMAE, R 1317/118.
5. Politisches Archiv des Auswärtigen Amtes. Akten der spanischen Botschaft Spanien (hereafter PAAA), B Madrid, 622, 10-a.
6. Deutsche Bauliche Vorbereitungen für Olimpia 1936; Kampfstätten der Olympischen Winterspiele in Garmisch; Der Führer Eröffnet das Winterhilfswerk 1934; Das Reichssportfeld Entsteht; Die Turnerischen Pflichtübungen, etc.
7. *Wo der rote Wein wächst*; *Allgäu in Sommer*; *Bauerntag in Bückenburg*; *Thuringen*; *Streifzüge durch Deutschland*; *Bayreuth, der Stadt der Wagnerfestspiele*; *Barockstadt Dresden*; *Dresdens Umgebund* y *Land und Leute im Erzgebirge*, among others.
8. 'Rutas de la decadencia. Cinema alemán', *Popular Film*, 10:5 (1935).
9. S. Saporta, 'El film como preocupación del gobierno', *Popular Film*, 20:4 (1933).
10. '... The credibility of certain information, attributed to the Third Reich Minister Dr. Goebbels, is doubtful and if there is any truth in it, it is the concept that light, entertaining films should preserve a certain spiritual level... and should not show... Germany too different from what it really is'. 'Sobre una campaña contra la producción alemana', *Popular Film*, 31:8 (1933). This was obviously based on Goebbels first speech to German film makers as Propaganda Minister which he delivered at the Kaiserhof on 28 March 1933. Speech in full reprinted

in D. Welch, *The Third Reich Politics and Propaganda* (London: Routledge, 2002 rev.), pp. 184–9. Goebbels was actually warning film-makers that if they wished to produce National-Socialist films 'they must capture the spirit of the time'.

11. 'La personalidad del animador de "S.O.S. Iceberg" ', *Popular Film*, 10:8 (1933).
12. The information was obtained through a systematic study of the film-related pages of *El Sol*.
13. 'La cinematografía documental en Alemania', *Arte y Cinematografía*, 6–7 (1932).
14. R. Vande Winkel, 'Nazi Newsreels in Europe, 1939–1945: The Many Faces of Ufa's Foreign Weekly Newsreel (Auslandstonwoche) versus the German Weekly Newsreel (Deutsche Wochenschau)', *Historical Journal of Film, Radio and Television*, 24:1 (2004), pp. 7–8.
15. R. Vande Winkel, 'La imagen de la España franquista en los noticiarios nazis extranjeros durante la Segunda Guerra Mundial', in J. Montero and A. Rodríguez (eds), *El cine cambia la historia* (Madrid: Rialp, 2005), pp. 155–75.
16. Of 512 censored pages (*Boletines Oficiales de Pamplona* y *La Coruña*), 60 correspond to those of *Ufa Tonwoche*.
17. Bundesarchiv (hereafter Barch), R 109 I/1663, *Gesellschaftsrechtliche Bindungen, Aufstellung und Erläuterung des in Spanien belegenen Ufa-vermögens*. Thanks to R. Vande Winkel for consulting these documents on our behalf.
18. R. Hidalgo, *La ayuda alemana a España, 1936–1939* (Madrid: Editora Nacional, 1975); G. Weinberg, *The Foreign Policy of Hitler's Germany. Diplomatic Revolution in Europe 1936–1939* (Chicago: Chicago University, 1970); A. Viñas, *La Alemania nazi y el 18 de julio* (Madrid: Alianza, 1977).
19. A. Cañada, *El cine en Pamplona durante la II República y la Guerra civil (1931–1939)*, unpublished doctoral thesis, Pamplona, 2003, p. 169.
20. A. Román, 'Cine y deporte en Alemania', *Radiocinema*, 30:6 (1938).
21. 'La antítesis de Sin novedad en el frente', *Radiocinema*, 15:1 (1939).
22. Vid. J. Cabeza, *El Descanso del Guerrero. El cine en Madrid durante la Guerra Civil Española (1936–1939)* (Madrid: Rialp, 2005), p. 119 and following.
23. PAA, B Madrid, 621, I.
24. Vid. R. Álvarez and R. Sala, *El cine en la zona nacional, 1936–1939* (Bilbao: Mensajero, 2000), pp. 207–9.
25. Barch, R 109/I, 1617, *Landeräkte Spanien*; Censorship cards at the Archivo General de la Administración, Alcalá de Henares.
26. PAA, B Madrid 621, 2.
27. Ibid.
28. Vande Winkel (2004), pp. 11–12.
29. A note (17 June 1942) from the Embassy to the Spanish government says, 'Since I have so far not received any response to the proposals made to Mr. Soriano on March 5, nor to my verbal answer referring to the reply of the Regulating Subcomission to the proposals of the German delegation from 12 November 1941, I would like to repeat . . .'. AMAE, R 3064-12.
30. Archivo de la Fundación Francisco Franco (hereafter FFF), 27183.
31. FFF, 27183.
32. Ibid.
33. AMAE, R 1347-86. The following films and prohibition dates are quoted: *Domino Verde* (*Green Domino*, 18 September 1940); *Dunia* (3 May 1939); *Baile en la Ópera* (*Dance in the Opera*, 11 May 1941); *Marido Ideal* (*Ideal Husband*, 16 January 1941), and *Estrellas del Río* (*Stars of the River*, 10 September 1940), substantial cuts in *Kora Ferry* and *Noche Embrujada* (*The Spell of the Night*).

34. E. Diez, *Historia Social del Cine en España* (Madrid: Fundamentos, 2003), p. 131.
35. Barch, R 109 I/1663, *Gesellschaftsrechtliche Bindungen, Aufstellung und Erläuterung des in Spanien belegenen Ufa-vermögens*.
36. B. Drewniak, *Der deutsche Film 1938–1945* (Düsseldorf: Droste Verlag, 1987), p. 769.
37. R. R. Tranche and V. Sánchez-Biosca, *No-Do: El tiempo y la Memoria* (Madrid: Cátedra/Filmoteca Española, 2002).
38. Vande Winkel (2005).
39. V. Sanchez-Biosca, 'Les actualités No-Do en Espagne', *Les Cahiers de la Cinémathèque*, 66 (1997), pp. 78–9.
40. AMAE, R 1724/74.
41. *Radiocinema*, 23:4 (1944); 21:5 (1944); 28:5 (1944); 2:7 (1944); 30:7 (1944).
42. See Note 36.

20
Swedish Film and Germany, 1933–45

Rochelle Wright

In the decade or so between Victor Sjöström's *Ingeborg Holm* (1913) and Mauritz Stiller's *The Story/Atonement of Gösta Berling* (*Gösta Berlings saga*, 1924), Swedish film attracted international attention for its narrative sophistication and innovative visual techniques. By 1924, however, both Sjöström ('Seastrom') and Stiller had relocated to Hollywood; the indigenous film industry subsequently underwent a precipitous decline both qualitatively and quantitatively, reaching a low point in 1929, when only six Swedish works premiered. The introduction of simultaneous sound and image recording at the beginning of the new decade brought far-reaching changes. With the language barrier virtually eliminating exports, filmmakers focused on the domestic market. During the 1930s, as going to the movies became a progressively more popular activity, film production increased again, averaging about 25 features a year. Svensk Filmindustri, specialising in 'quality' films, continued to dominate, but a spate of other production companies arose, including the hugely successful Europa Film, where the focus was on 'folksy' entertainment. Following the model already established by Svensk Filmindustri, Europa Film consolidated its position by establishing a chain of movie theatres to show its own films. Another high-profile company, Sandrews, proceeded in reverse, expanding from theatre ownership into film production by the end of the decade.[1] These three corporations, Svensk Filmindustri, Europa Film, and Sandrews, remained the leading Swedish film producers for many years.

The Swedish film industry and relations with Germany

Though imported films accounted for more than 90 per cent of the releases throughout the 1930s, ranging from 250 to 325 titles annually, Swedish films represented a proportionately larger share of the market, about a third overall.[2] Swedish audiences, especially outside major metropolitan areas, favoured films in their own language, a predilection that may be correlated with the industry-wide preference for subtitles rather than dubbing. Among the imports, American entertainment films maintained a clear dominance, representing about 65 per cent of the total and an even higher percentage of the major hits.[3] Except for a dip in 1939, German features held steady at around 8 per cent of the releases between 1935–40.[4]

Despite the relative insularity of the Swedish film industry, events on the wider European scene had repercussions at home. Shortly after Hitler's rise to power in 1933, *Landsorganisationen* (LO), the umbrella labour union affiliated with the Social Democratic Party, demanded a boycott of all German products, including film. The boycott endeavour officially continued until 1940 without having much direct effect on movie attendance, but it vexed German film producers and appears to have reinforced the inclination of the Swedish film industry to avoid controversial subject matter.

In 1935, Sweden became a founding member of the Nazi-dominated International Film Chamber (*Internationalle Filmkammer*, IFK) which necessitated a restructuring of the Swedish film bureaucracy to meet German specifications.[5] This concession was largely a matter of form rather than substance; the newly formed Swedish Film Chamber (*Svenska Biograf- och Filmkammare*) could not in actuality function in the same manner as the analogous German Reich Film Chamber (*Reichsfilmkammer*, RFK), since Sweden's film industry, unlike Germany's, was not controlled by the state. Cooperation was nevertheless close between Sweden's leading production company and the international organisation. Olof Andersson, head of Svensk Filmindustri, served not only as president of the Swedish Film Chamber but also as one of the three vice presidents of the IFK.

Andersson and other representatives of Sweden's film industry did not share the overtly pro-Nazi political and racial goals of the IFK, but hoped to side-step German propaganda efforts by steering clear of politically sensitive stances of any kind. The Swedish industry found a common cause in the collective attempt to counteract American dominance of the market. Swedish participation in the IFK was nevertheless in stark contrast to the refusal of several other nations, including Great Britain and the Netherlands. (The latter joined the (revived) IFK after it was occupied by Nazi-Germany.[6])

The IFK languished after the war began, but at Goebbels's directive it was revived in 1941. Though the Swedish Foreign Ministry, concerned about maintaining neutrality, did not sanction continued Swedish involvement, it had no objection to representatives of the Swedish film industry attending meetings of the IFK as observers. Sweden's position was difficult. With no other reliable source of film stock, the industry was loath to alienate Germany, but the IFK's new and insistent demand for a complete ban on American films was clearly against Swedish interests. The import of American films had declined by about 15 per cent after 1939, largely because of transport problems, but Hollywood productions still represented a large and lucrative share of the Swedish market, compensating in part for the collapse of the French film industry. Though German imports peaked in 1941, at 37 films or 12.3 per cent of the total, German features could not possibly fill in the gap if American films were prohibited.[7]

Continued cooperation with Sweden through the IFK was advantageous to Germany for propaganda purposes since most other affiliated countries were Axis controlled. There were also practical, economic incentives. Ufa and Tobis each had a branch in Stockholm: AB Ufa Film and Tobis Film AB (though Tobis Stockholm, like Tobis branches elsewhere in Europe, was subsumed by Ufa (the Ufi Concern) in the summer of 1942).[8] Goebbels hoped not only to promote German film in Sweden, but also to import more Swedish features to fill Germany's screens. Consequently Sweden was able to maintain a semi-official affiliation with the IFK without complying with the ban, the only country granted this concession. Simultaneously the Swedish industry began exploring alternative sources of film stock, eventually finding a conduit to import Kodak film from the United States. When the ban on American productions led to an acute shortage of feature films elsewhere in Europe, the Swedish industry profited from increased export of its own products and leveraged this position to resume importation of film stock from Germany. (The Swedish film *Kalle at Spången* (*Kalle på Spången*, 1939), starring the popular comedian Edvard Persson, played for a year and a half in occupied Copenhagen, where the Danes considered it a matter of honour to prevent it from being replaced by a German product.[9]) The war did not hamper Swedish film production, which reached an all-time high during the 1940s, averaging more than 40 features a year and accounting for between 40 and 50 per cent of the domestic market through 1945.[10] Beginning in 1943, the import of German feature films dwindled precipitously and as the outcome of the war became increasingly apparent, the IFK ceased to be a significant factor.

The opportunistic collaboration of Sweden's film industry with the IFK was motivated by economic self-interest but had extremely questionable political and ideological implications. As film historian Jan Olsson concludes, hypersensitivity to German demands was in conflict with a policy of strict neutrality and undercut freedom of expression to an objectionable degree.[11]

Both before and during the Second World War, however, industry self-censorship and Statens Biografbyrå, the indigenous State Censorship Board, had a greater effect both on domestic film production and the fate of foreign films than did the IFK, though that organisation often applied pressure both directly and indirectly.[12] In practice, German attempts to influence Swedish film censorship policy sometimes proved unnecessary, since Censorship Board guidelines called for the prohibition of films that might have a negative effect on Sweden's relationship with foreign powers, and the Board, in turn, was under the watchful eye of the State Information Department (*Statens Informationsstyrelse*, SIS), which represented the interests of the Foreign Ministry. Swedish foreign policy focused on maintaining neutrality but in the early years of the war also took into account an anticipated German victory. The Board had already banned *Confessions of a Nazi Spy* by July 1939, a month before the German delegation in Stockholm conveyed such a request through diplomatic channels. That same month the German Reich Film Chamber moved more quickly, alerting Olof Andersson to the presumed propagandistic qualities of Chaplin's *The Great Dictator* (1940) while the film was still in production. Andersson's cautious reply, while stressing that the Swedish Film Chamber had no control over foreign releases, suggested that if advance reports were accurate, the film probably would not clear the censors.[13] In fact *The Great Dictator* (1940) was not brought before the Censorship Board until September 1945, when it was approved without controversy.

Though the majority of the films forbidden by the Censorship Board were American or British, this stance was not pro-German *per se* but rather reflects the preponderance of English-language films scrutinised. Certain German features deemed offensive were banned as well, for instance Veit Harlan's notoriously anti-Semitic *Jew Süss* (*Jud Süss*, 1940) in 1941. Documentaries glorifying German war victories were considered on a case-by-case basis, with inconsistent outcomes. *Baptism of Fire* (*Feuertaufe*, 1940) was banned in 1940, while the following year *Campaign in Poland* (*Feldzug in Polen*, 1940) and *Victory in the West* (*Sieg im Westen*, 1941) were released with only minor cuts. The Board responded to an influx of propaganda newsreels after the outbreak of war by prohibiting those with Swedish texts or sound tracks. Though some exceptions were made, this ban contributed to Ufa's decision in 1941 to set up a branch office of the German Newsreel Company (*Deutsche Wochenschau GmbH*) in Stockholm, where a Swedish-language version of the Foreign Weekly Newsreel (*Auslandstonwoche*, ATW) could be produced locally. German newsreels continued to be shown in Sweden in conjunction with the screening of feature films throughout the war.[14] Ufa advertisements appeared regularly in the industry publication The Cinema Owner (*Biografägaren*) until May 1945.[15]

The most popular star of foreign films shown in Sweden during the 1930s was the Swedish-born Greta Garbo, who appeared primarily in apolitical melodramas designed to showcase her beauty and mystique. From the late 1930s, however, Swedish actresses who achieved fame outside their homeland played significant roles on both sides of the propaganda war. Ingrid Bergman's Hollywood films included two with an obvious anti-fascist message, *Casablanca* (1942) and *For Whom the Bell Tolls* (1943). Zarah Leander and Kristina Söderbaum, in contrast, were major stars in Germany, often acting in films that explicitly promoted Nazi ideology.[16]

After Marlene Dietrich 'defected' to Hollywood, Leander was launched as her replacement. A relatively minor luminary at home, Leander became the highest paid actress of the period in Germany, appearing in 10 Ufa productions before returning to Sweden in 1943. Among the most popular was Homeland (*Heimat*, 1938). All of Leander's films were vehicles constructed around her performance as a singer and her persona as a glamorous, foreign-born vamp, but the Leander character generally underwent a transformation during the course of the film, eventually embracing the traditional female role endorsed by the state by giving up her career. Leander was associated with the Nazi cultural elite through her participation in public events, social functions and radio shows, activities that undercut her later claim to have been uninvolved in politics.

Söderbaum, blond, blue-eyed, fresh, innocent, and natural, with a girl-next-door quality, embodied the Nazis' feminine ideal. An unknown when Ufa director Veit Harlan, a favourite of Goebbels, discovered and married her, she appeared exclusively in features directed by her husband. These included melodramas like *The golden City* (*Die goldene Stadt*, 1942) as well as overt propaganda films such as *Jew Süss* and *Kolberg* (1945); regardless of genre, Söderbaum's characters tended to be victims obsessed with sacrifice and death, often by drowning, hence her nickname 'Die Reichswasserleiche' (the Reich Water Corpse). Unlike Leander, Söderbaum remained in Germany after the war, though after Harlan's death she attempted to distance herself from her earlier career.

Melodramas starring Leander – *Homeland* (*Heimat*, 1938), *Enchanted Evening* (*Es war eine rauschende Ballnacht*, 1939), *The Great Love* (*Die grosse Liebe*, 1942) – and Söderbaum – *The golden City*, *Lake of Bees* (*Immensee*, 1943) – were shown in Sweden, with the stars attending the Stockholm premieres to considerable fanfare, but their association with the Nazi political agenda seems to have made at least some segments of the contemporary Swedish audience uneasy. Neither Leander nor Söderbaum was ranked among the top stars of the period in Sweden and after the war both were reviled as collaborators.

Film subject matter and the Third Reich

During the 1930s, domestic film production in Sweden took little direct notice of political and social developments on the continent, but the choice of subject matter nevertheless reflected contemporary concerns.[17] Like much of the rest of the world, Sweden experienced an economic depression in the early years of the decade, but it was also then that the fundamental legislation of the Welfare State was put into place. The film industry responded to uncertainty and social change by offering images of security and focusing on the stable and familiar. The dominant genre of the period was comedy, intended to entertain and distract. Virtually all films provided the reassurance of a conventionally 'happy' ending that rewarded virtuous characters and punished villains, or indeed anyone who threatened the status quo. This idealised image of Swedish well-being and happiness conveys a sense of insularity and ethnocentricity that is reinforced by the derogatory depiction of outsider groups.

The outsider figure who appears most frequently is the Jew, inevitably portrayed in a stereotypical and negative manner as a Shylock out to take monetary advantage of ethnic Swedes.[18] The prevalence of this motif is particularly striking given the relatively small Jewish population in Sweden, around 7000. Clearly the many pejorative film portrayals are correlated to an increase in Swedish anti-Semitism during the 1930s; an intriguing question is whether this phenomenon, in turn, was influenced by Nazi ideology.

The Nazi party was not politically significant in Sweden, but indigenous anti-Jewish prejudice was reinforced by propaganda disseminated from Germany. Among mainstream Swedish political parties, the Farmers' League incorporated statements about racial purity in the party platform and the Social Democrats were sometimes swayed by eugenic arguments. The pseudo-science of racial biology was particularly influential in Sweden during this period; negative traits previously attributed to Jews on religious grounds were now construed as racially or genetically determined and hence immutable. Though the climate of the times brought anti-Semitism into the open, contemporary manifestations also built on a long tradition of anti-Jewish sentiment in Swedish literature and folk humour. Anti-Semitism in Sweden nevertheless did not reach the virulent pitch promoted by Nazi rhetoric.

Jewish figures were especially common in Swedish films of the early 1930s; they embody an anti-Semitic stereotype that had international currency but is placed in an entirely Swedish context. Though individuals are rarely identified as Jewish in the dialogue, there are many specific ethnic markers that the audience is intended to recognise, including physical appearance, gestures and body language, accent and profession. With one exception, however – the anomalous and little-seen *Panik* (*Panic*, 1939) – these Swedish films were not intended to be malicious or provocative and do not appear to have been influenced by anti-Semitic propaganda films from Germany, the most infamous of which appeared towards the end of the decade and furthermore were not released in Sweden. Rather, the Swedish–Jewish characters are stock figures functioning within the predictable narrative formulas of domestic film comedy, and were accepted as such by contemporary critics and audiences. Many films in which such characters appear were extremely popular, with viewer statistics of 750 000 to 1 million.

The fiction that these anti-Semitic stereotypes were harmless caricatures became difficult to maintain when the Swedish film *Pettersson & Bendel* (1933) attracted the personal attention of Hitler and was shown in Germany as part of the intensifying anti-Semitic campaign of the mid- and late 1930s.[19] Though the film had no overt political agenda, in this different context it could be used in a deliberately manipulative way for invidious political purposes; screenings of the film in Germany led directly to acts of violence against Jews. Subsequent debate in Sweden contributed to a heightened awareness of the dangers of ethnic stereotyping, and as the full ramifications of Hitler's racial policies became clear, anti-Semitic characterisations receded and then, with few exceptions, vanished from Swedish film.

In the 1930s, a popular subcategory of film comedy was the military farce. Since Sweden had not been directly involved in a war since the

Napoleonic era, poking fun at military incompetence was harmless escapism bearing little relation to contemporary reality. Circumstances changed after hostilities engulfed the continent and the war came uncomfortably close to Sweden's borders. Swedish sentiment was overwhelmingly in support of Finland during the Winter War of 1939–40, and while pro-German feeling was not negligible, most Swedes also sympathised deeply with the plight of their fellow Scandinavians after Norway and Denmark were occupied in the spring of 1940. Swedish neutrality was nevertheless preserved at the cost of certain concessions to Germany, including the transport of German troops through Swedish territory.

With a sizeable section of the adult male population drafted into military service, Sweden's defence was no longer a laughing matter. Beginning in 1940, films focusing on the military acquire a more sober tone, highlighting camaraderie, patriotism and the necessity of sacrifice. The war does not figure directly and the political orientation and national allegiance of spies and potential saboteurs is never specified, but the possibility of armed combat is present in the background.[20] Overall, Swedish film during the war period is more inclined than previously to consider serious subject matter, not infrequently based on literary sources.

Despite heightened censorship restrictions, politically provocative material was occasionally allowed, provided it was packaged as historical drama or allegory. *Ride This Night* (*Rid i natt*, 1942) depicted a peasant uprising against German estate-owners in southern Sweden during the seventeenth century but alluded directly to the situation in occupied Europe. The film, like the 1941 novel on which it is based, helped crystallise anti-fascist sentiment in Sweden.

Several films from the war years give sympathetic portrayals of the plight of refugees fleeing Nazi Germany.[21] In *Dangerous Ways* (*Farliga vägar*, 1942), the family of displaced persons – not explicitly identified as Jewish, though reviewers understood the subtext – have been stripped of their citizenship and cannot obtain work permits, but eventually the adult daughter finds both employment and personal happiness in Sweden, while the others are able to emigrate to America. This positive resolution, while emotionally satisfying, was an ironic contrast to the restrictive policies of Swedish authorities towards actual refugees from the Third Reich.

In October and November 1942, there were mass arrests and deportations of Norwegian Jews to Auschwitz. In the fall of 1943, however, most Danish Jews escaped that fate by fleeing to Sweden. These events brought home the horrifying reality of Hitler's racial policies and led to an increased sense of solidarity with Sweden's occupied neighbours. By 1943–44, when five films set in occupied countries appeared, such topics could be addressed relatively openly.[22] Though only one film, *His Excellency* (*Excellensen*, 1944), identifies the occupied land (Austria) and makes specific reference to a German takeover, the generic military uniforms and lack of geographic specificity in the other films was not ambiguous to contemporary audiences, who immediately recognised parallels to, in particular, the situation in Nazi-occupied Norway.

The first occupation film, *My Land Is Not Yours* (*Mitt land är icke ditt*, 1943), in many ways set the pattern for the others by personalising the conflict; all but one incorporate a love story between a military officer serving in or cooperating with the occupying forces and a woman resident of the subjugated land. When forced to choose, the woman eventually places loyalty to country and/or fidelity to ideals ahead of love. *Live Dangerously* (*Lev farligt*, 1944) downplays romance, instead highlighting an actual heroic exploit of the Norwegian resistance movement when commandos parachuted into dangerous territory to sabotage a heavy water plant. That the film's director and lead actor, Lauritz Falk, was himself a refugee from occupied Norway underscored the anti-German thrust.

The Invisible Wall (*Den osynliga muren*, 1944) focuses on a woman who becomes directly involved in the rescue of her Jewish neighbours, an action that in the end necessitates her own flight across the border. As a foreign national in the occupied land, she represents neutral Sweden, illustrating that it is not enough to be a sympathetic observer. In *His Excellency*, the Jewish motif is less significant, but the title character, a famous writer, is himself imprisoned in a concentration camp, where he is tortured and eventually shot. The graphic concentration camp sequences exposing Nazi sadism and brutality make this film more forthright and daring than any other Swedish production of the war years. Both *The Invisible Wall* and *His Excellency* argue convincingly for the moral necessity of resistance, even at great personal cost.

Since the occupying forces are clearly understood to be Nazis, these films all convey an obvious anti-German bias. This negative image is nevertheless partially countermanded in four of the films by the relatively sympathetic qualities of the military officer who is the love interest, the contrasting 'good German' who suggests the possibility of individual if not collective redemption. By 1944, Swedish films could promote anti-German sentiment with impunity regardless. The Censorship Board required no cuts in *His Excellency*, and though the film's release elicited repeated strong protests from the German ambassador in Stockholm to the Swedish Foreign Minister, there were no repercussions.[23]

The cinematic portrayal of Swedish Nazi sympathisers generally postdates the war by many decades, but one contemporary reference deserves mention: *Torment* (*Hets*, 1944), directed by Alf Sjöberg from a script by Ingmar Bergman. The film establishes a parallel between the hierarchical, authoritarian, regimented structure of the bourgeois family and the equally rigid school system, connecting these microcosms to fascist ideology through the sadistic Latin teacher Caligula, who is shown reading the Swedish Nazi newspaper *Dagsposten* (The Daily News) and made up to

Das Asta-Theater in den Den Haag bei der Vorführung des Ufa-Films „Heimat"

Ufa-Filmwerbung an den Haltestellen der Pariser Untergrundbahnen

The Swedish actress Zarah Leander was never considered a top-rank actress in her home country, but became an internationally successful actress (and singer) during the Second World War. These pictures show several advertisements for Leander: in The Hague for *Home* (*Heimat*, 1940); in Copenhagen for *The Heart of the Queen* (*Das Herz der Königin*, 1940); in the Parisian subway, also for *The Heart of the Queen*. *Source*: H. Traub, *Die Ufa. Ein Beitrag zur Entwicklungsgeschichte des deutschen Filmschaffens* (Berlin: Ufa-Buchverlag, 1943), p. 253 [The Hague], 255 [Copenhagen] and 257 [Paris].

resemble Himmler. The film does not belabour these political implications, but Caligula's psychological collapse and the prospective social reintegration of his victim suggest – quite literally, in the final scene – that a new day is dawning.

Notes

1. L. Furhammar, *Filmen i Sverige: en historia i tio kapitel* (Stockholm: Bra Böcker/ Filminstitutet, 1998), pp. 127–61, gives an informative account of the Swedish film industry during the 1930s. See also P. O. Qvist, *Folkhemmets bilder: modernisering, motstånd och mentalitet i den svenska 30-talsfilmen* (Lund: Arvik förlag, 1995), pp. 26–61.
2. L. Furhammar (1998), p. 134.
3. Ibid., p. 159.
4. J. Olsson, *Svensk spelfilm under andra världskriget* (Lund: Liber Läromedel, 1979), p. 17.
5. Ibid, pp. 23–61, provides a detailed analysis of Swedish dealings with the IFK.
6. See Chapter 2.
7. J. Olsson (1979), p. 17.
8. Bundesarchiv (Barch), R 109 I/1893, *Auslands-Gesellschaften*.
9. L. Furhammar (1998), pp. 164–5.

10. Ibid., p. 185.
11. J. Olsson (1979), p. 61.
12. See R. Skoglund, *Filmcensuren* (Stockholm: Svenska Filminstitutet/Norstedts, 1971), pp. 211–18. L. Furhammar (1998) also covers censorship issues; see especially pp. 166–9.
13. Andersson's letter is quoted in Olsson (1979), p. 35 and Skoglund (1971), p. 213.
14. R. Vande Winkel, 'Nazi Newsreels in Europe, 1939–1945: The Many Faces of Ufa's Foreign Weekly Newsreel (*Auslandstonwoche*) versus German's Weekly Newsreel (*Deutsche Wochenschau*)', *Historical Journal of Film, Radio and Television* 24:1 (2004), p. 11.
15. J. Olsson (1979), p. 57.
16. C. Romani, *Tainted Goddesses: Female Film Stars of the Third Reich*, trans. Robert Connolly (New York: Sarpedon Publishers, 1992), summarises the careers of Leander and Söderbaum. For a reading of their respective star personas in the context of Nazi ideology, see A. Ascheid, *Hitler's Heroines: Stardom and Womanhood in Nazi Cinema* (Philadelphia: Temple University Press, 2003).
17. An excellent typology of Swedish film in the 1930s is J. Schildt, *Det pensionerade paradiset* (Stockholm: Norstedts, 1990). A more detailed consideration of subject matter and ideology is found in P. O. Qvist (1995). See also L. Furhammar (1998), pp. 127–61.
18. See R. Wright, *The Visible Wall: Jews and Other Ethnic Outsiders in Swedish Film* (Carbondale: Southern Illinois University Press and Uppsala: Centrum för multietnisk forskning, 1998), pp. 1–68, for a full discussion of Jewish figures in films of the 1930s.
19. For more information on the fate of *Pettersson & Bendel* in Germany, see J. Olsson (1979), p. 61; P. O. Qvist (1995), pp. 444–7 and R. Wright (1998), p. 58.
20. J. Olsson (1979), pp. 62–111 traces the shift from farce to serious drama in military films of the period. For an overview of film production during the war years, see L. Furhammar (1998), pp. 162–97.
21. R. Wright (1998), pp. 69–94 examines the depiction of refugees in films of the 1940s.
22. J. Olsson (1979), pp. 112–96 analyzes the occupation films in detail.
23. R. Skoglund (1971), p. 216.

21

Film Propaganda and the Balance between Neutrality and Alignment: Nazi Films in Switzerland, 1933–45

Gianni Haver

Switzerland is a country with a German-speaking majority. In the 1941 census, 72.6 per cent of inhabitants declared themselves to be German speakers, against only 20.7 per cent French speakers. In the same period there were 338 cinemas: 60 per cent in the German-speaking regions and 27 per cent in the French-/Italian-speaking areas.[1] Largely due to language, the country constituted a logical outlet for the German cinema, well before the National-Socialists came to power. At the end of the silent era, in 1928, 375 American films, 300 German films, 60 French films and 20 from various other countries were imported.[2] Furthermore, in this period the widespread use of bilingual French/German subtitling meant there could be quite a uniform distribution throughout the whole country. It was the arrival of sound films which was to erect barriers between the regions, even if it was not uncommon in the early 1930s for German language films to be shown in French-speaking parts, accompanied by a summary of the plot in French.

Framework

Hitler's coming to power caused a certain apprehension in the Swiss cinema world: its own national film output was low, and Germany was its second supplier. A Swiss film trade-journal expressed this fear: 'Because of the regime change in Germany, the rumour has been rife more or less everywhere that the only films that will be made in the German studios will be nationalist and politically biased propaganda ones.'[3] The statements from those in charge at Ufa reported in the same journal, aimed, however, to reassure the Swiss cinema owners by stressing that the production of feature films would continue and would be encouraged, which was in fact in line with Goebbels'spolicy regarding the cinema.

In 1934 the changeover to sound films was complete in Switzerland. German feature films continued to hold second place.[4] They were to lose this position to France in the course of the 1930s, however. On the eve of war, Germany accounted for only 14.7 per cent of full-length feature films, against 23.7 per cent for France and 55.9 per cent for the United States. However, the studios of the Reich did not limit themselves to feature films. These figures change significantly if one adds the accompanying items (documentaries, short films, newsreels), which were regularly included in cinema programmes at that time. Germany's contribution thus rose to 26 per cent of all imported films, when taking into account a mixture of all sorts of films.[5]

The outbreak of war imposed changes on the Swiss cinema market and more widely on the economic and political situation of the country. In fact, the hostilities brought about the immediate establishment of a national censor (who took precedence over the former local ones) and disrupted the usual way in which Swiss cinemas were supplied with films. During this period, this small neutral state constituted an interesting destination to which the Nazi cinema could export its productions. Not only was it the only German-speaking country not under the control of the Reich, but it also counted among its inhabitants a large community of ex-patriot Germans. Following the fall of France and the entry of Italy into the war, the Swiss Confederation was entirely surrounded by Axis countries. Therefore its economic policies were aligned with those of its powerful northern neighbour: its armament factories would supply the Wehrmacht, and the two countries enjoyed close financial exchanges. In such a framework, the presence of German films in Swiss cinemas gave Berlin the chance of establishing a cultural, even ideological understanding with Switzerland. The distribution of Nazi films in Switzerland has given rise to much questioning, and deserves a wide-ranging study on how these were received. Yet research in this area is still limited to case studies or to regional analyses.[6] Therefore this chapter is essentially going to sketch a general picture of the distribution of German films in Switzerland during the war years.

Distribution companies

In the interwar period, the traditional importer of Ufa films was EOS-Film in Basle; indeed from 1926 it had exclusive rights on these. It was an important firm in the distribution sector since it had also managed to secure the distribution monopoly over Paramount films. Being an independent company, it escaped direct control from Berlin; what is more, it was owned by the Jewish Rosenthal family, which was certainly not to the taste of the Nazi authorities. In 1938 the commercial director of EOS, Emil Reinigger, a Swiss who had taken German nationality in 1933 and who had converted to National-Socialism, left his job to become director of Nordisk-Film of Zurich, which belonged to the Reich. From then on, Nordisk became the sole distributor of Ufa and Terra films.[7] This change would allow the Nazi authorities much more direct control than previously over the exploitation of their films in

Switzerland. As for the EOS, it would continue to distribute certain Ufa films made before 1939, among which were to be found popular successes, much appreciated by the Swiss public, such as those which starred Zarah Leander (*To new Shores* (*Zu neuen Ufern*, 1937), *La Habanera* (1937) and *Homeland* (*Heimat*, 1938)) and even titles with ideological connotations like *Traitors* (*Verräter*, 1936) and *Patriots* (*Patrioten*, 1937) by Karl Ritter.

Still in Zurich, the local subsidiary of Tobis distributed its productions as well as those of Bavaria Film AG, to which it also added, after the annexation of Austria, those of Wien-Film. Having been managed since 1935 by the German Jews Armand Palivoda and Wilhelm Karol, it was to be 'Aryanised' in 1937. From 1938, Reinegger took over the management of Tobis too, thus taking control of a fundamental part of German film production distributed in Switzerland. Nordisk and Tobis, as real antennae of German cinematography, shared a minor, but solid, part of a market which was otherwise dominated by the big American film companies. The remaining German films were distributed by Pandora Film and above all by Neue Interna-Film, two companies which had close links with both the Nazi regime and the Swiss extreme right.[8] Taking advantage of favourable contracts with Berlin, several of these firms charged dumping prices, which made their films very attractive to the exhibitors. Furthermore, following the defeat of France in June 1940, the German authorities were in control of that country's film exports as well. The new French films, highly valued on the French-speaking Swiss market, were to be rare from now on, and were to be listed in the Nordisk and Tobis catalogues. Most notably, these took over the films of Continental Paris, a German-controlled firm. Its productions were to be among the few rare new French films to be distributed in Switzerland during the war. The two distributors were to seize this opportunity to impose German films on the francophone market, as such films were now available in French, since they had been dubbed for distribution in France.

Feature films

Just under one-fifth of full-length feature films imported into Switzerland in 1939 came from German studios. In this year, between a troubled peace and phoney war, Germany was in second place, with 92 films. France was not far behind, but the gap with the United States was considerable.[9] However, this dominance by Hollywood did not really prejudice the Swiss market against German and French productions. In as far as one can compare these figures, it is striking to note that the number of films imported from these two countries represented about 90 per cent of their production for that same year.

During the war, the importation of films from Germany was hardly affected, which was not the case for its competitors. Of course, imports became fewer as the fighting went on (which can be partially explained by the drop in production), but in relative terms the number of films imported grew. The effects of the occupation of France, which gave the Nazi cinema the chance to increase its lead, have already been alluded to. Three years later, with the 1943 armistice between Italy and the Allies, and the subsequent occupation by the Wehrmacht of a good part of its former ally's territory, it was the American cinema's turn to experience difficulties. These events blocked the import of American films, which, thanks to an agreement with the Italian authorities, came through the port of Genoa. In other words, throughout the period 1940–44, the conditions for the German cinema to really assert itself in Switzerland all came together. The supply difficulties experienced by films from other sources would mean that in 1944 Germany was in first place. This was, however, a precarious situation, as the following year the balance swung in favour of the Hollywood cinema, which flooded the Swiss market with 381 films (Table 21.1).

These figures, however, do not give the full picture of what was actually shown in Swiss cinemas. They fail to inform us of the number of copies in circulation, of how long they were shown in cinemas, nor of their geographical distribution. To have a clearer idea of the German cinema's position in Switzerland, one must take into account its role in cinema programming. All in all, at the start of the war the situation in Switzerland was as would be expected: the cinema which dominated at world level – Hollywood – was equally dominant in the Swiss market as a whole, Germany and France occupying second place in their respective linguistic zones. This restriction to the German-speaking region was very clearly defined for German films. Indeed, in Zurich, at the beginning of 1939, whilst there were three times as many imported American films as German ones, the frequency with which they were shown in cinemas was the same, that is a third each.[10] In French-speaking Switzerland this strong presence of German films in the main German-speaking town was not at all duplicated. In the same year, in Lausanne, German films only accounted for about 1 per cent of all films shown.[11] Furthermore, at that time the war had not yet imposed restrictions on the cinema-owners choices.

Table 21.1 Import of full-length feature films into Switzerland

Year	USA	Germany	France
1939	265	92	89
1940	179	74	41
1941	323	65	17
1942	241	57	21
1943	99	60	13
1944	14	50	24
1945	381	22	127

In 1941, the arrival of films dubbed in French increased the amount of German films in Lausanne cinemas, which rose to about 4.5 per cent for the period 1941–44. This is a proportion which nonetheless remained limited. In German-speaking Switzerland the number of German films shown stabilised at about 25 per cent.

Propaganda feature films

In Germany the full-length feature film was used to support direct political propaganda. Even though there were not huge numbers of these films, they nevertheless represent an important body of work. Whatever the country, it is not easy to define what separates works of propaganda from others. In Hitler's Germany, however, we have a framework which allows us to make such a distinction. This we can do precisely thanks to the practice instituted by the German authorities of awarding certain films 'predicates' depending on their political alignment and their adherence to the regime's political line.

Ernest Prodolliet[12] was able to establish that, of the 90 films belonging to the categories *staatspolitisch besonders wertvoll* (politically especially valuable) and *staatspolitisch wertvoll* (politically valuable)[13] between 1933 and 1945, there is written evidence remaining in Switzerland of 58 of them. Prodolliet was able to find traces in the daily and specialised press, and on occasion he could trace them through a decision to ban them taken by the censor. For the period from 1939 to 1945, going on the production year, rather than that of the first showing in Switzerland, Prodolliet counted 33 films. Nine of these were banned by the military censor over the entire national territory. These were *Enemies* (*Feinde*, 1940) by Viktor Tourjansky; *Jew Süss* (*Jud Süss*, 1940) by Veit Harlan; *Carl Peters* (1941) by Herbert Selpin; *Homecoming* (*Heimkehr*, 1941) by Gustav Ucicky; *Riding for Germany* (*. . . reitet für Deutschland*, 1941) by Arthur-Maria Rabenalt; *Stukas* (1941) by Karl Ritter; *Wetterleuchten um Barbara* (*Summer Lightning about Barbara*, 1941; a justification of the Nazi annexation of Austria) by Werner Klingler; *Fronttheater* (1942) by Arthur-Maria Rabenalt and *Germanin* (1943) by Max W. Kimmich. One film only arrived after the end of the war: the big Agfa colour production *Kolberg* (1945) by Veit Harlan. The remaining 23 films were certainly shown in Switzerland, largely in cinemas in German-speaking towns.[14]

While within Germany, the Propaganda Ministry considered them useful, many of these films depicted a world vision already widely shared by the majority of the European middle classes. Values such as motherhood, family, sacrifice, patriotism, and dedication to work were not necessarily considered a priori as an ideological intrusion by the Nazis into Switzerland, especially when they were not shown directly in connection with events linked to the war or to its military and political antecedents. However, it should be noted that more than a third of full-length feature films regarded as ideologically important by the Nazi regime were shown in Switzerland, and that they were well received, by both critics and the general public. Some films about the German army's engagement in the conflict were also shown. *Squadron Lützow* (*Kampfgeschwader Lützow*, 1941), for example, ran for 2 weeks in Zurich in December 1941 and *The Great Love* (*Die Grosse Liebe*, 1942), starring Zarah Leander, became a great wartime success. It was shown for several weeks in prestigious cinemas and received very favourable reviews. Other films on the war without 'predicates' were also on release, such as *U-Boats Westwards* (*U-Boote Westwärts*, 1941), one of the offerings from Nordisk's catalogue of films. But the war as seen through German cameras was present to an even greater extent when one was no longer in the realm of the feature film.

News and documentaries

The German *Kulturfilm* was a genre very popular in Switzerland. During 1939, alongside the 502 feature films, 303 documentary films were imported.[15] One-third came from Germany (109), which took first place in front of France (91) and the United States (47). The main German war documentaries may have been banned (*Campaign in Poland* (*Feldzug in Polen*, 1940), *Baptism of Fire* (*Feuertaufe*, 1940), *Victory in the West* (*Sieg im Westen*, 1941)) but others most certainly were shown, for instance *Weapons of the Blitzkrieg* (*Waffen des Blitzkrieges*, 1940?) and *Paratroopers* (*Fallschirmjäger*, 1939). Sadly, we have little information on the screening of documentaries, as cinemas more often just advertised the main film. On the other hand, newsreels can be more easily traced, for their very direct link with the events of the conflict meant that they were commented on in the press and that they attracted the censor's attention.

Up to August 1940 there was no national newsreel in Switzerland and the cinemas subscribed to whichever they chose from among the imported newsreels. The Ufa newsreel (Ufa's *Foreign Weekly Newsreel* or *Auslandstonwoche*, ATW)[16] was already shown in Switzerland before the war. In September 1939, Nordisk had at its disposal four copies, one of which was in French. This same firm distributed the news magazines *Ufa Magazin* and *Europa Magazin*,[17] both productions of the Deutsche Wochenschau GmbH. At this time the newsreel market was dominated by American companies – Fox Movietone circulated 12 copies and Paramount circulated 9, closely followed by their French competitors – Pathé-Journal and France-Actualités Gaumont – with 9 and 8 copies respectively. However, the German newsreels (ATW) were developing rapidly. At the end of December 1939, they were already present with seven copies, of which one was in French, and at the end of March of that year they had eight copies, still with one in French. However, the popularity of these newsreels really took off after the fall of France which meant that the arrival of French and Allied newsreels was temporarily halted. Ufa took advantage of the situation to set up long-term contracts with as many cinemas as possible. This practice of taking over and occupying the market created an obstacle for the newsreels of other countries when they reappeared on the Swiss market.[18]

With the German advance in the west, Nordisk sent a circular to cinema managers throughout Switzerland on 5 June 1940. It was signed by the head of Nordisk, Emil Reinegger, who used a tone mid-way between threat and commercial promotion:

> Dear client, Today every one of us looks with the greatest attention towards the events of the present war. [. . .]The Ufa news cameramen stand alongside the soldiers. Ufa news is therefore able to show reports never before imagined [- - -] You too will sooner or later show our news in your programme. And so we urge you in your own interest to sign the contract without delay. We can still follow up special requests today and we can accept new orders. [. . .][19]

In July 1940, the ATW was for some time the only newsreel to be imported into Switzerland; there were at the time 21 copies of which 7 were in French. The high point of German exportations was reached on 30 September 1940, when 14 copies in German and 8 in French came on to the Swiss market. Subsequently, these numbers stabilised at around 21 copies in all.[20] In German-speaking Switzerland, Nordisk was able to put pressure onto cinema owners into including ATW newsreels in their programmes, by using as a bargaining tool – their large stock of German-language feature films. When after the occupation of Paris this company became the distributor in Switzerland of feature films produced by Continental, it did not hesitate to use the same methods to put pressure on cinema owners in French-speaking Switzerland. On 27 June 1944, after the Normandy landings, the head of the film section of the censorship board stated

> I can tell you on the basis of reliable information that the German film distribution subsidiaries are exerting strong pressure on cinema owners in French-speaking Switzerland in as much that they are refusing to lend French language films if the cinema owner does not agree to show the Ufa news along with them. It is therefore not true that Berlin no longer attaches any importance to the distribution of Ufa news in Switzerland.[21]

Due to its wide circulation, the fact that its newsreels were longer than others, because they were shown regularly, and also they were available in the two main languages of the country, Ufa's ATW was probably the main means by which Berlin's voice was heard in Switzerland. Even though the political authorities, careful not to upset their powerful neighbour too much, allowed this propaganda, the audience sometimes showed they were disturbed by it: in Lausanne a police inquiry in October 1942 revealed that the public sometimes whistled at the German news and applauded the other news (Allied and Swiss).[22]

Film showings for the German community

Germans formed an important community in Switzerland (in 1941, it numbered 78 274 ex-patriots, and was the largest after the Italian community);[23] this was a potential public that the Nazi regime had no intention of neglecting. Film showings had already been part of the activities of the German associations in Switzerland during the First World War. With the arrival of Hitler, most of the German associations came under the wing of the NSDAP. The cinema programming also adapted itself accordingly. The first propaganda films, like *Hitler Youth Quex* (*Hitlerjunge Quex*, 1933), were already in circulation in 1934. At the beginning they hired public halls, as in Lausanne on 29 June, and then the associations acquired sound projectors. At the start of the war, the German Legation in Berne negotiated with the Swiss authorities about permission to screen propaganda films for their own people. According to these agreements, the Germans were to be able to organise screenings of films normally forbidden on Swiss territory. For their part, they committed themselves to not advertising in the press and to reserving entry into these film-shows exclusively for their ex-patriots. These commitments were not always respected. In fact, the Swiss authorities soon found themselves confronted with continual infractions: the ban on publicity was not respected, and this even after the military censorship board had brought the matter to the attention of the minister for Germany.[24] What is more, the police were continually pointing out that Swiss citizens were present at these screenings, which exalted the exploits of the 'Thousand Year Reich'. On 7 May 1941, in Bienne, during the screening of *Baptism of Fire* a stricter than normal check made it possible to establish that 'half of the spectators were Swiss citizens, in particular former members of the Swiss National Movement'.[25] The Swiss National Movement, one of the many 'frontist' organisations, was founded in June 1940 and allied itself with various pro-Nazi groups. Contrary to other fringes of the extreme right of the time, which operated on a regional basis, this movement had ambitions on a nationwide level. It would be dissolved in November 1940, at a time when it already consisted of 2200 members divided into 162 local groups.[26] What happened at the Bienne screening seemed to show an attempt to keep the organisation going by taking advantage of the structures that Hitler's Germany had put in place in Switzerland (Table 21.2).

The importance of these screenings is far from merely anecdotal: Table 21.2 gives a total of 1804. This is all the more striking if it is taken into account that the figure could actually be higher, since some German film screenings escaped the Swiss authorities' control.[28] The missing figures for 1939 and 1940 are regrettable, as they could have provided information on whether the astounding success of the Wehrmacht at the start of the war had any rousing effect on the German colony in Switzerland. The great interest in these screenings came to a head in the first half of 1942. It appears that

Table 21.2 Screenings for the German community in Switzerland estimated on the basis of reports from the police of the cantons[27]

Period	Number of screenings	Number of spescators	Average number of spectators per screening
1 April–30 June 1941	133		
1 July–31 August 1941	123		
1 October–31 December 1941	93	16,185	175
1 January–31 March 1942	146	43,800	300
1 April–30 June 1942	163	50,530	310
1 July–30 September 1942	109	12,032	110
1 October–31 December 1942	169	19,230	114
1 January–31 March 1943	130	10,663	81
1 April–30 June 1943	104	10,301	99
1 July–30 September 1943	82	7788	95
1 October–31 December 1943	125	10,851	87
1 January–31 March 1944	146	13,706	93
1 April–30 June 1944	75	6064	81
1 July–30 September 1944	79	6606	83
1 October–31 December 1944	75	8005	107
1 January–31 March 1945	52	4310	83

this success was seen as a sign of encouragement to increase the number of screenings after the summer break. And yet, when they started again in October 1942, while the number of screenings was the highest of all, an obvious drop in attendance was noticeable. From now on, the Germans in Switzerland would no longer follow so keenly these shows that were screened especially for them. Should we deduce from this a certain lassitude on the part of the spectators, or rather waning enthusiasm as the first defeats of Nazi Germany were registered?

The aim of these film shows was not only to spread propaganda, but also to gather together German ex-patriots around Nazi institutions. So the main film could be pure entertainment, as was the case for the screening organised in the premises of the German colony of Lausanne on 28 February 1940. On this occasion, 45 spectators were present at the screening of the Ufa newsreel no. 441 (not the ATW, but the 'inland' newsreel of the Reich: the uniform newsreel that would soon afterwards carry the title of *German Weekly Newsreel* (*Die Deutsche Wochenschau*, DW), which was accompanied by the Heinz Rühmann comedy *Come on, Don't you Know Korff?* (*Nanu, Sie kennen Korff noch nicht?* 1938)).[29] Apart from the newsreel, the event was not strictly speaking of a political nature. In fact, this comedy, a Terra production, was not banned in Switzerland; it could have been shown in any cinema in the country.

While on the subject of this screening in Lausanne, it should be noted that prestigious film shows were also organised in hired halls. The German

An advertisement from Nordisk, which distributes productions from Ufa, Terra and ACE (Paris). *Source*: *Annuaire de la cinématographie suisse* (Genève: Editions Film Press, 1940).

colony even hired the Métropole, which, with its 1500 seats, was the largest in the city and one of the biggest in the country. In such cases, propaganda films were usually involved. For instance, on Sunday 15 June 1941, a screening was organised at the Métropole. The film shown was the documentary *Victory in the West.* Forbidden by the censor, this film dealt with the conquest of Western Europe and had been made under the patronage of the German Army High Command.[30] On this occasion, the police of the Canton complained, 'it has come back to us that many young Swiss have received invitations for next Sunday's screening either from the German or the Italian colony'.[31] On 1 September 1941, still at the Métropole, *Squadron Lützow,* a fiction film glorifying the bombers of the Polish campaign was screened. On 26 October of the same year, at the Bel-Air, *Enemies* was shown. This film was made as a justification for the invasion of Poland by Germany. As such, it depicted the German populations resident in Poland before the war as the victims of persecution. Its propagandistic nature did not escape the censor, who banned it from being shown in public in Switzerland. On 22 February 1942, 450 people attended the screening of the aviation film *Stukas* at the Bel-Air. On this occasion the Swiss citizens wanting to see the film were turned back. This film too was banned by the censor.

Conclusion

In general, the Second World War was beneficial for the distribution of German films in Switzerland. This happened at several levels: feature films kept their market share in German-speaking Switzerland, while gaining ground in the French-speaking areas. As for the German newsreels (ATW), they enjoyed a quasi-monopoly for long periods in the war. The Swiss authorities did not really hinder their circulation, as they were concerned to keep good relations with Berlin. The possibility of forbidding all foreign news, at a time when this offered no diversity, was discussed by the censors, without anything concrete coming of it. Therefore the censorship committee just limited itself to cutting certain scenes or to banning the most heavily tendentious films. What is more, these limits did not apply when the screenings were organised by Nazi associations. It would be wrong to say that Swiss cinemas were swamped by productions from Berlin, since the American cinema would always keep its dominant position, particularly in the area of the feature film. This was made possible even in hard times, thanks to the many repeats of old films by the cinemas and because of the reserves built up by the distributors. Nevertheless it is clear that Nazi films did make a substantial contribution to Swiss cinema programmes. It remains difficult to draw conclusions as to their ideological impact, just as it remains difficult to separate 'politically committed' works from those of 'pure entertainment', when film production in general was dedicated to 'invisible propaganda', in line with Goebbels's wishes. It can only be noted that the German feature film posed far fewer problems and sparked far fewer polemical discussions than did German newsreels. The most revealing attitude was adopted towards propaganda feature films: depictions of German military might and the deeds and gestures of soldiers posed problems in a feature film, to the extent that they were often banned by the federal censor. On the other hand, films bearing the most prestigious Nazi 'predicates', but without a war-like character, were allowed onto programmes. Such films found success with the public and critics alike. The threatening military power of Germany did pose problems, while at the same time the moral and ideological values of these Nazi films seemed to fit in well with the model valued at that time in Switzerland.

Notes

1. Federal Statistics Office *Annuare statistique de la Suisse* (Basle: Birkhäuser, 1947), p. 33 and (1942), p. 170.
2. R. Cosandry, *'Cinema', 19–39. La Suisse romande entre les deux guerres* (Payot: Lausanne, 1986), p. 264. These figures are based on an estimation dating from 1933.
3. L'Effort cinématographique suisse, *no.31–32–33* (April–May–June 1933), p. 52.
4. *Annuaire de la cinématographie suisse* (1940), p. 64. Switzerland imported 256 films from the United States in 1934, 136 from Germany, and 135 from France out of a total of 578.
5. Ibid. Figures calculated over the period 1 January–31 March 1939.
6. For example: Y. Zimmermann, 'Just Entertainment! The Press and Feature Films of the Third Reich in German-speaking Switzerland', in G. Haver (ed.), *Le cinema au pas .les productions des pays autoritaires et leur impact en Suisse* (Lausanne: Antipodes, 2004), pp. 63–78; G. Haver, *Les lueurs de la guerre* (Lausanne: Payot, 2003).
7. H. Dumont, *Histoire du cinema Suisse. Films de fiction 1896–1965* (Lausanne: Cinémathèque Suisse, 1987), pp. 211–12.
8. Ibid., p. 211.
9. The figures on film imports are taken from F. Aeppli, *Der Schweizer Film 1929–1964. Die Schweiz als Ritual* (Zurich: Limmat Verlag Genosenschaft, 1981), pp. 155 and 201.
10. Based on an examination of the cinema programming reported during the first 10 weeks of the year by the *Neue Zürcher Zeitung,* which concerns 16 cinemas.
11. Not included in this figure are films added on to the basic programme of the cinemas. Certain cinemas offered the German-speaking community of this town (about 15 per cent of the population) undubbed German serial films, which we did not take into account. We have analysed the cinema programming in Lausanne in Haver (2003).
12. E. Prodolliet, *Die Filmpresse in der Schweiz.Bibliographie und Texte, Freiburg* (Universitätsverlag: Freiburg, 1975).
13. See also Chapter 1.
14. For the French-speaking town of Lausanne, I have indexed the showing of 5 of these 23 films. These are *A Mother's Love* (*Mutterliebe,* 1939) by Gustav Ucicky; *Robert Koch* (1939) by Hans Steinhoff; *Annelie* (1941) by Josef von Báky, 1941; *The Great Love* (*Die Grosse Liebe,* 1942) by Rolf Hansen and *Titanic* (1943) by (Werner Klingler and) Herbert Selpin.

15. Swiss Cinema Chamber, *Statistiques des films importés en 1939,* Berne (10 April 1940). The copy can be found in the *Cinégram,* box 1939–41, deposited in the Swiss Film Archive of Lausanne.
16. R. Vande Winkel, 'Nazi Newsreels in Europe, 1939–1945: The Many Faces of Ufa's Foreign Weekly Newsreel (Auslandstonwoche) versus the German Weekly Newsreel (Deutsche Wochenschau)', *Historical Journal of Film, Radio and Television,* 24:1 (2004), pp. 5–34.
17. 'Gekürzte Filme', Archives Fédérales Suisses (Swiss Federal Archives, AFS), E4450, No. 5803.
18. Quarterly report no. 5 of the Press and Radio Division from 1 January to 31 March 1941. AFS, E4450, no. 245.
19. AFS, E4450, no. 5887. Here is to be found a copy of the circular in French, dated 5 June 1940 and another in German dated the following day. The underlining was in the original.
20. Undated statistics from the Film Section, probably drawn up at the beginning of the year 1944. AFS, E440, no. 5857.
21. Report from Sautter of 27 July 1944. AFS, E4450, no. 5801.
22. Report of 28 October 1942 by the Police of the Commune of Lausanne. The document cites episodes recorded at the Métropole cinema from 28 June of the same year. Archives Cantonales Vaudoises (Archives of the Canton of Vaud ACV), Police and Justice Department, S66.
23. *Annuaire statistique de la Suisse* (Berne: Federal Statistics Office, 1968).
24. Letter of the 21 December 1940 from the head of the Film section to Colonel Perrier. AFS, E4450, no. 5798.
25. Letter from head of Film Section Sautter to Colonel Perrier, of the 21 May 1941. AFS, E4450, no. 5798.
26. C. Cantini, *Les Ultras* (Lausanne: Editions d'en bas, 1992), p. 22. See also W. Wolf, *Faschismus in der Schweiz* (Zurich: Flamberg Verlag, 1969), pp. 81–4.
27. Quarterly reports, AFS, E4450, no. 24, no. 1982/76.
28. Notably those organised in the German Legation which took advantage of the Statute of Extra-territoriality.
29. Lausanne City Archives [AVL] Police force, box 818, no. 1415.
30. T. Sakmyster, 'Nazi documentaries of intimidation: "Feldzug in Polen" (1940), "Feurtaufe" (1940) and "Sieg im Westen" (1941)', *Historical Journal of Film, Radio and Television,* 16:4 (1996), pp. 485–514.
31. Letter of 12 June 1941 from Vaud Justice and Police Department to the Chief of Police of Lausanne asking them to take necessary controlling measures to prevent Swiss people gaining entry. AVL, Police Force, box 818, no. 1415.

22
'A Thin Stream Issuing through Closed Lock Gates': German Cinema and the United Kingdom, 1933–45

Jo Fox

> [I]f the exclusion of German films is by no means watertight, the proportion that trickles through is somewhat like the thin stream issuing through closed lock gates compared with the cascade that came through when the sluices were open.
>
> 'Open Letter to the Reich Revivalists',
> *To-day's Cinema, 11th June 1935.*[1]

As this comment made in the trade newspaper *To-day's Cinema* suggests, it was noticeable that, by 1935, German film exports to the United Kingdom were not as they had been. Britain had been an important consumer of German films of the silent era, praising and appreciating the talent emanating from the 'second Hollywood' located at the heart of Europe, with the likes of Ernst Lubitsch, Erich Pommer and Fritz Lang producing some of the most memorable and defining films of the 1920s. Nevertheless, the rise of the *Nationalsozialistische Deutsche Arbeiterpartei* (NSDAP) had profound implications for the political and cultural life of the 'new Germany', as well as its artistic exports. This chapter traces the cinematic relationship between Britain and Germany from the *Machtergreifung* (seizure of power) in 1933 to the fall of the Reich in 1945. In many ways, the history of their shared filmic past mirrors wider Anglo-German relations in this period, moving from an initial attempt to understand each other's form of government and the vague hope of reconciliation to disquiet about the Nazi regime's racial policies and its implications to the era of appeasement and finally to the outbreak of another European conflict, concluding in 1945 with both nations standing at the poles of defeat and victory. Their cinematic relationship was characterised by profound mistrust and a prolonged attempt by British film-makers to make sense of their new export partner, a series of significant events indicating the broader tensions between them. This was not so very far from the wider social and political environment in which

Anglo-German relations operated in the inter-war years, indicative of the construction of art reflecting life, in the truest sense.

Early relations

The filmic relationship between Britain and Nazi Germany was heralded by a rather turbulent and inauspicious start. The first major film export to Britain from the Third Reich, Gustav Ucicky's 1933 film *Dawn* (*Morgenrot*), caused a great deal of consternation. Such was the public excitement over the film that *The Times* covered the premiere in February. Seeing the occasion as indicative of the wider political climate, *The Times* reported that 'in a scene typical of the moment', Hitler, Alfred Hugenberg and Franz von Papen attended the first screening of the production which controversially dealt with submarine warfare during the Great War. However, of greatest concern, reported the newspaper, was the unfriendly depiction of the British warriors in contrast to the 'noble German submarine commander'.[2] It was clear to the newspaper's correspondent in Berlin that the film put 'all the chivalry on the German side and all the treachery on the British side'.[3] This sparked a minor diplomatic incident. Three days after the premiere, *The Times* published an article which claimed that Ernst Hanfstängl, Head of the Foreign Press Division, had been authorised to state that Hitler disapproved 'of the political tinge' in the film, '[deprecating] the unimaginative dishing up these days of old wartime propaganda, clichés and controversies', and adding that, although he was proud of his troops' effort in the Great War, the film was 'not representative of the outlook of the new, the coming Germany which he leads'. Indeed, the correspondent added that Hitler was certain that 'even the most nationalistic Germany of today does not . . . look upon Great Britain in that light [and] takes the line that bygones should be bygones'. *The Times* added that 'Herr Hitler's opinion . . . coincides with that of many moderate people, who deprecate this naïve and dangerous type of propagandist production'.[4] Two days passed, after which Hitler's statement was curiously retracted, Herr Hanfstängl apparently having been the 'victim of a misunderstanding'. This came as 'no surprise' to *The Times'* correspondent who had begun to notice that 'conciliatory statements intended for abroad have not always coincided with views expressed for home consumption', a product of the 'hastily cemented coalition' of the early Nazi era which needed time to 'settle down to work'.[5]

Despite the furore, *Dawn* was eventually released in Britain, after continued postponements due to numerous protests. It was initially screened at the Academy and the Curzon cinemas and eventually toured Britain on the non-theatrical circuit through the national network of film societies, although distribution was extremely limited.[6] Although *The Cinema's* booking guide for July 1933 claimed that Ucicky's film was 'good entertainment for better-class popular halls',[7] the press reaction was mixed. *The Times* complained that 'the object of the film is to school the public mind in the virtues of war and as usual the characterisation suffers for the sake of propaganda'.[8] Nevertheless, *Picture-goer Weekly* lauded its 'wonderfully convincing presentation of submarine warfare'. In a rare moment of praise for the depiction of the German commander and his men, the critic noted that 'none of us who fought in the war would, I think, hesitate to admire courage and devotion to duty'. Moreover, the film was perceived to be the epitome of Anglo-German filmic cooperation, *Picture-goer Weekly* claiming that 'both German and British naval authorities were called to supervise the technical detail' of the film.[9] The UK distribution of *Dawn* was a strangely appropriate beginning for this complex cinematic relationship.

It was *The Times'* identification of the propagandistic strand of Ucicky's production which came to dominate the cinematic discourse after 1934 in both the trade newspapers and the wider press. It increasingly became apparent that the regime was indeed 'bedding down' as *The Times* had suggested in 1933 and that the direction the 'new Germany' was taking became rather more sinister, particularly in its racial policies which impacted upon the film industry and strained the filmic relationship between the two nations still further. The *Entjudung* (removal of Jews) of the German film industry and the decision by the *Reichsministerium für Volksaufklärung und Propaganda* (RMVP) to prohibit Jewish performances and productions created difficulties in terms of the British export market. This problem came to the fore with the release of the 1934 film *Catherine the Great* directed by Paul Czinner and starring Elisabeth Bergner, a prominent German–Jewish actress who had been forced to leave the Reich. Bergner had been one of Germany's most popular actresses before the NSDAP came to power, drawing 'tremendous crowds to the theatres and [arousing] the enthusiasm of men and women of all ages among the art-loving population' of Berlin with her stage performances of George Bernard Shaw's *Saint Joan*, and nationally on the silver screen in *Ariane* (Paul Czinner, 1931) and *Dreaming Lips* (*Der Träumende Mund*, Paul Czinner, 1932), thought by contemporaries to be 'among the consummate achievements of German filmcraft'.[10] However, as *Picture-goer Weekly* commented in January 1934, 'politics in Germany have, in the last few months, dealt very [harshly] with Elisabeth Bergner. She is a Jewess and, as is well known, Herr Hitler no longer has any use for Jewsesses, however valuable their services to Germany.'[11] This was a forewarning of the problems the industry was to face in future.

Bergner's plight became national news in Britain in 1934 with the release of *Catherine the Great*. Given the film's international success, British producers were openly expecting a similar reaction from German audiences, especially as the film was eagerly awaited by Bergner's fans with many seats for the first screenings sold out in advance.[12] However, with the RMVP's determined prevention of Jewish cultural activity, *Catherine the Great* was released amongst a storm of controversy both in Germany and in Britain. On 9 March

1934, *The Times* reported that there had been widespread disturbances at the premiere of Czinner's film, 'which culminated in a dramatic announcement to "the public" . . . that the Prussian Government had decided to forbid the film as from tomorrow'. In a characteristic stunt in which pressure for censorship seemed to come from the people prompted by announcements in the press in the days leading up to the premiere, members of the *Sturmabteilung* marched into the theatre only to be repelled by the 'field police', forcing them out onto the steps of the Memorial Church in Berlin where they proceeded, surrounded by a large crowd, to denounce the film and, in particular, its Jewish star.[13] Unsurprisingly, the following day, the Reich Film Chamber announced that, due to the activities of the previous evening, *Catherine the Great* would not be permitted to run in Reich film theatres, even though the film had been passed by the censor. This, reported *The Times*, was the work of a 'few hundred young [SA] men' and Nazi zealots, and had little to do with a popular rejection of the film, its correspondent recording that 'the ordinary picture-going public asks nothing better than to see the film . . . [P]reliminary announcements . . . have been received with spontaneous applause . . . [and] audiences were enthusiastic'.[14]

For British film-makers, there was an important consequence of the ban. The film's producers, London Films, protested to the British Ambassador to Germany, claiming heavy financial losses as a result of events in Berlin. This had significant implications for British film exports, which were finding box-office popularity in Germany with productions such as Alexander Korda's *The Private Life of Henry VIII* (1933). The film industry voiced suspicions that the Germans had instigated a trade war with the United Kingdom. However, more problematic was the issue of employing Jewish actors and producers in the British film industry. The choice appeared to be relatively simple: either cease employing Jews or face financial losses in the German export market. This was unacceptable, and led to questions in the House of Commons. Sir John Simon, secretary of state for foreign affairs, was asked 'whether compensation would be paid to the company concerned' and whether any 'British film in which Jewish actors or actresses took part would in future be permitted to be shown in Germany'. Simon 'could not say'. The diplomatic implications of the incident were also considered, and the M.P. representing Torquay asked for reassurance that the Right Honourable Gentleman 'would not stir up trouble with Germany because the film [had] been censored'. Once again, the Secretary of State failed to answer.[15]

Despite the reluctance of the Government to address the issue before them, the film industry continued to voice its unease at the policy of *Entjudung* and the implications for British film exports in their newspapers and journals, as well as in the production of anti-Nazi films from 1933.[16] Probably the most famous of these was Lothar Mendes' *Jew Süss* (1934), based on the novel of Lion Feuchtwanger and rather favourable towards the historical agent (18th-century Süss Oppenheimer) the book was loosely based on.

Jew Süss (1934) would serve as an uncredited stylistic model to Veit Harlan's virulently anti-Semitic *Jew Süss* (*Jud Süss*, 1940).[17]

In June 1935, *Kinematograph Weekly* lamented that in the first 11 months of the contingent year 1934–35, four British films had been banned: *Catherine the Great, Blossom Time* (1934), *The Iron Duke* (1934) and *Nell Gwyn* (1935). Censorship had been due to the fact that the productions were 'not in conformity with . . . Nazi racial doctrines and other ethical principles'.[18] However, Ivor Montagu, member of the Film Society's council, observed that:

> Some of the incidents connected with the various bannings are so ludicrous that they would make angels weep. The Flaherty film *Man of Aran*, for example, for which Goebbels wrote a special foreword stating that it 'exemplified all the virtues of simplicity, courage and endurance that Hitler wished to become characteristic of the German people' was purchased from its predominantly Jewish-directed producers, Gaumont-British, only on condition of the deletion from the credit titles of the names of Louis Levy, the composer, and John Goldman, its cutter.

Montagu continued, 'Martha Eggert, who has one Jewish grandmother, although allowed to appear in *My Heart is Calling You* (*Mein Herz ruft nach dir*, 1934) as a secretary, was forbidden to appear in another as a princess!' Perhaps most bizarrely, he drew attention to the case of 'the Scots-produced comedy with the 100 per cent Yorkshireman Arthur Riscoe . . . ; the only cause that could be [ascertained] was Riscoe's ambiguously proportioned (though still in truth good Yorkshire) nose'.[19] It became clear to film-makers that film exports to and from Germany were to be a contested space in the 1930s.

German film exports to the United Kingdom: Distribution and impact

Although British exhibitors were keen to export their films to Germany, it remained unclear as to whether British film houses wished to reciprocate, particularly as UK distributors were having considerable difficulty obtaining their royalties from British films screened in the Reich.[20] The list of German films imported into Britain from the Third Reich remained very limited indeed. Of the films exported by Germany to the United Kingdom, few were on commercial release. Naturally, some major productions of the Third Reich were screened in the United Kingdom, the most notable being Gustav Ucicky's *Joan of Arc* (*Das Mädchen Johanna*, 1935), Gerhard Lamprecht's *Barcarole* (1935), Gerhard Lamprecht's *Spies at Work* (*Spione am Werk*, 1933), Hans Steinhoff's *The Young and the Old King* (*Der alte und der junge König*, 1934), Gustav Ucicky's *Refugees* (*Flüchtlinge*, 1933), Carl Lamač's *Little Dorrit*

(*Klein Dorrit*, 1934), Luis Trenker's *The Kaiser of California* (*Der Kaiser von Kalifornien*, 1936), Veit Harlan's *The Ruler* (*Der Herrscher*, 1937), Gustav Ucicky's *The Broken Jug* (*Der Zerbrochene Krug*, 1937) and, of course, Ucicky's *Dawn* in 1933.[21] The films tended to be screened at smaller cinemas, such as the Everyman, the Berkeley and the Curzon cinemas in London, the latter an 'international cinema' opened in 1934 with the capacity to seat about 500 film-goers. This cinema, in particular, was regarded as the first purpose-built 'art-house' cinema in the capital, and thus addressed itself to selective patrons.[22] Such limited seating and target audiences meant that German films reached a restricted clientele and that commercial distribution and therefore export royalties were limited. The royalty receipts from some of the key German films screened in Britain give some indication of their limited appeal. *Refugees* raised £459.1s.7d, *So Ended a Great Love* (*So endete eine Liebe)* £1085, *The Old and the Young King* £930.4s.6d, *Barcarole* £570.18s.10d, whilst Erich Waschneck's *Music in the Blood* (*Musik im Blut*, 1934) only managed £539.10.s.11d.[23]

There were, of course, other channels of non-theatrical distribution within the United Kingdom and here German films found wider audiences through the network of film societies across the country, the largest being the Film Society based in London, which regularly showcased foreign films.[24] Although the Film Society was keen to show a selection of German films, particularly those reflecting artistic innovation or those which afforded a window on life in the 'new Germany', the Council were confronted with a number of obstacles to importing specific German features, having to negotiate with the German Embassy for the rights to screen productions. Such was the case with *Hans Westmar* (1933), based on the life of Nazi martyr Horst Wessel.[25] The Film Society began to communicate with the Embassy in January 1934,[26] and reported in March that 'Prince Bismarck of the German Embassy had sent a set of stills of *Hans Westmar*' to further whet the appetite of the Council.[27] Just days later, the Society was informed that Germany was not 'proposing to import a copy of this film' and that 'if the Society wishes it to be brought over it will have to be done at [their own] expense'.[28] Eventually, members of the Council, among them Ivor Montagu and Thorold Dickinson, viewed a print of the film in June. They recorded that 'some of those present would be in favour of showing the first two reels and the last reel for the Society's programme of mixed propaganda'. The German Embassy, who had arranged for the copy to be sent to the Council, had requested that the film be immediately returned for despatch to Germany, and informed the Society that if they wanted to screen the film they would have to 're-import it'. It further transpired that 'the Embassy submitted the film to the [British] censor but it was rejected and... the censor asked them to return it to Germany as soon as possible'. This had implications for the Society should they wish to screen *Hans Westmar*, for first they would need the necessary permissions and secondly, 'in the event of consent not being given . . . , a drawback of duty [could not] be claimed'.[29] A similar set of obstacles faced the Society on trying to import and screen Leni Riefenstahl's *Olympia* (1938), where they were informed that Tobis were preparing 'to hold a premiere as soon as the political situation warrants [and] so do not wish [the Society] to show the film first'.[30] Thus, there were a number of factors, political and financial, which made the import of German films, even by those who were keen to screen them, a tiresome process. The Society did not experience the same kinds of interventions when screening Soviet films, symbolically winding up the organisation with a screening of Sergei Eisenstein's *Alexander Nevsky* (1938) in 1939, even though its members complained that the programme was too loaded with left-wing propaganda and that the Society had imported a 'surfeit of Russian films'.[31] That said, the Film Society did screen some German films of interest, in particular the films of Lotte Reiniger and some of the main features.[32] Commercial screenings of main features were replicated across the country by film societies, bringing films such as *Refugees, The Triumph of the Will* (*Triumph des Willens*, Leni Riefenstahl, 1935), *Joan of Arc, The Old and the Young King, The Student from Prague* (*Der Student von Prag*, 1935) *Dawn* and *Barcarole* out into the regions.[33] As this suggests, distribution of German films was, indeed, 'somewhat like the thin stream issuing through closed lock gates', a mere trickle when compared to the age of the silent cinema.[34]

A number of factors explain this change. Broadly speaking, as indicated above, the British film industry objected to the Nazi regime and recognised that German film was not as celebrated as it had been under the Weimar Republic. Commentators began to question why Goebbels' famous prediction of the new cultural dawn of German cinema, and its masterpiece, the 'National Socialist Potemkin', had not yet transpired.[35] Indeed, some suggested publicly that 'the great German industry which produced *Vaudeville, The Last Laugh, Destiny* and *Caligari* is only a memory. The industry which evolved Pommer and Lubitsch, Grune and Veidt, is but a shadow, an insipid and meaningless reflection of its masters' will.'[36] The collapse in German film exports to the United Kingdom in the mid-1930s and the lack of interest in German films generated after the *Machtergreifung* was directly attributed to the policy of *Entjudung*. The trade newspaper *To-day's Cinema* addressed Goebbels directly, informing him that he

> had made a very grave error . . . in victimising the Jewish members of the industry . . . Where is your foreign film trade? It is virtually non-existent. Here and there, in a few – a very few – scattered quarters a German film is showing – mainly to an exclusive and highbrow audience. What few there are take some finding. We do not know of one in England at the moment.[37]

The refusal to allow Jewish artists to work in the industry had, in the opinion of the British film industry, led to an irrevocable decline in the quality of German cinema. In a hand-written manuscript dated c. 1936–37, Ivor Montagu listed over 80 producers, directors, scenarists, art directors, cameramen, composers and actors who had been exiled from the Reich and associated territories, among them some of the great names of German cinema such as Erich Pommer, Fritz Lang, G. W. Pabst, Max Reinhardt, Arnold Fanck, Walther Reitsch, Conrad Veidt, Peter Lorre, Gitta Alpar, Lucie Mannheim and Elisabeth Bergner.[38] (Montagu correctly identified the exile of artistic personnel as a problem for the German industry, but was not very well informed. For instance, Fanck did not leave Germany[39] while Pabst returned from the United States to Europe in 1936.) Montagu noted that 'a great industry which in the . . . early days of the Republic contributed unforgettably to the promotion of the cinema now has no name to give the world comparable to Clair, Hitchcock, Corda [sic.]'. He lamented that 'Nazi Germany has one world name only' and that even this was 'regarded as a proof of Nazi cinema' as a 'hopeless fake': Leni Riefenstahl. Montagu regretted that Riefenstahl had undermined her 'justly admired performances' in the films of Fanck by becoming 'Hitler's favourite'. He asserted that:

> In more than three years of the Third Reich, Riefenstahl's work has been confined to the marshalling of a corps of cameramen to produce a documentary – a film which . . . had to be held up from going abroad lest its goose-stepping should cause ridicule, in accordance with Hitler's fine euphemism: 'national enthusiasm does not survive export'.[40]

This was at the heart of the problem. British exhibitors complained of the overt propaganda content of films such as *Refugees*, described by the *Monthly Film Bulletin* as 'primarily propaganda' and inappropriate for the English audience. The reviewer noted that:

> . . . many English people find its psychology crude, occasionally even absurd and a trifle boring: and those who lived through 1914–18 will find the tune of 'Pack up your Troubles' something inappropriate in the mouths of Germans and with German words. Yet those who want to see a self portrayal of Nazi ideals and convictions will find *Refugees* very well produced and thoroughly characteristic.[41]

The same was said of *The Ruler*.[42] *Today's Cinema* pointed out that German films had 'dropped their export figures merely because they have ceased to matter as entertainment', testament to the Nazi '[obsession] with the mission and purpose of German might' and leading to the view that 'every output is suspect'. The trade newspaper reminded the RMVP that 'one paramount reason why your films, even your less obnoxiously Hitlerite films, are devoid of any art or entertainment value is that you have dismissed or banished many of the finest and most creative minds in the business' and warned the Nazis

> not to attempt to cut in on our markets by producing English versions of your supers... You have a very poor chance of succeeding in selling them. This superficial schmooze will delude nobody. The industry which has seen your treatment of its people in Germany is not likely to want your tarnished product here. Go back and wipe the steam from your spectacles. You can see no further than your noses.[43]

It was for this reason, argued the trade newspapers, that the German Statistical Bureau reported a fall in film exports year on year in the mid-1930s.[44] However, German film exports to the United Kingdom had not collapsed purely due to ideological objections to the Nazi regime. It was also the natural consequence of the advent of sound and the problems created by language. With few exceptions, Josef von Sternberg's *The Blue Angel* (*Der blaue Engel*, 1930) being one, German films had already ceased to be popular even before the *Machtergreifung*. As Rachel Low has indicated in her study of British film in the 1930s, by the 1931–32 film season, there was already a noticeable decline in the box office for foreign films. She rightly emphasised that 'film-makers forgot the technique of visual story-telling and relied more and more heavily on a soundtrack loaded with dialogue'. It was in this environment that 'foreign language films virtually disappeared' from Britain.[45] There were some attempts to forestall this crucial development, such as the production of English versions of Lilian Harvey musicals primarily made for export to Britain, with the star appearing alongside English leading men, Laurence Olivier among them in one of his first film parts, and the work of British International Pictures. However, the German film industry eventually succumbed to the sound era and the inevitable dominance of Hollywood.[46] Translation did little to add to the appeal of the German film, with subtitled foreign productions only 'of interest... to an educated minority audience'. As Low pointed out, by the mid-1930s, 'the term "specialised" began to creep into the reviews, and before long the stars of Continental films were unknown to the majority of the British public'.[47] It was no surprise, therefore, to find that the Film Society and specialised cinemas resorted to re-running the classics of the German cinema such as Fritz Lang's *The Testament of Dr. Mabuse* (*Das Testament des Dr. Mabuse*, 1933), *The Cabinet of Dr. Caligari* (*Das Cabinet des Dr. Caligari*, 1920), *Siegfried* (1924), *Waxworks* (*Das Wachsfigurenkabinett*, 1924) and *The White Hell of Piz Palü* (*Die Weiße Hölle vom Piz Palü*, 1929).

It is clear that the filmic relationship between Britain and Germany in the years from 1933 to 1937 was turbulent, characterised as it was by frequent clashes of interest, a fundamental dislike of each other's cinematic outputs, politically, culturally and ideologically motivated disagreements and few moments of cooperation, such as the congress of the International Film Chamber in Berlin in April 1935.[48] The Third Reich found that exporting to Britain was extremely problematic, but did not ease matters by throwing bureaucracy in the way of genuine interest in their films, such as that encountered by the Film Society in the mid-1930s. On the other hand, the RMVP could have done little to salvage German film exports to English-speaking countries where the dominance of the Hollywood talkie had already taken hold. The decline was not purely of their making and their propagandistic output was not solely to blame.

By 1937, industry concerns had been subordinated to national exigency. The British film industry and particularly its primary censor, the British Board of Film Classification (BBFC), were sensitive to the international crisis and possibility of war. Banning the production of films overtly hostile to Germany, the BBFC were keen to avoid heightening tensions between the two nations. This was aptly demonstrated by their objections to the *March of Time* film, *Inside Nazi Germany* (1938), which arrived on the desk of the censor in February 1938. Colonel J. C. Hanna, Vice-President of the BBFC, noted of the script that 'the public exhibition of this picture in England would give grave offence to a nation with whom we are on terms of friendship and which it would be impolitic to offend'.[49] Many British pictures fell victim to the regulations, only to be resurrected after September 1939, the most notable being *Pastor Hall* (1940) and *Freedom Radio* (1941). Similar concerns were voiced about Charlie Chaplin's *The Great Dictator* (1940), the News Department of the Foreign Office contacting the British Consulate in Los Angeles in April 1939 to assess the status of the production. The BBFC informed the Foreign Office in June that the Hollywood studios had been warned that a 'delicate situation might arise . . . if personal attacks were made on any living European statesman', hoping that the executives would 'realise the delicacy of the situation'.[50] The colonies too were concerned about aggravating German opinion, the consulate in Hong Kong wondering what action should be taken regarding the exhibition of the American film, *Confessions of a Nazi Spy* (Anatole Litvak, 1939). Despite the desire to calm relations with the Nazi State, the authorities in Hong Kong were adamant that the film was propaganda of a 'rather cautious kind in so far as it is only an entirely accurate account of events that took place in America last year', adding 'if Germany doesn't like it, she must watch the manners of her secret police in foreign countries'.[51] Besides, the colonies were less sensitive to their protestations, by the later 1930s refusing permission for Herbert Selpin to film *Carl Peters* (1941) in Tanganyika. (The film was based on the life of Carl Peters (1856–1918), who acquired colonies on the African continent for Germany.) It would, they claimed, incite local protests, the protagonist being 'a pretty fair scoundrel', and inflame relations between German and English sections of the European population. In any case, they questioned 'can one imagine the Germans allowing a British propaganda film to be taken in territory under German control?' With this in mind, they decided 'the Germans . . . would have no real cause for complaint'.[52]

The impact of war

With the outbreak of war in September 1939, the British film industry was no longer required to humour German sensibilities. Thoughts turned to propaganda and German film was not to be used for entertainment but rather as a psychological weapon. The British authorities were now concerned with importing captured German footage for information and for use in home-front and neutral propaganda shorts. Various screenings of captured Nazi newsreel footage (sometimes obtained through British embassies in neutral countries[53]), beginning in 1941, were organised for British audiences in order to stress the brutality of the enemy and to inspire both home and front in the fulfilment of their national duty. In order to ascertain how effective the screening of enemy footage was in this task, the Home Intelligence Division collated a variety of responses from across the United Kingdom on film shows in September 1941. It was notable that publicity for enemy films had been overstated, leaving many audiences disappointed at the 'mildness of the scenes chosen for the first release'. Audiences longed for images of 'unprovoked aggression' on the Soviet front, with numerous film-goers complaining that they had been 'let down' by the 'lack of horrors and morbid incidents'. The films were considered 'rather tame' and 'flat'. More worryingly for British propagandists, audiences began to comment that 'the Nazis didn't seem to be doing any worse things than our own men do', and some noted that 'if they were British soldiers, we'd probably be cheering'. Although many film-goers were distinctly unimpressed, cinema owners noted that audiences commented that they wanted 'more short films of this type to shake the people up and prevent that feeling of complacency'.[54]

This was delivered by a second batch of captured footage shown in the same period, but not heralded by a similar degree of publicity, indicating the development of a degree of subtlety on the part of British propagandists. These films had more success. Audiences did not arrive at theatres with a high degree of expectation and thus were left to form their own opinions of the footage. Many left the cinema 'stupified', 'horrified' and 'revolted', questioning why the 'German people are expected to applaud acts of brutality by their own army'. The propaganda effect appeared to be significant, with many regions reporting that patrons had begun to comprehend 'what would happen if the Germans invaded Britain', the films succeeding in '[awakening] the apathetic to a realisation of what total warfare means'. Mass-Observation noted that 'in some people the reaction to the horrors of the film was an aggressive one, making them long to "get at the swine" or to wonder whether they were really doing their bit'. The second batch of films released in 1941 were so popular that a Cambridge film theatre reported that the 'takings broke all records'. The only factor that the manager could identify was that 'the public were coming to see this newsreel itself'. In this atmosphere, it was unsurprising that many felt that this was 'the best single piece of propaganda up to date'. Regret was voiced that the newsreels were edited, however, and audiences expressed the wish that ' "real horror" films of Nazi doings should be shown as often as possible, and that they should not be watered down. "If the Nazis paint themselves black, we should not whiten them by cutting their horrors" '.[55] By 1943, captured newsreels were being shown in full in film theatres throughout the country.[56]

Importing captured German film was a sensitive task. From October 1943, the British Ministry of Information (MoI) began to organise the administrative apparatus to exert control over enemy film materials, extending their remit beyond newsreels, with specific uses in mind, notably 'to see what the enemy is producing in the way of propaganda films, to see what he is producing in the way of "entertainment" for the German people and for the people of occupied countries, to make use of any suitable material in our own propaganda [and] to prevent the circulation or exhibition in this country, or any Allied countries, of enemy film that might be harmful'.[57] The import of such material was conducted with the utmost secrecy, and the proposed enemy film library at Pinewood in conjunction with the Crown Film Unit was to employ a custodian 'who should be at least SAS and possibly specialist rank'.[58] When it became clear that the Armed Forces were arranging special screenings of captured materials, the Ministry protested that the War Office, the Air Ministry and the Admiralty should hand over the footage as the films were 'considered an important source of propaganda as well as information to government departments'.[59] This was duly arranged. By 1943, German feature films were once again being screened in British cinemas, although in quite a different atmosphere. The MoI and the Armed Forces arranged special 'Films in Prize' screenings for selected government and military personnel, the first being Karl Ritter's 1938 film, *For Honour* (*Pour le Merité*). A succession of screenings followed and continued throughout 1944 and into the final year of the war. The programme, running at numerous locations in London including the MoI cinema in Malet Street, the Curzon and the War Office Cinema, was varied. Authorised personnel were treated to comedies and musicals such as *Hallo Janine* (1939), *Frau Luna* (1941) and *We Dance around the World* (*Wir tanzen um die Welt*, 1939), to popular dramas, *Goodbye Franziska* (*Auf Wiedersehen Franziska*, 1941), *The Journey to Tilsit* (*Die Reise nach Tilsit*, 1939) and even to *Titanic* (1943), which had not been fully released in Germany. The most propagandistic and overtly political productions of the Reich were also shown, many of which had a distinctly anti-British flavour, such as the notorious *Baptism of Fire* (*Feuertaufe*, 1940), *Uncle Krüger* (*Ohm Krüger*, 1941), *The Fox from Glenarvon* (*Der Fuchs von Glenarvon*, 1939) and *Linen from Ireland* (*Leinen aus Irland*, 1939).[60] Exiled in the first wave of persecution of the German film industry, Heinrich Fraenkel was asked to 'cover [the] whole jamboree' and submit reports to the Political Warfare Division of Supreme Headquarters Allied Expeditionary Force (SHAEF). The reports, he was informed, should include 'any significant sentences in the dialogue . . . and all political background information'. They should not be 'written in a facetious vein, but should be as factual and objective as possible'.[61] Careful not to contravene copyright laws, the MoI confirmed that 'it has apparently been decided that a clause will be inserted in the Treaty of Peace protecting any exhibitor within the UK . . . against action for breach of copyright by enemy nationals'.[62] The floodgates were open. In all, over 100 films were viewed in private screenings over the final 2 years of the war.

Naturally, with such a plethora of unseen films, many of which had been reported upon in the trade press, the British film industry were keen to be invited to the screenings to study techniques of an industry which had received heavy investment from the RMVP. The MoI began to receive letters from prominent filmmakers requesting an invitation to view significant German productions. By far the most sought-after ticket was for the German colour film, Josef von Baky's *Münchhausen* (1943), starring Hans Albers. Although SHAEF were not keen to organise a screening of this film, Paul Rotha,[63] David Lean, Ronald Neame and Bob Krasker,[64] photographer for *Henry V*, all requested special dispensation to view von Baky's piece. This was testament to the continued interest in German filmic techniques, despite the turbulent years of the early 1930s. It was ironic that the greatest variety of German films exhibited should occur as a result of the collapsing Reich. This was certainly not what Goebbels had hoped for in terms of distributing German films abroad. Whether German films of the Nazi era should be distributed commercially was now in the hands of SHAEF, who began a denazification process in the aftermath of the ceasefire.

The filmic relationship between Britain and Germany, then, mirrored wider social, political and cultural developments. Unsure of the 'new Germany' in 1933, there was an atmosphere of hope balanced by a fear for the future, a fear realised when it became clear that the racial policies of the Nazi regime were to have a profound impact on the cinematic community and beyond in Britain and Germany. The United Kingdom now became home to many exiled artistes who greatly enriched Britain's own national cinema. At the same time, the industry was saddened and angered by developments in Germany, particularly when they began to affect British productions and exports. The distribution of German films prior to the Second World War was limited by the regime's insistence on exporting propaganda features, problematic for the UK markets, by its continued persecution of their colleagues and by objections to the politics of the Third Reich. Germany's export market to the United Kingdom was further undermined by declining popular interest in foreign features, sound altering public desires irrevocably and the dominance of Hollywood. Although film producers reluctantly accepted the BBFC's decision to limit anti-Nazi films during the years of crisis from 1937–39, they threw themselves wholeheartedly into the war effort. Films then became a means of conducting warfare, and it

Lilian Harvey, born to a British mother and a German father, was a big musical star in the German cinema of the 1930s. She starred in multilingual films and was popular in Germany, but also in France and Great Britain. Harvey often paired with Willy Fritsch. *Source*: Vande Winkel/De Paepe Collection.

was in this vein that German films were screened in Britain once more. The history, therefore, of German exports to the United Kingdom is chequered, much like Anglo-German relations in this period. It was characterised by hope, protest, appeasement and finally anger, and explains why German film exports were nothing more than a footnote to film history compared to the glory days of Lang, Lubitsch and the greats of the silent screen.

Notes

1. 'Open Letter to the Reich Revivalists', *To-day's Cinema* (11 June 1935), p. 2.
2. 'Herr Hitler sees a war film', *The Times* (3 February 1933).
3. 'German Anti-British War Film: Herr Hitler's Disapproval', *The Times* (6 February 1933).
4. Ibid.
5. 'Herr Hitler's Criticism of a War Film: Statement "Unauthorised"', *The Times* (8 February 1933).
6. For reports on the screening at the Curzon, see *The Times* (17 April 1934). *Sight and Sound* regularly carried reports of film society screenings, and Ucicky's film seems to have had a very limited distribution.
7. *The Cinema*, booking guide, vol. 3 (July 1933), p. 23.
8. 'German Naval War Film: *Morgenrot*', *The Times* (2 May 1933).
9. 'War "backgrounds" to the fore', *Picture-goer Weekly* (20 May 1933), p. 8.
10. 'Will Bergner be the Bernhardt of the Talkies?' *Picture-goer Weekly* (6 January 1934), p. 8.
11. Ibid.
12. '*Catherine the Great* in Berlin', *The Times* (7 March 1934).
13. '*Catherine the Great:* Nazi Disturbances in Berlin', *The Times* (9 March 1934).
14. '*Catherine the Great:* Film Suppressed by the Nazis', *The Times* (10 March 1934).
15. 'House of Commons', *The Times* (15 March 1934).
16. For details of British proposals for anti-Nazi films, see J. Richards, 'The British Board of Film Censors and Content Control in the 1930s: Foreign Affairs', *Historical Journal of Film, Radio and Television*, 2:1 (1982), pp. 39–48. Here, pp. 40–2.
17. S. Tegel, 'The Politics of Censorship: Britain's "Jew Süss" (1934) in London, New York and Vienna', *Historical Journal of Film, Radio and Television*, 15:2 (1995), pp. 219–44; S. Tegel, 'Veit Harlan and the origins of Jud Süss, 1938–1939: opportunism in the creation of Nazi anti-semitic film propaganda', *Historical Journal of Film, Radio and Television*, 16:4 (1996), pp. 515–31.
18. *Kinematograph Weekly* (27 June 1935).
19. British Film Institute Special Collections. Ivor Montagu Collection, Item 56. MS article on 'The Decline of the German Film Trade under National Socialism', c. 1936–37.
20. National Archives (hereafter NA PRO) BT 11/863. Anglo-German payments agreement: provision of exchange for payment for film rents, 31 May 1938. British producers were awaiting payments for the following films: *Henry VIII* (2123.73 RM); *Don Juan* (12 079.55); *The Scarlet Pimpernel* (4857.30); *Sanders of the River* (45 100.39); *Lions Starve in Naples* (7956.98).
21. Others included *Anna und Elisabeth* (Frank Wysbar, 1933), *Reifende Jugend* (Carl Froelich, 1933), *Musik im Blut* (Erich Waschneck, 1934), *Der Student von Prag* (Artur Robison, 1935), *Letzte Rose* (Karl Anton, 1936), *Das Schloß in Flandern* (Geza

von Bolvary, 1936), *Versprich mir nichts!* (Wolfgang Liebeneiner, 1937), *Savoy-Hotel 217* (Gustav Ucicky, 1936), *Der Schimmelreiter* (Carl Oertel and Hans Deppe, 1933), *Schwarze Rosen* (Paul Martin, 1935) and *Wenn die Musik nicht wär* (Carmine Gallone, 1935).

22. For more on this, see D. Atwell, *Cathedrals of the Movies. A History of British Cinemas and their Audiences* (Architectural Press: London, 1980).
23. NA PRO BT11/863 Amounts paid or owing by British importers of German films during the 12 months ending 31 October 1935.
24. For more on the Film Society, see J. Samson, 'The Film Society, 1925–1939', in C. Barr (ed.), *All Our Yesterdays: 90 Years of British Cinema* (Bfi Publishing: London, 1986), pp. 306–13.
25. D. Welch, *Propaganda and the German Cinema 1933–45* (London: IB Tauris, 2001 rev.), pp. 61–71.
26. British Film Institute Special Collections. Film Society Collection. Item 4C. Minutes of the meeting of 24 January 1934.
27. British Film Institute Special Collections. Film Society Collection. Item 4C. Minutes of the meeting of 13 March 1934.
28. British Film Institute Special Collections. Film Society Collection. Item 4C. Minutes of the meeting of 20 March 1934.
29. British Film Institute Special Collections. Film Society Collection. Item 4C. Minutes of the meeting of 13 June 1934.
30. British Film Institute Special Collections. Film Society Collection. Item 4C. Minutes of the meeting of 24 November 1938.
31. British Film Institute Special Collections. Film Society Collection. Item 10. Member Survey, 1939.
32. The German films screened from 1933 to 1939 by the Film Society were *Anna und Elisabeth* (Frank Wysbar, 1933), *Carmen* (Lotte Reinger, 1933), *Reifende Jugend* (Carl Froehlich, 1933), *Deutschland – zwischen gestern und heute* (Wilfired Basse, 1934), *Das Rollende Rad* (Lotte Reiniger, 1934), *Das Gestohlene Herz* (Lotte Reinger, 1934), *Das Kleine Schornsteinfeger* (Lotte Reiniger, 1935), *Galatea* (Lotte Reiniger, 1935), *Der Jager Toni Schafft's* (Ferdinand Diehl, 1936), *Kleines Tier groß gesehen* (Karl Metzner, 1934), *Opta empfängt* (Alexeieff, 1936), *Graf von Carabas* (Lotte Reiniger, 1936) and *Düsseldorf* (Walter Ruttmann, 1936), as well as a number of technical films produced by *Tobis-Klangfilm*. A full list of the Film Society's programmes can be found in *The Film Society Programmes, 1925–1939* (Arno Press: New York, 1972).
33. *Sight and Sound* reported the following screenings in the regions (reference in brackets): *Flüchtlinge* (Glasgow, vol. 4, no. 13, Spring 1935, p. 40; Tyneside, vol. 4. no. 16, Winter 1935–36, p. 199), *the Triumph des Willens* (Tyneside, vol. 4. no. 16, Winter 1935–36, p. 199), *Das Mädchen Johanna* (Leicester, vol. 5, no. 18, Summer 1936, p. 57; Ayrshire, vol. 5, no. 19, Autumn 1936, p. 111), *Der alte und der Junge König* (Edinburgh, vol. 5, no. 19, Autumn 1936, p. 111), *Der Student von Prag* (Dundee, vol. 5, no. 19, Autumn 1936, p. 111; Tyneside, vol. 5, no. 19, Autumn 1936, p. 113), *Morgenrot* (Southampton, vol. 4, no. 13, Spring 1935, p. 41; Leicester, vol. 4, no. 14, Summer 1935, p. 95), *Deutschland – zwischen Gestern und Heute* (Billingham, Co. Durham, vol. 4, no. 14, Autumn 1935, p. 146), *Der Schimmelreiter* (Glasgow, vol. 4, no. 16, Winter 1935–36, p. 198; Tyneside, vol. 5, no. 18, Summer 1936, p. 57) and *Barcarole* (Southampton, vol. 4, no. 15, Autumn 1935, p. 137).
34. 'Open Letter to the Reich Revivalists', *To-day's Cinema* (11 June 1935), p. 2.

35. British Film Institute Special Collections. Ivor Montagu Collection, Item 56. MS article on 'The Decline of the German Film Trade under National Socialism', c. 1936–37.
36. *To-day's Cinema* (22 June 1935), p. 3. The films referred to were Destiny (*Schicksal*, 1925); *Vaudeville* (*Variété*, 1925); *The Cabinet of Dr. Caligari* (*Das Cabinet des Dr. Caligari*, 1920) and *The Last Laugh* (*Der letzte Mann*, 1924).
37. Ibid.
38. British Film Institute Special Collections. Ivor Montagu Collection, Item 56. MS article on 'The Decline of the German Film Trade under National Socialism', c. 1936–37.
39. See Chapter 13.
40. See note 38.
41. *Monthly Film Bulletin*, 1934, p. 105.
42. *Monthly Film Bulletin*, 1937, p. 151.
43. *To-day's Cinema* (30 August 1935), p. 3.
44. See, for example, *Kinematograph Weekly* (4 April 1935), p. 39.
45. R. Low, *The History of the British Film, 1929–1939: Filmmaking in 1930s Britain* (George Allen & Unwin: London, 1985), p. 91.
46. Ibid., p. 92. For more on these films of the early 1930s and in particular the role of British International Pictures, see pp. 92–100.
47. Ibid., p. 100.
48. See Chapter 2.
49. British Film Institute Special Collections. BBFC scenarios (1938/19). J. C. Hanna quoted in Richards (1982), p. 40.
50. J. Brooke-Wilson (BBFC) to R. Kenney, Foreign Office, 21 June 1939. Quoted in K. R. M. Short, 'Documents: Chaplin's *The Great Dictator* and British Censorship', *Historical Journal of Film, Radio and Television*, 5:1 (1985), pp. 85–90. Here, p. 89.
51. NA PRO 859/6/9, Memo on *Confessions of a Nazi Spy*, Lord Dufferin (2 August 1939).
52. NA PRO 822/70/15, German film expedition – *Peters, the Kingmaker*. Lee to Bowyer/Calder, n.d.
53. K. Gladstone, 'British Interception of German Export Newsreels, and The Development of British Combat Filming, 1939–1942', *Imperial War Museum Review*, 2 (1987), pp. 30–40.
54. NA PRO INF 1/292, 'Public Reactions to the Captured German Films', Home Intelligence, 24 September 1941.
55. Ibid.
56. *Kinematograph Weekly* (14 January 1943), p. 27.
57. NA PRO INF 1/633, Watson to Nunn-May, n.d.
58. NA PRO INF 1/633, Fletcher to Nunn-May, 25 October 1943.
59. NA PRO INF 1/633, Beddington to the War Office, 15 November 1943; he asks again on 19 November 1943.
60. NA PRO INF 1/633. A full list of films can be found in this file.
61. NA PRO INF 1/633, Lefebre to Nolbandov, 24 May 1945.
62. NA INF PRO 1/633, Nunn-May to Watson, 21 February 1944.
63. NA INF PRO 1/633, Rotha to Beddington, 7 September 1945.
64. NA INF PRO 1/633, Anthony Havelock-Allen to Beddington, 1945.

23

German Films in America, 1933–45: Public Diplomacy and an Uncoordinated Information Campaign

David Culbert

The impact of German feature and documentary films on American attitudes between 1933 and 1945 is part of what these days is commonly referred to as 'public diplomacy', a term which was apparently first used in 1965, though a process very much part of the foreign policy of Nazi Germany, in which identity creation and image projection (what is sometimes termed 'nation-branding') were of enormous concern. The problem for Germany, however, was related to an uncertainty as to what image was to be projected – peaceful, powerful, energetic – or threatening, frightening, brutal. As a recent student of the subject notes, 'the aims of public diplomacy cannot be achieved if they are believed to be inconsistent with a country's foreign policy or military action'.[1] Germany had no overall direction of its information campaign for America. As a result, actions clearly at cross-purposes, and a lack of coordination, meant that specific images and actions were placed within framing devices provided by various groups in America, and often used to sharpen negative perceptions of both Adolf Hitler and Nazi Germany.

America, 1933–45, was a society shaped by Franklin D. Roosevelt, president for this entire period. It was a time of economic depression through 1940, and then of wartime prosperity, 1941–45. It was a society shaped by the mass media – newspapers, still photography, magazines, radio and film. Film's weekly audience was some 80 million in a country of 230 million. The country was too vast for any single newspaper to reach a national audience. Radio, thanks to its low cost, emerged by the late 1930s as the central medium of communication, for both entertainment and news. The surprise Japanese attack on Pearl Harbor, 7 December 1941, meant war with Japan. Hitler then declared war in America, and Nazi Germany became one of America's enemies in a time of total war. Germany's image, and the impact of German films in America, was transformed by total war.

The image of Nazi Germany in the United States

For many Americans, the image of Germany was seen in newsreels where the words – and in particular the uniforms – of the Nazis made it easy for the average person to consider Germany and its leaders in an unfavourable light. Frank Capra later said that the Nazi uniforms, brown or black, made it easy to show viewers the presumptive 'bad guys'.[2] One of the best-publicised examples of negative publicity for Germany inside America involved the FBI's arrest of a Nazi spy ring in New York City on 26 February 1938. Those arrested included members of the German–American Bund (see below). The spy ring's leader, Dr Ignatz T. Greibl, escaped to Europe aboard the *Bremen*, a German passenger ship. The FBI arrests formed the basis of a best-seller by Leon G. Turrou, *Nazi Spies in America* (1938), which in turn led to the most outspoken anti-Nazi feature film produced in America before the attack on Pearl Harbor: *Confessions of a Nazi Spy*, released by Warner Bros on 28 April 1939. The film was directed by Anatole Litvak, a Ukrainian of Jewish origin who had worked (as Anatole Lutwak) for Ufa but left Germany in 1933. The film contained newsreel footage of Joseph Goebbels, the German–American Bund, and excerpts from Leni Riefenstahl's *Triumph des Willens* (*Triumph of the Will*, 1935), her propaganda film glorifying Hitler and the

An advertisement from Ufa Inc., New York. *Source*: J. Alicoate (ed.), *The 1939 Film Daily Year Book of Motion Pictures* (New York: The Film Daily, 1939), p. 1130.

1934 Nuremberg Party Convention. *Confessions of a Nazi Spy* did badly at the box office, but resulted in an immediate forceful complaint by the German charge d'affaires in Washington, DC.[3]

After the attack on Pearl Harbor, several other anti-Nazi feature films were produced.[4] One of the most successful was *Hangmen also Die* (1943), Fritz Lang's box-office success based on the assassination of Reinhard Heydrich in Prague in May 1942, and the resulting destruction of the entire village of Lidice by the Germans. Berthold Brecht wrote the script; Hanns Eisler wrote the music. A number of German Jewish emigrants ended up playing the parts of brutal Nazis, as Lang hoped to build empathy with American viewers by giving the parts of Czech partisans to American-born actors and actresses. American wartime viewers had a number of anti-Nazi feature films to choose from, each with cardboard Nazi characters. Among the more successful of such films, one might mention *To Be or Not to Be* (Ernst Lubitsch, 1942) or *Hitler's Madmen* (Douglas Sirk, 1944).[5]

For many, the American face of Hitler's Germany was seen in the German–American Bund, headed after 1936 by Fritz Kuhn. Particularly memorable was a rally of thousands of Bund supporters at New York's Madison Square Garden, 20 February 1939. Kuhn told his enthusiastic listeners: 'I have just returned from a tour out West and we now have 100 Nazi units in the United States.' The newsreel footage of this rally, replete with Nazi flags and hundreds of Nazi uniforms, was recycled many times after 1941.[6] It was hard to balance footage of this rally with requests for peace and amity which came from the German embassy in Washington, DC, or the German consul general in New York City. It is worth noting that there is no direct evidence linking the activities of the German-American Bund with some larger German information campaign for America.

It is difficult to state precisely what the average American thought of anti-Jewish violence in Germany, but no one could be in doubt as to the feelings of Hamilton Fish III, ranking Republican in the House of Representatives' Committee on Foreign Affairs (and a long-time political enemy of Franklin D. Roosevelt). Fish spoke about Germany in a CBS radio broadcast on 25 November 1938:

> I speak tonight not as a Jew or a German but as an American who loathes and abhors all forms of political economic racial, and religious repression and persecution, whether in this country or elsewhere. . . . These are the identical words used by my grandfather, Hamilton Fish, in 1872, when as Secretary of State . . . he protested the outrages and persecution of the Jews in Rumania at that time. . . . Hitler has become stark raving mad on the Jewish issue. . . . Hitler, Goebbels, and other fanatical Nazis are undermining the fundamentals of civilisation.[7]

The documentary *Victory in the West* (*Sieg im Westen*, 1941) presented a triumphalist view of the German conquest of Western Europe (1940). The film made a forceful – indeed, too forceful-impression on American viewers. *Source*: Culbert Collection.

Fish was an outspoken isolationist, but no listener could have been in doubt as to his distaste for Nazi Germany in November 1938, and what public relations gesture from any member of the German diplomatic service in America might have provided a framing device to place such anti-Semitic actions in a 'kindly' light?

American films in Germany, 1933–41[8]

During the so-called *Kampfzeit* ('time of struggle'), some members of the Nazi party displayed hostility towards Hollywood. The simple fact that all American majors were owned or had been founded by European émigrés of Jewish origin[9] made Hollywood an easy target for ideologues such as Alfred Rosenberg, who vilified the American film industry as a classic example of Jewish capitalism. Hollywood was held responsible for producing 'anti-German' films such as Universal's *All Quiet on the Western Front* (1930) which despite *Nationalsozialische Deutsche Arbeiterpartei* (NSDAP) protests became one of the top 10 films in German theatres (1931–32).[10] In the eyes of such party members, 'apolitical' Hollywood productions were suspect too for they promoted the American way of life which was incompatible with National-Socialist values. Other factions, dominated by Hermann Göring, Joseph Goebbels (and Adolf Hitler) were equally critical of films such as *All Quiet on the Western Front* but admired American entertainment films and therefore followed a more moderate course vis-à-vis Hollywood.

When the Nazis came to power, this ambiguous attitude towards Hollywood and American films continued. Hardliners within the National-Socialist party, such as Himmler's SS, would repeatedly call for a total ban on American films in the Third Reich. Propaganda minister Goebbels was, however, not inclined to indulge such radical requests. American films were needed because the German film production and the import of European features were quantitatively (and qualitatively) unable to satisfy the demand of the German market. Goebbels, who attached great importance to offering the German people entertainment and escapism through the movies, initially sought to maintain a healthy relationship with Hollywood and hoped to stimulate (in the long run) German film export to the United States. Only by the end of 1936 did the propaganda ministry give up all hope of establishing a successful export of German films to the United States. Nevertheless, Goebbels and his collaborators, who in the words of Markus Spieker 'manoeuvred between dogmatism and pragmatism',[11] allowed local branches of the American majors to pursue their activities. This continued American presence in the German film market was only possible because the German branches of Hollywood majors that had not left Germany by 1937[12] – MGM, Paramount and Fox – complied with the rules imposed by the new regime and, for instance, fired their Jewish employees.

Fifty-two per cent of the films Nazi Germany imported in 1933–38 were American productions[13] that had been dubbed, as the law required, in

Germany by German actors. It was Goebbels who decided personally which American productions were fit for German screens.[14] Initially, B-films as well as top list productions were granted access to German cinemas. As a result, the American presence on the German film market reached unplanned heights in 1935–36. For instance, the most popular films screened in cinemas of the Reich capital (Berlin) in 1935 and 1936 were not German, but American: respectively Frank Capra's *It Happened One Night* (1934) and Roy Del Ruth's *Broadway Melody of 1936*.[15] From 1937–38 onwards, when the charm campaign surrounding the 1936 Olympic Games had come to an end, Goebbels made it more difficult for American A-films to enter German cinemas. Henceforth mainly American B-films (mostly productions of MGM, Paramount and Fox) which were weaker competitors to German productions were imported.[16] Nevertheless, *Broadway Melody of 1938* (also by Roy Del Ruth) was the most successful film shown in Berlin in 1938. In smaller towns, American films were less successful. As the *Motion Picture Herald* phrased it in 1937: 'The bigger the [German] city, the higher the result for the American-made film.'[17]

From 1938, the Hollywood production of anti-Nazi films contributed to deteriorating German–American film relations. It was no coincidence that such films were only made by companies that were no longer active in Germany. (United Artists had already left Germany when it released Chaplin's *The Great Dictator* in 1940.) For these and other reasons, Adolf Hitler ordered in January 1939 the gradual disappearance of American films from German cinemas. Goebbels 'half-heartedly' followed the order.[18] The import of American films was decreased by various measures, such as more severe censorship, resulting in embargos against particular productions. Germany imported 41 films in 1938; in 1939, 20; in 1940, 6.[19] In spite of aggressive anti-American offensives launched by the SS,[20] it took a long time before the last US production disappeared from German screens.

In May 1940, the final American film premiere in the Third Reich occurred. The honour befell on Eugene Forde's *Midnight Taxi* (1937), a B-film from the Fox Studios.[21] Within less than 6 months, between July and September 1940, the German branches of Fox, MGM and Paramount were closed.

German films in the United States, 1933–41

In spite of early successes such as *The Blue Angel* (*Der Blaue Engel*, 1930), an English-language version of which was shot simultaneously with the German 'original', the advent of sound made it nearly impossible for Germany or any other European film-producing country to conquer or otherwise dominate the American film market as it had been possible during the early days of cinema. Nevertheless, Germany did export some films to the United States, and Ufa, Germany's most important film company, had a branch in New York City.

Ufa-Films Inc. had been founded in September 1924 as an American company but virtually all of its shares were controlled by the Berlin parent company.[22] It had a total monopoly, in the United States as well as in Canada over the use of the Ufa name as well as on the distribution of all Ufa productions made after September 1924. In return, Ufa, the Berlin parent company, received most of the profits made by those films. Such profits were mostly non-existent. One year after its foundation, Ufa Films Inc. reported a loss of 95 000 dollars. The company nevertheless remained in business until 1941.

Quantitatively, a relatively high number of German productions were exported to the United States: 70 in 1936; 67 in 1937; 89 in 1938; and 95 in 1939.[23] But none of these managed to reach large audiences. Original distribution of German films in America, 1933–41, was restricted to the select few; those whose native tongue was German, often persons, one can presume, who found it difficult to adjust to life in America because of a language barrier.[24]

In December 1935, an Ufa Films Inc. subsidiary was created. The Amerfilm-Corporation, also located in New York, 'hired' films (free of charge) from Ufa Films Inc. and travelled to cities with German colonies, where movie theatres were rented to organise screenings. Another subsidiary, Ufa Theaters USA Inc., had been established in 1931 but apparently never really owned a theatre.[25] Independently organised screenings of German films were in small, financially precarious theatres. The public pronouncements of Hitler and the Nazi hierarchy pretty much guaranteed that the image of Germany in America was negative. In sum, the bad triumphed over the good, and efforts at favourable image building were no match for Fritz Kuhn or Hitler's anti-Semitic tirades. In such a situation, public diplomacy played a very small role.

The distribution of German films in America, actively protested against since 1933 by the Anti-Nazi League,[26] was largely restricted to a small number of theatres patronised by German speakers. The opposition of Hollywood moguls to anti-Jewish actions within Germany meant that between 1933 and 1945 Germany was never able to sell a commercial hit for American distribution, with necessary synchronisation into English. Instead, distribution of German feature films was restricted to the German-speaking part of New York City (Bronxville), where the leading theatre had but 500 seats, and to even smaller theatres in Chicago, Milwaukee, and a suburb of San Francisco. An anonymous German identified as 'e' toured American cities in the summer of 1938, and prepared, on his return, a long report about the actual audience for German-language films in America. 'E' included numerous anti-Semitic references in his report, presumably to meet the expectations of his superiors, but concluded that there was hardly any substantial German-speaking film audience in America outside of sections of New York City and Chicago, as in other cities first-generation Germans were living all over a given metropolitan area, and thus remote from a particular theatre. 'E' noted, with official disdain, that theatre owners of German-language theatres were Jewish, a number from Budapest.[27]

The biggest influence Nazi Germany exercised on Hollywood was an unintended effect of its racial policy. As many as 1500 members of the German film industry immigrated to Hollywood, a process which began in the early 1920s, but which accelerated between 1933 and 1939. Such notable actors and actresses as Marlene Dietrich, Conrad Veidt and Peter Lorre, such film composers as Franz Waxman and Friedrich Hollaender and, such directors as Fritz Lang, Otto Preminger, Billy Wilder, Ernst Lubitsch and Joseph Von Sternberg found success in Hollywood equal to or greater than the success they had enjoyed in Europe. These were the success stories. But many others, forced by racial laws to emigrate, never did quite fit into Hollywood, in part because of difficulties learning a new language. As Jan-Christopher Horak notes, it is difficult, in retrospect, to distinguish between genres such as the 'exile film', and the 'anti-Nazi' film, and it is hard to integrate the achievements of Hollywood's German exiles into a proper history of either the German film industry or that of America. Horak speaks of films in which the language is English but the spirit German.[28]

In November 1938, Leni Riefenstahl arrived in New York City, to try and sell commercial distribution of her four-hour *Olympia* film (1938) about the 1936 Olympics. Her arrival, just after news of the so-called *Kristallnacht*, the orgy of destruction of Jewish property and synagogues in Germany, guaranteed her a stony reception in America, though she did show her film at selected private 35 mm theatres in Washington, DC, Chicago and San Francisco. Walt Disney tried to help Riefenstahl, but in Hollywood she received not just a cold shoulder, but, thanks in part to members of the German film colony, was the subject of denunciation in such publications as the *Hollywood Reporter*.[29]

The most effective use of German film in America is related to three feature-length documentary films representing Nazi triumphalism: the German military victories over Poland (in *Campaign in Poland* (*Feldzug in Polen*, 1940) and in *Baptism of Fire* (*Feuertaufe*, 1940)) and over Western Europe, including the defeat of France (in *Victory in the West* (*Sieg im Westen*, 1941)). These films were shown in the Bronxville section of New York City in 1940 and the spring of 1941. Efforts were made to prevent the showing of what was deemed enemy propaganda, but the films were shown for many weeks. Obviously these films, made with the thought of terrorising neutral European countries by revealing the effectiveness of the *Blitzkrieg*, were only of use in promoting a negative or warlike image of Germany.

In August 1940, the American chargé in Berlin confirmed that American films were now barred from distribution within Germany and most German-occupied territories – that is, of Europe. On 11 September 1940, a representative of the motion picture industry met with Breckinridge Long, Assistant

Secretary of State. A Colonel Herron, representing Will Hays, president of the Motion Picture Producers and Distributors of America, told Long that his group was unlikely to seek retaliation by trying to block distribution of German films within America: 'He said he personally hated to see the propaganda films which the Germans were exhibiting here, particularly on the east side of New York. However they had little circulation.'[30]

Matters did not take a turn for the better. The American chargé in Berlin, on 25 October 1940, spoke with a 'competent official' in the Propaganda Ministry about the blocking of Hollywood films in Europe. The charge reported the burden of the conversation:

> It was quite apparent from the conversations that his Ministry has no intention of allowing established American distributors for producers who are classified as making so-called anti-Nazi films to resume operations in any of the countries under German military occupation and it was intimated that the property attached and the prints seized by the German authorities would not be returned unless the interested American companies agreed to cease producing anti-German films and came to some arrangement whereby German films would be shown in the United States.... The Propaganda Ministry is increasingly subsidising German films and welcomes the opportunity offered by military occupation to stop American competition and establish the Reich's film industry in Europe.[31]

In spite of Germany's desire to remove Hollywood films from European cinema screens, Ufa Films Inc. was allowed to continue its activities on American soil. A shipment with new German film prints was confiscated in the harbour of New York in August 1940, but the American Ufa branch kept on distributing older films.[32] It was only after the attack on Pearl Harbor that all German film activities were immediately stopped. Ufa Films Inc. and its subsidiaries – considered German property – were confiscated. The company director, George Nitze, was arrested, as was Georg Gyssling, Nazi Consul General in Hollywood.[33] The Alien Property Custodian, operating under the provisions of the draconian 1917 'Trading with the Enemy Act', seized over 200 German films from the New York office of Ufa, with the assistance of the Treasury Department. Copyright to all films Ufa Films Inc. had ever released was confiscated too. The film prints ended up being transferred to Washington, DC, for the use of Frank Capra, though Iris Barry of the Museum of Modern Art made strenuous efforts to gain control over these German films herself, particularly as she had been able to employ Siegfried Kracauer as a research assistant, thanks to funding from the Rockefeller Foundation.[34]

After the attack on Pearl Harbor, Nazi feature films, newsreels, *Kulturfilme* and the films about the Polish and French campaigns found a new use: as visual evidence for the brutality of Nazi Germany in Frank Capra's *Why We Fight* series, seven orientation films intended to show the typical American soldier the reason he was fighting a war against Germany, Italy and Japan. German footage was re-edited, re-cut and provided with new music and a new voiceover, to show the brutal face of the enemy. A large percentage of the footage in Capra's second and third films, *The Nazis Strike* (1942) and *Divide and Conquer* (1943), uses footage from *Campaign in Poland, Baptism of Fire* and *Victory in the West.*[35] And it is in this wartime depiction of the evil Nazi that American viewers see excerpts from Leni Riefenstahl's *Triumph of the Will.* The Film Library of the Museum of Modern Art, New York City, had purchased a 35 mm print of *Triumph of the Will* in Berlin in 1936, but screenings were restricted to programmes for cineastes at the museum's theatre.[36] It was only in wartime that millions of Americans first saw excerpts of the film, in a very different manner from the original version. Additional German footage, much of it from feature films, was also shown to American troops in a film first titled *Know Your Enemy—Germany*, but reworked as *Your Job in Germany* (1945).[37]

It seems clear, then, that the greatest impact of German film on American viewers was in re-edited and re-cut form, as visual evidence for the nature of the enemy in wartime documentary films intended for orientation. Here the evidence is clear: most Americans got their ideas of what Hitler and Nazi Germany were like from German footage recycled for wartime depictions of the nature of the enemy. Above all, Leni Riefenstahl's *Triumph of the Will* was the 'perfect' source for showing the regimentation of a society in which 'everyone' stood at attention in Nuremberg crowd scenes.

Notes

1. J. Melissen (ed.), *The New Public Diplomacy: Soft Power in International Relations* (Hampshire: Palgrave Macmillan, 2005), pp. 3–9.
2. Author's telephone interview with Frank Capra, 18 January 1977.
3. M. E. Birdwell, *Celluloid Soldiers: Warner Bros.'s Campaign Against Nazism* (New York: New York University Press, 1999), pp. 57–86.
4. J.-C. Horak, *Anti- Nazi- Filme der deutschsprachigen Emigration von Hollywood 1939–1945* (Münster: MAKS, 1995 rev.).
5. Ibid., pp. 101–18.
6. S. Dickstein (D—New York), US Congress. *Congressional Record*; House (24 February 1939), p. 1884.
7. H. Fish, CBS radio broadcast, 25 November 1938, reprinted in Appendix, *Congressional Record* (1939), pp. 31–2.
8. This section is, unless otherwise noted, based on M. Spieker, *Hollywood unterm Hakenkreuz. Der amerikanische Spielfilm im Dritten Reich* (Trier: Wissenschaftlicher Verlag Trier, 1999). Thanks to Roel Vande Winkel for valuable information from this source and from the Bundesarchiv documents cited below.
9. N. Gabler, *An Empire of Their Own: How the Jews Invented Hollywood* (New York: Crown Publishers, 1988).

10. J. Garncarz, 'Hollywood in Germany: The Role of American Films in Germany, 1925–1990', in D. W. Ellwood and R. Kroes (eds), *Hollywood in Europe: Experiences of a Cultural Hegemony* (Amsterdam: VU University Press, 1994), pp. 94–135. T. Hanna-Daoud, *Die NSDAP und der Film bis zur Machtergreifung* (Köln–Weimar–Wien: Böhlau, 1996), pp. 23–9. See also T. J. Saunders, *Hollywood in Berlin: American Cinema and Weimar Germany* (Berkeley: University of California Press, 1994) for very different conclusions, based, it seems, on an inaccurate assessment of attendance figures.
11. M. Spieker (1999), p. 89.
12. Warner Brothers (1933), United Artists (1934–35), Universal (1934), Columbia (1937) and RKO (1937) stopped their activities, either because their films were unsuccessful or because German censors would not allow their productions (the horror films of Universal for instance). Spieker (1999), pp. 90–3.
13. 248 out of 473. G. Stahr, *Volksgemeinschaft vor der Leinwand? Der nationalsozialistische Film und sein Publikum* (Berlin: Verlag Hans Theissen, 2001), p. 202.
14. F. Moeller, *The Film Minister. Goebbels and the cinema in the 'Third Reich'* (Stuttgart–London: Edition Axel Menges, 2000), p. 32.
15. M. Spieker (1999), pp. 340–1. According to Bernd Kleinhans, the presence of American films was weaker in provincial cinemas. B. Kleinhans, *Ein Volk, ein Reich, ein Kino: Lichtspiel in der braunen Provinz* (Köln: Papyrossa-Verlag, 2003), p. 103.
16. See M. Spieker (1999) and B. Drewniak, *Der deutsche Film 1938–1945: Ein Gesamtueberblick* (Düsseldorf: Droste, 1987), no. 896, pp. 814–27. Few specialists in American films of the 1930s will recognise many of the obscure titles listed by Drewniak, who makes no effort to indicate how many Germans saw these American films.
17. Cited in M. Spieker (1999), p. 110.
18. Ibid., p. 283.
19. Ibid., pp. 357–60.
20. Ibid., pp. 298–303. See also G. Stahr (2001), pp. 203–8.
21. M. Spieker (1999), p. 304.
22. The history of Ufa Films Inc., Amerfilm-Corporation and Ufa Theatres New York Inc. is, unless otherwise noted, based on Bundesarchiv (hereafter Barch), R 109 I/1663, Ufa-Films Inc.
23. M. Spieker (1999), p. 180.
24. For a list of such films, mostly not major commercial hits in Germany, see B. Drewniak (1987) no. 895, pp. 794–6. Drewniak is short of data on this fascinating subject—as is everyone else—see how he presents a bit of information from the *New York Daily Mirror* on p. 796.
25. Officially, Ufa Theaters USA Inc. was owned by the NV Neerlandia Maatschappij voor Film- en Bioscoopbedrijf Amsterdam, a Dutch subsidiary of the Berlin parent company.
26. M. Spieker (1999), pp. 180–3.
27. Barch, R109 I/1611, *Der deutsche Film in USA*. It is possible to locate some of the theatres visited by 'e' in the list of theatres for 'New York City', in N. Schenck, *Your Priceless Gift* (New York: National Motion Picture Committee, 1946), unpaginated. For theatres for which an exact match is possible, one notes that 'e' overstates seating capacity.
28. J.-C Horak, 'Exilfilm, 1933–1945', in W. Jacobsen *et al.* (eds), *Geschichte des deutschen Films* (Stuttgart: Metzler, 1993), pp. 10l–18.

29. C. C. Graham, '"Olympia" in America, 1938: Leni Riefenstahl, Hollywood, and the Kristallnacht', *Historical Journal of Film, Radio and Television*, 13:4 (1993), pp. 433–50.
30. Memorandum of Telephone Conversation by Breckinridge Long, 27 August 1940; Memorandum of Conversation by Breckinridge Long, 11 September 1940, *Foreign Relations of the United States 1940*, vol. II (Washington: GPO, 1957), pp. 668–9.
31. Charge in Germany (Morris) to Secretary of State Cordell Hull, 30 October 1940, *Foreign Relations of the United States 1940*, vol. II, pp. 670–1.
32. M. Spieker (1999), p. 317.
33. Ibid., p. 318.
34. D. Culbert, 'The Rockefeller Foundation, the Museum of Modern Art Film Library, and Siegfried Kracauer, 1941', *Historical Journal of Film, Radio and Television*, 13:4 (1993), pp. 495–511. For the seizure of the UFA films, see Barry to Rockefeller, Document 63, in D. Culbert (ed.), *Film and Propaganda in America*, vol. III, *World War II, Part 2* (Westport: Greenwood, 1990), pp. 207–18.
35. For surviving draft and final scripts (with information as to sources of footage), see documents M-72 through M-82 in D. Culbert (ed.), *Film and Propaganda in America: A Documentary History*, vol. V (microfiche supplement) (Westport: Greenwood Press, 1993). Document M-82 records the responses of captured German POWs to seeing *The Nazis Strike and Divide and Conquer* in American captivity. See also S. A. Stouffer *et al.*, *Studies in Social Psychology in World War II: Vol. III. Experiments in Mass Communication* (Princeton: Princeton University Press, 1950).
36. Iris Barry showed her MOMA print of Riefenstahl's *Triumph of the Will* to Frank Capra and members of his staff at the 5th-floor theatre, National Archives, Washington, DC, March 1942. See I. Barry to N. A. Rockefeller, 3 February 1943, Document 63 in Culbert (1990), pp. 207–18. For the contract from 1936 for MOMA's purchase of *Triumph des Willens* see 'German folder—UFA', Central Files, Museum of Modern Art Film Library, New York, NY.
37. D. Culbert, 'Note on Government Paper Records', in B. Rowan (ed.), *Scholars' Guide to Washington, D.C. Film and Video Collections* (Washington, DC: Smithsonian Institution Press, 1980), pp. 236–9. *Mission to Moscow* (Michael curtiz, 1943) contains footage from *Triumph of the Will*.

Select Bibliography on the German Cinema, 1933–45

Albrecht, G., *Nationalsozialistische Filmpolitik. Eine soziologische Untersuchung über die Spielfilme des Dritten Reiches* (Stuttgart: Ferdinand Enke Verlag, 1969).

Albrecht, G., *Der Film im 3. Reich* (Karlsruhe: Doku Verlag, 1979).

Ascheid, A., *Hitler's Heroines: Stardom and Womanhood in Nazi Cinema* (Philadelphia: Temple University Press, 2003).

Baird, J. W., 'Nazi film propaganda and the Soviet Union', *Film & History*, 11:2 (1981), pp. 34–41.

Baird, J. W., 'Goebbels, Horst Wessel and the myth of ressurection and return', *Journal of Contemporary History*, 17:4 (1982), pp. 633–50.

Baird, J. W., 'From Berlin to Neubabelsberg: Nazi film propaganda and Hitler Youth Quex', *Journal of Contemporary History*, 18:3 (1983), pp. 495–515.

Barkhausen, H., *Filmpropaganda für Deutschland im Ersten und Zweiten Weltkrieg* (Hildesheim: Georg Holmes Verlag AG, 1982).

Bartels, U., *Die Wochenschau im Dritten Reich: Entwicklung und Funktion eines Massenmediums unter besonderer Berücksichtigung völkisch-nationaler Inhalte* (Frankfurt am Main–Berlin–Bern–Bruxelles–New York–Oxford–Wien: Peter Lang, 2004).

Becker, W., *Film und Herrschaft. Organisationsprinzipien und Organisationsstrukturen der nationalsozialistischen Filmpropaganda* (Berlin: Verlag Volker Spiess, 1973).

Beyer, F., *Die Ufa-stars im Dritten Reich: Frauen für Deutschland* (München: Wilhelm Heyne Verlag, 1991).

Bock, H.-M. and M. Töteberg (eds), *Das Ufa-Buch* (Frankfurt am Main: Zweitausendeins, 1992).

Bock, H.-M., W. A. Mosel and I. Spazier (eds), *Die Tobis 1928–1945: Eine Kommentierte Filmografie* (München: Edition text + kritik, 2003).

Brandt, H.-J., *NS-Filmtheorie und dokumentarische Praxis: Hippler, Noldan, Junghans* (Tübingen: Max Niemeyer Verlag, 1987).

Carter, E., *Dietrich's Ghosts: The Sublime and the Beautiful in Third Reich Film* (London: British Film Institute, 2004).

Culbert, D., 'Leni Riefenstahl and the diaries of Joseph Goebbels', *Historical Journal of Film, Radio and Television*, 13:1 (1993), pp. 85–93.

Culbert, D., 'The impact of anti-semitic film propaganda on German audiences: Jew Süss and the Wandering Jew (1940)', in R. A. Etlin (ed.), *Art, Culture and Media Under the Third Reich* (Chicago–London: University of Chicago Press, 2002), pp. 139–57.

Culbert, D. and M. Loiperdinger, 'Leni Riefenstahl's "Tag der Freiheit": the 1935 Nazi party rally film', *Historical Journal of Film, Radio and Television*, 12:1 (1992), pp. 3–40.

Cuomo, R., *National Socialist Cultural Policy* (New York: St Martin's Press, 1995).

Delage, C., *La vision nazie de l'histoire à travers le cinéma documentaire du troisième reich* (Lausanne: Editions de l'Age d'Homme2, 1989).

Distelmeyer, J. (ed.), *Tonfilmfrieden/Tonfilmkrieg: Die Geschichte der Tobis vom Technik-Syndikat zum Staatskonzern* (München: Edition text + kritik, 2003).

Drewniak, B., *Der deutsche Film 1938–1945* (Düsseldorf: Droste Verlag, 1987).

Fox, J., *Filming Women in the Third Reich* (Oxford–New York: Berg, 2000).

Fox, J. *Film Propaganda in Britain and Nazi Germany: World War II Cinema* (Oxford–New York: Berg Publishers, 2006).

Fröhlich, E. (ed.), *Die Tagebücher von Joseph Goebbels. Teil I: Aufzeichnungen 1923–1941; Teil II: Diktate 1941–1945* (München: KG Sauer, 1993–2006).

Fulks, B. A., 'Walter Ruttmann, the avant-garde film and Nazi modernism', *Film & History*, 14:2 (1984), pp. 26–35.

Giesen, R. and M. Hobsch, *Hitlerjunge Quex, Jud Süss und Kolberg. (Die Propagandafilme des dritten Reiches: Dokumente und Materialien zum NS-Film)* (Berlin: Schwarzkopf & Schwarzkopf Verlag, 2005).

Graham, C. C., ' "Olympia" in America, 1938: Leni Riefenstahl, Hollywood, and the Kristallnacht', *Historical Journal of Film, Radio and Television*, 13:4 (1993), pp. 433–50.

Hachmeister, L. and M. Kloft (eds), *Das Goebbels-Experiment* (München: Deutsche Verlags-Anstalt, 2005).

Hake, S., *Popular Cinema of the Third Reich* (Austin: University of Texas Press, 2001).

Hanna-Daoud, T., *Die NSDAP und der Film bis zur Machtergreifung* (Köln–Weimar–Wien: Böhlau, 1996).

Happel, H.-G., *Der historische Spielfilm im Nationalsozialismus* (Frankfurt: R.G. Fischer Verlag, 1984).

Hoffmann, H., *'Und die Fahne führt uns in die Ewigkeit.' Propaganda im NS-Film* (Frankfurt: Fischer Verlag, 1991). Translated as *The Triumph of Propaganda. Film and National Socialism 1933–1945* (Providence–Oxford: Berghahn Books, 1996).

Hollstein, D., *'Jud Süss' und die Deutschen: Antisemitische Vorurteile im nationalsozialistischen Spielfilm* (Frankfurt/M–Berlin–Wien: Ullstein, 1983 rev.).

Hornshøj-Møller, S., *Der ewige Jude. Quellenkritische Analyse eines antisemitischen Propagandafilms* (Göttingen: Institut für den Wissenschaftlichen Film, 1995).

Hornshøj-Møller, S. and D. Culbert, ' "Der ewige Jude" (1940): Joseph Goebbels' unequalled monument to anti-Semitism', *Historical Journal of Film, Radio and Television*, 12:1 (1992), pp. 41–67.

Hull, D. S., *Film in the Third Reich. A Study of the German Cinema 1933–1945* (Berkeley–Los Angeles: University of California Press, 1969).

Kanzog, K., *Staatspolitisch besonders wertvoll: ein Handbuch zu 30 deutschen Spielfilmen der Jahre 1934 bis 1945* (München: Diskurs-Film-Verlag, 1994).

Kinkel, L., *Die Scheinwerferin: Leni Riefenstahl und das 'Dritte Reich'* (Hamburg–Wien: Europa Verlag, 2002).

Kleinhans, B., *Ein Volk, ein Reich, ein Kino: Lichtspiel in der braunen Provinz* (Köln: Papyrossa-Verlag, 2003).

Koepnick, L., *The Dark Mirror: German Cinema Between Hitler and Hollywood* (Berkeley–Los Angeles–London: University of California Press, 2002).

König, S., H.-J. Panitz and M. Wachtler, *Bergfilm: Dramen, Trick und Abenteuer* (München: F.A. Herbig Verlagsbuchhandlung, 2001).

Kramer, T. and D. Siegrist, *Terra. Ein Schweizer Filmkonzern im Dritten Reich* (Zürich: Chronos Verlag, 1991).

Kreimeier, K., *Die Ufa story. Geschichte eines Filmkonzerns* (München: Wilhelm Heyne Verlag, 1992). Translated as *The Ufa Story* (Berkeley–Los Angeles–London: University of California Press, 1999).

Krenn, G., *Die Kulturfilme der Wien-Film 1938–1945* (Wien: Österreichisches Filmarchiv, 1992).

Leiser, E., *'Deutschland, erwache!' Propapaganda im Film des Dritten Reiches* (Reinbek bei Hamburg: Rowohlt Taschenbuch Verlag, 1968). Translated as *Nazi Cinema* (New York: Macmillan, 1974).

Liebe, U., *Verehrt, verfolgt, vergessen: Schauspieler als Naziopfer* (Weinheim–Berlin: Quadriga Verlag, 1992).
Loacker, A. (ed.), *Willi Forst: ein Filmstil aus Wien* (Wien: Filmarchiv Austria, 2003).
Loiperdinger, M., *Rituale der Mobilmachung: der Parteitagsfilm 'Triumph des Willens' von Leni Riefenstahl* (Opladen: Leske + Budrich, 1987).
Loiperdinger, M. (ed.), *Märtyrlegenden im NS-Film* (Opladen: Leske + Budrich, 1991).
Lowry, S., *Pathos und Politik. Ideologie im Spielfilm des Nationalsozialismus* (Tübingen: Max Niemeyer Verlag, 1991).
Maiwald, K.-J., *Filmzensur im NS-Staat* (Dortmund: Nowotny, 1983).
Margry, K., '"Theresienstadt" (1944–1945): The Nazi propaganda film depicting the concentration camp as paradise', *Historical Journal of Film, Radio and Television*, 12:2 (1992), pp. 145–62.
Möller, F., *Der Filmminister: Goebbels und der Film im Dritten Reich* (Berlin: Henschel, 1998). Translated as: Moeller, F. *The Film Minister. Goebbels and the Cinema in the 'Third Reich'* (Stuttgart–London: Edition Axel Menges, 2000).
Noack, F., *Veit Harlan: des Teufels Regisseur* (München: Belleville, 2000).
O'Brien, M.-E., *Nazi Cinema as Enchantment: The Politics of Entertainment in the Third Reich* (New York–Woodbridge: Camden House, 2004).
Offermanns, E., *Internationalität und europäischer Hegemonialanspruch des Spielfilms der NS-Zeit* (Hamburg: Verlag Dr. Kovac, 2001).
Paret, P., '"Kolberg" (1945) as historical film and historical document', *Historical Journal of Film, Radio and Television*, 14:4 (1994), pp. 433–48.
Paul, G., *Aufstand der Bilder. Die NS-Propaganda vor 1933* (Bonn: Diets Nachf. GmbH, 1990).
Petley, J., *Capital and Culture. German Cinema 1933–1945* (London: British Film Institute, 1979).
Phillips, M. S., 'The Nazi control of the German film industry', *Journal of European Studies*, 1:1 (1971), pp. 37–68.
Reeves, N., *The Power of Film Propaganda. Myth or Reality?* (London–New York: Cassell, 1999).
Reimer, R. C. (ed.), *Cultural History Through a National Socialist Lens: Essays on the Cinema of the Third Reich* (Rochester-Suffolk: Camden House, 2000).
Rentschler, E., *The Ministry of Illusion. Nazi Cinema and its Afterlife* (Cambridge–London: Harvard University Press, 1996).
Romani, C., *Le Dive Del Terzo Reich* (Roma: Gremese, 1981). Translated as *Tainted Goddesses: Female Film Stars of the Third Reich* (Rome: Gremese, 2001).
Rother, R., *Leni Riefenstahl – Die Verführung des Talents* (Berlin: Henschel Verlag, 2000). Translated as *Leni Riefenstahl: The Seduction of Genius* (London–New York: The Continuum, 2002).
Sakmyster, T., 'Nazi documentaries of intimidation: "Feldzug in Polen" (1940), "Feurtaufe" (1940) and "Sieg im Westen" (1941)', *Historical Journal of Film, Radio and Television*, 16:4 (1996), pp. 485–514.
Schulte-Sasse, L., *Entertaining the Third Reich: Illusions of Wholeness in Nazi Cinema* (Durham NC: Duke University Press, 1996).
Segeberg, H. (ed.), *Mediale Mobilmachung I: Das Dritte Reich und der Film* (München: Wilhelm Fink Verlag, 2004).
Singer, H. J., '"Tran und Helle". Aspekte unterhaltender Aufklärung im Dritten Reich', *Publizistik*, 31:3–4 (1986), pp. 347–56.
Spieker, M., *Hollywood unterm Hakenkreuz. Der amerikanische Spielfilm im Dritten Reich* (Trier: Wissenschaftlicher Verlag Trier, 1999).
Spiker, J., *Film und Kapital* (Berlin: Verlag Volker Spiess, 1975).

Stahr, G., *Volksgemeinschaft vor der Leinwand? Der nationalsozialistische Film und sein Publikum* (Berlin: Verlag Hans Theissen, 2001).

Stamm, K., 'German wartime newsreels (Deutsche Wochenschau): The problem of authenticity', *Historical Journal of Film, Radio and Television*, 7:3 (1987), pp. 239–45.

Stamm, K., 'Panorama. Farbige Auslands-Filmpropaganda 1944/45', *Filmblatt*, 5:12 (1999/2000), pp. 30–8.

Taylor, B. and W. Van der Wille, *The Nazification of Art. Art Music, Architecture and Film in the Third Reich* (Winchester: Winchester Press, 1990).

Taylor, R., *Film Propaganda. Soviet Russia and Nazi Germany* (London–New York: fI.B. Tauris Publishers, 1998 rev.).

Tegel, S., *Jew Süss – Jud Süss* (Trowbridge: Flicks Books, 1996).

Tegel, S., 'Veit Harlan and the origins of Jud Süss, 1938–1939: opportunism in the creation of Nazi anti-semitic film propaganda', *Historical Journal of Film, Radio and Television*, 16:4 (1996), pp. 515–31.

Theuerkauf, H., *Goebbels' Filmerbe. Das Geschäft mit den unveröffentlichten Ufa-Filmen* (Berlin: Ullstein, 1998).

Trimborn, J., *Riefenstahl – Eine deutsche Karriere* (Berlin: Aufbau-Verlag, 2002).

Vande Winkel, R., 'Nazi Germany's Fritz Hippler (1909–2002)', *Historical Journal of Film, Radio and Television*, 23:2 (2003), pp. 91–9.

Vande Winkel, R., 'The Auxiliary Cruiser Thor's Death and Transfiguration: A case study in Nazi wartime newsreel propaganda', *Historical Journal of Film, Radio and Television*, 23:3 (2003), pp. 211–29.

Vande Winkel, R., 'Nazi newsreels in Europe, 1939–1945: The many faces of Ufa's foreign weekly newsreel (Auslandstonwoche) versus the German weekly newsreel (Deutsche Wochenschau)', *Historical Journal of Film, Radio and Television*, 24:1 (2004), pp. 5–34.

Vande Winkel, R., *Nazi Newsreel Propaganda in the Second World War* (Gent: Academia Press, 2007).

Volker, R., *'Von Oben sehr erwünscht': Die Filmmusik Herbert Windts im NS-Propagandafilm* (Trier: Wissenschaftlicher Verlag, 2003).

Von Papen, M., 'Opportunities and limitations: The new Woman in Third Reich cinema', *Woman's History Review*, 8:4 (1999), pp. 693–728.

Weinberg, D., 'Approaches to the study of film in the third reich: A critical appraisal', *Journal of Contemporary History*, 19:1 (1984), pp. 105–26.

Welch, D. (ed.), *Nazi Propaganda. The Power and the Limitations* (Kent: Croom Helm Ltd, 1983).

Welch, D., 'Goebbels, Götterdämmerung and the Deutsche Wochenschauen', in K. R. M. Short and S. Dolezel (eds), *Hitler's Fall. The Newsreel Witness* (London–New York–Sydney: Croom Helm, 1988), pp. 80–99.

Welch, D., ' "Jews out!" Anti-semitic film propaganda in Nazi Germany and the "Jewish question" ', *The British Journal of Holocaust Education*, 1:1 (1992), pp. 55–73.

Welch, D., *Propaganda and the German Cinema 1933–45* (London: IB Tauris, 2001 rev.).

Welch, D., *The Third Reich Politics and Propaganda* (London–New York: Routledge, 2002 rev.).

Wetzel, K. and P. Hagemann, *Zensur – Verbotene deutsche Filme 1933–1945* (Berlin: Volker Spiess Verlag, 1978).

Witte, K., *Lachende Erben, toller Tag. Filmkomödie im Dritten Reich* (Berlin: Vorwerk 8, 1995).

Witte, K., 'The indivisible legacy of Nazi cinema', *New German Critique (Special Issue on Nazi Cinema)*, 25:2 (1998), pp. 23–30.

Witte, K., 'Film im Nationalsozialismus: Blendung und Überblendung', in W. Jacobsen, A. Kaes and H. H. Prinzler (eds), *Geschichte des deutschen Films (2., aktualisierte und erweiterte Auflage)* (Stuttgart–Weimar: J. B. Metzler, 2004 rev.), pp. 117–66.

Wulf, J., *Theater und Film im Dritten Reich* (Gütersloh: Sigbert Mohn Verlag, 1964).

Zimmermann, P. and K. Hoffmann (eds), *Geschichte des dokumentarischen Films in Deutschland. Band 3: 'Drittes Reich' (1933–1945)* (Stuttgart: Philipp Reclam, 2005).

Index